Donated by
The Chester Garden Club
2006

the complete book of
Herbs and Herb Gardening

the complete book of
Herbs and Herb Gardening

Jessica Houdret

LORENZ BOOKS

To Jeremy

This edition is published by Lorenz Books

Lorenz Books is an imprint of Anness Publishing Ltd
Hermes House, 88–89 Blackfriars Road, London SE1 8HA
tel. 020 7401 2077; fax 020 7633 9499
www.lorenzbooks.com; info@anness.com

© Anness Publishing Ltd 2003, 2004

UK agent: The Manning Partnership Ltd, 6 The Old Dairy, Melcombe Road, Bath BA2 3LR;
tel. 01225 478444; fax 01225 478440; sales@manning-partnership.co.uk

UK distributor: Grantham Book Services Ltd, Isaac Newton Way, Alma Park Industrial Estate,
Grantham, Lincs NG31 9SD;
tel. 01476 541080; fax 01476 541061; orders@gbs.tbs-ltd.co.uk

North American agent/distributor: National Book Network,
4501 Forbes Boulevard, Suite 200, Lanham, MD 20706;
tel. 301 459 3366; fax 301 429 5746; www.nbnbooks.com

Australian agent/distributor: Pan Macmillan Australia, Level 18,
St Martins Tower, 31 Market St, Sydney, NSW 2000;
tel. 1300 135 113; fax 1300 135 103; customer.service@macmillan.com.au

New Zealand agent/distributor: David Bateman Ltd, 30 Tarndale Grove, Off Bush Road, Albany,
Auckland; tel. (09) 415 7664; fax (09) 415 8892

A CIP catalogue record for this book is available from the British Library

Publisher: Joanna Lorenz
Senior Editor: Doreen Palamartschuk
Designers: Ruth Hope, Lilian Lindblom and Patrick Mcleavey
Photographer: Andrea Jones
Illustrator: Madeleine David
Production Controller: Julie Hadingham

Previously published as *The Ultimate Book of Herbs and Herb Gardening*

1 3 5 7 9 10 8 6 4 2

p.1: A group of herbs, including clary sage and Jacob's ladder against a wall.
p.2: Red and white valerian contrast with the blue of cornflower.
p.3: A colourful herb display with fennel in the foreground. Above: Elderberries and
bergamot. p.6: A selection of containers suitable for herbs.
p.7: A planted-up herb pot.

Contents

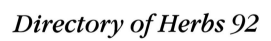

Introduction

Herbs are a diverse and versatile body of plants, which have been appreciated through the centuries for their many uses. In the past they were the main source of raw materials for medicines, nutritional supplements and culinary flavourings as well as fulfilling a wide variety of household needs. They provided fragrance in the home, were added to bath and beauty preparations, used as dyes, cleaning agents, insect repellents and other similar products which we have become used to buying ready made.

Although few people now would presumably want to give up the benefits of modern medical science or the convenience of contemporary technology and goods, there is an increasing revival of interest in herbs and their uses, which has been gathering momentum since the 1980s. Alternative therapies and herbal healing have gained ground and many more people add herbs to their cooking as a matter of course. This may be partly due to a current inclination towards natural products and natural practices, and partly due to increased travel and communications, which have brought the cuisines and ingredients of the world before a wider audience.

In addition, in more recent times, a new element has emerged: herbs have gained respectability. They are no longer seen as solely the preserve of eccentrics, nor are herbal remedies universally dismissed as superstitious nonsense. The reason is that much traditional herbal folklore has been vindicated by modern research. Scientific studies have proved that many herbs have antibacterial, antifungal, antidepressant and other medicinal properties and that some help to lower blood pressure or act on the hormonal systems of the body. Many plants are now recognized by the medical establishment as providing the key to discovering new drugs to combat the major modern illnesses such as cancers and AIDS.

Not only are herbs objects of academic study, they are also living plants, scented, exuberant and colourful – there to grow, to use and, above all, to enjoy.

Growing your own herbs is immensely rewarding, with the added advantage of having fresh material to hand, for use in home remedies and recipes, which you know has not been sprayed, adulterated or polluted. This book begins with a background history, ideas for schemes and layouts and a section on growing herbs and making the most of these useful plants in an ornamental setting.

The herb directory gives detailed information on individual plants. Under each entry, the history and traditions of the herb are dealt with first. Some of the stories or myths associated with the herb are mentioned, the origins of the name, or past uses, and, where relevant, how this is linked to present uses, properties and status. The rest of the information covers practical points on growing and usage for today. There is a description to help with identification, a note on where the plant originated (which often helps in the understanding of cultivation needs) and requirements for growth and propagation.

It would take many volumes to detail every plant that could possibly be construed as having herbal properties, even if all of them were known. In remote areas of the world there are many plants not yet classified, some, perhaps, whose medicinal uses are familiar only to a few local healers. So the decision on which herbs to include has necessarily been subjective. The ones chosen are those which are generally the most useful, the most popular, of special historical interest, or of current significance because of properties discovered by modern scientific research.

The aim is to provide accessible information on a wide range of herbs and the inspiration to take pleasure in them.

Jessica Houdret

History of Herbs

The first question explored here is what is meant by the term "herb"? This is followed by some guidelines on restrictions in using these powerful plants and a detailed explanation of plant classification, how it began and developed, and the helpfulness of using Latin names to avoid confusion. A background history of herbal knowledge and use through the centuries comes next. The chapter concludes with a summary of some of the landmarks in herbal literature.

Above *A topiary spiral emphasizes the symmetry of the raised stone urns in a small formal herb garden.*

Left *An arched walkway shelters raised beds, thickly planted with herbs, in a reconstruction of a medieval cloister garden.*

What is a Herb?

The definition of the term "herb" has varied over the centuries. At one time it meant primarily grass, green crops and leafy plants. This concept entered into many dictionaries, where the definition was narrowed to a plant that does not have a woody, persistent stem, but dies down to the ground after flowering – a herbaceous plant, in other words. This was clearly inadequate, because it excluded some of the most obvious and common herbal examples such as rosemary, thyme and sage .

A herb is now generally understood to mean a plant, some part of which, roots, stem, leaves, flowers or fruits, is used for food, medicine, flavouring or scent. This wide category covers much more than a few plants with small green leaves; and includes some trees, shrubs, sub-shrubs or woody-stemmed perennials. Annuals, even ferns and fungi, as well as the herbaceous group, could also fit the general description.

Right *Watermint and bogbean in a pond.*

Below *A detailed illustration of St John's wort,* Hypericum perforatum, *from W. Curtis's* Flora Londinensis, *1826.*

Most of the plants included in this book have a long herbal history, their therapeutic uses having been recorded in early manuscripts or published works written by the specialists of the time. Some of these uses seem very far-fetched or downright dangerous in the light of modern knowledge. Expressed in colourfully poetic language, the early records often deal with bizarre conditions and unfamiliar illnesses, from attacks by "flying venom" and "elf-shot" to agues, fluxes and St Anthony's fire – as well as coughs, fevers and more recognizable medical problems.

However, the remarkable fact is that many herbs have been found under modern analysis to vindicate our fore-fathers' faith in them. Recent research studies have established the antibacterial, antiseptic, anti-inflammatory or other medicinal properties of large numbers of common herbs.

Herb chemistry is very complex. Each individual variety of plant is unique in its make-up, even closely related species are quite distinct. They all contain many active constituents which work together to affect the functions of the body, when used for medicinal purposes. This holistic (or synergistic) method of using the whole plant, as opposed to taking a concentrated extract, is the gentlest and safest way to benefit from herbs.

Aconitum napellus, *or monkshood (top), and* Atropa belladonna, *deadly nightshade (above), are highly toxic in any quantity.* Cannabis sativa *(right) is one of the plants subject to legal restrictions in most countries.*

Restrictions on Herbs

Safety in use

Many plants are highly toxic and can be dangerous in use. Self-medication is not advised and it is always best to seek the advice of a qualified medical practitioner before herbs are used as a treatment. Plants can look very similar and common names are often misleading – there is a danger of mistaking one herb for another. Before collecting a herb, ensure that it has been correctly identified and do not interchange similar species for a particular purpose, as they may not have the same properties. It is also essential to use only the part specified, usually the leaf, stem, flower or seed and occasionally root. Some plants classified as herbs are highly poisonous in any form or quantity, monkshood, *Aconitum napellus*, being an example. It should be remembered that many apparently benevolent substances, for example vitamins, can be toxic if taken to excess. This principle applies to herbs too and includes the common culinary ones, such as thyme or rosemary. It is difficult to ingest a harmful amount in the form of the whole leaf, and most are totally safe if used, fresh or dried, in the quantities recommended in recipes. However, in the form of essential oils, which are concentrated extracts of the active principle, they can be highly toxic.

Poisonous and toxic plants in this book are shown under a caution box in individual entries.

Legal restrictions

There are legal restrictions both on the use or trade and on the collection or cultivation of various herbs. Restrictions also cover certain herbal extracts and preparations, and their permitted concentrations and doses, as well as those people allowed to administer, prescribe or supply them.

Growing herbs that are capable of producing illegal drugs, or cultivating species considered to be noxious weeds, is against the law in some countries. It is also a criminal offence to collect or uproot wild plants that are protected by law. See the caution box under individual herb entries for plants likely to be restricted by law.

Plant Names

Herbs are listed in this book under their Latin, or botanical, names. This helps to avoid confusion, as most have several common names which vary according to country, or even from one local region to another. Sometimes the common name used in one country refers to a totally different plant in another country. The Latin names have the advantage of being international. *The International Code of Botanical Nomenclature*, set every five years following an international conference, ensures that all countries accept the same botanical names.

In recent years, however, there has been a spate of reclassifications of plants by botanists in the light of new studies or detailed analysis of specimens. For example, the plant always known as *Mentha rotundifolia* var. 'Bowles', (or Bowles' mint), has now become *Mentha* x *villosa* f. *alopecuroides*. As far as possible the most current name is listed, but changes are ongoing.

Common Names
The most usual common name is also given in this book, along with variations and synonyms where applicable. Both Latin and common names are often a lively indication of a herb's history, properties or use.

Above *Cultivars of* Achillea millefolium.

Plant Classification
The system of plant classification by Latin names in use today was developed by Carl Linnaeus, 1707–1778, a Swedish botanist and professor of medicine at Uppsala University, near Stockholm. He divided plants into groups, according to common characteristics.

Some modifications have since been introduced, but the system remains essentially the same as at its inception. Under the Linnaeus system all plants have a double name. The first is the name of the genus, or wider grouping, to which they belong, and the second denotes their individual species. Generic names, like all Latin names, are either masculine, feminine or neuter.

Thus *Achillea* = genus, *millefolium* = species. The second part of the name also indicates whether a plant is a hybrid or cultivar, or has been subdivided, according to finer differences, as a subspecies, variety or form.

Plant Divisions

FAMILY – A group of plants, made up of a number of genera with characteristics in common, usually decided by the structure of flowers, fruits or seeds e.g., ROSACEAE. Some families have alternative names, such as COMPOSITAE also known as ASTERACEAE. The first is the traditional name, which, although it remains valid at present, is being superseded by a newer name, designed to fit into a standardized system of nomenclature, whereby all family names end with "aceae", preceded by the key genus of the family, as ASTER-ACEAE.

GENUS – A group, made up of a number of related species, such as *Achillea*, but which may also contain only one species, such as *Anethum graveolens* (denoted by the first part of the Latin name).

SPECIES (spp.) – Individual plants that are alike and breed naturally with each other, such as *Achillea millefolium* (the species is denoted by the second part of the Latin name).

HYBRID – A cross between two species, or genera, indicated by a cross, such as *Lavandula* x *intermedia*.

CULTIVAR – A variant of the species or hybrid that has a special characteristic, such as leaf variegation, developed and maintained under cultivation. For instance, *Melissa officinalis* 'All Gold', a golden-leafed lemon balm. The name of the cultivar is printed in roman type, within inverted commas (single quotation marks).

VARIETY (var.) – A subdivision of species and hybrids, often with a distinctive difference (such as flower or foliage colour), but with only minor variations in botanical structure, such as *Lavandula dentata* var. *candicans*.

SUBSPECIES (subsp.) – A variant of a species, such as *Lavandula stoechas* subsp. *pedunculata*.

FORM (f.) – Has only minor, but often noticeable, variations from the species, such as flower colour, e.g. *Lavandula stoechas* f. *leucantha* – a white-flowering form of *L. stoechas*. (Note that, once a genus has been stated, it can then, as here, be represented by its initial.)

System of plant classification

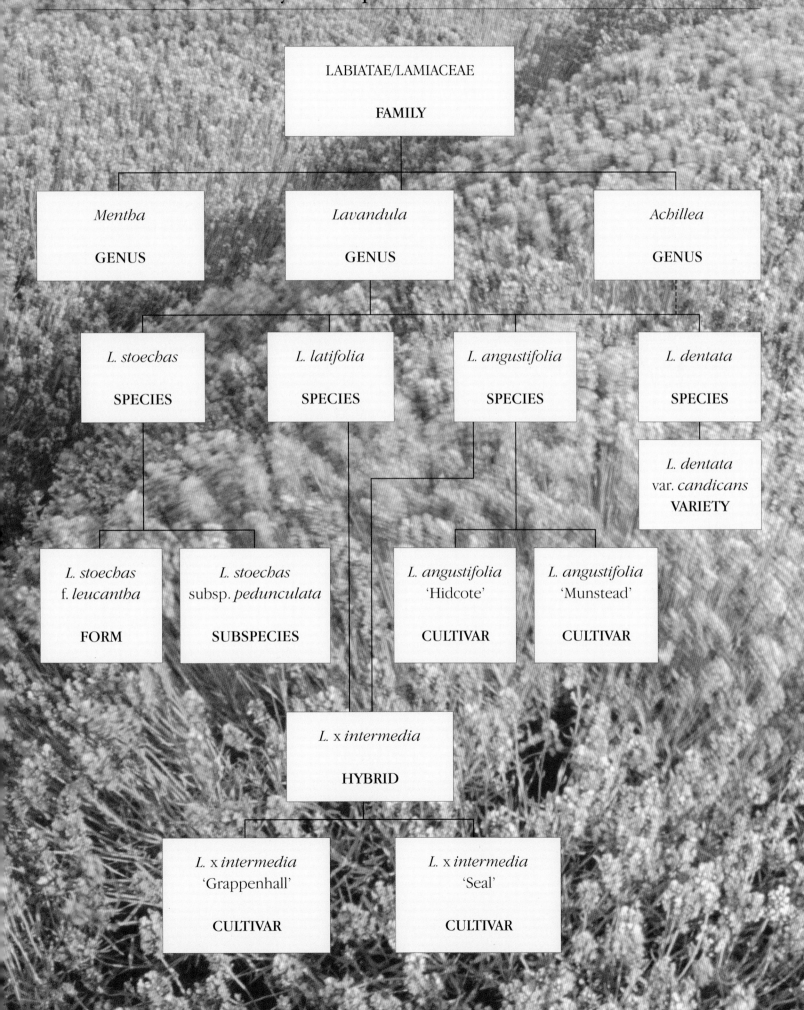

LABIATAE/LAMIACEAE

FAMILY

Mentha

GENUS

Lavandula

GENUS

Achillea

GENUS

L. stoechas

SPECIES

L. latifolia

SPECIES

L. angustifolia

SPECIES

L. dentata

SPECIES

L. dentata
var. *candicans*

VARIETY

L. stoechas
f. *leucantha*

FORM

L. stoechas
subsp. *pedunculata*

SUBSPECIES

L. angustifolia
'Hidcote'

CULTIVAR

L. angustifolia
'Munstead'

CULTIVAR

L. x *intermedia*

HYBRID

L. x *intermedia*
'Grappenhall'

CULTIVAR

L. x *intermedia*
'Seal'

CULTIVAR

Herbs in History

There is ample evidence of the herbal use of plants by the civilizations of ancient Egypt, over a period from 3000 BC to the reign of Cleopatra, which began in 48 BC. Papyri dating from 2800 BC record the medicinal use of some familiar herbs, including juniper, mint and marjoram. The wall paintings of tombs and temples reveal the use of aromatic plants, spices and gums in religious and funerary rites and on social occasions. Also an inscription in the temple of Karnak relates Ramses III's plea to the god Amun for victory in battle, reminding him of the pharaoh's generous sacrifice of 30,000 oxen, quantities of "sweet-smelling herbs and the finest perfume". Archaeologists have also found the physical remains of plants, flowers and seeds used for food and flavouring, as votive garlands and in cosmetic and embalming ointments.

Offerings made to the sun god Ra, at Heliopolis, included a concoction of 16 herbs and resins. Known as *kyphi* or *khepri*, it was adopted by the Greeks, and then the Romans, and was described by Dioscorides. Later analysis confirmed that it contained among its ingredients *Acorus calamus*, cassia, cinnamon, peppermint, juniper, acacia and henna.

The Greeks, the great period of whose culture overlapped with the end of the Egyptian dynasties, adopted Egyptian skills in making ointments from aromatic plants, as their literature often confirms. The cosmetic use of plants was a frequently described theme:

> He really bathes
> In a large gilded tub, and steeps his feet
> And legs in rich Egyptian unguents;
> His jaw and breasts he rubs with thick
> palm oil,
> And both his arms with extract of
> sweet mint;
> His eyebrows and his hair with
> marjoram,
> His knees and neck with essence of
> ground thyme.
> – Antiphanes

Above *Plants being ground in a mortar, from a 10th-century French herbal.*

The Romans have left many records of their use of herbs for flavouring food, in perfumery, for decoration and strewing at social events. Medicinal uses are discussed in the works of writers such as Pliny. The vast spread of their empire also meant that the Romans took Mediterranean plants to northern areas that had never known them before and where many became naturalized.

After the fall of Rome, in the period sometimes known as the Dark Ages, AD 476–c.1000, herbal knowledge was nurtured and kept alive in Christian monasteries. In Britain during this time, Anglo-Saxon writings show a wide knowledge of herbs and evidence of correspondence with centres in Europe.

The Eastern Connection

During the 10th century a great Muslim empire stretched from the eastern Mediterranean, taking in Arabia, Persia, parts of Spain and North Africa. Arab academics were paramount in the medicinal practice of the time and Avicenna, born in Persia, AD 980, was one of the most famous. He was the first to describe the making of attar of roses by distillation, was instrumental in the discovery of plant essential oils, and his *Canon* became a standard medical text. Crusaders from Britain, who set out to destroy the Muslim influence, brought home the new plants and exotic spices from the Near East.

Above *A relief at the Temple of Karnak in Luxor, Egypt, depicting a botanical garden showing plants brought from Syria by Pharaoh Tutmosis III.*

In India, where so many medicinal and scented plants grow, there is a long tradition of using spices and aromatic herbs in cookery, for perfumes and cosmetics. An 18th-century Italian traveller wrote that "nowhere do the women pay greater attention to their cleanliness than in the East, bathing frequently and massaging all parts of their body with perfumed oils". Ayurvedic medicine, practised in India, is an ancient system based on herbs and shares many similarities of concept with Chinese herbal medicine, whose longest unbroken tradition of practice is often considered to be the most ancient in origin. The Yellow Emperor, Huang Ti, born *c.* 2000 BC, wrote a medical treatise which is often cited as the earliest herbal on record. Chinese herbalism is currently enjoying a revival in the West.

The Renaissance and the Discovery of the New World

With the Renaissance, the great revival of learning marking the birth of modern Europe, came advances in medicine and the study of the healing properties of plants. The 16th and 17th centuries were the age of great herbalists and herbals: Turner, Gerard and Parkinson in Britain; Brunfels, Fuchs and Bock in Germany; Clusius, L'Obel and Dodoens in the Netherlands; Mattioli and Porta in Italy.

Above *A man and woman harvesting sap, from* Le Livre des Simples Médecines, *a 15th-century French herbal.*

Above *Collecting herbs to use in the stillroom.* Spring *by Lucas van Valkenborch, 1595.*

At the same time the use of herbs in cookery, perfumery and for cosmetics was widespread and well documented in many books on household skills, such as Sir Hugh Platt's *Delights for Ladies*, 1594, and T. Dawson's *The Good Housewife's Jewel*, 1585. It should be remembered, however, that the line between perfumery for pleasure and health was a narrow one. It was generally accepted that a fragrant smell was in itself proof against infection and many recipes in the stillroom books for perfumed powders and pot-pourris, which would now be considered fripperies, had a serious underlying purpose.

In the 16th and 17th centuries a huge quantity of new plants, many of which were used by the Native Americans in their traditional medicine, were brought to Europe from the Americas. Seeds were taken the opposite way by the early colonists keen to establish, in their new country, gardens stocked with the familiar herbs of home – including parsley, savory and thyme.

The Modern Era

Up until the 18th century, botany and medicine were closely allied, but with the rise of modern scientific enquiry they drew apart as separate disciplines. During the 19th century the medical establishment turned away from plant-based remedies, and synthetic drugs, produced in the laboratory, began their ascendancy. This is not to say that old herbal remedies and culinary and cosmetic recipes disappeared: traditions were kept alive in many country districts and in some countries never fell from use. In Europe the day-to-day use of herbs remained more widely practised than it did in Britain.

Mrs Grieve, whose famous herbal was published in 1931, did much to promote the renewed interest in herbs in Britain in the 20th century, as did Eleanour Sinclair Rohde, who wrote many books on herbs and became a popular lecturer on the subject in the United States, following World War II.

In the latter part of the 20th century the revival of interest in all things herbal continues. Emigration and accessibility of travel have spread the use of culinary herbs and spices across many countries and cultures. There is wide recognition among scientists today of the value of plants as the basis for drugs to combat major diseases, such as cancer and AIDS, and much research is being carried out. However, the drugs under development depend on isolating and copying active plant compounds. This takes a different direction from the use of the whole plant as practised in traditional herbal medicine.

Old Herbals

Old herbal manuscripts make fascinating reading. They give an insight into how herbs were used in the past and increase our general understanding of the subject. Not all are readily available and are kept in specialist libraries, but some have been reissued in modern editions and facsimiles and many are widely quoted from by modern authors. The following are some of the more important works on herbs written in the West.

Early Manuscript Herbals

c. **320** BC *Historia Plantarum* and *De Causis Plantarum* – by Theophrastus, *c.* 370–286 BC, Greek philosopher and pupil of Aristotle. (Edited and translated as *The History of Plants* and *The Causes of Plants* by Sir A.F. Hort, Loeb Library, 1916.)
c. AD **60** *De Materia Medica* – written by Dioscorides, a Greek physician, living in Rome. Describes 600 herbs and their healing properties. It became the standard work on medicine, influencing most herbals that followed for over 1,500 years. (English translation by John Goodyer, 1655.)

c. AD **77** *Naturalis Historia* – by Pliny the Elder, contemporary of Dioscorides. A massive, 37-volume work, 16 concern trees, plants and medicines.
AD **400** *The Herbal of Apuleius* – Author unknown. Originally written in Latin it drew quite heavily on Dioscorides and Pliny, adding pagan prayers and superstitions. It was much copied over the years. (Anglo-Saxon translation made in 11th century.)
c. AD **900** *The Leech Book of Bald* – compiled by a Saxon physician. Reveals a wide knowledge of native plants and includes prescriptions sent by the Patriarch of Jerusalem to King Alfred.
c. **1150** *Physica* – by Hildegard of Bingen. Unique as a book on the medicinal properties of plants by a woman and had great influence on the famous German "fathers of botany", Brunfels, Fuchs and Hieronymus Bock.
c. **1248–1260** *De Proprietatibus Rerum* by Bartholomaeus Anglicus, an Englishman living in Paris, then Saxony. A huge encyclopedia in 19 sections, number 17 being on plants and trees and their herbal properties.

Printed Herbals

1491 *Hortus Sanitatis* – compiled by publisher Jacob Meydenbach of Mainz. The last of the medieval works on herbs.
1500 *Liber de Arte Distillandi de Simplicibus* – by Hieronymous Braunschweig. The first major work on the techniques of distillation "of the waters of all manner of herbes". (English translation by L. Andrewes 1527.)
1525 *Banckes's Herbal* – anonymous, a quarto volume published by Richard Banckes. Earliest English printed herbal, based on earlier manuscript herbals.
1530 *Herbarum Vivae Eicones* – by Otto Brunfels, a former monk, Lutheran preacher, botanist and also physician. Published in Strasbourg, with realistic illustrations, it began the movement towards a more scientific mindset.
1539 *Kräuter Buch* – by Hieronymus Bock. Rather than repeat Dioscorides, Bock wrote about native plants and was the first to attempt a system of plant classification.
1542 *De Historia Stirpium* – written by Leonhard Fuchs. A scholarly work, which sought to clarify identification of medicinal plants mentioned by Dioscorides, through carefully observed illustrations. Records many new plants introduced to Germany from other parts of the world.
1551–68 *The New Herball* – by William Turner, credited as the "father of English botany". Based on his own observations of native plants but using many of the woodcuts from Fuchs' work.
1554 *Cruydeboeck* – by Rembert Dodoens, physician to the Holy Roman Emperor Maximilian II and professor of botany at Leyden University. A work of botanical importance, which borrowed Fuchs' pictures. (Many English editions, *A Niewe Herbal or History of Plants*, by Henry Lyte in 1578.)
1563 *Coloquios dos Simples* – by Garcia de Orta, a Portuguese doctor who spent time in Goa and produced a book on the plants and medicines of India.

Above *Collecting herbs for the Apothecary's preparations, from a Latin manuscript version of the Herbal of Apuleius.*

Above *Frontispiece to* The Herball, *1597, by John Gerard.*

1569 *Dos libros, el uno que trata de todas las cosas que traen de nuestras Indias Occidentales* – by Nicholas Monardes, a Spaniard, who never himself visited America. His book on the plants of the "New World" became better known by the title of the first English edition: *Joyfull Newes Out of the Newe Founde Worlde,* 1577.

1597 *The Herball or Generall Historie of Plantes* – by John Gerard, gardener and botanist. Based on Dodoens' work, it remains one of the most popular, widely quoted from herbals of all time for the grace of its Elizabethan language.

1629 *Paradisi in Sole Paradisus Terrestris*; **1640** *Theatrum Botanicum* – by John Parkinson. The emphasis in the first is on ornamental planting, the second lists 3,800 plants and their medicinal properties.

1652 *The English Physician* – by Nicholas Culpeper, an astrologer, considered a charlatan by the medical establishment of his day. His book is one of the most popular herbals of all time.

1656 *The Art of Simpling*; **1657** *Adam in Eden* – by William Coles. Less popular, but more readable than Culpeper, who Coles thought was "ignorant". Includes much herb lore.

Later Herbals

With the break between botany and medicine, few great medicinal herbals appeared after the 17th century. Those of note included:

1710 *Botanologia, The English Herbal or History of Plants* – by William Salmon.

1838 *Flora Medica* – written by John Lindley, botanist and lecturer to the Society of Apothecaries, who wrote several important horticultural works.

1931 *A Modern Herbal* – by Mrs M. Grieve. Seminal work on herbs of the 20th century.

Stillroom Books

As well as the learned tomes, written by the medical men of their day, there is a long tradition of more homely recipe (usually spelled "receipt") books, which include instructions on the culinary and cosmetic uses of herbs as well as medicinal remedies. They are sometimes known as "stillroom books". Throughout the 17th and 18th centuries all the big country houses had their own stillroom and women were supposed to be fully conversant in the art of making herbal and culinary preparations.

1585 *The Good Housewife's Jewel and Rare Conceits in Cookery* – by T. Dawson. A comprehensive, informative compilation of herbal recipes.

1594 *Delights for Ladies* – by Sir Hugh Platt. A book to fit in the palm of the hand, subtitled "to adorne their Persons, Tables, Closets & Distillatories with Beauties, Banquets, Perfumes & Waters".

1654 *The Art of Cookery* – by Joseph Cooper, recipes of Charles I's head chef.

1655 *The Queen's Closet Opened* – by W. M. (cook to Queen Henrietta Maria). Includes perfumed, culinary and medicinal preparations.

1668 *Choice and Experimental Receipts* – by Sir Kenelm Digby, Stuart diplomat, with a side interest in cookery, alchemy and herbalism. **1669** *The Closet of Sir Kenelm Digby Opened*. Many medicinal and fragrance recipes.

1719 *Acetaria* – written by John Evelyn. Cookery book by the prolific author and diarist, with a large section on the virtues of salad herbs, picked from the garden.

1719 *The Accomplished Lady's Delight* – by Mrs Mary Eales (confectioner to Queen Anne). Includes recipes for candying many flowers and fruits as well as for perfumes and scented waters.

1723 *The Receipt Book of John Nott* – competent, often workable recipes of the cook to the Duke of Bolton.

1732 *Country Housewife and Ladies Directory* – by R. Bradley. Intriguing cookery recipes.

1775 *The Toilet of Flora* – Anonymous. The title page states: "The Chief Intention of this performance is to point out, and explain to the Fair-Sex, the Methods by which they may preserve and add to their charms." But it is also for "Domestic Economy" and gives methods of preparing herbal baths, essences, pomatums, powders, perfumes, sweet-scented waters and opiates for preserving and whitening teeth.

1784 *The Art of Cooking* – by Mrs Glasse.

1845 *Miss Leslie's Directions for Cookery* – by Eliza Leslie (published USA). Primarily culinary recipes, but also contains directions for making oil of flowers, sweet jars, perfumes and scented bags.

Above *A medieval garden from* Rustican de Cultivement des Terres, *also known as* Les Livres des Prouffits. *British Library.*

Herb Garden Design

A look at traditional herb gardens and their influence on styles for today, followed by how to choose a design and whether to go for a formal or informal approach. Practical projects include step-by-step instructions on making a knot garden, raised bed and herb wheel. There are examples of themed gardens for inspiration, with detailed plans.

Above *A herb garden bounded by trees and a hedge creates an air of mystery.*

Left *Clipped box hedges, geometric lines and topiary re-create 17th-century formality in this design.*

Traditional Herb Gardens

Herbs have been grown in gardens since ancient times, as evidenced in Egyptian frescoes and descriptions of the Roman *Hortus*. However, it is really the monastery gardens of the early Christian era, following the fall of Rome, which begin the Western tradition of the herb garden.

A plan of the Benedictine monastery of St Gall in Switzerland, dating from AD 812, provided a blueprint of the style of garden attached to religious houses and which became central to their life and ministry. There were three distinct areas in this early plan: A physic garden of medicinal plants, which included sage, rosemary, rue and roses, was close to the infirmary. On the other side of this building was the vegetable garden, divided into 18 plots, each designated a single species of plant, many of which we would call herbs. There were cabbages, lettuce, onions, celery, coriander, dill, poppy, radish, garlic, parsley, chervil and fennel. The orchard adjoined, with a large, cross-shaped path at the centre, and included burial plots. At the centre of the enclosed cloister garden was an

Above *Reconstruction of a Tudor garden, with a central "knot", at Southampton, England.*

area of lilies, roses and scented flowers for decorating the church, often known as a "paradise garden".

Monastery gardens were by their nature enclosed. This was a feature, too, of privy gardens belonging to a palace or castle in the medieval period. However, the emphasis here was on enjoyment, with scents, seats and arbours.

Another characteristic of the monastic gardens, which was carried into the designs of the Renaissance period beginning in the 16th century, is the rectangular layout of symmetrical paths, with the cross as a central motif. It has often been noted, however, that the Islamic and Persian tradition of a garden on a grid pattern (probably set out this way for ease of watering by irrigation channels) was also an influence.

In England the fashion for knot gardens began at the outset of the reign of Henry VIII, in the early 16th century, and was popular for over 200 years. Some of the patterns, depicting interlaced ribbons, were extremely complicated and set out in clipped hedges of wall germander, hyssop, cotton lavender and box, infilled with coloured stones or scented herbs and

flowers. By the 17th century the more expansive and open French parterre, with its elaborate swirls of curls and loops, became fashionable.

It was during the 17th century that a host of new plants arrived in Europe, brought back by explorers and traders. Many of the new arrivals were from North America, including nasturtiums and sunflowers. They were planted in physic gardens and the gardens of the great houses, as well as in large botanical gardens throughout Europe, where the study of botany and medicine still went hand in hand. It was a two-way traffic as plants from the "old world" were also taken to North America.

The landscape movement and "natural" school of garden design in the 18th century swept away the intricate knots and parterres; and physic gardens declined in importance as medicine moved apart from botany. Herbs were still grown, of course, but retreated to the cottage garden. Here, they largely remained until the early 20th century when Vita Sackville-West and Gertrude Jekyll started the fashion for informal planting of old-fashioned species, and restored herbs to centre stage.

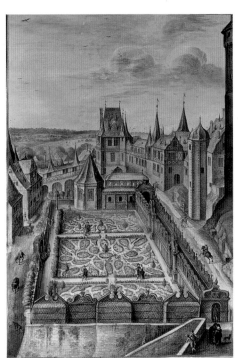

Above *An elaborate 17th-century garden, from a painting by Johan Walter, 1660.*

Herb Gardens for Today

When planning a herb garden today there is a vast choice of styles and influences to choose from. As herbs and plants cover such a wide range, they are often grown throughout the garden in ornamental beds and borders or among vegetable plots. But a designated herb garden with a range of medicinal, culinary and aromatic plants and its own boundaries always makes a rewarding feature. In a very small garden, of course, it may well be designed to take up the whole area.

Historical precedents provide much inspiration for a herb garden in the formal style, with rectangular beds, straight paths and edgings of clipped box. It could be based on the medieval garden, with narrow, raised beds filled with a single species, divided by wide alleys. Or you could draw inspiration from the romantic enclave of a castle garden; or a cloister or paradise garden. And, the striking pattern of a knot garden or parterre is always effective.

Informal designs based on curves and irregular shapes give scope for imaginative planting schemes with a

Above *A beautiful, scented cloister garden at Château de Vandrimare in France.*

bold use of colour and texture; and the cottage-garden style, with its profusion of plants crammed into a small space, is another option.

In any scheme a place to sit, either a simple bench or intricate covered arbour, is a must. A sundial or urn as a centrepiece provides a good focal point.

Whatever the style, some kind of enclosure adds an extra dimension, setting the herb garden apart. It could be a low fence or herbal hedge or, for a larger area, high trelliswork or a wall may be more appropriate. Herbs may be practical plants, for particular purposes, but they also add a little mystery and magic to the world and deserve a special place of their own.

Left *A sundial makes a traditional focal point in an informal planting of herbs and roses, with a statue in the background.*

Choosing a Design

Working out the design of a new herb garden is an exciting project. But before you begin there are several questions you need to answer to ensure that the end result is a success. Space is the first consideration. How much room are you prepared to devote to herbs? Do you have a large enough area to make a garden within a garden? Perhaps you would like to turn most, or all, of your existing space over to herbs? Or would a bed or border of herbs be more appropriate?

Plan how the design is going to fit in with your surroundings. Think about your house and current garden, as this will dictate the overall style you choose; formal, informal, old-fashioned or state-of-the-art or of the 21st century.

Consider how much time and energy you have for upkeep. Beware of choosing a large and complicated scheme if from a practical point of view your needs are for a low-maintenance garden. A simple knot of box hedging, filled in with gravel needs clipping only twice a year. But be wary of putting in

other traditional clipped herbs, such as santolina and germander, unless you are prepared to trim the plants frequently. A formal potager, which needs constant replanting and tending to keep it in shape, can be very time-consuming. But a carefully thought-out border of shrubby herbs and perennials needs little upkeep. Containers of herbs can provide extra space and variety.

Consider which category of herbs is your chief interest – culinary, medicinal or scented and aromatic? Your preference here may dictate size, layout and planting plans. If your main aim is to produce a good supply of culinary herbs, a small, formal patch may be sufficient. But if your ambition is to include as many species as possible, a more extensive scheme is inevitable.

Left *A colourful archway and large containers of pelargoniums mark the entrance to an inviting garden bounded by a high hedge.*

Below *Topiary and architectural plants of contrasting foliage lend height and interest to a mixed scheme of herbs.*

Formal Gardens

Taking their inspiration from the Renaissance gardens of France and Italy, formal designs depend on straight lines and geometric shapes, on symmetry and regularity. Balance is the key, with elements arranged around a central axis. The strict pattern of paths, which form the structure, is all-important. Paths may be of brick, stone, gravel or grass, but make sure they are wide enough to walk on comfortably and to take a wheelbarrow. A metre (about three feet) is a minimum width for straight sections, with some wider areas to create a feeling of spaciousness and for extra manoeuvrability. Planting schemes echo the geometry of the layout, with corresponding blocks of colour filling the beds. Foliage plants, especially those with a dense habit of growth such as thyme, are often more suitable than those with a profusion of flowers and a tendency to sprawl.

Large pots and ornaments or statues provide focal points at the ends of vistas. If placed to line a path edge or in a regular pattern they will provide visual links, drawing the scheme together and reinforcing the regularity. Topiary and plants growing over a shaped framework are used in much the same way. They also introduce a theatrical element which underlines the style. But beware of cramming in too much – for this look to be successful, understatement and simplicity are best.

Above *The low-growing silver thyme in the foreground forms a block of colour to reinforce the geometry of the design.*

This plan is for a garden about 11 x 9.50 m (36 x 31 ft), enclosed by a brick wall to one side and trelliswork at each corner supporting a scented, white-flowered jasmine. If you do not have a site where a wall can be used as one boundary, the trellis can be extended. An archway, clothed in the coppery pink climbing rose, 'Albertine', forms the main entrance, with a bench seat under a jasmine arbour on the opposite side, against the wall. Topiary in pots – box trees clipped in spheres and rosemary globes – mark the points of entry, add height to the scheme and increase the sense of regularity.

A sundial surrounded by a chamomile lawn, of the non-flowering cultivar *Chamaemelum nobile* 'Treneague', makes a focal point at the centre, emphasized by the square beds of creeping thymes, bronze-purple 'Russetings' and the white-flowering *Thymus serpyllum* var. 'albus'. Chamomile is quite difficult to establish as a lawn and needs constant weeding, so is best kept on a small scale, as it is here. Paths are of stone slabs with brick or tiling edges to the beds.

The emphasis of the planting is on scented herbs with a purple, silver and white colour scheme predominating. Dark-green hyssop, which has blue flower spikes in summer, along with feathery bronze fennel, provide contrast and texture. Golden hops, trained against the wall, echoed by golden sage, lend brightness. Each of the main beds is edged with a low-growing lavender and has a standard rose at the centre.

Plan for a formal herb garden

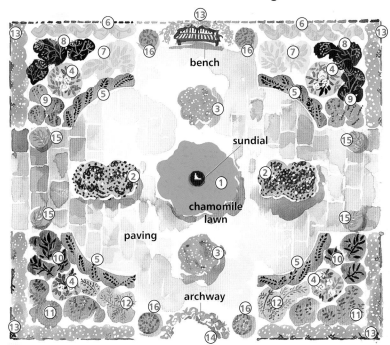

Key to planting plan

1. *Chamaemelum nobile* 'Treneague' – non-flowering chamomile
2. *Thymus serpyllum* 'Russetings' – creeping thyme (mauve-flowering)
3. *Thymus serpyllum* var. 'albus' – creeping thyme (white-flowering)
4. *Rosa* 'Félicité Perpétue' – as a weeping standard
5. *Lavandula angustifolia* 'Hidcote' – low-growing lavender
6. *Humulus lupulus* 'Aureus' – golden hops
7. *Salvia officinalis* 'Icterina' – golden sage
8. *Foeniculum vulgare* 'Purpureum' – bronze fennel
9. *Hyssopus officinalis* – hyssop
10. *Salvia officinalis* Purpurascens Group – purple sage
11. *Salvia sclarea* – clary sage
12. *Artemisia absinthum* – wormwood
13. *Jasminum officinale* – jasmine
14. *Rosa* 'Albertine' – rose 'Albertine'
15. *Rosmarinus officinalis* – rosemary trained over a globe frame
16. *Buxus sempervirens* – box trained as a "lollipop"

Formal Beds and Borders

Beds edged with low hedges of clipped, dwarf box are a sure way of providing a formal, structured look. This works well for several beds, each being one element of a larger, overall design, or for a single herb border to stand alone.

A large border may also be subdivided by a pattern of internal hedges for a more interesting effect. The spaces in between construct individual planting areas for different species of herb. Timber or tiling edges are another way to give beds a neat finish in a formal scheme.

Right *Tightly clipped box hedging provides an orderly framework for herbs.*

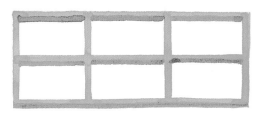

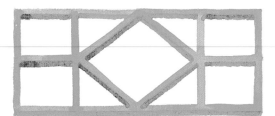

Left *Various designs for long, rectangular borders which are sub-divided by low, internal hedges. Diamonds and squares create satisfying patterns as border divisions and can be filled with a variety of other herbs.*

Clipped Mounds

Clipped mounds of plants such as cotton lavender, or golden or variegated dwarf box, may be used to great effect, either as edgings or to infill a whole bed. This kind of scheme has more impact if punctuated by clipped plants of a contrasting shape and colour: such as a large bed filled with mounds of silvery santolina, set against pyramids of dark-green box bordering a path.

A formal effect can also be achieved by planting blocks of herbs to make up a simple pattern of squares or triangular shapes, which can be repeated. This works most successfully for herbs of contrasting foliage colour and similar heights and habits: silver posie thyme, perhaps, with the dark green of wall germander, or golden and purple sage.

Above *Pyramids of box and tiling edges give beds a neat finish in a formal scheme.*

Topiary Herbs

Standard "mop-head" box or bay trees, pyramids or spiral shapes are an instant way to add formality. If you have time and patience you can train your own to shape, but it may be easier to buy them ready-grown. Topiary and citrus fruit trees in tubs were a popular feature in Tudor and Renaissance gardens, and can still work well in a modern scheme. Placed at strategic points in a geometric scheme, they add an old-fashioned touch and increase the sense of order and regularity. They can also be very useful for introducing the all-important dimension of height and visually linking the various elements of a garden.

Effective herbs for potted topiary include: bay, wall germander, mintbush (*Prostanthera rotundifolia*), rosemary, scented-leaf pelargoniums – especially *P. crispum* – myrtle and box.

Right *A bay tree clipped into a spiral emerges from a sea of lavender.*

Below *Box hedging punctuated by finials, tall clipped shapes in the beds and the trim, rounded heads of an avenue of* Quercus ilex *add up to topiary on a grand scale.*

Knot Gardens

Pattern is very satisfying to the eye and a knot garden always makes a stunning feature. The historic ideal consisted of four elements, each of a different pattern, but it would be as well to start with something simpler.

An area 3–4 m (10–13 ft) square will be large enough to contain an interesting, interwoven pattern. If possible it should be sited where it can be viewed from above – an upstairs window, neighbouring mound or raised level in the garden. It could also form an attractive centrepiece of a sunken garden. A sunny position and well-drained soil will suit it best. The old pattern books include a wide variety of hedging plants for knot gardens. To do the job effectively the

plants need to be evergreens with small leaves, dense growth and an ability to withstand close clipping. Although they all have attractive flowers and are not as neat and compact as box, excellent results can be obtained with the following herbs:

Teucrium chamaedrys has glossy, dark-green foliage, shaped like oak leaves. It is fully hardy and tolerates hard trimming, and is easy to grow from cuttings. Plant 23 cm (9 in) apart.

Santolina chamaecyparissus has silvery foliage. This responds well to close clipping and regenerates from old wood. Plant cuttings approximately 23 cm (9 in) apart. *Santolina rosmarinifolia* and *Santolina viridis* have acid-green leaves, treat these as *S. chamaecyparissus*.

Hyssopus officinalis has dark green foliage and is semi-evergreen. This often loses its leaves where winters are hard, but regenerates from old wood. Clip it regularly to avoid straggling and replace plants every four or five years. Plant 23 cm (9 in) apart.

Lavandula angustifolia 'Hidcote' – A low-growing lavender with silvery foliage. Immediately after flowering clip back to shape. However, do not cut into any old wood.

Using box for knot gardens

Box is ideal for knot gardens as its neat habit of growth means that it retains a clipped shape better than most plants. However, it is relatively slow-growing, and an instant finished effect is not easy to achieve.

Buxus sempervirens 'Suffruticosa' has bright-green leaves and is a compact plant, ideal for all edging work.

Buxus sempervirens 'Elegantissima' with small, silver-edged, olive-green leaves is slow-growing and makes a good contrast for darker leaves. *Buxus microphylla* 'Koreana' is low-growing and has dense, dark-green leaves.

It is best to choose compact varieties of box such as these, or the garden will soon grow unwieldy. Using all box makes a more manageable scheme than interspersing other knot garden plants, with different rates of growth and heights when mature.

'Elegantissima'   'Suffruticosa'   'Koreana'

Above *This striking pattern in the form of a foot maze at Hatfield House, England, symbolizes the complexities of following the Christian path through life.*

Right *A stunning and colourful knot garden of clipped box, with spaces between hedges filled with roses, lavender and scented herbs.*

To make a simple knot garden

Tips for success:

- Prepare the site well. Dig in some garden compost or manure, as it will be difficult to add organic matter once the plants are established.

- Make sure the area is completely level – use boards and a carpenter's spirit level.

- Accuracy of measuring out the design and putting in the plants is essential. A large set square, made of lengths of wood nailed together in the proportion of 3:4:5, ensures accurate 90° angles at the corners.

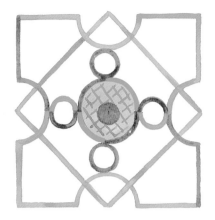

1 *Draw the plan out on graph paper in measurements to suit your plot (3–4 m or 10–13 sq ft). Colour in the design to represent the plants to be used to achieve the effect of interwoven ribbons.*

2 *Using the plan as a guide, mark out the squares on the ground using the tape measure, string and short lengths of cane. A builder's square will ensure accurate right angles.*

3 *Find the centre point of each side of the outer square and mark the semicircles by drawing arcs with string attached to a cane. The string should be the length of the radius of the semi-circles.*

4 *Mark out the semi-circle with the pointed canes and attach the string tautly to define the curve. This provides an accurate guide to follow when delineating the design in sand.*

5 *Mark out the rest of the design with string and canes, measuring everything carefully. To define the pattern, fill a plastic bottle with fine sand and pour it out evenly along the lines of the string and all markings. Remove the string and canes.*

6 *Put in the plants, spacing them evenly, 15 cm (6 in) apart and keeping accurately to the markings. Follow the colour code on the plan, making sure the interwoven effect is achieved by putting the right colour plant at the intersections.*

7 *It will take two to three years for the plants to develop and close the gaps. In the second year, pinch out the centres and trim lightly to encourage growth. Once filled out, clip twice a year (late spring and early autumn). Avoid clipping if there is any danger of frost, as the new soft growth will be damaged by it.*

Informal Gardens

Designs based on fluid shapes and an irregular layout give plenty of scope for growing a variety of herbs. They often fit better than formal schemes with the style of a contemporary house and surroundings. Paths may be offset and gently curving, with beds and borders placed seemingly at random. Areas of hard material are often broken by greenery and flowers. Plants spill over on to the paths and spring up among the pea shingle; gaps are left among the paving stones of a terrace to be filled with creeping, aromatic herbs. Bare expanses of plant-free gravel are not in keeping with this style of garden.

Planting should be exuberant: forests of poppies, stands of valerian, a vibrant jumble of flowers and foliage. Pruning and trimming are, of course, essential, but the close-clipped look is less acceptable here.

This is not to say that the structure of the informal garden has to be completely irregular. A relaxed look is frequently achieved by the planting schemes as much as by the layout of beds and paths. This has its roots in the cottage garden genre of gardening, where a central path divided two rectangular areas, and lack of space forced an eclectic mix of plants.

In many informal gardens a regular framework works well. But it has to be simple – four rectangular beds, divided by intersecting paths, perhaps. There is little room for complex patterns and rigid symmetry.

Above *Exuberant planting in a cottage garden style.*

Above *Irregular circular shapes and a gently winding path in a display garden at the National Herb Centre, England.*

Plan for an informal herb garden

This has been designed as a peaceful, rustic retreat as well as being an all-purpose herb garden containing a wide variety of plants. A path of circular logs, laid at the side of the central sweep of gravel, leads around the edge of a pond to a wooden decking area for seating and a table. Creeping thymes are planted in pockets among the log paving, and architectural spires of mullein, *Verbascum thapsus*, spring up at random in the gravel.

The borders at either side are planted for colour and to provide a selection of culinary herbs as well. A further collection of culinary herbs in containers is sited near the seating area, and an olive tree in a tub (so that it can be moved to a protected area for winter) is near the entrance. This is surrounded by shrubby herbs: thyme, sage, prostrate rosemary and winter savory in a gravel mulch, which echoes the main area of gravel.

For early summer colour there are swathes of red and white valerian and opium poppies, to be followed later in the season by brilliant red bergamot, *Monarda didyma* 'Cambridge Scarlet'. A broad band of blue catmint, *Nepeta* x *faassenii*, leads the eye up to the pond, where the fine mossy growth of Corsican mint, *Mentha requienii*, spills over the logs, with clumps of chives and gold and green variegated gingermint nearby. An ornamental form of sweet flag, *Acorus gramineus* 'Variegatus', which does not grow as large as the more authentic sweet flag, *Acorus calamus*, is planted in the pond with some water lilies.

Behind the pond, the spearmint is planted in a bucket with no base to prevent it spreading. Angelica, lovage and fennel provide height and texture as well as being valuable culinary herbs. At the top of the garden, just on its boundaries, is a common elder, with golden and fern-leafed varieties for extra interest.

To complete the countryside feel of the garden and continue the timber theme the boundary could be further defined by traditional wicker screening.

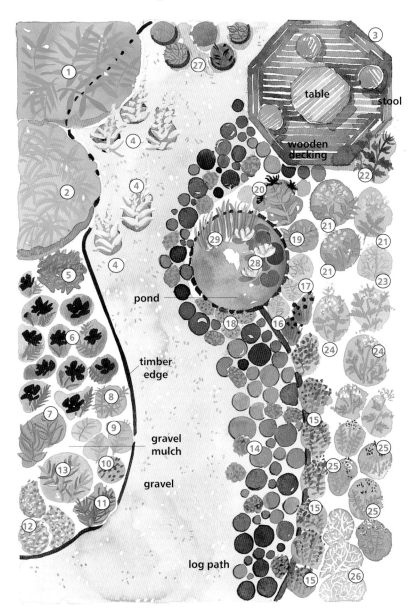

Key to planting plan

1. *Sambucus nigra* – common elder
2. *Sambucus nigra* 'Aurea' – golden elder
3. *Sambucus nigra* f. *laciniata* – fern-leafed elder
4. *Verbascum thapsus* – mullein
5. *Origanum onites* – pot marjoram
6. *Papaver somniferum* – opium poppy has white or lilac flowers, but there are many attractive cultivars in reds and pinks
7. *Salvia officinalis* – common sage
8. *Artemisia dracunculus* – tarragon
9. *Satureja montana* – winter savory
10. *Thymus vulgaris* – common thyme
11. *Rosmarinus officinalis* – prostratus group – prostrate rosemary
12. *Thymus vulgaris* 'Silver Posie' – silver posie thyme
13. *Olea europaea* – olive tree
14. *Thymus serpyllum* 'Bressingham Pink' – creeping thymes and *T. serpyllum* Coccineus
15. *Nepeta* x *faassenii* – catmint
16. *Allium schoenoprasum* – chives
17. *Mentha* x *gracilis* 'Variegata' – gingermint
18. *Mentha requienii* – Corsican mint
19. *Mentha spicata* – spearmint
20. *Monarda didyma* 'Cambridge Scarlet' – bergamot, red flowering
21. *Angelica archangelica* – angelica
22. *Levisticum officinale* – lovage
23. *Foeniculum vulgare* – fennel
24. *Valeriana officinalis* – white valerian
25. *Centranthus ruber* – red valerian
26. *Helichrysum italicum* – curry plant
27. A selection of culinary herbs in pots
28. *Nymphaea odorata* – white water lily
29. *Acorus gramineus* 'Variegatus' – variegated sweet flag

Herbal Beds and Borders

Island beds or long borders can make gratifying small herb gardens where space is limited. They are ideal for providing a supply of herbs for cooking, or a colourful medley of medicinal and aromatic herbs for general household use. In larger beds, paths or narrow brick divisions may be appropriate as visual separations and to prevent invasive species from growing into each other. Stepping stones, placed in a random pattern, provide easy access to the plants for picking or weeding.

When planting island beds, tall subjects, such as angelica and lovage, may be placed at the centre, with lower growing plants surrounding them. In a border against a wall or hedge, plant heights look best graduated, with the tallest at the back and dwarf and creeping plants at the front. Introducing height with statuesque plants adds interest. Standards, especially of plants with irregular growth patterns – olive trees, lemon verbena, old-fashioned roses – also add extra height. Scented climbing plants, such as jasmine, hops or honeysuckle, trained over tepees of canes or wooden sticks, make unusual punctuation marks in a large border.

Above *A simple, rectangular border with paved divisions, set in a gravel surround, makes a self-contained herb garden.*

Left *Bronze fennel contrasts well with white-flowering* Galega officinalis '*Alba*'.

Below *A river of creeping thymes, flanked at right by gallica roses* (R.g. *var.* officinalis *and* R.g. '*Versicolor*'), *makes an imaginative and decorative feature.*

Above *Closely-packed herbs provide a riot of midsummer colour.*

Right *Alternating clumps of purple and green-leafed sage,* Salvia officinalis.

Below *A pocket of mixed thymes, set in golden stone.*

Raised Beds

These have many advantages. They can be used to provide ideal conditions where garden soil is unsuitable. If your garden is on heavy clay, which most herbs dislike, especially the shrubby, Mediterranean varieties, a raised bed can offer the requisite free-draining environment. Where soil is poor and dry, a raised bed can be filled with a good moisture-retentive growing medium for herbs that need damp ground. Beds at a higher level can also make gardening easier and more rewarding for the disabled or elderly. For everyone, they allow plants to be seen from a new perspective so that flowers, foliage and scents can all be appreciated more closely.

Heights of raised beds may be varied according to intended purpose or preference. Old illustrations reveal the popularity from medieval times into the age of the Renaissance garden, of beds raised from the surrounding paths by no more than a few inches. For old-style physic gardens and formal potagers, low raised beds, edged with timber, are both practical and decorative.

Above *A brick-built raised bed provides a free-draining environment, which suits many herbs, especially those of Mediterranean origin.*

There are various materials that can be used for constructing raised beds:

Timber – use planks that are wide enough to sink into the ground. Screw or nail together securely at the corners and treat with wood preservative suitable for plants.

Railway sleepers (railroad ties) can be used for a rustic, informal look. Clean off any tar and preservatives, which are toxic to plants, with solvent. A plastic membrane may be necessary for heavily impregnated sleepers. No foundations are necessary as their weight makes them stable. Lay them flat, rather than on edge, for stability and fix together at the corners with steel rods, driven through them and into the ground.

Bricks are durable and attractive in a variety of settings (especially old bricks). Check they are frostproof as ordinary housebricks may not be suitable.

Above *A raised bed made of timber with feverfew and grasses.*

Above *Marjorams growing in a bed walled with stone.*

Above *Herbs flourish in a brick-built raised bed.*

Making a raised bed

Raised beds can be laid out as functional squares and rectangles, in decorative shapes or made to fit a corner of the garden such as this bed for culinary herbs.

YOU WILL NEED

Short stakes or dowel; string; builder's set square; fine sand or line-marker paint; tape measure; cement; ballast; builder's sand; pointing trowel; approximately 90 bricks; spirit level; waterproof paint; paintbrush; rubble; gravel or pea shingle (pea stone); 3 bags of topsoil; potting medium; a selection of herbs

1 *Mark out the shape of the bed on the ground, using a short, pointed stake or dowel and string. Use a builder's set square to ensure correct right angles. Define the lines with a dribble of fine sand, or use line-marker paint.*

2 *Dig out the soil along the markings to a depth and width of 15 cm (6 in). Fill in with concrete to within 5 cm (2 in) of the top. Firm down, level and leave for 24 hours to set completely. For concrete, use one part cement to four parts ballast.*

3 *Build up four or five courses of bricks, and set into mortar, carefully checking with a spirit level at each stage. (Mortar is one part cement to four parts sharp or builder's sand.)*

4 *Clean up the mortar, while it is still wet, with a pointing trowel. Leave it to harden.*

5 *Before filling with soil, coat the inside of the wall with a waterproof paint.*

6 *Put in a layer of rubble, topped with gravel or pea shingle for drainage. Fill in with bought topsoil and stir in a top layer of a good potting medium.*

7 *Plant up the raised bed with your chosen herbs.*

8 *The completed raised bed planted with a selection of culinary herbs and wild strawberries.*

Herb Wheels

These were a feature of numerous Victorian gardens, when old cartwheels (wagon wheels) were plentiful. They provided frameworks of little beds containing kitchen herbs, the spokes prevented the different varieties from encroaching on each other. If you are using an old cartwheel, it must be treated with a plant-friendly preservative to prevent the timber from rotting. The spokes may also be a little close together to be practical, so consider removing some of them.

A brick-built wheel is long-lasting and the sections can be more effectively allocated. Choose a location in full sun if possible, and if it is for culinary herbs, put it near the kitchen.

Above *An intriguing design for a herb wheel at the Henry Doubleday Research Association.*

Above *Nasturtiums are good in salads.*

Above *Pot marigolds add bright colour to a herb garden.*

Above *Chives and golden marjoram.*

Herbs for a cook's herb wheel

Medium- to low-growing herbs of similar heights make for a balanced effect.

Perennial selection:

Allium schoenoprasum – Chives. Mild onion flavour herb with attractive, purple flowers.

Origanum onites – Pot marjoram. Warm-flavoured leaves, with pinkish-purple flowers.

Satureja montana – Winter savory. Makes an aromatic, neat pillow of dark-green foliage with white flowers.

Thymus x *citriodorus* – Thyme. Delicious, lemon-scented thyme.

Salvia officinalis Purpurascens Group – Purple sage. Bold purple and green foliage; strong, savoury taste.

Foeniculum vulgare – Fennel. Tall, feathery plant with an aniseed flavour for central pot.

Petroselinum crispum – Parsley. Biennial. It is also suitable for growing as an annual.

Annual selection to sow from seed:

Calendula officinalis – Pot marigold. Well worth including for the brilliance of its flowers. Self-seeds.

Anthriscus cerefolium – Chervil. A delicately flavoured herb, which is fully hardy and can be sown successfully for a continuous supply. Self-seeds.

Coriandrum sativum – Coriander (Cilantro). Spicy flavour. Thin out seedlings and keep moist.

Tropaeolum majus – Nasturtium. Grow it for the bright flowers and use them in salads.

Ocimum basilicum 'Purple Ruffles' – Purple basil. The foliage provides a foil for other green herbs. Good basil flavour.

Satureja hortensis – Summer savory. This is more subtly flavoured than the perennial variety and it goes very well with beans.

Anethum graveolens – Dill. Plant in the central pot for its feathery foliage and delicate taste.

Making a raised brick herb wheel

1 *Using a length of string equal to the radius of the bed, attached to a piece of pointed cane, mark out a circle on the ground. Then shorten the string and mark a small inner circle at the centre. Sink a length of earthenware (clay) sewage pipe (from builder's merchants or building supply stores) in the centre. Then measure off equal points on the circumference to form the spokes, marking them out with canes and string.*

2 *Trace over the whole design with fine sand or line-marker paint.*

3 *Dig a trench for the bricks and fill with sharp or builder's sand.*

4 *Construct as for the raised bed (steps 3–5), putting in one or two layers of bricks, set in mortar, to form the outer circle and spokes.*

5 *Fill in the sections of the wheel and the earthenware pipe with rubble, then gravel or pea shingle, topsoil and compost (soil mix).*

YOU WILL NEED

String; short canes or dowel; earthenware (clay) sewage pipe; fine sand or line-marker paint; tape measure; sharp sand; approximately 90 bricks; cement; builder's sand; ballast; pointing trowel; spirit level; waterproof paint; rubble; gravel or pea shingle; 3 bags of topsoil; compost (soil mix); a selection of culinary herbs

6 *Plant the herb wheel with a selection of culinary herbs such as wild strawberry, thyme, sage, rosemary and lemon verbena.*

Themed Gardens

A themed garden can make a vibrant and colourful display for herbs. In the following section there are plans for various styles of gardens – an old-fashioned medieval garden, a decorative Shakespearean garden with a small knot garden of clipped box, and a pot-pourri garden with many different fragrant herbs and scented flowers. The cook's or kitchen garden is not only productive but will look good too.

The potager is intended mainly for culinary use but with bold use of colour, it makes an excellent ornamental layout. The plan for a traditional apothecary's garden with small, individual plots of medicinal herbs shows how to make a functional, but very eye-catching, herb garden, that needs the bare minimum of maintenance.

Right *A re-creation of a medieval pleasure garden with scented herbs, at Tretower Court, Wales.*

Medieval Garden

Above *Herbs such as valerian and feverfew grow in the raised beds of this medieval-style garden. When gardens like this were laid out, beauty was not a consideration, but with their symmetry, and the colours and shapes of the plants, the effect is delightful.*

In gardens of the Middle Ages herbs were often grown in small beds, each devoted to a single species. This made it easy to tend and harvest the plants, as well as to identify them, and was the chosen style of monastery and physic gardens, whose primary purpose was practical.

By the 12th and 13th centuries pleasure gardens, based on cloister gardens, became a feature of palaces and castles. These usually took the form of a small enclosed "privy" garden, for the benefit of the lady of the house and her attendants. King Henry III installed one for his queen, stipulating that it should have a pleasant herbery and high walls so that no one should enter except the Queen. There are narrow beds at the side, and a seat or an arbour is standard, and often there is a fountain splashing in the corner.

Plan for a medieval garden

This small garden, designed to take up approximately 6 x 8 m (19 x 26 ft), is surrounded by a trellis, with a low fence on one side and a Gothic arch as entranceway. Since a "flowery mead" would be an impractical proposition in this space, the path is made of gravel, with a central bed of pot marigolds, surrounded by a chamomile lawn.

Two chamomile seats, made as raised beds, are separated by a gallica rose, with further gallica roses at opposite corners.

Rosa eglanteria, the eglantine rose of Chaucer's day, climbs over the trellis, but a compromise has been made with the other climbing rose, 'Noisette Carnée'. This rose, unlike the others, is not ancient enough to be a true medieval rose, but has a delicate old-fashioned form and the great benefit of repeat flowering to provide interest over a longer period.

Narrow beds against the perimeter are planted with a froth of lady's mantle, flax (with its profusion of dainty blue flowers),

feverfew, wild strawberries and other plants common at the time – though a modern cultivar, *Achillea millefolium* 'Moonshine', has been substituted for wild yarrow, which would be too invasive for the area and not very attractive. There is a small fountain and shallow pond in one corner, with the moisture-loving *Iris versicolor* planted at its margins. White Madonna lilies, popular in the medieval era as a symbol of purity and associated with the Virgin Mary, are planted in pots.

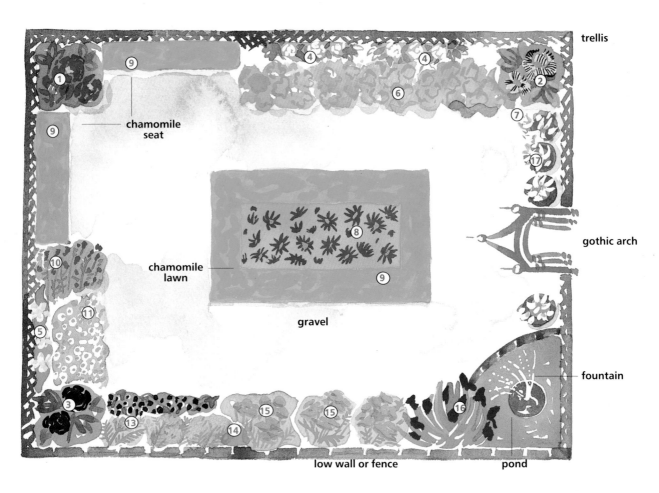

trellis

chamomile seat

gothic arch

chamomile lawn

gravel

fountain

low wall or fence

pond

Key to planting plan

1. *Rosa gallica* var. *officinalis* – the fuschia-pink apothecary's rose
2. *Rosa gallica* var. *officinalis* 'Versicolor' – pink-and-white-striped gallica rose
3. *Rosa gallica* var. *officinalis* 'Tuscany Superb' – dark-crimson, double gallica
4. *Rosa* 'Noisette Carnée' (syn. 'Blush Noisette') – pale-pink repeat-flowering climber

5. *Rosa eglanteria* – sweet briar rose, a vigorous climber with simple, palest pink blooms.
6. *Alchemilla mollis* – lady's mantle
7. *Thymus vulgaris* 'Silver Posie' – thyme with silver-variegated foliage
8. *Calendula officinalis* – pot marigold
9. *Chamaemelum nobile* 'Treneague' – a non-flowering chamomile

10. *Linum usitatissimum* – flax
11. *Tanacetum parthenium* – feverfew
12. *Fragaria vesca* – wild strawberry
13. *Tanacetum vulgare* – tansy
14. *Thymus vulgaris* – thyme
15. *Achillea millefolium* 'Moonshine'
16. *Iris versicolor* – blue flag
17. *Lilium candidum* – Madonna lily

Shakespearean Garden

For those with a literary bent, a garden based on the herbs and flowers included in the works of Shakespeare makes an exciting project. No other poet and playwright can have made so many references to these plants, nor indicated such a delight in them and knowledge of their uses and characteristics. There is also scope for a comprehensive selection, as over 130 plants are mentioned, some under two or three different names.

Culinary herbs include "saffron to colour the warden pies", "a dish of caraways" (caraway seeds) to eat with apples and "parsley to stuff a rabbit". Garlic gets several mentions, usually in connection with its odour on the breath, and onions are linked with tears.

Medicinal uses of plants make frequent entrances – though the portrait of the downtrodden apothecary (in *Romeo and Juliet*) with his "old cakes of roses" and other accoutrements "thinly scattered to make up a show" is hardly a flattering one. The narcotic properties of poppies and mandrake are referred to several times and the myth that mandrakes scream when uprooted is perpetuated. The power of the witch's brew is noted, with its deadly "root of hemlock digged i' the dark". The symbolic associations of herbs are acknowledged such as wormwood for bitterness, and also rosemary for remembrance.

Household uses of herbs include polishing chairs with juice of balm in *The Merry Wives of Windsor*; and the soothing power of scented flowers is memorably evoked in Oberon's description of Titania's bower in *A Midsummer Night's Dream*:

I know a bank whereon the wild thyme blows,
Where oxlips and the nodding violet grows
Quite over-canopied with luscious woodbine [honeysuckle],
With sweet musk-roses, and with eglantine.

Who could resist re-creating this for themselves? For researching the full extent of Shakespeare's references to herbs, *Shakespeare Concordance* by A. Bartlett, 1894, is a great help.

Other works include: *The Plant-lore and Garden Craft of Shakespeare* – by Rev. Henry N. Ellacombe, 1884; *The Flora and Folklore of Shakespeare* – by F.G. Savage (Shakespeare Press, 1923); *The Shakespeare Garden* – by Esther Singleton (William Farquhar Payson, New York, 1931); *Shakespeare's Wild Flowers* – by Eleanour Sinclair Rohde (the Medici Society 1935); *The Flowers of Shakespeare* – by Doris Hunt (Webb and Bower, 1980).

Above *Box and cotton lavender form intertwining ribbons in a garden edging.*

Plan for a Shakespearean garden

The plan is for a garden approximately 9 x 13 m (29 x 43 ft) in the formal style that was popular in Shakespeare's day. At the centre is a small knot garden of clipped box, surrounded by narrow borders of lavender and pinks. Three spacious steps lead to an arbour on a higher level, so that the knot can be viewed from above. Creeping thyme is planted in pockets on the stone slabs in front of the seat, and over the steps. The arbour is clad in honeysuckle and roses and surrounded by the 'wild thyme' and other flowers and herbs of Titania's bower. Raised beds, with brick-retaining walls, form the boundaries and topiary trees in tubs visually link the garden and mark the entrance points. Poisonous plants such as hemlock, henbane, aconitum and others have not been included in this garden for safety reasons. The two rue bushes are at the back of the border, where they are least likely to be accidentally brushed. Rue can cause blistering on contact, but has long been a popular aromatic plant.

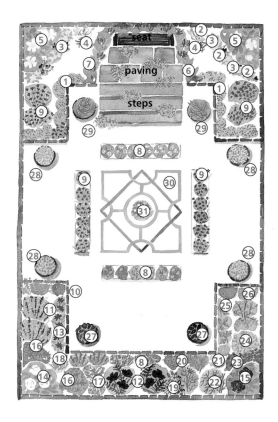

Key to planting plan

1. *Thymus serpyllum* – wild thyme
2. *Viola odorata/Viola tricolor* violets and heartsease
3. *Primula veris/Primula vulgaris* – cowslips/primrose
4. *Lilium candidum* – Madonna lily
5. *Rosa moschata* – musk rose
6. *Rosa eglanteria* – sweet briar rose
7. *Lonicera periclymenum* – honeysuckle
8. *Dianthus caesius/Dianthus deltoides* – pinks
9. *Lavandula angustifolia* 'Hidcote' – lavender
10. *Satureja montana* – winter savory
11. *Consolida ajacis* – larkspur
12. *Papaver somniferum* – opium poppies
13. *Calendula officinalis* – pot marigold
14. *Rosa x alba* – white rose of York
15. *Rosa gallica* var. *officinalis* – red rose of Lancaster
16. *Ruta graveolens* – rue
17. *Artemisia absinthum* – wormwood
18. *Hyssopus officinalis* – hyssop
19. *Origanum onites* – marjoram
20. *Mentha* spp. – mint
21. *Carum carvi* – caraway
22. *Foeniculum vulgare* – fennel
23. *Borago officinalis* – borage
24. *Melissa officinalis* 'Aurea' – variegated lemon balm
25. *Petroselinum crispum* – parsley
26. *Sanguisorba minor* – salad burnet
27. *Laurus nobilis* – standard bay
28. *Buxus sempervirens* – standard box
29. *Rosmarinus officinalis* – rosemary (trained as topiary)
30. *Buxus sempervirens* 'Suffruticosa' – dwarf box
31. *Myrtus communis* subsp. *tarentina* – dwarf myrtle

Top *The flower stems of silvery blue* Sempervivums *create an intricate pattern.*

Above *Lavender grows very well in the free-draining soil of a bed with raised timber edge.*

Opposite *An Elizabethan knot garden, closely planted with colourful flowers for a richly embroidered effect, at Stratford-upon-Avon, England.*

Pot-pourri Garden

There is a long tradition of drying scented flowers and aromatic herbs for sweetening the air. Stillroom books of the 17th and 18th centuries include many recipes for scented powders and "perfumes" as pot-pourri was more usually known then. The term as currently used to describe a mixture of dried fragrant petals and leaves did not become common until the 19th century. It comes from the name of a Spanish stew, *olla podrida* (literally meaning "rotten pot"), and the French translation of pot-pourri came to mean any medley or mixture.

An area of scented herbs and flowers, which can be picked for pot-pourri, makes a rewarding garden feature. Stock it with plenty of roses – pink and red ones are best as they retain good colour when dried.

"Rose-leaves ... were gathered even as they fell to make into a pot-pourri for someone who had no garden." (*Cranford* by Mrs Gaskell).

Above *A pergola covered in old-fashioned roses provides plenty of petals for drying.*

Plan for a pot-pourri garden

This plan would fit into an area about 8 m (26 ft) square to make a scented garden with plenty of material to cut for making pot-pourri. The four corner beds, set in a grass path, are edged with dwarf box and filled with colourful flowers and fragrant herbs. The central circular area is brick-paved, with pockets for a low-growing double chamomile and vivid caraway thyme. The gazebo supports a richly perfumed, dark crimson 'Ena Harkness' climbing rose and a cloud of jasmine. There is room beneath it for a seat, or a small table and some stools, and it is surrounded by pots of colourful, scented pelargoniums, pineapple sage and lemon verbena.

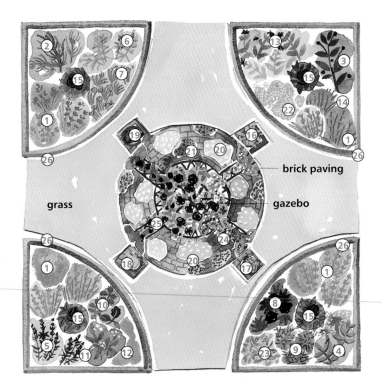

grass

brick paving

gazebo

Key to planting plan

1. *Lavandula angustifolia* 'Munstead' – dark blue, low-growing lavender
2. *Rosmarinus officinalis* – rosemary
3. *Myrtus communis* – myrtle
4. *Angelica archangelica* – angelica
5. *Agastache foeniculum* – anise hyssop
6. *Hyssopus officinalis* – hyssop
7. *Dianthus* 'London Delight' – an old-fashioned pink
8. *Paeonia officinalis* 'Rubra Plena' – a rich red paeony
9. *Artemisia abrotanum* – southernwood
10. *Coriandrum sativum* – coriander (cilantro)
11. *Tanacetum balsamita* – alecost
12. *Consolida ajacis* – larkspur
13. *Monarda* 'Croftway Pink' – a pink bergamot
14. *Iris germanica* var. *florentina* – Orris
15. *Rosa* 'François Juranville' – a gold-pink rose, as a weeping standard
16. *Aloysia triphylla* – lemon verbena
17. *Pelargonium tomentosum* – peppermint scented
18. *Pelargonium* 'Lady Plymouth' – scented-leaf geranium, with cream margins
19. *Salvia elegans* – pineapple sage
20. *Chamaemelum nobile* 'Flore Pleno' – dwarf, double-flowered chamomile
21. *Thymus herba-barona* – caraway-scented thyme
22. *Thymus vulgaris* 'Silver Posie' – a silver-leafed thyme
23. *Mentha* x *gracilis* 'Variegata' – gingermint
24. *Jasminum officinale* –the white-flowering jasmine
25. *Rosa* 'Ena Harkness' – dark-red climbing rose
26. *Buxus sempervirens* 'Suffruticosa' – dwarf box

To make a rose pot-pourri

Making your own pot-pourri is a rewarding and creative experience. The results will have individuality and a more pleasant fragrance than shop-bought.

YOU WILL NEED

3 cups dried rose petals;
2 cups mixed dried flowers;
15 ml (1 tbsp) dried lavender;
1 cup mixed dried herbs: mint,
marjoram, thyme and angelica;
5 ml (1 tsp) cloves; 2.5 ml/½ tsp)
ground allspice; 10 ml (2 tsp)
ground orris root; 5–10 drops
rose essential oil

1 To dry the plant material, pick everything on a dry day. Spread out on newspaper and leave in a warm, airy place (out of direct sunlight) for 5–7 days, until papery to the touch.

2 To make the pot-pourri, combine all the ingredients, mix thoroughly and put them in an airtight container. Leave in a dry, warm place for 2–3 weeks, shaking the container occasionally.

Above *A traditional rose garden in full bloom and (right) a garden of scented herbs and flowers for making pot-pourri.*

Cook's Garden

A small border or bed can provide a surprisingly good selection of herbs to meet basic culinary needs, especially if supplemented by a few tubs and containers. A sunny location is important as the herbs will thrive and have a better flavour. For convenience the kitchen garden should be sited as close to the kitchen door as possible so that herbs can be harvested without you having to trudge too far.

Plan for a cook's garden of herbs

A semicircular-shaped bed against a wall allows space for 13 useful herbs, with bay, basil and mint in containers: tender basil is much easier to grow in a pot, and mint is inclined to spread into its neighbours. A narrow brick path divides the space and makes it easier to reach the plants when tending or picking them.

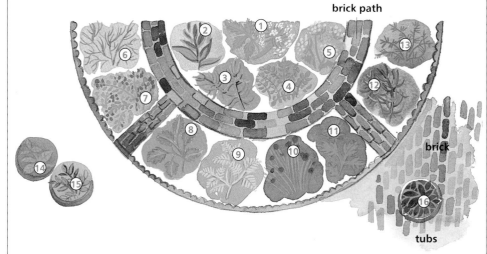

brick path

brick

tubs

Key to planting plan

1. *Angelica archangelica* – angelica
2. *Salvia officinalis* – sage
3. *Artemisia dracunculus* – tarragon
4. *Origanum onites* – pot marjoram
5. *Levisticum officinale* – lovage
6. *Anethum graveolens* – dill
7. *Thymus vulgaris* or *Thymus x citriodorus* – thyme or lemon thyme
8. *Coriandrum sativum* – coriander (cilantro)
9. *Anthriscus cerefolium* – chervil
10. *Allium schoenoprasum* – chives
11. *Petroselinum crispum* – parsley
12. *Rosmarinus officinalis* Prostratus Group – prostrate rosemary
13. *Satureja montana* – winter savory
14. *Ocimum basilicum* – sweet basil
15. *Mentha spicata* – spearmint
16. *Laurus nobilis* – bay

Above left *An informal kitchen herb garden with nasturtiums and coriander (cilantro).*

Far left *A pot of golden and purple sage provides a ready source of leaves for cooking.*

Left *Sweet basil is a traditional complementary flavour for tomatoes and is frequently used in culinary dishes.*

Potager

A potager is a garden where vegetables and herbs are grown together in an ornamental layout. Early cooks' gardens contained as many herbs as "vegetables" – as we now call them – with little distinction being made between the two. "Sallet"(salad) herbs in Elizabethan times included a wide variety of unusual leaves and colourful flowers. They were also made into stuffings and uncooked sweet and savoury sauces: flower petals pulverized with ground almonds and sugar, or potent mixtures of green herbs pounded together in vinegar.

Growing herbs and vegetables together is practical and ornamental at the same time. Mixed plantings of this nature suffer less from pests because the bright flowers of many herbs attract beneficial insects, such as lacewings and ladybirds (bugs). At the same time, aromatic plants deter aphids and other insects. If vegetables are intermingled with strong-smelling herbs, rather than planted in huge blocks on their own, they become a less obvious target for the pests normally attracted to them.

As with all vegetable growing, allowance must be made for rotation of crops and there will inevitably be bare patches at intervals to accommodate this. But the garden is afforded a permanent structure by the framework of paths and perennial herbs.

Paths may be of gravel, brick, stone or any hard material. The central one should be at least 1 m (3 ft) wide and the divisions between the beds no less than 0.5 m (20 in). Beds should be no more than 1.5 m (5 ft) wide so that they are easy to reach; timber or tiling edges give them a neat finish and link the elements of the garden together.

Archways for climbing plants at the entrance or at the centre of the garden add height and visual appeal. Espaliered fruit trees at the perimeter make a practical and decorative screen. A tunnelled archway of apples or pears is a traditional feature.

Plan for a potager garden

This potager is both practical and ornamental, with beds about 1.5 m (5 ft) in length and paths 0.5 m(20 in) wide. The plan below allows for perennial herbs, such as lavender, rosemary and sage, to be planted at the ends of each bed.

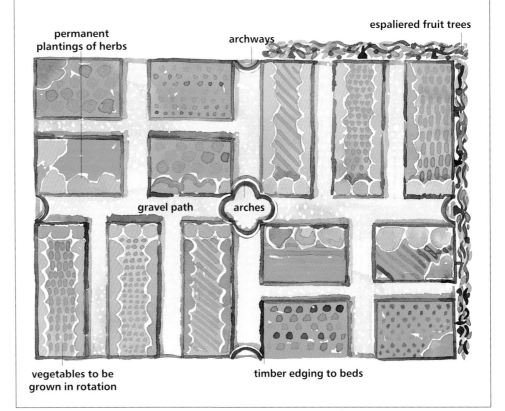

permanent plantings of herbs

archways

espaliered fruit trees

gravel path

arches

vegetables to be grown in rotation

timber edging to beds

Above *A formal potager of box-edged beds, packed with sturdy vegetables, ruby chard (foreground), sweetcorn, marrow and beans, interspersed with aromatic rosemary.*

Apothecary's Garden

Also known as a "physic garden", the apothecary's garden was the source of raw materials for making medicines to heal the sick.

In the tradition of the monasteries, a range of "simples", or medicinal plants, were grown in their own little plots. These were sometimes prescribed to be used on their own, or, more frequently, the apothecary concocted compounds from them, consisting of several ingredients. The advantage of keeping each herb in its separate bed in this way was to make identification easier when it came to picking, as well as being an efficient method of cultivation on a small scale. It also provided easy access for planting, weeding and watering.

When making their remedies, the apothecaries were guided by a variety of herbals: the earliest of which was written in China nearly 5,000 years ago. They also studied the works of the great physicians of ancient Greece – Hippocrates, Galen, Theophrastrus and Dioscorides – and the texts from the Dark Ages which were

copied by generations of monks, and given a new lease of life by the invention of printing in the mid-15th century.

The role and influence of the apothecary began to wane during the 16th century as European herbalists started to base their work on empirical observations of plants. John Gerard's *Herball or Generall Historie of Plantes* was in this tradition of enquiry and was first published in England in 1597. Apothecaries established their own society at the beginning of the 16th century and were the pharmacists of the time, dispensing drugs for the physicians and giving out medical advice to patients.

Above *Herbs growing in little beds, created by gaps in paving slabs, make an attractive and practical medicinal garden.*

Left *A collection of herbs in sunken pots, carefully labelled to ensure correct identification.*

A modern garden of herbs for making home remedies, which draws on the best of these traditions, has understated charm and is a low-maintenance way to grow herbs. Filled with traditional herbs, such as bright gold pot marigolds (*Calendula officinalis*), neatly patterned houseleek (*Sempervivum tectorum*), aromatic lavender, rosemary, thyme and sage, laid out in a simple configuration of beds, it will be both functional and eye-catching.

Top *Houseleek is a useful plant for soothing skin irritations.*

Above *Pot marigolds are picked for drying before they have a chance to go over.*

Plan for an apothecary's garden

This garden of medicinal plants is based on the old idea of individual plots for each herb, but simplified and brought up to date by setting the herbs among paving slabs. The plan is uncomplicated by the need to lay paths, or put in edgings. All that is required is a level, completely weed-free site, some paving slabs and a base of sand and cement to bed them into. The design will fit a space of 4.5 x 6 m (15 x 19 ft).

Key to planting plan

1. *Calendula officinalis* – pot marigold – for soothing creams
2. *Sempervivum tectorum* – houseleek – for chapped skin and insect bites
3. *Myrtus communis* – myrtle – for sinusitis and bronchial infections
4. *Foeniculum officinalis* – fennel – for indigestion
5. *Marrubium vulgare* – horehound – for coughs
6. *Tanacetum parthenium* – feverfew – for migraines
7. *Salvia officinalis* – sage – for mouth and gum infections
8. *Lavandula stoechas* – lavender – for tension headaches
9. *Rosmarinus officinalis* – rosemary - for colds and depression
10. *Thymus vulgaris* – thyme – for sore throats
11. *Origanum onites* – pot marjoram – for arthritis
12. *Allium sativum* – garlic – for warding off colds
13. *Valeriana officinalis* – valerian – for insomnia
14. *Hypericum perforatum* – St John's wort – for anxiety and nervous tension

Boundaries

A herb garden with its own distinct boundaries becomes a secluded retreat, a place to sit and relax away from the pressures of the outside world. The key point is that the enclosing wall, fence or hedge does not have to be very solid, or even high – so as not to cast too much shade, which is usually better for gardens. It is the illusion of a place apart that counts, which can be achieved just as effectively with a low balustrade fence or plant-clothed pergola. And even a low division still provides some shelter, reduces the wind-chill factor and helps to retain and intensify the fragrance of the plants.

Above *A simple construction of posts and cross-rails divides areas of a kitchen garden.*

Above *Trelliswork, in the foreground, makes an effective internal division in a secluded garden bounded by a wall and plant-clothed walkway.*

A garden entirely enclosed by high brick walls enjoys its own warm microclimate. But in order not to be overpowering it has to cover a reasonably large area, as in the walled kitchen gardens of the grand houses of the past. In the smaller gardens of today, it is sometimes possible to make use of a high brick wall as one boundary, but other internal walls are best kept to a height of about 60 cm–1 m (2–3 ft).

Fences are a useful way to provide an instant screen and come in a wide range of materials. Choose one that is sympathetic to the overall style of your herb garden. A simple balustrade fence can work very well, or a traditional picket fence, popular in many American herb gardens: these are often painted white, but also look good with a green or blue finish. Wattle or wicker screens, as used in medieval enclosures, are another congenial fencing material.

Trelliswork, also known as treillage, makes a versatile boundary. It adds elegance and romance and works in formal or informal settings. Trellis comes in different patterns, may be painted in a range of colours and provides a frame for climbing plants. It is important, as for all fences, that the support posts are solid and firmly installed. The easiest and longest-lasting method of securing posts is to bed them into a custom-made pointed metal base set into the ground, or set them into a rubble and concrete base. Timber posts should be treated with preservative – choose one that does not harm plants. (If you use creosote, planting must be delayed for a year, as it can harm plants.)

Pergolas are another way of making a visual boundary, rather than a solid screen, and will suit a small garden as well as a large one. A covered or semi-covered walkway, clothed in plants, was a traditional feature of many 17th-century gardens and it was usually called an "arbour" or "herber". Strictly speaking a pergola should be constructed as a double row to form an arched walkway with a curved or rectangular top. But it can also be made as a single row of posts and cross-rails, to act as a support for climbers and to make an internal fence or division.

Espaliered fruit trees trained flat against a system of posts with wires strained horizontally between them provide an openwork, living screen as a boundary or division. They can be planted in a single row or a double one to form a walk. They also look good trained against a wall. Plant as young trees, removing any side shoots and training the branches along the wires as they grow.

Hedging Plants

Hedges make the ideal boundary for many herb gardens. They divide different areas and delineate paths. They may be formally clipped, or left to a more natural pattern of growth, and reach different heights to provide a high dense screen or a low division. Low, clipped hedges form knot-garden patterns. Choose from a selection of the following:

• *Taxus baccata* – Yew. Slow-growing, but makes a superb screen and its dark green provides a foil for many plants.

• *Buxus sempervirens* – Box. Makes an excellent hedge for a neat, clipped finish. Formal hedges – low to medium height.

• *Buxus sempervirens* 'Suffruticosa' – Dwarf box. Much more compact than the common box, ideal for knot gardens.

• *Santolina chamaecyparissus* – Cotton lavender. A silver plant which responds well to clipping into mounds or low hedges.

• *Teucrium chamaedrys* – Wall germander. The dark-green foliage needs frequent trimming to keep it in shape. Can be grown as an informal hedge and left to flower.

• *Origanum vulgare* 'Aureum' – Golden marjoram. Although it can be clipped to form mounds, its relaxed habit of growth makes it less suitable as a conventional formal hedge.

• *Rosmarinus officinalis* – Rosemary. Can be clipped to a squared-off hedge shape, or trimmed as an informal hedge.

• *Rosa rugosa* – Rose. This forms a dense, impenetrable barrier of medium to full height.

• *Artemisia abrotanum* – Southernwood. Light-green, feathery foliage makes a delightful informal hedge that needs trimming only once or twice a year.

• *Hyssopus officinalis* – Hyssop. It is possible to clip this to a formal shape, but the blue flower spikes make it worth growing in its natural form, lightly trimmed. Cut back in the spring.

• *Lavandula* spp. – Lavender. There are different heights to choose from. Makes a fragrant hedge, needing little attention, apart from cutting back firmly (but not into old wood) after flowering.

Planting a hedge

1 *Dig out a shallow trench along the line of the proposed hedge and fork over the soil at the base of it to ensure good drainage.*

2 *Add plenty of garden compost, digging it lightly into the soil, and just before planting, fork in a sprinkling of blood, fish and bone organic fertilizer, wearing gloves and a respirator mask.*

3 *Mark the centre line of the hedge with string and pegs, put in the plants, spacing them evenly by using a measured length of wood – 23 cm (9 in) apart is suitable for most. Fill in the soil, firming it around each plant, and water.*

4 *The hedge will soon become established, ready for its first trim in the second year. Give it a mulch of compost in subsequent years or add a little organic fertilizer to the soil, watering it in.*

Above *Rosemary forms a good hedge-like boundary in this enclosed herb garden.*

Focal Points

The design of the herb garden will be stronger and have more impact with the inclusion of focal points to draw the eye. They may be in a central position or at the end of a path or vista. A sundial is a traditional feature in many herb gardens. Birdbaths and fountains introduce the soothing element of water. A stone urn overflowing with trailing or flowering herbs is always a simple but effective centrepiece, and standard topiary trees in tubs make versatile and movable points of interest.

An arbour, in the sense of a covered seat or shelter, strikes just the right note in an ornamental herb garden. It provides a focal point as well as being a frame for climbing plants, and introduces the all-important dimension of height. At the same time it adds a hint of mystery and makes a secluded place to sit and enjoy the sights and scents of the surroundings. Sited at the end of a walk, in a far corner or high vantage point, it becomes an inevitable attraction that has to be visited. Arbours may be constructed from many types of materials including posts and rails, trellis, metal frames, or, for a more rustic look, wickerwork.

Archways can be sited to emphasize an important feature, such as a statue, within the garden itself, or to frame a distant view .

Right *The elegant façade of a distant house is framed by an archway of roses.*

Opposite *A fountain makes an attractive centrepiece in a sheltered garden.*

Below *A water-lily pond provides the focal point in the centre of a cloister herb garden.*

Choosing Herbs

When working out planting schemes it pays to think about the colour and texture of the herbs you choose and to group them for best effect. They will flourish and make a better show, too, if given the right conditions – damp or dry, sun or shade. One of the many advantages of a herb garden is that it has quite a long season of interest – often provided by the colour of the leaves (many of which are evergreen). Foliage colours available include silver, or silvery-blue, bronze, purple and gold as well as all the greens.

Above *Rue and curry plant in flower.*

Silver

Artemisia abrotanum – Southernwood. Greeny-grey, feathery leaves.

Artemisia absinthium – Wormwood. Silvery-grey, finely indented leaves.

Artemisia ludoviciana 'Silver Queen' – Western mugwort. Fine, silvery lanceolate leaves.

Artemisia pontica – Roman wormwood. Silver, upright, foliage spikes.

Dianthus spp. – Pinks. Foliage colouring varies, most are blue-grey.

Eucalyptus globulus – Eucalyptus. Silvery-blue, smooth oval leaves, round when immature.

Helichrysum italicum – Curry plant. Silver, spiky leaf clusters.

Lavandula dentata var. *candicans* – Lavender. Woolly, finely toothed silvery-grey leaves.

Marrubium vulgare – Horehound. Greeny-grey, rounded, textured leaves.

Ruta graveolens 'Jackman's Blue' – Rue. Steely-blue, strikingly indented foliage.

Salvia officinalis – Sage. Greeny-grey, oval, rough-textured leaves.

Santolina chamaecyparissus – Cotton lavender. A good strong silver, finely indented foliage.

Thymus vulgaris 'Silver Posie' and *T.* x *citriodorus* 'Silver Queen' – Best of the silver thymes, with delicate variegations.

Bronze and Purple

Ajuga reptans 'Burgundy Glow' – Bronze bugle. Glossy, bronze foliage.

Above Thymus x citriodorus *'Silver Queen'.*

Above *Feathery, bronze fennel.*

Atriplex hortensis 'Rubra' – Red orache. Purple-red, smooth, pointed leaves.

Foeniculum vulgare 'Purpureum' – Bronze fennel. Golden-bronze foliage.

Ocimum basilicum 'Dark Opal' – Purple basil. Glossy, purple leaves.

Ocimum basilicum 'Purple Ruffles' – Purple basil with purple, frilly leaves.

Salvia officinalis Purpurascens Group – Purple sage. Purple-green leaves.

Sambucus nigra 'Guincho Purple' – Purple-bronze elder with indented foliage.

Gold

Many of these are variegated, but the predominant effect is gold.

Above Origanum vulgare *'Aureum'.*

Buxus sempervirens 'Latifolia Maculata' – Golden box. Small golden leaves.

Laurus nobilis 'Aurea' – Golden bay. Smooth, oval golden leaves.

Melissa officinalis 'All Gold' – Golden lemon balm. Bright golden-yellow leaves, splashed with green.

Melissa officinalis 'Aurea' – Variegated lemon balm with gold and green leaves.

Mentha x *gracilis* 'Variegata' – Gingermint. Boldly-patterned gold-and-green-striped leaves.

Origanum vulgare 'Aureum' – Golden marjoram. Yellow-gold, oval leaves.

Salvia officinalis 'Icterina' – Golden sage. Gold and grey-green variegation.

Thymus spp. – Thymes. Several of these have strong gold foliage. Among the best are *Thymus.* x *citriodorus* 'Archer's Gold', *T.* x *citriodorus* 'Aureus', *T.* 'Nitidus' and olive-green and gold *T.* 'Doone Valley'.

Above Mentha suaveolens '*Variegata*'.

Variegated

Agave americana 'Variegata' – Agave. Yellow margins to spiky, blue-grey leaves.
Ajuga reptans 'Multicolor' – Bugle. Green, pink and cream variegated foliage.
Armoracia rusticana 'Variegata' – Variegated horseradish. A cultivar with striking, creamy-white stripes on green.
Mentha suaveolens 'Variegata' – Pineapple mint. Creamy-white margins to leaves.
Pelargonium crispum 'Variegatum' – Scented geranium. Crinkly, golden-edged leaves.
Pelargonium 'Lady Plymouth' – Scented geranium. Light-green leaves with creamy margins.
Ruta graveolens 'Variegata' – Variegated rue. Foliage dappled green and cream.
Salvia officinalis 'Tricolor' – Tricolor sage. Striking variegations of pink, greeny-grey and cream.

Above Ruta graveolens '*Variegata*'.

Herbs with Colourful Flowers

Many herbs have colourful flowers which transform the garden when they are in bloom. Even those that do not have large flowers like their cultivated cousins, such as *Hypericum perforatum*, put on a good show in a mass planting.

Above *Red and white valerian with catmint.*

Ajuga reptans – Bugle. Blue flower spikes.
Alchemilla mollis – Lady's mantle. Frothy, greeny-yellow flowers.
Borago officinalis – Borage. Tiny, star-shaped flowers provide a mist of blue when planted en masse.
Calendula officinalis – Pot marigold. Brilliant, orange-yellow blooms.
Dianthus spp. – Pinks. Deep reds and pinks.
Helichrysum italicum – Curry plant. Bright-yellow button flowers.
Hypericum perforatum – St John's wort. Bright-yellow star-shaped flowers.
Hyssopus officinalis – Hyssop. Deep-blue flower spikes.
Inula helenium – Elecampane. Yellow, daisy-like flowers.
Lavandula spp. – Lavender. A range of misty-blues, mauves and purples.
Monarda didyma – Bergamot. There are many cultivars which come in a range of pink, red, purple and white.

Above *Sunflowers and nasturtiums.*

Nepeta x *faassenii* – Catmint. Mauve-blue flowers, spectacular in a mass planting.
Origanum onites, Origanum vulgare – Pot marjoram and oregano. Clusters of purple-red flowers.
Rosa spp. – Rose. Old-fashioned varieties have pink, red and white blooms.
Salvia officinalis – Sage. Massed purple-blue flower spikes.
Santolina chamaecyparissus – Cotton lavender. Bright yellow button flowers.
Thymus spp. – Many of the thymes have mauve to pinkish-red flowers.
Tropaeolum majus – Nasturtium. A range of bright yellows and oranges and a long-flowering season.

Above *Old-fashioned pinks (*Dianthus *spp.).*

Above *A variety of white-flowering herbs.*

Above *Bronze fennel and rosemary standing tall over a bed of low-growing herbs.*

Herbs with White Flowers

A garden of white-flowering herbs has a restful quality, especially if combined with silver-leafed plants and white and green variegated foliage. Many herbs have white flowers, others, such as borage, lavender and sage, have white-flowering forms. This is a selection:

Achillea millefolium – Yarrow. Small creamy-white umbels.

Allium tuberosum – Garlic chives. White star-shaped flowers.

Borago officinalis 'Alba' – A white-flowering borage.

Chamaemelum nobile – Chamomile. White daisy-like flowers.

Digitalis purpurea f. *albiflora* – White foxglove. Creamy-white spires.

Galium odoratum – Sweet woodruff. Small white stars.

Lilium candidum – Inimitable pure-white lilies.

Myrrhis odorata – Sweet cicely. Large white umbels.

Thymus serpyllum var. *albus* – A creeping, white-flowering thyme.

Valeriana officinalis – Valerian. Effective in a mass planting.

Right *Tall herbs – elecampane, fennel and a white-flowering goat's rue at the back of a border.*

Tall Herbs

When it comes to planning beds and borders it helps to know the eventual height and spread of plants. The ultimate size of individual herbs is indicated in this book, but the selection below are a reminder of "what not to put at the front". They are also useful for adding height to a scheme.

Angelica archangelica – Angelica. A classic for adding architectural impact.

Cynara cardunculus Scolymus Group – Globe artichoke. Earns a place in any scheme for the decorative value of its striking, purple heads.

Foeniculum vulgare – Fennel. A graceful feathery plant, which needs plenty of room.

Levisticum officinale – Lovage. Large clumps of glossy, green leaves need space to spread sideways and upwards.

Onopordum acanthium – Scotch thistle. The patterned leaves are relatively low-growing, but the flower stalks rise to a height of 2 m (6 ft 6 in).

Climbers

Another way to add the dimension of height to an otherwise flat design is by training creeping plants over arbours, archways, obelisks and twiggy tepees. Herbal creepers to choose from include:

Humulus lupulus – Hops. There are both green and golden-leaved varieties.
Jasminum officinale – Jasmine. This has star-shaped, perfumed white flowers in midsummer.
Lonicera periclymenum – Wild honey-suckle with creamy flowers, borne throughout summer. There are also many cultivars to choose from.
Rosa spp. *R. eglanteria* – Eglantine rose. Has very short-lived flowers. An old-fashioned climber, such as Mme Alfred Carrière, might be more rewarding. *R. gallica* 'Complicata' reaches 2 m (6 ft 6 in) and may be used as a pillar rose.

Top Humulus lupulus *'Aureus'*.

Above *A bay tree with climbing roses.*

Above *Creeping thymes make effective and appealing ground cover.*

Ground-cover Herbs

For the front of a border, to fill an awkward corner, or as paths and lawns, ground-cover plants are invaluable.

Arctostaphylos uva-ursi – Bearberry. A mat-forming evergreen shrublet.
Chamaemelum nobile 'Treneague' – Non-flowering lawn chamomile. A non-flowering cultivar.
Juniperus communis 'Prostrata' – Juniper. Forms a dense, neat carpet, which no weed can penetrate.
Symphytum ibericum – Dwarf comfrey. A fast-spreading plant. Also comes in a gold and green variegated form.
Thymus serpyllum – There are many creeping thymes, ideal for paths, lawns and ground cover.
Vinca minor – Periwinkle. The dark-green leaves form dense, weed-defying cover. Cheerful blue flowers in spring.

Dry or Damp Soil?

It is usually easier to fit the plant to the right environment, rather than the other way about. Changing the soil and microclimate to accommodate a plant's particular preference can often be difficult and costly. The good news is that herbs are relatively easy-going plants and will often adapt to and grow well in conditions they would not choose in the wild. But to make things easier, it usually pays to give them what they want.

Dry, or certainly well-drained, soil suits the majority of plants, especially the shrubby herbs such as rosemary and thyme.

Damp-lovers to watch for include angelica, the *Mentha* genus and *Monarda didyma*. The mints and angelica will also grow happily in shade or semi-shade.

Herb Containers

Growing herbs in containers has many advantages. Where space is limited there is always room for a few pots, even in the smallest of gardens. Sited near the house, they provide the added convenience of being handy for harvesting – important for culinary herbs. As part of a garden scheme, containers can be placed in a bed to fill a temporary bare patch, used as focal points or arranged symmetrically to link different elements of a design.

Their mobility is a definite plus. Of course it must be borne in mind that very large pots, or those made of stone, will be too heavy to move. But, unlike static planting in a bed, small and medium pots, or those made of a lighter material, can be moved around to make a change. This is also useful for plants past their best, which need a less prominent position in which to recuperate. Tender and half-hardy herbs in containers can be moved under cover for winter protection.

Above *Comfrey has deep roots and needs a tall container (left back). Marjoram (centre) and thyme thrive in smaller pots.*

Planting

Growing a single species in a container gives plants room to develop and to provide plenty of leafy growth. For larger specimens, such as bay, sage and lemon verbena, it is essential that they do not

Above *Large pots planted with angelica add impact to a parterre.*

have to share a pot if they are to be left undisturbed for several years. The pot should be large enough to allow roots to spread. Mixed herb pots make very attractive features and are a good way of growing a variety of plants in a small space, but plants are inevitably cramped; roots become congested and annual replanting is usually necessary for a mixed planting.

Good drainage is one of the keys to success. Before you start, check that there is a large hole in the base of the pot, or several holes in the case of plastic pots and troughs. Put in a layer of crocks (broken terracotta pots), then cover with a layer of sand or grit (gravel) before filling with potting compost (soil mix).

Most herbs flourish in a free-draining environment and, as a general rule, a 3:1 mixture of soilless compost (planting mix) and loam-based compost (soil mix) gives the best results. For shrubby herbs, such as bay, sage and rosemary, and for scented pelargoniums, add a few handfuls of grit (gravel) to the mix to improve drainage. Do not be tempted to use garden soil; it will not provide enough nutrients and might harbour weeds and pests.

Maintenance

Extra fertilizer must be added after about four weeks, with subsequent weekly feeds throughout the growing season. An organic plant food based on seaweed extract is preferable, but slow-release fertilizer granules save time as they are added when potting up.

Pot-grown plants need frequent watering during the growing season. As a general rule, it is better to let them almost dry out and then give them a good soaking, rather than to keep dribbling in small amounts of water. Water-retaining gel mixed into the growing medium at the time of planting makes watering less of a chore. During the winter months pot-grown perennials should be given the minimum amount of water possible.

Plants that are kept in the same container for several years should have the top layer of compost, about 5 cm (2 in), scraped off and replaced with fresh every year. They will need re-potting in a container one or two sizes larger as roots become congested – try not to leave it until the plant is obviously suffering, with roots bursting out of the pot, yellowing leaves and poor, straggly growth.

Above *Herbs growing in separate pots with* Lavandula stoechas *at rear right.*

Planting a pot of mixed culinary herbs

1 Mix slow-release fertilizer and water-retaining gel, following instructions, into a potting medium made up of 3:1 parts of soilless compost (planting mix) and loam-based compost (soil mix).

2 Put a layer of crocks (broken terracotta pots) in the bottom of the pot.

3 Fill to the first hole with the potting medium, settling it evenly.

4 Tap a plant out of its pot and feed it gently through the hole, working from the inside outwards.

5 Cover the roots with more compost and firm it down before adding a further layer of plants.

6 Put in more plants until all the holes are filled and finish with one or two plants on top. Water in thoroughly.

YOU WILL NEED
Slow-release fertilizer; water-retaining gel; soilless compost; loam-based compost; trowel; terracotta pot; crocks (broken terracotta pots); a selection of culinary herbs

Right Marjoram (top), alpine strawberry, thymes and parsley go well together in a pot of herbs for culinary use.

Potting Composts

Potting composts (soil mixes) come in two main types: based on sterilized loam, and the soilless composts (planting mixes), based on peat or peat substitutes such as coir. Soilless composts are lighter and easier to handle, but they do not retain nutrients as long as the loam-based ones. They provide a more moist environment, but, if left unwatered, they also dry out more quickly, and are difficult to remoisten. Both types of potting compost are available containing nutrients in a range of proportions: "seed and cuttings" formula contains the least and a "potting" formula the most, with "all-purpose" in between.

Indoor Herb Gardening

Some herbs adapt well to being grown as houseplants. In regions with cold winters which suffer frosts, it is one way of cultivating tender herbs successfully. A conservatory gives scope for keeping a wider range, but is by no means essential. Give indoor plants as much natural light as possible and regular liquid feeds in summer, and do not overwater, especially in winter.

Vigorous and colourful, easy-to-grow scented pelargoniums are a rewarding group to grow this way as they come in such a variety of scents and leaf forms. Don't be afraid to prune them hard if they become straggly and never keep them too damp. Tender pineapple sage (*Salvia elegans*) does well indoors and produces scarlet flowers in late autumn or winter just when colour is welcome. It needs a big pot and more water than most. *Aloe vera* adapts well to an indoor regime, requiring the minimum of attention. A gritty, free-draining compost (soil mix) suits it best and infrequent but thorough watering. Myrtles do not always survive frosts and are another good choice. The dwarf *Myrtus communis* 'Tarentina', having a compact and tidy habit of growth, is eminently suitable, and *Myrtus communis* 'Variegata', being even less hardy, is well worth growing inside.

Herbs on the Windowsill

A supply of indoor culinary herbs is a great convenience. It is possible to grow them on the kitchen windowsill as long as you take into account the stress this puts on the plants. If you put a young plant into a small pot and then keep cutting off its leaves, it will be hard pressed to survive. At the same time, it is being kept short of air, the atmosphere may be too hot and steamy and changes of temperature extreme. From the point of view of flavour, there is little sun to bring out the essential oils.

The best way to counteract these problems is to alternate pots kept on the windowsill with another set left standing outside. Keep the different herbs in individual pots and group them together. They grow better in close proximity to one another because transpiration from the massed leaves increases the overall humidity.

Standing the pots on a gravel tray, or in a container with a layer of gravel on the base, keeps them cool and helps to retain moisture, without the plants becoming waterlogged.

Above Herbs grouped together on the windowsill are handy for cooking.

Far left Scented pelargoniums and lemon verbena grow well as houseplants.

Left Culinary herbs in separate pots, standing in an outer container of gravel.

Herbs in the Greenhouse

It is perfectly possible to grow many herbs without any form of winter protection or artificial heat. But in colder regions a small, frost-free greenhouse is a great help in extending both the season of growth and the range of plants it is possible to grow.

It is often easier to raise plants from seed sown in trays. Under controlled conditions, the success rate is usually higher. With a greenhouse you can start sowing much earlier than if you had to wait for the right outdoor conditions. But remember that young plants, grown on from seedlings, must be acclimatized gradually to being outside, before they are finally planted in the garden. Do this by standing them outside in the daytime for a short period, or transferring them to a cold frame.

Parsley is a good candidate for sowing under glass. Although it is reasonably hardy, it needs heat to germinate (about 18°C, 65°F), which is why it takes so long to emerge when planted straight into the garden early in the year before the soil has warmed up. Germination will be much quicker and more reliable if the seeds are started in trays in the greenhouse, with a view to transplanting outside once grown.

Basil is almost impossible to raise from seed in temperate regions without the benefit of glass. But it is not difficult to get good results if you follow a few guidelines:

• Do not start too early in the year; allow spring to get well under way first, when it will be easier to supply a temperature of 15–18°C (60–65°F).

• Scatter seeds as sparsely as possible, so that little thinning-out is required later and root disturbance minimized.

• Provide the seedlings with adequate ventilation and do not overwater to reduce risk of "damping-off" disease.

• Grow plants on in a large container, rather than planting them directly into the soil. They can then be kept outside or moved into a greenhouse, according to current weather conditions.

Above Capsicum frutescens *'Gipsy', in flower, in a greenhouse.*

Summer Herbs

Unless the summer is exceptionally cool and wet, sweet basil (*Ocimum basilicum*) will usually grow well in a pot outside, but the purple-leafed kinds seldom reach their full potential unless kept under glass.

Chilli peppers (*Capsicum* spp.) also need to be grown in the greenhouse in cooler climates if they are to produce mature, ripe fruits. In parts of the United States chilli peppers can be grown outside. Other herbs to try are the popular Japanese salad plants known as shiso (*Perilla frutescens* and *P. frutescens* 'Crispa') and the culinary flavouring plant, lemon grass, much used in Thai cookery (*Cymbopogon citratus*).

Adequate shading and copious watering are necessary for plants grown under glass in the summer.

Winter Protection

For container-grown plants that are not fully frost-hardy, such as bay, lemon verbena and myrtle, as well as more tender subjects such as scented pelargoniums, a cold greenhouse, provided it is frost-free, gives enough protection to keep them alive through the winter. In the summer months they can stand outside in the garden, as long as they are moved under cover before the first winter frosts.

Many of these plants will lose their leaves, even if they remain evergreen in warm climates. Once they have been moved into the greenhouse in the autumn, cut them back or trim lightly, according to individual requirements. Over the succeeding winter months give them a minimal amount of water and no fertilizer to ensure dormancy.

Growing Herbs

Once the design and overall style have been chosen, it is time to turn them into reality. Practical guidance is included in this chapter on how to do so, through the stages of planning and preparing the site, laying out paths and hard surfaces, to putting in the plants themselves. There are tips on successful propagation and how to train plants into standards or over frames. There is advice on maintenance and seasonal tasks, with a final section on dealing with pests and diseases.

Above *Tools of the trade in an old-style potting shed.*

Left *A supply of freshly-cut material for recipes is one of the rewards of growing your own herbs.*

Planning Your Planting

Many of the most familiar herbs are Mediterranean in origin and grow best where there is plenty of sun. Bear this in mind when deciding on the location for your herb garden. Choose an area that has the sun for most of the day and where there is little dense or permanent shade. Take the time to watch the movement of the sun, so that you know exactly where shadows fall. This will help with planning the planting, allocating the right areas for herbs needing sun, shade or semi-shade and deciding where to site features such as a sundial, arbour, fountain or a seat. If you are at the survey stage in winter when the trees have no leaves, don't forget to take into account the deep shade cast by summer foliage.

Shelter is also important. Chilly winds, particularly in winter, can be devastating to many shrubby herbs such as thyme and rosemary. You may be able to make good use of an existing boundary wall to act as a windbreak. Consider putting in hedges, trelliswork or wicker fences to provide a sheltered, secluded environment, but remember that they will cause some shade and loss of light to plants. It may be better to install them on one or two sides only, according to prevailing wind direction, leaving other sides open or with low balustrade fencing.

If productivity is the main objective it is best not to overdo the number of low hedges, central features and dividing pathways, all of which will diminish the amount of space available for cultivation. Nevertheless, the plot can still achieve considerable charm if the production is arranged in an orderly fashion and by building in a feature or two that will add overall interest.

Top *A carefully planned bed, with silvery spokes of* Santolina chamaecyparissus *in a wheel of block planting.*

Right *Herbs flourish in a garden sheltered by a high brick wall.*

Soil and Site Preparation

Time spent preparing the site by improving the soil and eliminating weeds will be repaid many times over. This is not as daunting as it might seem. Improving the texture of the soil (though not weed elimination) applies only to the planting areas and does not have to be carried out where paths and hard surface areas are to be laid.

A light, free-draining soil is best for most herbs. It warms up quickly in spring and does not become as cold and waterlogged as heavy soil in winter. But if it is too porous, moisture and nutrients will be quickly leached away, resulting in a soil so poor and dry that few plants will flourish. Forking in organic matter – garden compost or leaf mould – will ensure better results. On heavy soil, if areas are inclined to become water-logged it is worth digging out trenches and filling them with rubble to form land drains. Chalk and sand both drain rapidly whilst clay retains moisture. The ideal is a crumbly loam which retains the right degree of water and nutrients.

Many herbs, including lavender, do not grow well in a heavy clay soil. One way to overcome the problem is to put

Above *A raised bed provides good drainage.*

in raised beds filled with loamy topsoil. But if you intend to plant straight into existing ground, once again it will be necessary to incorporate organic matter.

For a very heavy soil, the addition of plenty of coarse grit helps to open up the texture further. Double digging, though hard work, is the way to do this most effectively. Take out a trench to the depth of two spades at one end of the plot, turning it straight into a wheelbarrow and removing it to the other end of the area to be treated. Add a layer of grit and

compost to the first trench, covering it with soil from the next section. Continue in this pattern until the whole area has been dug over and organic matter incorporated. When the last trench is reached fill this with the soil from the first trench. After digging, tread down the soil lightly to ensure that no air pockets remain and that the soil does not subsequently settle unevenly. Rake over in several different directions until the surface is level and leave it for a week or so before planting.

Beware of overmanuring ground where herbs are to grow. The object of digging in bulky organic matter is to improve texture and drainage. For the majority of herbs, heavy feeding with rich farmyard manure or artificial fertilizers encourages soft growth, reduces aroma, and lays the plants open to attack by pests and diseases.

Another factor to consider is the alkaline or acid content of the soil, measured by the pH factor. A figure of seven is taken as neutral – anything higher is alkaline, anything lower is on the acid side. An inexpensive soil-testing kit will tell you what you have. Herbs are a disparate group, but as a rule most will grow in a neutral soil.

Weeding

Eliminating perennial weeds as thoroughly as possible before putting in plants pays great dividends. Another advantage of double digging is that you can take out deep roots and every speck of greenery you see as you go along. Fork out all weeds as painstakingly as possible. For stubborn or dense weed growth, cover the area for a full season with a layer of thick black polythene (plastic). Once this is removed, all but the most persistent weeds will be obliterated.

If you would rather get started on the planting immediately, put down a layer of black polythene (plastic), cut with holes for planting pockets, making sure these are completely weed free. Then put in the plants and cover the surface of the polythene with a mulch of gravel or bark chippings.

Above *Forking out weeds.*

Above *Double digging eliminates weeds and improves soil texture.*

Above *Removing all trace of roots helps keep the soil clear for longer.*

Laying Out a Garden

The first thing to do is to make a plan to fit your plot and requirements. You can take it from an existing design in a book, but you will need to tailor it to fit your own site. Check that you have the space to carry out your chosen scheme, that it will complement its surroundings and not be too cramped. Then measure the site and note the position of any existing walls, trees or other features that are to be kept.

Decide on a scale and draw up the plan on graph paper, but remember that it is all too easy to put in too much, too close together. It may look good on paper but will not work in reality. Keep checking as you go along that the layout you have drawn is feasible on site. The simpler it is and the fewer fussy elements you include, the more impact the finished garden is likely to have.

Marking Out a Garden

Once you have worked out the design and chosen the site, it is time to lay it out on your plot and put in hard surfaces.

Take your paper plan on to the chosen area and mark the key points on the ground with stakes. Designate the boundaries and outline the beds and paths with string and pegs, measuring carefully and ensuring that right angles are accurate with a builder's square. A length of garden hose is useful for marking out curves. At this stage it is possible to check that the proportions are right, that the whole scheme is well balanced and that other parts of the garden do not intrude or clash with the general concept. An upstairs window is often the best place to get a good overall view. Now is the time to change anything that does not look right – it will be difficult and costly to alter later on. It is best to decide on the order of work before you start:

• Changes of levels or major earthworks, including digging out ponds, need to be done first.
• Construction work, paths, terraces, hard surface areas, herb wheels and raised beds come next.
• Boundaries need to be clearly marked before you start, and, if putting in a wall, you may want to do this first, as well as putting in fence posts. But for ease of access and wheelbarrow movement it usually pays to leave fences till after the hard construction is done. Hedges, too, should be put in at a later stage with the bulk of the planting.
• Features such as pergolas, arbours and fountains may be put in at the same time, or after the hard-surface construction.
• Preparation of the soil in the beds should be done a few days in advance of planting if possible.
• Planting the herbs is practically the last stage.
• Finishing touches include adding container plants to the scheme and movable features such as sundials.

Above *Contrasting coloured stones, in this cobbled surface, pick out a star motif and decorative border.*

Putting in Paths and Hard Surface Areas

All paths and hard surface areas require a firm, level base. This can be done by marking a series of pegs with a line 5 cm (2 in) from the top. Hammer the pegs into the ground across the area to be levelled, tapping them in until the tops are flush with each other (using a spirit level to check). Then level and firm down the soil to the mark on the pegs.

Above *Drawing out the design on paper helps to achieve a successful result.*

Above *A random pattern of paving stones.*

Above *Bricks provide a colourful surface.*

Gravel is a relatively inexpensive, quickly laid surface. It comes in a range of colours and in two main types: crushed stone from quarries and pea shingle (pea stone) from gravel pits. It should be laid on a level, well-compacted base of soil covered with a layer of dry concrete, eight parts ballast (gravel) mixed with one part cement, which has been left to dry off for several days. Hessian mesh (burlap), laid over the path before the gravel is spread, prevents weeds.

Stone slabs are a good surface for a terrace or large paved area. They are also useful for using as stepping stones in a wide border and for a mixed surface path of gravel and paving slabs. Bed them into mortar on a hardcore base (stones and broken bricks), as for the brick path, below.

Cobblestones are an attractive finish for a small scale area. They can be used to fill in round shrubs and trees or to lay in conjunction with other hard-surface materials. Pack them together as closely as possible, set in a bed of mortar on a hardcore base.

Bricks must be hard, impermeable and resistant to frost. Reclaimed bricks, from specialist merchants, have the best mellow colour. They must be laid on a firm, hardcore surface or they will expand and lift with the moisture in the soil and form an uneven path. For a path with less heavy wear a sand base without hardcore is sufficient.

To lay a main brick path

This construction will be suitable for main paths in a herb garden and should withstand average domestic use and weather conditions.

YOU WILL NEED
Timber boarding; wooden pegs; mallet; spirit level; hardcore (stones and broken bricks); ballast; cement; rake; hard, impermeable bricks (about 24 for an area 60 cm (2 ft) wide by 1 m (3 ft) long); sand, a large broom

1 Dig out soil for the path to a depth of one brick plus 10 cm (4 in) for the base. Tread it down till level. Put in an edging of timber boards, held in place with hammered-in pegs, with their upper edges at the level of the finished path. Spread a 7.5 cm (3 in) layer of hardcore, rolling it in until firmly compacted.

2 Cover the hardcore base with a dry mix of eight parts ballast to one part cement, approximately 2.5 cm (1 in) thick, lightly tamp it with the head of the rake to fill in any gaps in the hardcore, and then rake to a loose, level surface.

3 Lay the bricks into the ballast and cement base, arranging them in a staggered pattern so that you don't have a line of joints. Tap each one down with a mallet, butting it as close to its neighbour as possible; check with a spirit level that the path is even in all directions as you go.

4 When all the bricks are in place, spread more ballast and cement over the surface, brushing it repeatedly into the joints to fill them, before cleaning off the surplus. Moisture from the soil will set the cement, but a light spray of water may be applied to hasten the process.

5 Before the cement hardens, ease sand from the joints to create pockets for prostrate herbs, then fill in with a little topsoil and sow seeds or plant divisions from established plants.

Planting the Garden

Once you have a stock of established perennials you will be able to increase them by propagation, and many annuals and biennials will conveniently seed themselves. But you are sure to need to buy some plants in order to get your herb garden started.

Buying Plants

Specialist herb nurseries should have many of the more unusual varieties, but many garden centres now offer a reasonable selection. As you will require several of each species for a good show, the initial outlay could be considerable, so make sure you buy only strong, healthy specimens and follow these tips to get the most for your money:

• Check that a plant has not been too recently potted and whether it lacks a strong root system, or conversely that it has not been too long in the pot and the roots have become congested. Make sure there are no weeds, algae or moss.

• Examine the plant carefully for pests – red spider mite and whitefly may not be obvious at first glance.

• Don't buy anything with discoloured , wilting or blotched leaves – it could be diseased.

• Never assume that a stunted, straggly and overgrown or poor and sickly specimen will improve once planted out. It won't.

• Resist the temptation to buy annuals potted up singly. Many do not transplant well and seed quickly in hot, dry weather – these include coriander (cilantro), chervil, dill and borage. Grow them yourself from seed. Once established they often self-seed.

• Look for annual flowering herbs, such as pot marigolds and nasturtiums, sold as bedding plants in trays, rather than in single pots – or grow them yourself from seed.

• It will probably be necessary to thin seedlings to give them room to develop; and keep them well weeded to prevent competition for moisture and nutrients.

Planting the Design

If you have drawn in the herbs on your plan, this can be very useful as a guideline. A pre-designed scheme helps to group plants effectively for colour, texture, height and so on. However, it is not always easy to visualize on paper how it will look on the ground. Standing the plants in their pots on the soil, and shifting them around as necessary, helps with spacing and final decisions on position which often leads to a happier end result. It cannot be stressed enough that plants always look best in groups, rather than being scattered about singly. A whole bed of purple sage makes a

Above *One healthy and one poor container-grown vervain plant.*

Top *A well-stocked herb garden.*

much more dramatic statement than one little clump lost in a mass of competing colour. A broad sweep of catmint or borage is a sight to savour.

The same principle applies to climbers grown over an arched walkway. With several different plants the result can be very haphazard. One variety will have impact.

Invasive Herbs

Be careful where you put invasive plants. Comfrey, horseradish, sweet cicely and other herbs with strong tap roots can be very difficult to eradicate if you later want to change the planting scheme.

Some herbs, particularly those with creeping roots, encroach on their neighbours. Mint is a well-known culprit; soapwort and tansy can also prove overpowering. It is best to confine them with divisions in the bed: bricks or tiles buried in the soil work very well for shallow-rooting invasive herbs.

Another way to curtail them is to grow them in a large container buried in the soil – but make sure it has adequate drainage holes, or the base removed, if the plants are not to become choked.

Planting a herb garden

1 *When you have put in all the hard surfaces in your garden and prepared the soil as necessary (see Soil and site preparation) it is time to plant up the scheme. Fork in a little organic fertilizer first, to give your herbs a good start, but avoid heavy manure.*

2 *Always water plants well in their pots first, as plants never take up moisture as well after planting if put in dry. Add water until it trickles out of the base of the pot – this is important for trees, shrubs and larger specimens, which may look damp on top but are dry at the rootball.*

3 *Mark your planting positions with sand. Tap each herb out of its pot, make a hole with a trowel, and put in the plant, firming the soil lightly around it afterwards. Water in well. Under very dry conditions it helps if you fill the planting hole with water first.*

4 *Keep the area free of weeds so that the newly set out herbs do not have to compete for moisture and nutrients.*

YOU WILL NEED

Garden fork; organic fertilizer; a selection of herbs; watering can; trowel; sand

Right *Recently planted aromatic herbs, set out in a knot pattern, surround a dwarf standard tree.*

Propagation

Propagating your own herbs is a rewarding occupation and the best way to replace plants and to stock your garden economically. The basic techniques are not difficult, but, as herbs are such a disparate range of plants, their requirements and the degree of difficulty in raising them varies. Some are much easier to propagate than others. Many respond better to one method than another so check for the optimum propagation method for each plant.

Raising from Seed

Many herbs are easy to grow from seed. Spring is generally the best time for sowing, but do not start too early: seeds sown when air and soil temperatures are warmer and light levels higher will grow into stronger plants. Some seeds are sown in autumn, as indicated here.

Annuals: All annuals – plants whose life cycle is completed in one year – can be grown from seed sown in spring. Hardy annuals, such as chervil (*Anthriscus cerefolium*), coriander (cilantro) (*Coriandrum sativum*) and pot marigold (*Calendula officinalis*) may also be sown in autumn to give them an early start the following spring. Half-hardy annuals, such as nasturtiums (*Tropaeolum* spp.), should not be sown until late spring or early summer in areas where there is frost. Basil (*Ocimum basilicum*) is tender and should be sown in seed trays under glass in late spring to early summer.

Biennials: These are planted in the late summer or early autumn of one year, to flower the following year – though some of them go into a third year, their life cycle is over once they have flowered. Although parsley is a biennial, it is worth sowing seed every year because the stems coarsen and it does not produce such good leaf in its second year. Biennials include angelica (*Angelica archangelica*), caraway (*Carum carvi*), clary sage (*Salvia sclarea*) and evening primrose (*Oenothera biennis*).

Perennials: These live for a number of years and many perennial herbs can be successfully raised from seed. But not all of them produce seed, such as French tarragon (*Artemisia dracunculus*) and the non-flowering golden sage (*Salvia officinalis* 'Icterina'). Many hybrids and cultivars do not come "true" from seed, which means they may vary considerably from the parent plant. This includes all the mints, most lavenders and ornamental thymes. These must be vegetatively propagated.

Vernalization: A few herb seeds need to be subjected to a period of intense cold before they will germinate. In the wild, this ensures their survival where winters are cold. To reproduce these conditions artificially, in a process known as "vernalization" or "stratification", put the seeds in a polythene (plastic) bag of moist sand and leave in a refrigerator or freezer for 4–6 weeks before sowing.

This is necessary for: aconitum or monkshood (*Aconitum napellus*), arnica (*Arnica montana*), agrimony (*Agrimonia eupatoria*), juniper (*Juniperus communis*), hawthorn (*Crataegus laevigata*), *Primula* spp., *Rosa* spp., sweet cicely (*Myrrhis odorata*), sweet woodruff (*Galium odoratum*) and sweet violet (*Viola odorata*).

Scarification: Some hard-coated seeds, such as those of legumes, which include broom, clovers and vetches, will germinate more readily if first rubbed with fine sandpaper. This breaks up the outer coating and allows moisture to penetrate, which all seeds require before they will germinate.

Left *Careful labelling prevents mis-identification when new seedlings emerge.*

Sowing in seed trays

The success rate for seeds sown in trays under controlled conditions is higher than for seeds sown outdoors. It is the best method for very fine seeds, such as parsley, and essential for raising tender plants, such as basil. It is also a good way to give many plants an earlier start.

YOU WILL NEED

Cellular seed tray; soilless seed and cuttings compost (soil mix); watering can; herb seeds; garden sieve; label; polythene (plastic) dome or plastic bag; 7.5 cm (3 in) pots

---

1 Fill a seed tray with soilless growing medium. A tray divided into cells makes it easier to sow thinly and to pot up seedlings with minimum root disturbance. Water first, then scatter two or three seeds in each compartment.

2 Cover the tray with a layer of sieved compost (soil mix). Never bury seeds too deeply, especially small ones such as parsley. Water again and don't forget to label the tray (tiny seedlings look similar).

3 Put a polythene (plastic) dome over the tray, or enclose it in a plastic bag, to retain moisture. Put the tray on a windowsill or in the greenhouse until the seedlings emerge.

4 When the seedlings come through remove the cover and put the tray in a light place out of direct sunlight. Keep moist, but never waterlogged.

5 As soon as the seedlings are large enough to handle, pot them up in 7.5 cm (3 in) pots filled with fresh potting compost (soil mix). When strong and bushy they can be planted out.

Sowing Outdoors

Many seeds can be sown outdoors directly into the soil where they are to grow, or in nursery beds for later transplantation. It is also the sensible way to raise herbs that do not respond well to being transplanted. These include coriander (cilantro), chervil and dill. It is as well to remember that there is a higher failure rate for seeds sown outdoors, rather than in a tray in the greenhouse, due to unexpected adverse weather conditions or the unwanted attention of birds or rodents. On the other hand it saves time and energy in pricking out, potting up and hardening off, and plants raised this way are often sturdier. For a good chance of success with outdoor seeds:

• It is best not to start too early in spring, if still cold. But to speed things up cover the area with cloches for a week or two in advance of sowing to warm up the soil.

• First weed the area thoroughly and rake it to a fine texture and level surface.

• Next make a shallow depression with a stake, or rake handle, in the soil and sprinkle in seeds as thinly as possible. Larger seeds, like nasturtiums or coriander (cilantro) can be placed individually rather than scattered.

• Cover seeds with a thin layer of soil, patting it down lightly, but beware of burying them too deeply.

• Don't forget to mark the area planted clearly. Sowing in straight lines, as appropriate for producing some culinary herbs, makes it easier to distinguish seedlings from weeds.

• Water well after planting and keep the area moist until the seedlings appear.

Above Calendula officinalis *grown from seed.*

Germination Requirements

For seeds to germinate successfully they require:

Moisture: The surface of the growing medium in seed trays must not be allowed to dry out, and outdoor seeds need frequent watering in dry spells.

Warmth: Most seeds need some degree of warmth to germinate, though temperature requirements can vary considerably. Most plants native to northern Europe and North America germinate at 10–13°C (50–55°F); plants from tropical and southern latitudes 15–21°C (60–70°F). Those herbs with special requirements include: lavender, exceptionally low at 4–10°C (40–50°F), parsley, 18–21°C (65–70°F), and rosemary, especially high at 27–32°C (80–90°F).

Light: Seeds should not be sown too deeply, in order that light may penetrate the soil and waken the seed into growth. This is particularly important for fine seeds – larger ones can be buried a little deeper. Light is crucial for thyme (*Thymus vulgaris*), winter savory (*Satureja montana*), poppies (*Papaver* spp.) and also sweet marjoram (*Origanum majorana*).

Air: A peat-based (or peat-substitute) growing medium is best for seeds, as the open texture allows air to circulate and oxygen to reach the developing plant. This is why breaking up the soil to a fine tilth is necessary for outdoor sowing and why seeds fail in compacted, water-logged soil.

Vegetative Propagation

Many perennial herbs are best propagated vegetatively, rather than by seed. This includes those that do not flower and set seed.

Above *Mint (in pot) grown from cuttings.*

Taking cuttings from the stems during the growing season is an effective method for many. Softwood cuttings are taken from soft, new growth in spring through to midsummer. They root quickly with warmth and humidity. Suitable for: *Origanum* spp., *Pelargonium* spp., *Santolina* spp., *Tanacetum* spp., *Mentha* spp. and *Salvia elegans*.

Semi-ripe cuttings are taken from harder, half-ripened wood in mid to late summer and can be taken from many shrubby herbs, including *Buxus* spp., *Citrus* spp., *Helichrysum italicum*, *Rosmarinus officinalis*, *Thymus* spp., *Lavandula* spp. and *Myrtus* spp. Some plants, including *Salvia elegans* and *Artemisia abrotanum*, root from stem cuttings taken at any time during the growing season.

Hardwood cuttings are taken from mature wood in mid to late autumn. They are slow to root (up to 12 months), and are usually kept in a cold frame over winter. This is suitable for trees, shrubs and roses.

Stem cuttings

Many herbs, such as rosemary and southernwood, are best propagated from cuttings. It is also the only way to perpetuate a special flower colour, such as pink-flowered hyssop, or a leaf variation, such as variegated rue. Stem cuttings are all taken in the same way. Do not cram in too many cuttings or put one in the middle of the pot.

YOU WILL NEED

Plants; sharp knife or secateurs (pruners); polythene bag; hormone rooting powder; 15 cm (6 in) pot; cuttings compost (growing medium); dibber (dibble), pencil or stick; plastic dome or bag

1 *Collect only a small amount of material at a time and be sure to keep in the shade in a polythene bag, to minimize water loss. Choose sturdy, non-flowering stems, with lots of leaves. Cut a section about 10 cm (4 in) just below a leaf joint and remove all but the top two or three leaves. These are necessary to supply the plant with nutrients as the root system develops.*

2 *Dip the cuttings into hormone rooting powder, tapping off any excess, and insert them into holes made with a dibber (dibble) round the edge of a pot filled with moist cuttings compost (growing medium). Water lightly and cover with a plastic dome or polythene bag held over a wire frame and sealed at the bottom – this is to maintain maximum humidity.*

3 *Once the cuttings have rooted – 2–4 weeks for softwood cuttings, 4–6 weeks for semi-ripe cuttings – repot into new compost and harden them off gradually before planting out.*

Root cuttings

A method of increasing herbs with creeping roots, such as mint (*Mentha* spp.), soapwort (*Saponaria officinalis*), bergamot (*Monarda didyma*) and herbs with taproots such as horseradish (*Armoracia rusticana*).

YOU WILL NEED

Garden fork; mint, or other suitable plant; secateurs (pruners); seed tray; cuttings or all-purpose compost (growing medium); watering can

1 *Lift a root of mint and cut it into 4 cm (1½ in) pieces. Try to cut at a point where there is a small bud from which a new plant can grow.*

2 *Fill a seed tray with cuttings compost. Lay the pieces of root on the surface, press them in and cover with a further layer of compost. Water and leave in a shady place. There is no need to cover the tray or enclose it in polythene, but do keep it moist.*

3 *Once there are plenty of leaves showing through, divide the new plants and grow them on in bigger pots or plant them out in the open ground.*

Division of roots

Herbs with fibrous or fleshy taproots are very easy to propagate by division. These include: chives (*Allium schoenoprasum*), oregano (*Origanum* spp.), lemon balm (*Melissa officinalis*), lovage (*Levisticum officinale*) and comfrey (*Symphytum* spp).

1 *Dig up a clump of chives. Divide it into several new pieces, pulling it apart with your hands or the aid of a small fork if necessary.*

2 *Cut off some of the top growth. Replant in open ground or firm each new piece into a pot filled with all-purpose compost.*

3 *Keep the new plants well watered. They will soon grow strongly to provide plenty of fresh leaf.*

Layering

A useful method of propagation for shrubby herbs such as bay, rosemary and sage. It works by inducing a side stem to develop new roots while still attached to the parent plant. Mound layering is particularly suitable for thymes, which become straggly after a few years. Pile gritty loam in a mound over the lower, leafless stems, leaving the crown of the plant showing. This stimulates new roots to develop at the base, when they can be separated and then planted in a different position.

1 *Trim the lower leaves from a side stem, attached to the shrub. Bend it over and bed into soil beside the plant.*

2 *Fasten it down with a staple or peg. Water in and leave for several months until roots have formed. Divide the new plant from the parent and replant it.*

Maintenance

Herbs are easy-going plants. Most are not difficult to grow, coming up year after year, or self-seeding exuberantly; but a herb garden, like any other garden, needs regular care and maintenance to keep it looking at its best. Keeping paths and gravel areas free of weeds makes all the difference to the overall appearance, especially in formal gardens, which depend on symmetry and orderliness for effect. If you don't like using weedkiller, there is nothing for it but to hoe out offenders as soon as you see them. Try not to let weeds seed or else the problem will be compounded.

Mulching is a good way to keep beds and borders weed-free. Use well-rotted garden compost, mushroom compost, leaf mould or bark chippings and pile it on thickly round plants. Weeds that come up through the mulch will be weak and easy to pull out. Gravel is also a suitable mulch and weed suppressant for thymes and many shrubby herbs. Grass clippings are useful for mulching round fruit bushes and the base of trees – they can be used fresh, added in a thick layer and allowed to rot down. For weeds with persistent roots, spreading heavy-duty black polythene (plastic) over the area for a full season helps to eradicate them by depriving the seedlings of light and air.

Deciding which plants are undesirable is not always straightforward, as plenty of herbs are wild plants and often described as "weeds". You may decide to keep some self-sown plants, either leaving them in situ or transplanting to a more convenient spot, and this can add to the interest of the garden. The main thing is to be in control and not to let unwanted plants take over and dominate the scheme.

Clipping

In a formal scheme keeping plants clipped is all-important. Some will need cutting only twice a year, but others may require more frequent light trims to keep them in shape.

Many herbs grow prolifically, if left to themselves, and need frequent cutting back if the garden is not to become untidy and overgrown. Pruned plants can often be harvested for culinary or household use and any spares should be added to the compost heap. Spring is a good time to do some initial tidying and trimming, but many plants will need further cutting back during the summer months or in autumn.

Watering

It should not be necessary to give extra water to fully grown herbs planted out in the garden, except under severe drought conditions. Many of the shrubby herbs of Mediterranean origin are resistant to a shortage of water – rosemary flourishes in the driest of summers. But moisture-lovers, such as angelica, bergamot and mint, may need some help at these times. And of course it is essential in dry spells to water newly-planted young herbs until they are well-established.

Mulching often helps to conserve moisture, but if it is to be effective for this purpose it must be added early in the season before the soil dries out.

The main task is to water container-grown herbs throughout the growing season. In their dormant period, during winter, they should be kept barely moist, or root rot may ensue.

Feeding

Although it is important to keep the soil "in good heart" with the addition of garden compost, heavy manuring and fertilizing with high-nitrogen inorganic products is to be avoided. It results in soft, sappy growth which is susceptible to blackfly infestation and will not withstand the stress of droughts or extreme cold. Worst of all the herbs will lack fragrance and aroma.

A slow-release organic fertilizer, such as blood, fish and bone, forked into the soil, helps to get new plants off to a good start. And any fruit and vegetables in the herb garden will require extra nourishment in the form of liquid seaweed or a comfrey fertilizer. Container-grown plants benefit from regular liquid feeds throughout the growing season, especially older plants that have been in the same pot for some time.

Above *A standard bay in a tub needs regular clipping with secateurs (pruners) and feeding.*

Opposite *A rotting compost heap.*

Above *A meticulously maintained garden.*

Comfrey Fertilizer

Comfrey is invaluable as a herb garden fertilizer, containing all the nutrients necessary for healthy plant growth in digestible form. It has a high potash content and is also a source of nitrogen, phosphorus and many other elements. Use it in the following ways:

• As a mulch by spreading freshly cut comfrey leaves round plants (blackcurrants and other fruit bushes benefit particularly). Topping the comfrey with a layer of lawn mowings adds bulk and speeds decay.

• Add comfrey leaves to the compost heap in thin layers – it doesn't add to the humus content, but works as an "activator", encouraging the breakdown of other plant material. Be careful to avoid adding roots and flowering stems, which will regenerate and form unwanted plants.

• As a liquid fertilizer, by filling a bucket to the halfway mark with comfrey leaves, fill it with water and cover with a lid – to exclude insects. Leave for 4–5 weeks, then strain off the liquid (which will be very smelly) and use it undiluted as an organic fertilizer for container plants, tomatoes and general garden use.

• A more concentrated version may be made by standing a bucket with a hole in the bottom over another container, filling the bucket with comfrey leaves and pressing them down with a weighted board. The bucket should then be covered with a lid and the leaves left to rot down for several weeks, until a black, tarry liquid seeps out. This should be diluted in water before use.

Above *A variety of garden clippings and fresh vegetable material is added to the heap, for a good supply of garden compost.*

Making a Compost Heap

A good supply of garden compost is always needed in the herb garden for improving the structure and fertility of the soil and as a mulch material.

Containers: There are many types of manufactured compost bins available in plastic, wood and other materials, suitable for gardens of varying sizes, but you can easily make your own. Build the heap straight on to the earth, with a surround of wire mesh, or timber boards to contain it. If using boards, leave airspaces between them.

Materials: Any plant material is suitable, such as, leaves, flowers, lawn clippings, straw, vegetable peelings. Woody stems should be included only if they have been mechanically shredded. Do not add difficult-to-eradicate perennial weeds, especially with their roots or main flowering stems attached. Annual weeds are best avoided if there is any chance of their seeding.

Construction: Build up the heap in layers, alternating lawn clippings with leaves and open-textured material – a variety of materials leads to a better texture. Add an activator every two or three layers – a sprinkling of chicken manure, seaweed meal, blood, fish, and bone, or comfrey leaves.

Processing: Covering up the heap with polythene (plastic), or a manufactured lid helps conserve moisture, so that the heap rots more rapidly. It is not usually necessary to "turn" the heap if it has been well constructed, but it does help to break up material added in clumps, such as lawn mowings. It will take 3–6 months to achieve a dark colour and moist crumbly texture.

Management: Have at least two heaps simultaneously at different stages of decay – one being for current use and one under construction. Dig out the compost from the bottom so that the old material is used first.

Spring Tasks

Propagating and planting are key tasks in what is the busiest and probably most exciting time of the year in the herb garden, with everything burgeoning into new growth. But the timing of "spring" varies greatly from one area to another and from one year to the next, so always take local conditions into account when carrying out suggested tasks.

Propagating

Early spring is the time for sowing seeds of hardy annuals in trays in a cold greenhouse, including borage, summer savory and pot marigold. You can also sow parsley if you can provide constant heat for germination; and perennials that are easy to raise by this method include fennel, sage (*Salvia officinalis* only), pot marjoram, winter savory and horehound. Of the thymes, only common thyme (*Thymus vulgaris*) and wild thyme (*T. serpyllum*) can be grown from seed. Others, which are cultivars, have to be vegetatively propagated.

Leave annuals such as basil, sweet marjoram and nasturtium until late spring, when they can be grown on outside without danger of frost. Seeds of herbs that dislike being transplanted should be sown outside, where they are to grow, including dill, chervil and coriander (cilantro).

Hardy annuals and perennials that are easy to raise from seed should not be sown outdoors until later in spring, when the soil has warmed up.

Now is the time to take root cuttings of mint, tarragon, bergamot and chamomile. There is no need to provide any extra heat.

To layer herbs, mound up earth around straggly thymes and sages, to encourage new shoots, or bed a single branch into soil until it roots to form a new plant.

Fibrous-rooted herbs and herbaceous plants can now be divided throughout the spring months to make vigorous new plants.

Care of Seedlings

Seedlings raised in trays will have to be pricked out and potted up into 7.5 cm (3 in) pots, to develop and harden off before they are finally planted out in the garden.

Outdoor seedlings need thinning out, so that the plants left have enough space to grow and thrive. This is the best time, once the weather has warmed up a little and the soil is still moist, for planting out pot-grown herbs bought from the nursery.

Weeding

Hoe weeds and unwanted plants out of paths and beds immediately as they appear. They will be much easier to control if they are not allowed to set seed or grow too big, especially those with strong taproots. Spread mulch now to suppress weeds and conserve moisture. A mulch is most effective when soil is damp.

Preparing Soil

Prepare beds for planting by forking over and incorporating garden compost or slow-release fertilizer. In heavy soils dig in manure or bulky organic material.

Pruning

Be careful not to start pruning hard too early in spring when frosts are still likely. This is because it will stimulate plants into new growth, which will be susceptible to frost injury. As soon as the weather is suitable and all risk of frost is over, prune shrubs and silvery herbs that have suffered winter damage back to new shoots. Cut out dead and straggly growth on sages and thymes, but trim thymes only lightly, after flowering, as they do not respond well to heavy pruning. Rosemary can be cut back quite hard, but leave it until it has flowered. Trim box hedges, bays and all formal topiary shapes.

Containers

Trim out any dead or old growth on container-grown plants and start to give them more water and a liquid feed. Replant if necessary into a large pot with fresh growing medium.

Above *Clipping a santolina hedge.*

Above *Seedlings and overwintered cuttings.*

Above *Lemon balm (*Melissa officinalis*) ready for dividing and replanting.*

Summer Tasks

Now is the time to enjoy the garden, when plants are in bloom and looking their best. It is also the time for harvesting and making use of the bounty available.

Propagating

Stem cuttings can be taken from many plants, starting with softwood cuttings from late spring to midsummer and continuing with semi-ripe cuttings from late summer to early autumn.

Above *Taking cuttings of purple sage.*

Collect seeds of annuals as they ripen, for use, or for sowing to produce a new crop, such as poppies, pot marigolds, nasturtiums, sunflowers, dill and coriander (cilantro); and of biennials and perennials, including angelica, caraway, sweet cicely (*Myrrhis odorata*), fennel and lovage. Clean the seeds, removing the seed husks, and store in clearly marked paper envelopes. Do not store in polythene (plastic), as moisture will form and they will rot or start into growth. Seeds should be sown within a year of collection, and angelica must be sown within a few months as the seed soon loses viability.

Weeding and Watering

Continue a routine of diligent weeding, to prevent anything undesirable becoming established. Allow plants to self-seed as appropriate; some can always be transplanted. Top up mulches as necessary. Water newly-planted herbs well and any moisture-lovers that may be suffering from drought. Water containers daily.

Above *Nasturtium seeds are collected for drying and replanting the following year.*

Harvesting and Pruning

Summer is the time to make maximum use of fresh-cut herbs in the kitchen and to harvest leaves for drying for winter use, as it is best to cut them before they come into flower. Leafy herbs, such as lovage and mint, should be cut down to ground level in early summer to midsummer, before they start to seed, in order to ensure a second crop. In very dry spells, watering may be needed to achieve this. Cut back chive flowers and stems for new leafy growth and dead-head roses and annuals to encourage new blooms. Cut aromatic foliage and flowers for drying to make pot-pourri.

For plants with variegations, such as variegated lemon balm, cutting out any stems that have reverted to all green helps to prevent the whole plant reverting. Variegated plants are mutants and less prolific in habit than the common version from which they were derived and if left alone the stronger-growing plain foliage will soon take over the whole plant.

Trim fast-growing herbal hedges, such as wall germander (*Teucrium chamaedrys*) and cotton lavender (*Santolina chamaecyparissus*), as often as necessary to keep them in shape during the growing season.

Above *If planting young herbs in summer, choose a damp spell and water well.*

Autumn Tasks

This is the season for clearing up and cutting back, preparing plants for dormancy and planning their protection through the colder months of winter. But there is still propagation to be done, too, if next year's garden is to fulfil its potential.

Propagating

Sow seeds of biennials, including angelica, clary sage (*Salvia sclarea*), anise and caraway in pots to keep in a cold frame or in a cold greenhouse over the winter. Seeds that require vernalization before they will germinate should be sown outdoors, either in pots or in the ground, including sweet cicely (*Myrrhis odorata*), aconite (*Aconitum napellus)*, primrose (*Primula* spp.) and sweet violet (*Viola odorata)*. The advantage of sowing in pots is that the seeds are less likely to disappear than if they were sown into the ground to be eaten by birds or to be washed away. Finish collecting seed heads for saving, as they ripen.

Above *Pot up French tarragon to encourage new shoots to appear in spring.*

Many perennials may be divided in autumn for replanting in the border or for starting off as new plants in pots. Dig up French tarragon, put it into a large pot and leave in the cold greenhouse over the winter, for dividing into new plants in spring.

Above *Hardwood rose cuttings.*

Hardwood cuttings of fully mature wood may be taken from shrubs and trees suitable for propagation by this method, including roses, blackcurrants and willow.

Clearing

Cut back dead top growth of hardy herbaceous perennials, which do not need winter protection, such as mint, lemon balm and pot marjoram. If left until spring, new growth is likely to come through before the old stems have been cut back, by which time it is difficult to cut them low enough without clipping into fresh, new foliage. Dig up and compost annuals, including pot marigold, borage, summer savory, sweet marjoram, and biennials in their second year, such as parsley and caraway.

Remove fallen leaves (to make compost or leaf mould) and garden debris – decaying material left lying on plants encourages fungal diseases.

Above *Remove annuals that have finished flowering.*

Pruning

In early autumn, well before the onset of frosts, give box hedges and formally clipped topiary a last trim. Many deciduous shrubs are pruned when they lose their leaves in late autumn to early winter. Common elder (*Sambucus nigra*) and its ornamental cultivars benefit from hard pruning at this time to encourage bushy new growth for the next season and to help retain a neat and controlled shape.

Soil Preparation

For new plantings, dig heavy soils and spread with manure to be broken down by winter frosts.

Above *Double digging the soil.*

Containers

Bring in tender and half-hardy container-grown plants before frosts begin. Cut back excess top growth and give them a minimal amount of water.

Plant Protection

Protect the crowns of French tarragon left in the ground, and other garden-grown plants that are not fully frost-hardy, with agricultural fleece or a coat of straw or bracken.

Dig up at least one tarragon root, to ensure its survival, and also tricolour sage and other less than hardy plants. Pot them up in John Innes compost (soil mix) or similar, and put to spend the winter in a cool greenhouse.

Winter Tasks

During the cold months, when there is less to do outside, take stock of current schemes and plan for the year ahead. In many ways this is the start of the gardening year. Cleaning equipment ready for the new season will be instrumental when it comes to getting an early start on the springtime propagating programme. Order new seed catalogues in good time and plan new garden layouts.

Above *Order seed catalogues and choose seeds for the next season.*

Propagating

If you have a greenhouse, even an unheated one, it is possible to force some herbs for an early crop. Mint and chives are ideal for this treatment. Dig up the roots in late autumn to early winter, divide and replant in a peaty growing medium in quite large pots. Tarragon will need some heat to bring it on early, but may be treated the same way. Plant trees, bare-rooted roses and hedges, such as hawthorn, during their dormant period, and plant garlic bulbs.

Above *Planting a beech hedge.*

Cleaning

Thoroughly wash and clean pots, seed trays and equipment for propagation, getting rid of scum and tidemarks (water stains). Clean out the greenhouse, wash the glass, and do not leave old bags of potting compost (soil mix) around to harbour pests and diseases. Oil and clean garden tools and equipment.

Above *Thoroughly clean pots before storing them until the spring.*

Construction

Provided the weather is not too severe, new paths, terraces or hard surface areas may be constructed, garden schemes laid out and beds prepared for planting. But heavy rain and frosts are not conducive to this work, so local conditions must be taken into account.

Containers

Protect terracotta and stone pots that have not been put under cover against severe temperatures by wrapping them in fleece or hessian. Roots of even relatively hardy plants are more vulnerable if grown in a container, and if the soil freezes it will expand, which is likely to crack the pot.

Give indoor container-grown plants the minimum of water, just enough to ensure the compost (soil mix) does not dry out completely, and do not feed.

Plant Protection

Check that outdoor-grown perennials, which are not totally hardy, such as lemon verbena (*Aloysia triphylla*) are adequately protected with fleece. Some of the ornamental thymes, such as *Thymus vulgaris* 'Silver Posie', will also benefit greatly from a light covering as they dislike cold winds and water-logged roots.

Above *Tying in branches to protect them from the weight of the snow.*

Above *Protecting a plant for the winter.*

Above *A polythene (plastic) plant cover.*

Topiary and Training

Shrubs and trees clipped into geometric shapes have been a garden feature since Roman times. They introduce an appearance of order and formality to the herb garden and provide a contrast for the exuberant growth of many of the other plants. Grown in a pot as a standard, one plant alone makes an interesting focal point, and several placed at strategic intervals lend unity to a scheme. Standards may also be planted in the soil of a parterre (rather than being container-grown) to add height and punctuate the design. Lower-growing herbs clipped into mounds as path edgings or to infill beds emphasize the structure of the design.

Above *An imposing display of topiary.*

J. c. 'Compressa' – A dwarf form of juniper that is suitable for lower topiary shapes.

Laurus nobilis – Bay, traditional herb-garden centrepiece as a "lollipop" or standard "mophead".

Myrtus communis – Myrtle responds well to clipping for all topiary shapes. Trim after flowering and give winter protection as it is not fully hardy.

M. c. subsp. *tarentina* – A dwarf form of myrtle ideal for compact globes and low mounds.

Rosmarinus officinalis – Rosemary, for training over wire shapes and clipping into formal hedges.

Ruta graveolens – Rue, effective clipped into mounds.

Santolina chamaecyparissus – Cotton lavender, much used in knot-garden work, also good for clipping into mounds and edges.

Satureja montana – Winter savory responds well to being clipped into low mounds or trained over a frame.

Taxus baccata – Yew, a traditional topiary tree and a favourite for hedging.

Teucrium chamaedrys – Wall germander, for knot gardens and central mounds.

Above *Mounds of clipped box .*

Herbs for Topiary

Shrubs or trees with small leaves and a tight habit of growth make ideal subjects for topiary work.

Buxus sempervirens – Box, easy to shape, is the favourite for taller standard trees, cones, spirals and pyramids. Also comes in gold- and silver-leafed varieties.

Buxus sempervirens 'Suffruticosa' – Dwarf box is best for miniature standards and small globes.

Juniperus communis – Juniper, for tall cones and pyramids. Prune in autumn and winter to prevent bleeding of sap.

Cones, Pyramids and Spheres

These are relatively simple to achieve as they require no complicated training and pruning, though it helps to have a good "eye"for the job and to stand back frequently, as you clip, to assess progress. Box is the most rewarding to work with as it produces a clean outline and is easy to shape. For a cone, start with a bushy young plant and clip it roughly to shape by eye in its first year. Feed and water it well so that it puts on new growth. In the second year, trim it into a more pronounced cone, using a tripod of canes, encircled with wires as a guide. Keep the shape by trimming twice a year in late spring and early autumn.

Above *Training rosemary over a frame.*

Wire-framed Globes

Plants with flexible stems can be trained to grow over a balloon-shaped wire frame. This works well for rosemary, curry plant (*Helichrysum italicum*), ivies, scented-leaf pelargoniums and climbers such as jasmine. Start with a young plant which has developed a reasonable length of stem. Repot it, cut out any middle growth and push the spiked end of the wire frame into the growing medium. Then tie the stems to the wire frame with twine, avoiding tight knots, which will damage the plant and impede its growth. Clip straggly stems to shape two or three times a year during the growing season.

Standards

Free-form standards: Lemon verbena (*Aloysia triphylla*) can be grown as a free-flowing standard, in contrast to formally clipped box and bay. It is more appropriate in an informal scheme where height and a structural element are required.

Select a young plant with a strong central leader. Remove any competing leaders and strong side stems, leaving higher shoots and some lower laterals to provide food, but shortening the lower laterals by half. Stake the stem to keep it straight. As the plant grows, the shortened laterals can be removed to leave a bare stem. As top laterals develop, pinch out the tips to encourage bushiness. When the plant has reached the desired height and developed a thick head of foliage, pinch out the leading shoot.

Rose standards: Old-fashioned roses trained as weeping standards make a romantic focal point in any scheme and lend colour and contrast to the strict pattern of a potager. Train them over a plastic-covered metal frame shaped like an umbrella for a more formal effect.

Aftercare

Topiary trees in containers all need regular watering and feeding throughout the whole summer to keep them healthy and growing actively. The roots of pot-grown plants are more vulnerable in cold weather than those grown in the soil, so wrap them in hessian (burlap) during frosty spells if they are hardy plants and if less than hardy move them to the protection of a cold greenhouse. Myrtle, bay, rosemary and lemon verbena are all best kept under cover during the winter months.

A mophead bay with a twisted stem

This shows how to make a standard bay with a twisted stem. For a version with a straight stem, simply cut off all side growth to leave one strong central leader, instead of three. Feed regularly throughout the growing season. Replace the top 5 cm (2 in) with fresh compost (soil mix) annually.

YOU WILL NEED

Large pot; multipurpose compost (soil mix); coarse grit (gravel); fertilizer granules; watering can; bay tree; secateurs (pruners); ratchet secateurs or pruning saw

1 *Fill a pot with free-draining, multi-purpose growing compost (soil mix), and add a few handfuls of grit (gravel) and a handful of slow release fertilizer.*

2 *Repot a sturdy bay tree with plenty of straight, flexible growth. Clip off side growth to leave three straight stems.*

3 *Using ratchet secateurs or a pruning saw remove lower shoots up to about two-thirds of the overall height.*

4 *Bend over the stems, twisting them carefully, to form a plait.*

5 *Clip the crown to your preferred shape during subsequent years with secateurs (pruners).*

Pests and Diseases

Herbs in general do not suffer greatly from pests and diseases. As predominantly wild plants, they have health and vigour and many are highly aromatic, which gives them inherent protection from insects, which do not like the strong smell. But bacterial and fungal diseases do occasionally strike and no garden is without its share of insect pests. They are, after all, part of a chain, providing food for predators: hedgehogs, birds, mice and other insects.

Above *Damage from red spider mites.*

Top *Scale insect on a bay leaf.*

Above *The damage caused by a scale insect.*

Pests

Aphids: Blackfly and greenfly, which suck the sap of a plant, weakening it, checking growth and often transmitting viral diseases. Greenfly are attracted to roses and the various species of black aphid to the new soft growth of many green plants. Encourage natural predators such as ladybirds (ladybugs), spray with soapy water, hose with plain water, or spray with derris dust or rotenone. (Black aphids, commonly known as blackfly, should not be confused with American bloodsucking black flies, which are a true fly, rather than an aphid.)

Whitefly: These are small winged insects which usually live on brassicas but can be a problem in the greenhouse. Spray with soft soap, hang up sticky traps (yellow attracts whitefly) or introduce *Encarsia formosa*, a parasitic wasp.

Red spider mite: Flourishes in hot, dry conditions, especially the greenhouse in summer. Difficult to detect without a magnifying glass – watch for bronzed or withered leaves and a fine cobweb mesh on the plants. Cut off badly affected leaves, hose off with plenty of water and spray with soft soap, or introduce a biological predator, another even smaller mite *Phytoseiulus persimilis*.

Scale insects: Flat, brownish insects which attach themselves to the undersides of leaves, suck the sap and spread a sticky substance, followed by a sooty mould. Bay is especially prone to attack. Cut off affected leaves and burn them, spray with insecticidal soap or introduce predatory wasp, *Metaphycus helvolus*, as a control.

Slugs: These do most damage in early spring and appear in the evenings. Pick them off by hand or sink jars filled with beer into the soil to attract and trap them.

Diseases

Powdery mildew: A fungal disease which thrives in high humidity. Bergamot, *Monarda didyma*, is prone to it. Don't overwater or overfertilize plants. Spray with Bordeaux mixture.

Botrytis: A fungus which attacks many plants, especially if grown under glass, including tomatoes, strawberries, roses and sunflowers. Seen as a grey mould, it thrives in high humidity. Spray with Bordeaux mixture, following the manufacturer's instructions.

Rust: Brownish-red pustules appear on the leaves and the plant wilts. It affects mint. Dig up and destroy plants if severely affected. Dust with a proprietary sulphur powder following manufacturer's instructions.

Damping-off disease: A fungal disease, it affects seedlings grown under glass. Prevention is best – sow seeds thinly, as overcrowding will encourage the condition, do not overwater, and provide adequate ventilation.

Above *Greenfly suck the sap of a rose.*

Above *Caterpillars on* Polygonatum odoratum.

Prevention

Healthy plants depend on good gardening practice. They should not be overcrowded, which deprives them of light and air. Keep them free of weeds and prune regularly – always using clean secateurs (pruners) and other cutting tools so that you do not pass diseases from one plant to another by mistake.

Vigilance is important – try to remove insect infestations before they build up, and cut out diseased leaves as soon as you see them and burn them. Overfeeding plants with chemical fertilizers will only weaken them and make for fresh, sappy growth which attracts insect pests, but an organic seaweed fertilizer, applied as a spray, helps to build up their resistance.

Correct watering, especially for greenhouse and indoor plants, is also a vital factor. Overwatering tends to lead to rotting plants and inadequate ventilation encourages mildews and botrytis.

Beneficial Insects

Lacewings, ladybirds (ladybugs) and the larvae of the hoverfly all prey on aphids. Grow plants to attract them.

Lacewings: These are attracted by yarrow (*Achillea millefolium*), golden rod (*Solidago virgaurea*) and chamomile (*Chamaemelum nobile*).

Ladybirds (ladybugs): These are attracted by yarrow (*Achillea millefolium*) and pot marigolds (*Calendula officinalis*).

Hoverflies: These are attracted by yarrow (*Achillea millefolium*), lovage (*Levisticum officinale*), dill (*Anethum graveolens*), sweet cicely (*Myrrhis odorata*), fennel (*Foeniculum officinale*), golden rod (*Solidago virgaurea*) and centaury (*Centaurium erythraea*).

Other insects which prey on specific pests can be bought in.

Encarsia formosa: Small parasitic wasps that control whitefly infestations.

Phytoseiulus persimilis: A Chilean mite smaller than its red spider mite prey.

Metaphycus helvolus: Predatory wasp for scale insects.

Aphidoletes aphidimyza: A parasitic midge which preys on aphids.

Above *Yellow sticky traps used for catching whitefly in a commercial greenhouse.*

Organic Pesticides

Sometimes sprays are the only way to control a situation. But the problem with chemical sprays is that they destroy all the beneficial insects as well as pests. They also upset the balance of nature as the predatory insects are less numerous, multiply less enthusiastically than their prey and do not recover. Therefore, the next generation of pests multiplies unchecked and the problem is compounded.

It is best to use organic sprays where possible, but the most effective of these destroy insects, not just pests.

Soap is the least harmful method. A household liquid soap is suitable. Horticultural insecticidal soaps are even more effective. Derris is made from a tropical plant, and available in liquid or powder form. It kills beneficial insects as well as pests so use with great discretion. Bordeaux mixture is an inorganic chemical fungicide, but not harmful to human or animal life.

Companion Planting

The insect-repellent properties of many herbs, owing to the high concentration of aromatic oils they contain, makes them ideal companions for protecting vulnerable plants such as roses, fruit and vegetables from insect attack. Plant them in a potager garden. Rue (*Ruta graveolens*), cotton lavender (*Santolina chamaecyparissus*), curry plant (*Helichrysum angustifolia*), tansy (*Tanacetum vulgare*) and southernwood (*Artemisia abrotanum*) are all strongly aromatic and can discourage many types of pests.

Chives and garlic are beneficial to roses. They give off an odour which discourages aphids and may help cut the incidence of the disease, blackspot.

Chamomile, once known as "the plants' physician", has a reputation for improving the health and vigour of those plants and herbs surrounding it.

Pennyroyal (*Mentha pulegium*) helps to keep ants away, planted among paving. Summer savory (*Satureja hortensis*), planted in rows next to broad beans (fava beans), provides some protection from blackfly.

French marigolds, *Tagetes*, are excellent at discouraging whitefly, especially in the greenhouse.

Nicotiana sylvestris works on a trap principle. It attracts whitefly, which are then caught by the sticky stems and leaves and can be disposed of.

Using Herbs

This chapter covers when and how to harvest your herbs, with guidelines on successful drying and storing for culinary and other uses. There are suggestions for different ways of preserving herbs in oil and vinegar, sugar and honey, in medicinal tinctures or by freezing them. There is a short section on essential oils; what they are and how they are produced, their history and current uses, with some practical suggestions for making the most of them.

Above *Aromatic resins, frankincense and benzoin from the styrax tree.*

Left *Dried herbs, pot marigold and lemon verbena, with cocoa butter (at centre) and other ingredients for making herbal preparations.*

Harvesting Herbs

Harvesting the herbs you have grown is a continuous process rather than a one-off annual event. Once established, most will grow strongly enough to allow plenty of repeat picking, which in itself encourages new growth in healthy, well-cared-for plants. It makes sense not to denude small, immature plants before they have much foliage, but many annuals and herbaceous perennials, such as lovage (*Levisticum officinale*), will produce a second crop once they have flowered, if they are cut back almost to the ground. When cutting perennial, shrubby herbs think of it as pruning and aim to improve the overall shape of the plant.

The optimum time for harvesting plant material to preserve it for later use depends on the growth pattern of the individual herb and the part of it that is required – leaf, flower, seed or root.

Usually it will be during the growing season, but a few herbs, such as thyme, rosemary and sage, may be lightly picked when dormant, although they will not have such a full flavour. Whether harvesting herbs to dry for culinary use, cosmetics and pot-pourri or for home remedies, the following guidelines will ensure good results:

• Choose a fine, sunny day for picking, so that the essential oil content, which gives the plant its flavour and scent, is at its best. Wait until any dew or residual raindrops have evaporated – herbs tend to go mouldy before the drying process is complete if picked when wet – but try to finish in the morning before volatile oils have been drawn to the surface by the heat and dissipated.

• Use only sharp scissors or secateurs (pruners) so as not to damage the plant and limit further cropping. Make sure that your equipment is clean and that sticky blades do not pass pest or disease problems from one plant to another.

• Pick only prime material from plants that are at their peak – avoid anything damaged, discoloured, diseased or spent with age.

• Pick herbs in small quantities, only as much as you can deal with at one time. Herbs should not be left in heaps, waiting to be processed, as even quite a small pile encourages heat and deterioration sets in. The idea is to preserve the plant before the active constituents start to break down and lose viability.

• Flowers and foliage must be wiped clean and be insect free before they are processed: they can be lightly sponged and patted dry with a paper towel, but do not try to wash them as this will impede drying.

Above *Cutting a head of angelica to collect the seeds.*

Left *A freshly-gathered harvest of garden herbs, ready to be preserved and stored in containers for future use.*

Leaves: Most should be picked before they come into flower, when leaf flavour and texture are at their best. Pick small-leafed plants on the stem for stripping later – larger leaves may be picked individually. Shrubby perennials which last through the winter should not be cut severely late in the season, as this will weaken them and leave them vulnerable to frost damage.

Flowers: These should be cut soon after they have opened when they are at their best, and not left to drop their petals, when colour and scent will be minimal. Pick single blooms or flower heads as appropriate and strip off petals or florets when spreading them to dry. Lavender should be picked with a long stem, and flowers such as borage, where only the tiny blue "star" is required, need careful individual collection.

Seeds: The pods or seed heads must be picked as soon as they are ripe, when they are no longer green, but before they fall. This means watching them carefully, as they can ripen and disperse very quickly.

Roots and rhizomes: These are usually collected during their dormant period in autumn or winter. When digging them up, try to leave some portion of the root so that the plant can regenerate. With some herbs, such as horseradish, this is not difficult, as it will regrow vigorously from the tiniest portion of root. Wash roots and rhizomes thoroughly with plenty of cold water and cut into pieces before processing.

Bulbs: These include garlic and onions. Dig them up in late summer to early autumn.

Bark: Bark should not be stripped from very young trees. They must never be ring-barked (stripped of bark all round the circumference of the trunk), nor should too much be taken in one year as this could kill the tree. Tools should be clean and sharp, and the lowest cut made at 1 m (3 ft) above ground level. Endangered or protected species should not be harvested at all.

Wild plants: Wild plants should be picked with the utmost caution, both for safety reasons and for the sake of the environment. Many wild plants are protected by law (check if this applies), and should not be touched – in any case none should be uprooted or overpicked, especially if less than common. Any that grow near crops should be treated with suspicion, as they may contain pesticide residues, and of course you must be confident of correct identification. If you are not sure, leave them alone.

Right *Fresh sage leaves tied up in small bunches for drying.*

Harvesting marjoram

1 *Cut bunches of healthy material at mid-morning on a dry day.*

2 *Strip off the lower leaves, which may otherwise become damaged.*

3 *Twist an elastic (rubber) band around the stems to hold them tightly together.*

4 *Gather as many bunches as you need, then the bunches can be hung in a dry, well-ventilated place where they are protected from light.*

Drying

Successful drying depends on removing the moisture in the fresh material without sacrificing the volatile oil content. The process has to be completed quickly so that oils are not lost through a natural process of decay, but not so quickly that they are destroyed by heat. The key to success is the right temperature and low humidity.

An average temperature for commercially dried herbs is 38°C (99°F), but this would be difficult to provide at home without special equipment. Between 20–32°C (68–90°F) works well and can be found in an airing cupboard, or a cupboard near a hot-water heater. A spare room, with an electric heater (not directed straight at petals or loose material), could also be used.

The place chosen should be dry and well ventilated (garages are not really suitable, but a clean shed may be ideal) and, for better colour preservation, dark. Sun drying is a traditional method in climates where air temperatures are high and humidity low, but it does lead to colour loss and there is also a greater risk of contamination than in an indoor, controlled environment.

Oven drying is generally too fierce for flowers and foliage, even at its lowest setting, but it is suitable for roots. Microwaving is not ideal as it is necessary to include a small container of water to prevent arcing, and this makes for humidity, which is counterproductive.

Green Herbs

Small-leaved green herbs may be dried on the stem and larger leaves dried individually. Spread them on slatted trays, or on fine netting stretched over a frame so that air can circulate beneath, and put them in a warm, dark place with some ventilation.

Leave the herbs until they are crackly-dry to the touch. The length of time will depend on the thickness and moisture content of the leaf, the level of heat provided and humidity in the air. The process takes from 3–4 days to a week at the most. Once dried, strip leaves off the stems, or crumble larger ones into small pieces ready to store. Wearing cotton gloves makes the job easier on the hands.

Herbs may also be tied in bunches with raffia or string and hung up in a clean, airy place to dry.

Above *Drying lavender commercially on a custom-built, movable frame.*

Flowers

Twist off heads of large blooms, such as roses, and spread out the petals on paper on slatted trays. Put in a warm place and leave them until papery dry.

Pot marigold (*Calendula officinalis*) flowers are easier to dry whole, then twist off the petals afterwards if required.

Lavender is best hung up in bunches, tied loosely with string or raffia, and with the heads in paper bags to exclude dust and catch petals that may fall as they dry.

Once the flowers are dried, they may be left whole, according to their intended use, or stripped from the stems in the same way as green herbs.

Chive flowers, or rosebuds that are required for decorative purposes, will keep a good shape if dried upright, with stems pushed through wire cake trays.

Specially treated dry sand or silica gel may also be used for drying flowers, resulting in a good colour and perfect shape. Place a flower on a thin layer of sand, sift more sand gently over it until covered and leave for three weeks in a warm, dry place. Uncover carefully.

Above *Herbs drying in a dark, clean and well-ventilated shed.*

Above *Lavender, tied in bunches for drying, is well spaced to allow air to circulate.*

Seeds

A good way to dry seeds is to pick the seed heads with stems attached. Tie them in bunches, insert the heads into paper bags and hang them up in a warm, airy place. When completely dry, clean off the pods or husks before storing in clearly marked envelopes. Seeds should not be stored in polythene (plastic), which encourages moisture.

Roots

Roots require a higher temperature than flowers and leaves for successful drying from 50–60°C (120–140°F). An oven, at a very low setting, with the door left open is suitable. Make sure the roots are scrubbed clean, then cut them in pieces and spread on baking trays. Put them in a cool oven and turn at intervals to ensure even heat. Leave until brittle, but test frequently as they should not become shrivelled and overbrown – length of time depends on the size and moisture content of root pieces.

Storing

Dried herbs and flowers deteriorate quickly, losing aroma and colour, if left exposed to light and air. Always store them in the dark and keep in a dry place. Flowers and foliage required for pot-pourri can be kept in paper bags, airtight tins or glass jars.

Above *Dried herbs retain colour and flavour stored in opaque containers.*

Above *Dried bay leaves in a jar.*

Right *Pot-pourri ingredients, stored in glass, are best kept in a dark cupboard.*

Preserving

Preserving the flavour and perfume of herbs in vegetable oils or in vinegar is easy to do and these have many uses in culinary and cosmetic recipes or in home remedies. A mixed-herb oil, or one with a single flavour, such as basil, adds interest to salad dressings, stir-fries, pizza and pasta dishes, grilled or barbecued meat, fish or vegetables. Rosemary oil is the ideal ingredient for bath lotions and beauty treatments and oil infused with garlic makes an effective liniment for relieving aches and pains.

Above *Finish off oil bottles by neatly winding cotton string around waxed paper and then tying it securely with a reef knot.*

Tips for success:

• Use a good-quality, mild-flavoured oil, such as sunflower or safflower, so that the taste of the oil doesn't compete with the flavour of the herbs. Extra-virgin olive oil, which has a strong flavour of its own, is not suitable.

• Always cover herbs completely with oil during the infusing process. Any bits left sticking out will start to deteriorate and affect the quality of the oil.

• It is important to remove the plant material before storage. If left it will start to decay and the oil will become cloudy and sour.

To make herb oil

1 *Put a good handful of herbs or flower heads into a clean glass jar – either a single herb, such as marjoram used here, or a mixture, such as oregano, rosemary and thyme – and crush them lightly to release the essential oils.*

2 *Pour in a mild vegetable oil until the herbs (or flowers) are completely covered, otherwise any that are not covered will go mouldy. Cover the jar and stand it in a warm place – a sunny windowsill is fine.*

3 *After about a week, strain off the herbs, replace with fresh ones and leave to infuse for a further week. This process can be repeated until the flavour is strong enough.*

4 *Remove the herbs and pour the oil into a clean, sterilized bottle with an airtight lid. The oil will keep for a few weeks if extra flowers have been added, or 6 months without extra flowers.*

> **YOU WILL NEED**
> A handful of fresh herbs or about 12 flower-heads; 400 ml/³/₄pt light vegetable oil; jar with top; filter

Herb Vinegars

Herb vinegar is made in the same way as a herb oil. A great variety of flavouring materials can be used: fresh or dried leaves, spices, chillies, garlic, fruit or flower petals. Tarragon vinegar is a classic for salad dressing. Fruit and flower flavours, such as raspberry, blackberry, lavender or rose petal, add sharpness to sweet dishes and are useful as home remedies. Raspberry vinegar helps to ease a sore throat, and lavender, applied as a compress, may relieve a headache.

Some herb vinegars can be used as antiseptics for cleaning surfaces or as poultices; some can be dabbed on the skin to counteract a range of conditions; others can be taken internally as a tonic or prophylactic.

An excellent ingredient for home-made cosmetics is cider vinegar; it restores the acid mantle of the skin and is a traditional ingredient in skin lotions and hair rinses. Use it to make a mint-and-marigold or rose petal vinegar, which is then diluted – two or three tablespoons in a basin of water – to splash over the face as a general toner.

To make herb vinegar: Fill a clean jar to about one-third with herb leaves, spices, fruit or flowers of your choice, top up with cider vinegar and leave to infuse for two or three weeks. It is not usually necessary to use more than one batch of herbs or other flavouring ingredient to obtain a strong enough flavour, as it is for oil.

Vinegar is a better preservative than oil, so it is possible to leave in some of the herb used, such as a sprig of tarragon, for decorative effect, but always replace the infused material with a fresh piece. Dried material can be left in vinegar indefinitely. Coloured peppercorns, rosemary, chillies and dried bay leaves look most attractive when left in a spiced vinegar.

Above *Fresh herbs add a spicy, aromatic flavour to vinegar. Clockwise from front, rosemary, sage and marjoram.*

Right *Tarragon (left) and a mixed herb vinegar with bay leaves.*

Preserving in Sugar

Sugar makes an excellent preservative and was a traditional method of retaining the properties of herbs and flowers. Old herbal manuscripts are full of recipes for herbal syrups and conserves made with sugar, or more often, honey.

Above *Sugar, flavoured with lavender flowers, is ideal for baking.*

Lavender sugar: This is a delicious way to impart a subtle fragrance to cakes, biscuits, meringues and other sweet dishes, without the coarse texture of the whole petals. To make lavender sugar, bruise dried lavender flowers, stripped from the stem, and add them to caster (superfine) or icing (confectioner's) sugar before storing in an airtight jar until required. Sieve out the flowers before use. Ten to 15 heads of lavender will be enough to lend fragrance to 450g (1 lb) of sugar.

Crystallized petals: Many edible flowers may be used for this purpose. To make the petals: Check the petals are dry, clean and insect-free. Spread them on a greaseproof-paper covered baking tray. Then paint them, using a fine artist's brush, with a thin coat of lightly whipped egg white (just broken up, rather than frothy), and sprinkle thickly with caster (superfine) sugar. Put in the bottom of a very low oven with the door left open, until completely dry and brittle, but not brown.

Top *Crystallized violas make delicate decorations for cakes and sweets.*

Above *Lavender honey is easy to make and has a subtly distinctive flavour.*

Herb honey: The finest honeys are those which are made by bees collecting from a single flower source such as lime blossom or thyme. Both honey from the hive and many herbs, such as rosemary and garlic, have antiseptic properties. In combination they are helpful for soothing sore throats and cold or flu symptoms, taken in teaspoonfuls. They can also be used as a sweetener for herb teas.

To make herb honey: Put a small handful of herbs, such as rosemary, thyme or lavender flowers, into a saucepan. Bruise with a wooden spoon, add the contents of a 225 g (8 oz) jar of honey and heat gently until melted but not boiling. Leave to infuse for about one hour before straining the mixture. Discard the herbs and pour the honey into a jar with an airtight lid for storage.

Freezing Herbs

A convenient way to preserve fresh herbs for later use is to freeze them in ice cubes for adding to soups, stews and other cooked dishes. Simply chop them finely, put into ice-cube trays and top up with water before freezing. Whole mint leaves or borage flowers may be frozen in the same way for floating in drinks.

Culinary herbs, stripped from the stems but not chopped, can be frozen packed in polythene (plastic) bags, or cartons, for short periods of time. They will not, of course, have the texture of fresh leaves once thawed. This is a useful method of preserving herbs that do not keep a good aroma when dried, such as basil, parsley, chives and mint.

Tinctures

Many herbs may be preserved in alcohol for medicinal use. They are best made as a cold infusion using dried herbs and alcohol with little flavour of its own, such as vodka. This makes a potent preparation, as the essential oils and active constituents of many herbs are soluble in alcohol. It should be taken in small doses of drops, or teaspoons, and, it is strongly suggested, as directed by a qualified practitioner.

To make a tincture: Put dried herbs in a jar and top up with a mixture of one part of water to two parts of vodka. As a general guideline, 15 g (½oz) of dried herbs to 300 ml (½ pint/⅔ cup) of alcohol and water mixed are standard quantities. Seal the jar and leave in a warm, dark place for one week, after which time the active constituents will have been extracted and the herbs will start to deteriorate. Strain out the herbs and rebottle.

Making herb ice cubes

1 Pick some mint leaves, selecting small undamaged ones, and strip them from the stem.

2 Put a single leaf into each compartment of an ice-cube tray, top up with water and freeze.

Left *From left to right: lavender, violet leaf and juniper tinctures.*

Above *Edible flowers and herb leaves make unusual ice-cubes for floating in drinks.*

Herbal Essential Oils

What are essential oils? The essential, or volatile, oil in a plant gives it its scent. Despite the name, essential oils are not oily – a drop applied to paper does not usually leave any mark. They are volatile liquids, which evaporate at normal air temperatures and are secreted from minute glands and hairs in the leaves, stems, flowers, seeds, fruit, roots or bark of plants and trees.

Some plants, such as roses, contain their essential oil mainly in the flowers; others, such as lemon balm (*Melissa officinalis*) mainly in the leaves. The orange tree (*Citrus aurantium*) contains three differently-named essential oils, in the flowers (neroli), the leaves (petitgrain) and the rind of the fruit (orange oil).

The organic chemical structure of plant essential oils is extremely complex. Analysis by gas liquid chromatography (GLC) reveals that peppermint oil, whose 50 per cent menthol content provides its minty smell, has 98 other constituents. Flower essential oils have as many as several hundred components. For this reason it is impossible to chemically reproduce an exact copy of a naturally occurring essential oil in the laboratory.

Above *The leaves of* Melissa officinalis *are distilled to produce a cheering, tonic essential oil.*

Above right *Essential oils have long been valued for their therapeutic properties.*

Production

Essential oils are soluble in fats, vegetable and mineral oils and in alcohol. For the most part they do not dissolve in water, though some of their constituents may do so. The main fragrance molecules of roses and orange flowers, for example, are soluble in water. Steam distillation is the most frequent method of extraction, and volatile solvents and alcohol are sometimes used in the process. A few fragile flower fragrances are still obtained by the centuries-old method of macerating the petals in trays of fat, and volatile oil from orange rind is extracted by expression: that is by pressing it out, nowadays by machine, but formerly pressed by hand. Quality is affected by varying soils, climates and harvesting conditions. Some oils may have been diluted or adulterated. It is not easy to tell, so look for a reliable source.

Using Essential Oils

Plant essential oils and extracts are widely used in the pharmaceutical, cosmetic and food industries. In the home they are used therapeutically in aromatherapy and herbal medicine, by taking them internally, by inhaling them in vaporizers and in fragrance products such as pot-pourri, by massaging them into the skin, by applying them in compresses, or by putting them in the bath. They are sometimes used in a domestic context to flavour food, but only in very small quantities, the whole plant being safer and usually more satisfactory for culinary use.

The important thing to remember is that, as extracts of the active principles of plants, essential oils are concentrated substances and should be taken internally only in controlled, drop-sized doses. When applied externally they must be diluted in a carrier oil.

Essential Oils in History

Essential oils take their name from the *quinta essentia*, or quintessence, a term coined by a Swiss physician Paracelsus, 1493–1541. He took the medieval theory of alchemy, which sought to isolate the *prima materia*, or elemental matter, of a substance, and applied it specifically to plants. His goal was to divide the "essential matter" of a plant from its "non-essential" components.

In ancient times, extracting plant fragrance by macerating it in oil or fat was common, and a technique of destructive distillation, such as that which produces oil of turpentine, was also known. At the beginning of the 11th century, steam distillation as a means of making plant-scented waters was discovered, usually credited to the physician, Avicenna, 980–1037, author of the *Canon of Medicine*. Arnald de Villanova, d. 1311, a Spanish doctor, further popularized the use of distilled herb waters for medicinal purposes.

Distillation was seen at the time as a means of refining plant material to its purest form, through fire, and alcohol was widely used in the process as producing the best results. But it was not until the mid-16th century that the nature of essential oils was understood and the process of separating them from the distillate put into practice.

By the beginning of the 17th century plant essential oils were available from professional pharmacies, as well as being produced on a domestic scale in the stillrooms of grand houses. Many herbals and old recipe books contained detailed instructions.

Inhaling Essential Oils

Breathing in the fragrance of essential oils has an immediate effect on mood and can be immensely therapeutic. An essential oil burner or vaporizer is one of the best ways to do this. You could also put a few drops of oil on a handkerchief to tuck under a pillow, or mix some into a pot-pourri of flowers and herbs.

To lift depression, anxiety and nervous tension try essential oil of frankincense, jasmine, neroli, rose or sandalwood. Sedative oils for insomnia include chamomile, juniper, lavender and marjoram. For stress and shock there is cedarwood, melissa or peppermint, and for mental fatigue and lethargy use basil, black pepper, cardamom or pine.

Bath Oils

Adding essential oil in drops to the bath water is another way to benefit from the fragrance. To make a bath oil for dry skins, mix about 20 drops of essential oil into a 10 ml (2 tsp) bottle of almond or sunflower oil which has first been infused with fresh flowers or herbs, such as chamomile or lavender.

A lavender bath is deeply relaxing, mildly antiseptic and helps to heal tiny cuts and scratches, bites or swellings. It is also soothing when you have a cold.

Right *A bath oil including essential oil of chamomile is soothing to sensitive skins.*

Below *Lavender, mixed with a light oil for massage, releases an aroma which will help ease stress headaches and promote calm and restful sleep. It also helps muscular aches and pains. To release the scent, warm the oil slightly before you begin.*

Insect Repellent Oils

Essential oil of lavender makes an effective insect repellent. Good quality and pure lavender and tea-tree oils are two of the few oils that may be applied directly to the skin. But if you are not sure of its provenance, or are likely to suffer from allergies, dilute it in a carrier (such as sunflower) oil first. Candles scented with citronella or eucalyptus help deter midges and flying insects.

Directory of Herbs

Each entry in this directory gives a brief history of the herb, its description, habitat, growth and cultivation, any related species and the principal uses. Medicinal uses described are for general interest only and should not be taken as practical recommendations. All herbs can be toxic if taken to excess, especially in the form of essential oils. Some may cause adverse reactions in certain people. Consult a qualified practitioner before using herbs medicinally.

Above *Chives with herb Robert.*

Left *Field grown herbs at the National Herb Centre, England, including from left, white foxgloves, wall germander and santolina.*

Growth Prefers moist but well-drained, slightly acid soil and does not flourish in polluted air. It may be propagated from seed, sown in late autumn or winter, with a period of stratification to aid germination.

Parts used *A. alba,* leaves, resin tapped from mature trees. *A. balsamea,* leaves, oleo-resin collected from blisters on the trunk. Essential oil from resin of both species.

USES Medicinal *A. alba* and *A. balsamea* have aromatic, antiseptic properties, stimulate circulation and increase blood flow and are expectorant and diuretic in action. They are common ingredients of proprietary remedies for coughs and colds, bath preparations, liniments and rubs for rheumatism and neuralgia. Oleo-resin from *A. balsamea* is used in North American traditional medicine for chest infections, cuts, burns, skin eruptions and venereal disease.

Cosmetic The essential oil is an ingredient of cosmetics, perfumes and soaps.

PINACEAE
Abies alba
Silver fir

History and traditions The silver fir was the source of "Strasbourg Turpentine", as described by the French doctor and botanist Pierre Belon in *De Arboribus coniferis,* 1553, and listed in the London *Pharmacopoeia* until 1788. Its manufacture is covered in the famous work on distillation techniques, *Liber De Arte Distillandi* by the Strasbourg physician Hieronymus Braunschweig, 1450–1534. Turpentine is now more usually made from a selection of several different species of pine, but both *Abies alba* and *A. balsamea* still have a place in many herbal medicines and modern pharmaceutical preparations.

Description It grows from 25–45 m (80–150 ft) and has glossy, dark-green needles, silver underneath. It is monoecious – that is, the small male cones and much larger female cones, which are reddish-brown when ripe and up to 15 cm (6 in) long, are produced on the same tree.

Related species *A. balsamea* has smooth grey bark, studded with resin blisters, and is strongly scented with balsam.

Habitat/distribution Native to mountainous regions of central and southern Europe, also found in North and Central America.

Above *Leaves of a silver fir.*

> CAUTION Silver fir is an irritant, which can cause skin reaction in sensitive subjects.

LEGUMINOSAE/MIMOSACEAE
Acacia senegal
Gum Arabic

History and traditions The ancient Egyptians imported what appears to be acacia gum, and it was referred to in the writings of the Greek physician, Theophrastus, in the 4th century BC. Gum Arabic is mentioned in many old herbals as an ingredient of pomanders and medicines.

Description *A. senegal,* which produces gum Arabic, reaches 6 m (19 ft) tall, has grey bark, pale-green pinnate leaves and small pale-yellow balls of flowers. There are over 1,000 species in the *Acacia* genus, often called wattles, many of which produce gums for commerce. *A. nilotica* (above) is the source of an inferior gum Arabic.

Habitat/distribution The genus is found in dry areas in tropical to warm-temperate zones of Africa, Asia, Australia, Central and South America.

Growth *A. senegal* is tender, requiring a minimum temperature about 15°C/60°F. It needs a slightly acid, well-drained soil and full sun and is propagated by seed, germinated at 21°C/70°F.

Parts used Resin of *A. senegal* (it dissolves in water to form a mucilage which makes a bonding agent).

USES Medicinal Gum Arabic is a demulcent, soothes inflamed tissues and is used in pastilles, lotions and pharmaceutical preparations.

Culinary Although it has no place in the domestic kitchen it is used in the food industry in a wide range of products, including confectionery and chewing gum.

> CAUTION There are statutory restrictions on cultivation of wattles in some places.

COMPOSITAE/ASTERACEAE

Achillea millefolium

Yarrow

History and traditions The generic name honours the legendary Achilles, whose soldiers are said to have staunched their wounds with this plant in the Trojan War, and it has a long tradition as a wound herb. *Millefolium* refers to the many segments of the finely divided leaves. This herb has attracted a wealth of folklore over the centuries, as its many common names reveal.

Description A pungent perennial with flat, creamy-white to pinkish flower heads rising on tough stalks 15–30 cm (6–12 in) above a mat of greyish-green, finely-divided leaves. With its creeping roots and efficient self-seeding it is extremely invasive.

Related species There are many ornamental cultivars of *A. millefolium* including 'Moonshine', with light yellow flowers and the rich crimson 'Fire King'. *A. ageratum* (formerly *A. decolorans*), English mace, is a little-known culinary herb with a mildly spicy flavour, used to flavour chicken dishes, soups, stews and sauces.

Habitat/distribution Widespread in temperate zones, found in grasslands, waste ground and by roadsides. Native of Europe and western Asia, naturalized in North America, Australia and New Zealand.

Growth Propagated by division of roots. The wild species is invasive and when grown as a garden plant it is advisable to keep it in a container or to restrict the roots by surrounding with tiles pushed into the soil.

Yarrow folklore

As "devil's nettle" or "devil's plaything", yarrow was supposed to be dedicated to Satan and widely used in charms and spells. It had a place in Druid ceremonies and was made into herbal amulets or strewn on the threshold of houses against witches and evil forces. A bunch hung on the door, and tied to the baby's cradle for good measure on Midsummer's Eve, was supposed to ensure an illness-free year ahead.

Several claims are made for yarrow's supernatural powers in the 15th-century "Book of Secrets", attributed to Albertus Magnus. If put to the nose it will protect "from all feare and fatansye or vysion" and rather more wildly, if the juice is smeared on the hands, when plunged into water they will act as magnets for fish.

Yarrow features in many traditional rhymes connected with finding true love:

Yarrow, yarrow, long and narrow,
Tell unto me by tomorrow,
Who my husband is to be.

Another rhyme, variously attributed to the county of Suffolk, in England and to eastern Europe (with slightly different words), refers to yarrow's propensity to cause a nosebleed (one of its common names):

Green 'arrow, green 'arrow, you bears a white blow,
If my love loves me my nose will bleed now.

And if eaten at the wedding feast, it was claimed that bride and groom would remain in love for seven years.

As well as its role as a wound herb, reflected in the names soldier's woundwort, herb militaris and carpenter's weed, it was credited with both stopping a nosebleed or bringing one on (a supposed way of relieving migraine), as occasion demanded. It has a pungent smell and, as "old man's pepper", was made into snuff.

Parts used The whole plant, fresh or dried.

USES Medicinal The essential oil contains azulene, which has anti-inflammatory properties. It increases perspiration and is taken internally, as a tea, for colds and feverish conditions; applied externally for wounds, ulcers and nosebleeds. It is also thought to lower blood pressure and to relieve indigestion.

Cosmetic A weak infusion of the flowering tops in distilled water makes a cleanser or refreshing toner for oily skins .

Other names Soldier's woundwort, herb militaris, carpenter's weed, old man's pepper, nose bleed, devil's nettle, milfoil and also thousand leaf.

Above right *The finely divided leaves of* Achillea millefolium, *also known as thousand leaf.*

Right Achillea ageratum, *English mace.*

CAUTION Large doses can cause headaches. Allergic rashes and skin sensitivity to sunlight may result from prolonged use.

RANUNCULACEAE
Aconitum napellus
Aconite

History and traditions The generic name is from the Greek for a dart (*akontion*) in recognition of its one time use as an arrow poison, but the species name, *napellus*, meaning "little turnip", is supposedly for the shape of the roots, and gives no hint of the deadly nature of this plant. The popular name, monkshood, describes the curious shape of the flowers, while the common name for *A. lycoctonum,* wolf's bane, is a reference to its ability to despatch this once much-feared animal by sprinkling the juice over raw meat as bait. Stories of the dangers of aconite abound in herbals through the ages, such as Gerard's account of the "ignorant persons" of Antwerp who were taken with "most cruel symptoms and so died" when served the leaves in a salad as a "lamentable experiment".

Description The helmet-shaped inky-blue flowers give this hardy herbaceous perennial a slightly sinister appearance appropriate to its properties. It has tuberous roots and delphinium-like foliage from which the flowering stems rise to a height of 1.5 m (5 ft).

Related species There are about 100 species, all of which are highly poisonous. *A. lycoctonum* has yellow, sometimes purple, flowers and *A. carmichaelii,* syn. *A. fischeri,* is sometimes used in Chinese medicine as a painkiller.

Habitat/distribution Widespread in Europe and in northern temperate regions, in damp woodlands, meadows and mountainous areas.

Growth Plant in moist, fertile soil and part-shade. Propagation is by division of roots in the autumn for flowering in the second year. Seeds sown in spring will not flower for 2–3 years.

Parts used Dried root tubers.

Other name Monkshood.

USES Medicinal The alkaloid, aconite, gives it toxicity. As a strong sedative and painkiller, it should be used only by qualified practitioners. A very small dose causes numbness of lips, tongue and extremities and can lead to vomiting, coma and death.

> CAUTION The whole plant is highly toxic and if ingested can kill. Contact with skin may cause allergic reactions – always handle with gloves. Subject to legal restrictions in some countries.

ACORACEAE
Acorus calamus
Calamus

History and traditions The first specimens to reach Europe were imported from Asia by the botanical garden in Vienna in the 16th century. Calamus, which means "reed" in Greek, then became popular as a scented strewing herb. Cardinal Wolsey used it extensively for this purpose in Hampton Court Palace. This was yet another example of his extravagance in the eyes of his contemporaries, due to its comparative rarity – at the time calamus was grown only on the Norfolk Broads some distance away. It was also one of the ingredients in Moses's instructions to make "an ointment compound after the art of the apothecary" as a holy anointing oil (Exodus 30:25).

Description A pleasantly aromatic perennial with a thick much-branched rhizome, it has similar-shaped leaves to the irises, although is not botanically related to them. The flower head is a spadix, emerging from the side of the leaf, but it is not usually fertile in Europe and cool northern climates, owing to lack of appropriate insects for pollination.

Related species *A. gramineus,* native to the Far East, is a miniature species, used in Chinese

medicine. Its compact size makes it suitable for growing in ornamental ponds.

Habitat/distribution *A. calamus* (above) is indigenous to central Asia and eastern Europe, and is now widespread in marshy areas and by shallow waterways of northern temperate zones.

Growth Vigorous and easy to propagate, it must have moist soil and plenty of water. Grows best by water margins. Propagate in spring or autumn by cutting rhizomes in small pieces, each with 2–3 buds, and planting in muddy ground.

Parts used Rhizomes, essential oil.

USES Medicinal Calamus can be taken internally, as an infusion for digestive problems and to dispel intestinal worms. It is slightly sedative to the central nervous system and is traditionally used in Ayurvedic medicine following strokes, and also for bronchial complaints. Externally it is used as an alcohol rub for aching muscles.

Aromatic The essential oil, separated by steam distillation, is a perfumery ingredient. Herbalists of old called it "*calamus aromaticus*", and the ground root was added to pot-pourris, scented sachets, tooth and hair powders.

Household In Asia it is sometimes used as an insecticide powder to deter ants.

Other names Sweet flag, sweet rush and myrtle grass.

> CAUTION Excessive dose causes vomiting.

HIPPOCASTANACEAE
Aesculus hippocastanum
Horse chestnut

History and traditions This spectacular tree was introduced to western Europe in the mid-16th century, when it was grown in Vienna from seeds brought from Istanbul by the botanist Clusius (Charles de L'Ecluse), although it does not seem to have been widely used for medicinal purposes until the late 19th century. The origins of the name are confused, but are all tied to the use of this tree as animal fodder. *Hippocastanum* is the Latin for "horse chestnut", which the Romans supposedly fed to their livestock.

Description A stately, deciduous tree, 30–40 m (98–130 ft) in height, it has palmate leaves, sticky resinous buds and candelabras of white or pink-tinged flowers in spring. The spiny, globular, green fruit contains glossy reddish-brown seeds (conkers, also chestnuts).

Habitat/distribution Occurs in eastern Europe, eastern Asia and North America, introduced to Britain and western Europe.

Growth Propagate by seeds, sown in autumn. Often self-seeds and grows rapidly in any soil.

Parts used Bark, seeds.

USES Medicinal Contains coumarin glycosides and saponins (of which aescin is the most important) giving it astringent, anti-inflammatory properties. It strengthens arteries and veins and is used against heart attacks, strokes, thrombosis, varicose veins and haemorrhoids. The active principles are extracted for use in pharmaceutical preparations.

> CAUTION The whole fruit is mildly toxic and should never be eaten. Only for use by qualified practitioners.

UMBELLIFERAE/APIACEAE
Aegopodium podagraria
Ground elder

History and traditions The specific name comes from the Latin word for gout, *podagra*, and it was grown in monastery gardens in medieval times as a cure for that disease. The name bishops' weed could be a reference to a one-time episcopal tendency to gout, due to high living and a rich diet of meat and alcohol, or to the plant's prevalence around ecclesiastical sites. It is dedicated to St Gerard, the patron saint of gout sufferers.

Description A herbaceous perennial with a creeping root system, it spreads rapidly, smothering other plants and self-seeds. Umbels of white flowers rise on long stems to 90 cm (36 in) above the leaves, 30 cm (12 in), in summer.

Related species *A. podagraria* 'Variegatum' is a variegated cultivar with cream patterning at the leaf margins. It is not as invasive as the common variety and makes a pretty border, especially when grown with white lilies or tulips.

Habitat/distribution Native to Europe, naturalized in North America; found in woodlands and wasteground.

Growth Ground elder is a rampant weed that grows in any soil and is almost impossible to eradicate once established. This plant is definitely not suitable for cultivation as it will take over.

Parts used Leaves, stems.

USES Medicinal An anti-inflammatory herb with mildly sedative properties, it has a long tradition as a treatment for gout, sciatica and rheumatism. It can be taken internally as an infusion, and is applied externally for stings and burns.

Culinary Though fairly unpleasant tasting, the young leaves and shoots can be added to salads, or cooked like spinach.

Other names Goutweed, bishops' weed and herb Gerard.

Above Aegopodium podagraria *'Variegatum' (Variegated ground elder) in the foreground with white, lily-flowered tulips.*

LABIATAE/LAMIACEAE

Agastache foeniculum

Anise hyssop

History and traditions A traditional medicinal herb of Native Americans, it became popular with colonists as a bee plant for the distinctive aniseed flavour it gave to honey.

Description A hardy, short-lived perennial with soft, ovate leaves, strongly scented with aniseed. Bold purple flower spikes last all summer. Clumps are 60–90 cm (24–36 in) in height.

Related species *A. rugosa*, known as Korean mint, or wrinkled giant hyssop, is also a hardy perennial, 1 m (3 ft) high, with pointed, mint-smelling leaves and mauve flower spikes.

Habitat/distribution *A. foeniculum* is native to North and Central America, and *A. rugosa* comes from eastern Asia.

Growth Grows best in rich moist soil in full sun. Although reasonably hardy, *A. foeniculum* will not stand prolonged frost or temperatures below -6°C (20°F). Propagate by division or softwood cuttings in spring.

Parts used Leaves, flowers – fresh or dried.

USES Medicinal The leaves have antibacterial properties and are taken as an infusion to alleviate coughs and colds, or as a digestive.

Culinary The leaves of both *A. foeniculum* and *A. rugosa* make refreshing tea with a minty flavour. They can be floated in soft drinks and fruit cups to add piquancy or snipped into salads. The flowers make a pretty garnish. The dried or fresh leaves may be added to cooked meat dishes and go well with pork.

RUTACEAE

Agathosma betulina

Buchu

History and traditions A prized medicinal plant of the indigenous people of South Africa, its virtues were discovered by colonists of the Cape who introduced it to Europe at the end of the 18th century. In the 1820s the dried leaves were exported in some quantity to Britain and thence to America, to be included in proprietary medicines and used to flavour cordials. John Lindley in his *Flora Medica*, 1838, records that several species of *Agathosma*, collected as 'bucku', were "found to be an excellent aromatic stomachic and very efficacious as a diuretic. The infusion is much praised as a remedy in chronic inflammations of the bladder and urethra and in chronic rheumatism." All of these uses remain valid in herbal medicine today.

Description A tender, evergreen shrub, 1–2 m (3–6 ft) in height, it has glossy, yellowish-green leaves, which are leathery in texture and studded with oil glands which smell of blackcurrants. White flowers appear in spring. A member of the rue family, it is highly aromatic, scenting the air wherever it grows in quantity.

Related species Several species are used, all indiscriminately termed buchu, or "buka", meaning powder in the local language. *A. betulina* is held to be the most effective for medicinal purposes, *A. crenulata*, oval buchu, has ovate leaves and *A. serratifolia*, long buchu, serrated, lance-shaped foliage. These plants were once classified as "barosma" and the term "barosma powder" for buchu is still sometimes used.

Habitat/distribution Dry hillsides of Cape Province, South Africa.

Growth Grown as a conservatory plant in temperate zones, a minimum temperature of 5°C (41°F) is required. Pot in ericaceous (lime-free) compost. It must not be overwatered, which can lead to rot, and should be cut back hard in spring to keep it in shape and control size. Grown outside in warm, frost-free regions, it needs well-drained, acid soil and full sun.

Parts used Leaves, which are harvested when the plant is in flower, and dried.

USES Medicinal The volatile oil contains up to 40% diosphenol, a strong antiseptic. Used internally for urinary infections, especially cystitis, coughs and colds, rheumatism, arthritis and digestive disorders. Applied externally for bruises and sprains.

Culinary Gives a blackcurrant taste to soft drinks and cordials and is used to flavour a local liquor "buchu brandy".

Household Made into a powder to deter ants and other insects.

Other name Round buchu.

AGAVACEAE

Agave americana
Agave

History and traditions Agave comes from the Greek for admirable. It gained the name "century plant" from the mistaken belief that it flowers only after a hundred years – but most bloom after ten years.

Description A tender succulent whose rosettes of spiky grey-green leaves are 1–2 m high (3–6 ft) with a spread of 2–3 m (6–10 ft). The tall bell-shaped flower spikes, resembling small trees, rise to 8 m (26 ft). Agaves should not be confused with aloes, and are not botanically related.

Related species *A. americana* 'Variegata' is a cultivar with yellow margins to the leaves.

Habitat/distribution Originally from tropical zones of the Americas, especially Mexico, this plant is now naturalized in southern Europe, India, and Central and South Africa.

Growth Needs well-drained soil, full sun and a minimum temperature of 5°C (41°F). Propagate by offsets. In cool climates it can be grown as a conservatory plant but takes up a lot of space.

Parts used Leaves, roots, sap.

USES Medicinal The sap has anti-inflammatory properties, and is applied externally for burns, bites and stings, by breaking open a leaf.

General The root has cleansing properties and is used for washing clothes and in commercial soap production. Fibres are woven into rope. The powdered leaf makes snuff and the whole plant is much employed as a stock-proof fence.

> CAUTION Can provoke an allergic reaction when used medicinally.

ROSACEAE

Agrimonia eupatoria
Agrimony

History and traditions The species name is from Mithradates Eupator, King of Pontus, who died in 64 BC. He practised magic, was a great believer in herbal potions and was thought to have rendered himself immune to injury by saturating his body with lethal poisons. The Anglo-Saxons also attributed magical powers to agrimony, including it in charms and dubious preparations of blood and pounded frogs. A sprig under the pillow supposedly brought oblivion, until removed. It was also credited with healing wounds, internal haemorrhages, snake bites, charming away warts and mending bad backs. Retaining its reputation through the centuries, it became the principal ingredient of *eau d'arquebusade*, a lotion for treating the wounds inflicted by the arquebus, a 16th-century firearm and forerunner of the musket. It was an essential ingredient of a springtime drink, still taken by country folk into the early years of this century as a "blood purifier".

Description A perennial with compound pointed leaves, covered in soft hairs. In summer and autumn it has small yellow flower spikes with a hint of an apricot scent. It grows to a height of 30–60 cm (1–2 ft).

Habitat/distribution Found on waste grounds and roadsides throughout Europe, Asia and North America.

Growth A wild plant which tolerates poor, dry soil, it can be propagated by seed sown in spring or by root division in autumn.

Above *Agrimony in flower.*

Parts used Dried flowering plant.

USES Medicinal Has anti-inflammatory, anti-bacterial and astringent properties and is taken internally for sore throats, catarrh, diarrhoea, cystitis and urinary infections. Applied externally as a lotion for wounds.

Household Yields a yellow dye.

Other names Church steeples, sticklewort and cockleburr.

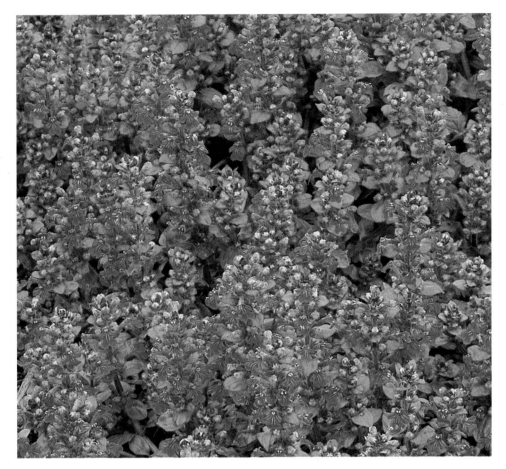

Above Aguja reptans *'Atropurpurea'*.

Below Aguja reptans *'Multicolor'*.

LABIATAE/LAMIACEAE

Ajuga reptans

Bugle

History and traditions The apothecaries knew it as "bugula" and along with self-heal, *Prunella vulgaris,* it was valued for many centuries as a wound herb. Culpeper thought highly of it: "if the virtues of it make you fall in love with it (as they will if you be wise) keep a syrup of it to take inwardly, and an ointment and plaster of it to use outwardly, always by you". He recommended it for all kinds of sores, gangrene and fistulas. Gerard, who found many specimens growing "in a moist ground upon Black heath, near London", backs him up, expressing the view that it is common knowledge in France "how he needs neither physician nor surgeon that hath Bugle and Sanicle".

Description A hardy perennial, 10–30 cm (4–12 in) high, growing on a creeping rootstock, it has attractive blue flower spikes in spring or early summer, growing from rosettes of basal leaves. White or pink-flowered mutants occasionally occur.

Related species Cultivars with richly coloured foliage make rewarding subjects for the herb garden. *A. r.* 'Atropurpurea' has purple-bronze leaves, *A. r.* 'Multicolor' has colourful variegated foliage of, pink, crimson and cream with a hint of green, and *A. r.* 'Variegata' has greyish-green leaves with creamy margins.

Habitat/distribution In damp ground in woodlands and meadows. Native to Europe and introduced elsewhere, it is also found in northern Africa and parts of the Middle East.

Growth Ajugas make excellent ground cover and are easy to propagate by separating and replanting the leafy runners at any time of the year, but preferably in spring or autumn when sufficient moisture can be provided. They do need a moist soil to flourish well and sun or partial shade.

Parts used Whole plant.

USES Medicinal Its reputation, sadly, has not stood the test of time and bugle is no longer widely used in herbal medicine today. But it is said to be mildly astringent and is sometimes still recommended, in the form of a lotion or ointment, for treating cuts and bruises.

Other names Carpenter's herb and sicklewort.

Habitat/distribution Found in mountainous areas, meadows, pasture lands and on rock ledges in Europe and throughout northern temperate regions.

Growth Grows in any soil in sun or partial shade. Self-seeds prolifically but germination of seed sown artificially is erratic. The easiest way to propagate is by division in spring or autumn. Species planted together hybridize readily.

Parts used Leaves.

USES Medicinal Has astringent and anti-inflammatory properties, controls bleeding and is taken as an infusion for menstrual and menopausal problems. Applied externally for vaginal itching, as a mouthwash or lotion for sores and skin irritation.

Culinary The leaves are edible and sometimes shredded and added to salads, but their slightly bitter, undistinguished taste hardly warrants this treatment.

Other names Lion's foot, bear's foot and leontopodium (in French, it is called Pied-de-Lion and in German, Frauenmantle).

Above Alchemilla mollis *has a froth of greeny-yellow flowers throughout summer.*

Right *The concave shape of* Alchemilla vulgaris *and* A. mollis *leaves forms a dip where drops of moisture collect.*

ROSACEAE

Alchemilla vulgaris
Lady's mantle

History and traditions This herb was unknown to the writers of the ancient classical world, but was a popular "magic" plant in northern Europe from earliest times, rising to prominence during the Middle Ages for its connections with alchemy. It was also sometimes associated with the Virgin Mary and dubbed Our Lady's mantle, subsequently shortened to lady's mantle, the scalloped leaves supposedly resembling a sculptured cloak. It was traditionally prescribed for infertility and "women's troubles" and was said to regulate the menstrual cycle and ease menopausal symptoms – as it still is prescribed by herbalists today.

Description A perennial 40–50 cm (16–20 in), it has hairy, branched stems and deeply lobed leaves (seven or nine lobes) with serrated edges and a froth of yellowish-green flowers in late spring and throughout summer.

Related species *A. alpina*, another medicinal species, is lower-growing, 10–20 cm (4–8 in) with star-shaped leaves. *A. mollis*, from the Carpathian mountains and known as "the garden variety", is the most attractive of the three with paler green, scalloped leaves and a more luxurious show of greeny-yellow flowers. It is widely grown in herb gardens, but has less medicinal value.

The alchemy connection

The magic of lady's mantle lies in its ability to hold moisture drops, often dew, trapped in the central dips of the leaves and by their waxy surface. Dew was a much-prized ingredient in the recipes of the alchemists of old and here was an accessible source. So the herb was named "Alchemilla" – the little alchemist.

In its narrowest and best-known sense, the primary concern of alchemy was the transformation of base metal into gold, but its wider significance is that it marked the beginnings of systematic chemistry. With origins in ancient Egypt, the science of alchemy passed to the Greeks of Alexandria, to the Arabs and then to the West. Leading alchemists of the 13th century were Albertus Magnus, Roger Bacon and Arnold de Villeneuve, who wrote widely on the subject. Although they believed in the "philosopher's stone" (the instrument capable of transmuting metals into gold), they were also pre-occupied with the discovery of a divine water, or elixir of life, capable of healing all maladies – with the purest dew as a necessary component.

In the 16th century, the Swiss physician, Paracelsus, took up some of the tenets of alchemy, including the concept of the "prima materia" and the "quinta essentia", the primary essence of a substance, but gave it a new direction. The chief objective was the making of medicines, not gold, dependent on a study of the properties of plants and their effects on the body.

LILIACEAE/ALLIACEAE

Allium

The onion genus provides us with some of the most useful medicinal and culinary herbs. The characteristic strong smell is a result of the sulphur compounds contained within, which are beneficial to the circulatory and respiratory systems and have antibacterial properties. It also makes them among the most popular and powerful flavouring agents in worldwide cuisine.

History and traditions Records of the use of both onions and garlic can be traced back to the ancient civilization of Babylonia as well as to Egypt, Greece and Rome. One variety of onion was accorded divine honours in Egypt, and the pyramid builders are said to have been sustained by daily doses of garlic.

Many of the old writers on herbs, from Pliny onwards, refer to the medicinal properties of garlic, but not everybody was unanimous in its praise. Horace made the outrageous claim that it is "more poisonous than hemlock", when he was ill following a meal containing garlic. And, in 16th-century Britain, the herbalist Gerard remained doubtful of its virtues. In this he was unusual, as the pungent smell of both onions and garlic ensured a widespread belief that their juice protected from infection and in times of plague they were much in demand. One old recipe book gives water distilled from onions as a treatment for the bites of a rabid dog. The smell of garlic is particularly lingering and all-pervasive and may well be responsible for superstitions about its capacity to ward off vampires and the devil.

Garlic breath

Chewing fresh parsley helps to disguise the smell of garlic on the breath. If you do not like the taste of garlic, but want to benefit from its healthy attributes, it can be taken in capsule form (available from good health stores or pharmacies).

Right Allium cepa *Proliferum Group, the tree onion, or Egyptian onion, produces little bulbs on its stems which are good for pickling.*

Allium cepa
Onion

Description Single bulbs at the base of each stem form the familiar culinary onion.
Related species There are numerous cultivars. *Allium cepa* Proliferum Group is the attractive tree onion, which is also known as the Egyptian onion, whose flowers produce large bulbils with leaves attached.
Habitat/distribution Origins unknown but probably originated in Central Asia, now grown worldwide.
Growth Propagate from sets in early summer or seed sown in spring or autumn. Plant in well-drained soil, rich in nutrients. Bend over tops in late summer to speed ripening and dry bulbs before storing.
Parts used Fresh bulb.

USES Medicinal See box.
Culinary Popular vegetable and flavouring agent.

Allium fistulosum
Welsh onion

Description Evergreen hardy perennial 60–90 cm (2–3 ft) tall, with hollow stems and leaves. Tightly packed greenish-white globes form the flowers in spring.
Habitat/distribution Native of Siberia, China and Japan. Widely grown elsewhere.
Growth Grow in well-drained, reasonably rich soil and divide clumps every three years. Seeds can be sown directly into the ground when frost no longer threatens.
Parts used Leaves, bulbs.

USES Medicinal The Welsh onion shares the decongestant, antibacterial properties of garlic and onions, but it is thought to be less concentrated and efficacious.
Culinary Pull the whole plant to make use of the bulb at the root, or cut the leaves and snip into salads and stir-fries.

Garlic bread

25 g/1 oz/2 tbsp butter or margarine
2–3 garlic cloves
1 tsp fresh parsley, finely chopped
1 tsp lemon juice
4 slices of bread, cut from a baguette

Peel the garlic cloves and put them through a garlic press. Mix the crushed garlic into the butter or margarine, with the parsley and lemon juice. Divide the mixture evenly and spread it over the slices of bread. Toast under a hot grill, or put on a baking tray in a hot oven, until browned.

Allium sativum
Garlic

Description A hardy perennial, it is often cultivated as an annual. Bulbs are made up of cloves, or bulblets, in a papery, white, or pinkish-white casing. The clump of flat leaves grows to 60 cm (2 ft). Flowers are greenish-white, but appear only in warm climates.

Habitat/distribution Originally from India or Central Asia, now grown worldwide, but does not flourish in cold, northern climates.

Growth Plant bulbs in autumn or winter in rich soil and a sunny position. Lift in late summer and dry in the sun before storing. Increase by dividing bulbs and replanting.

Parts used Bulbs, separated into cloves.

USES Medicinal See box.
Culinary Popular flavouring agent.

Allium schoenoprasum
Chives

Description A hardy perennial with clumps of cylindrical leaves growing from small bulblets to 30 cm (12 in). The leaves do not withstand very cold winters. Purple flower globes appear in early summer. There are both fine and broad-leafed cultivars.

Habitat/distribution Native to cool regions of Europe, naturalized in North America. Found in dry, rocky situations as well as damp grasslands and woods.

Parts used Leaves, flowers.

USES Culinary A prime culinary herb, with no medical applications, it has a milder flavour than its onion cousin, *Allium cepa*. Snip leaves into salads, sauces and soups. Flowers can be used as a garnish.

Allium tuberosum
Garlic chives

Description A perennial with sheaths of coarse, flattened leaves growing from a rhizome to a height of 50 cm (20 in). Star-shaped white flowers appear in late summer.

Parts used Fresh leaves.

USES Culinary Use as chives.

Allium
schoenoprasum

Medicinal use of garlic and onions

Helps lower blood pressure and blood cholesterol

Both garlic and onions may help to lower blood pressure and blood cholesterol. They are also thought to raise levels of beneficial high-density lipoproteins in the blood – these are molecules which play a part in clearing cholesterol from body tissues.

Helps prevent blood clotting

Research studies have also found that eating onions and garlic inhibits blood clotting and helps prevent circulatory diseases such as coronary heart disease, thrombosis and strokes. Studies using animals revealed that a garlic compound, allyl disulphide, helped prevent growth of malignant tumours – but the case for garlic as a cancer preventive in humans is as yet unproven.

Acts as a decongestant

Garlic and onions reduce nasal congestion and ease cold symptoms, especially when eaten raw, as volatile components are lost in cooking.

Has antiviral and antibacterial properties

The juice of a freshly-cut onion is a useful first-aid measure to relieve insect bites, bee stings and the itching of chilblains.

Left *Garlic bulbs – the oil makes an excellent flavouring for herb oil.*

LILIACEAE/ALOEACEAE
Aloe vera syn. *A. barbadensis*
Aloe vera

History and traditions The medicinal value of this plant was recognized by the Egyptians and used as an embalming ingredient. One story goes that Aristotle tried to persuade Alexander the Great to conquer the Indian Ocean island of Socotra (near the Gulf of Aden), for its aloes, being the only known place where they grew at the time. The plant was introduced to Europe in the 10th century and became established over the centuries as an important ingredient in proprietary medicines.

Description A tender succulent, 60–40 cm (2–3 ft) tall, with clusters of elongated, very fleshy, greeny-grey leaves, spiked at the edges, and tubular yellow flowers.

Related species Of the 300 species of aloes only a few have medicinal properties, including *A. perryi* and the South African, *A. ferox*, which has red spikes at the leaf edges. But *A. vera* is the most potent.

Habitat/distribution Origins are uncertain, but it is widespread in tropical and subtropical regions in dry, sunny areas.

Growth It needs a well-drained soil, full sun and a minimum temperature of 5°C (41°F). In cold climates it can be successfully grown as a conservatory or house plant. Pot up in gritty compost (soil mix), do not overwater, and allow to dry out completely between waterings.

Parts used Leaves, sap. The leaves are cut and the sap is used fresh, preserved and bottled or dried to a brown crystalline solid for use in creams, lotions and medicinal preparations.

USES Medicinal It is the mix of constituents in this plant that gives it exceptional healing properties. It contains anti-inflammatory and antimicrobial agents; long-chain polysaccharides which boost the immune system; minerals; antioxidant vitamins C, E, B^{12} and beta-carotene and lignin, a woody substance which aids penetration of the skin and tissues. *A. vera* gel from the leaf is applied externally to promote healing of wounds, burns, sunburn, eczema and skin irritations. It is taken internally for digestive tract problems and there is also some evidence that it may help conditions where the immune system is not functioning well. It has laxative properties and "bitter aloes" is the name for the strong, purgative medicine that is made from the leaves.

Cosmetic It is an ingredient of many commercial cosmetic products.

Other names Aloes, Barbados aloe, Cape aloe and Curacao aloe.

CAUTION Should not be taken internally by pregnant women. Subject to legal restrictions in some countries. Not to be taken in large doses.

VERBENACEAE
Aloysia triphylla syn.
Aloysia citriodora
Lemon verbena

History and traditions This lemon-scented shrub from South America was introduced to Europe in the 1790s. It is said to be named after Maria Louisa, wife of Carlos IV of Spain, Aloysia being a corruption of Louisa. The Victorians took to it for its long-lasting lemon fragrance, calling it "the lemon plant", and dried it for use in scented sachets.

Description Frost- to half-hardy deciduous shrub with rough-textured, strongly lemon-scented, spear-shaped leaves, dotted on the underside with oil glands. Racemes of tiny mauve-white flowers appear in late summer. In warm climates, where no frost occurs, it grows to 4.5 m (15 ft), but in cooler regions it is unlikely to grow to more than 1.5 m (5 ft). It is closely related to the *Lippia* genus, with which it was once classified.

Habitat/distribution Native to Chile and Argentina, it is widely grown in tropical and subtropical zones of the world, in Australia, New Zealand and temperate regions of Europe.

Growth It will usually survive a minimum temperature of -5°C (23°F), provided it is grown in a sheltered, south-facing site in well-drained soil. It will not tolerate prolonged cold and frost, especially if grown in a heavy soil. May be grown as a pot plant if given winter protection.

Aloysia
triphylla

Right *Lemon verbena in flower – it keeps its scent well when dried.*

New leaves do not appear until late spring or early summer. Cut back hard in spring, when it will regenerate from old wood. It is propagated from cuttings, taken in late summer, but needs heat to produce roots and during development of the seedlings.

Parts used Leaves, essential oil.

USES Culinary The leaves (fresh or dry) make a refreshing tea. If used with great discretion, as the taste is strong, they can be included in savoury stuffings and sauces, or used to flavour cakes and ice cream.

Aromatic The benefit of this herb is that the leaves retain their lemon scent, when dried, for several years. They help to deter insects and are ideal for sachets and making pot-pourri. The essential oil was widely used in perfumery, but has been discovered to sensitize the skin to sunlight.

Lemon verbena pot-pourri

dried peel of 1 lemon
2 cups dried lemon verbena leaves
1 cup dried chamomile flowers
15 cm/6 in cinnamon stick, crushed
1 cup dried pot marigold petals
1 tsp orris root powder
2–3 drops essential oil of lemon verbena (optional)

To dry the lemon peel, scrape it off the fruit with a vegetable peeler, spread on paper and put in a warm place (such as an airing cupboard) for about two weeks, until crisp.

Mix the ingredients together. Seal in a tin and put in a warm place for 2–3 weeks, shaking occasionally. Put in a bowl to scent the room, covering when not in use to retain the scent, or in drawstring sachets to hang in a wardrobe.

Lemon verbena essential oil will give the pot-pourri a stronger fragrance. It is also useful for adding zest to the mixture at a later date, as it will lose strength when constantly exposed to light and air.

ZINGIBERACEAE
Alpinia officinarum
Galangal

History and traditions Very similar to ginger, this plant has a long history as a spice and medicinal plant and has been used in Ayurvedic and Chinese medicine since ancient times. 'Galangal' comes from the Arabic word *Khalanjan*, which could in turn be derived from a Chinese word meaning "mild ginger". Known in Europe since the 9th century, it was probably introduced by Arab or Greek physicians.

Description A tropical evergreen with tall clumps of ovate to lanceolate leaves growing from ginger-scented rhizomes to a height of 1.2 m (4 ft). Flowers are pale green and white. *A. officinarum*, lesser galangal, is the more important species for both medicinal and culinary purposes.

Related species *A. galanga*, greater galangal, is a larger plant, growing to 2 m (6 ft), and has a less marked ginger aroma.

Habitat/distribution Found in tropical rainforest and grassland areas of southeast Asia and Australia.

Growth It can be grown only in climates with high humidity and minimum temperatures of 15–18°C (59–64°F). Needs well-drained soil and partial shade. Propagated by division of the rhizomes when new shoots appear.

Parts used Rhizome, oil.

USES Medicinal A good digestive, it also has antibacterial and antifungal properties, is used for feverish illnesses and fungal infections. *A. galanga* is considered less effective medicinally.

Culinary Both species are used as a ginger-like flavouring in Thai and southeast Asian cookery.

Growth Prefers moist to wet soil and a sunny situation. Propagated by division in autumn or by seed sown in late summer, though germination is often erratic.

Parts used Leaves, roots, flowers.

USES Medicinal The whole herb contains a sweet mucilage that is soothing and softening. Relieves inflamed gums and mouth, gastric ulcers, bronchial infections and coughs. Applied externally for ulcers, boils, inflammation of the skin and insect bites.

Culinary At one time the young roots and leaves were boiled, then fried with onions as a spring vegetable, or added to salads – but neither is very palatable.

Althea officinalis

MALVACEAE
Althaea officinalis
Marshmallow

History and traditions The generic name comes from the Greek, *altho*, meaning "to cure". The family name, Malvaceae, is also of Greek derivation, from *malake*, meaning soft, both indicating the emollient, healing properties of this plant, which have long been recognized. Pliny remarked: "Whosoever shall take a spoonful of Mallows shall that day be free from all diseases that may come to him." Early recorded uses include poultices to reduce inflammation and spongy lozenges to soothe coughs and sore throats – from which the modern confectionery is descended, though it no longer contains any of the herb. Marshmallow root was eaten as a vegetable by the Romans and in many Middle Eastern and European countries was a standby in times of famine when food was scarce. In more recent times it was a springtime country tradition to eat the young shoots, or make them into a syrup, to "purify the blood".

Description A hardy perennial with soft, downy leaves and pale pink flowers in summer, it reaches 1–1.2 m (3–4 ft) in height. It has large, fleshy taproots.

Habitat/distribution Found in salt marshes, near sea coasts and in moist inland areas, throughout Europe, in temperate regions of Asia, North America and Australia.

Related species

MALVACEAE
Alcea rosea formerly *Althaea rosea*
Hollyhock

This spectacular biennial, which first came to Europe from China in the 16th century, is closely related to *Althaea officinalis* and used to be classified in the same genus. It too has soothing properties and the flowers were once used to make cough syrups and to treat chest complaints, but the medicinal properties of its less showy relative are now considered superior. It is still worth its place in the herb garden for its old-fashioned grace and large colourful blooms (pink, purple, yellow or white) on towering spikes. It is easy to grow in well-drained soil and a sunny position from seeds sown *in situ* in spring or late summer.

Below left and right Alcea rosea, *the garden hollyhock, has racemes of single blooms in pink, purple and white. There are also many cultivars with double flowers.*

ANACARDIACEAE
Anacardium occidentale
Cashew nut

History and traditions A native of South and Central America and the Caribbean islands, this well-known nut tree was introduced to India from Brazil by Portuguese colonists in the 16th century, who originally planted it to prevent soil erosion on hillsides in Goa.

Description An evergreen tree, reaching 12 m (40 ft), it has dark-green, rounded, oval leaves. Panicles of pinkish-green flowers are followed by the fleshy fruit, known as the cashew apple, each of which has a kidney-shaped nut suspended from its base, containing a white seed.

Habitat/distribution Naturalized and cultivated in tropical zones worldwide.

Growth Tender trees which need well-drained, sandy soil, periodic high rainfall and a minimum temperature of 18°C (64°F).

Parts used Leaves, bark, fruits, seeds.

USES Medicinal Bark and leaves are used in treating malaria, especially in parts of Africa. Oil from the nut shell has been applied externally for ringworm and ulcers and to remove corns and warts – but its caustic action makes this a hazardous treatment.

Culinary The nut, or kernel, is rich in minerals and is a high-protein food. Juice from the fruit is made into soft drinks and distilled to produce spirits.

Other The outer shell of the nut produces a thick, tarry black oil used in engineering, and as a timber preservative to protect against insects.

CAUTION Oil from the cashew nut shell is an irritant and can cause painful skin blistering.

UMBELLIFERAE/APIACEAE
Anethum graveolens
Dill

History and traditions An ancient herb known in biblical times and described both by Pliny, AD 23–79, and by the Greek physician Dioscorides, AD 40–90, in *De Materia Medica*. It appears in the 10th-century writings of Alfric, Archbishop of Canterbury, and was a favourite herb in Anglo-Saxon charms against witchcraft, at which time it was also burned "to disperse thunder clouds and sulphurous air". The common name is likely to have come from the Saxon word *dillan*, to lull, for its ability to soothe colicky babies and for the ancient Greek tradition of covering the head with dill leaves to induce sleep. The culinary connection with cucumber goes back a long way. Charles I's cook, Joseph Cooper, records a recipe for pickling cucumbers in dill in his book of 1640. It has a long tradition of use in India and Eastern countries as a medicinal and culinary herb.

Description An aromatic annual, 1 m (3 ft) tall, with a single stem and feathery leaves. It has terminal umbels of tiny yellow flowers in midsummer and elliptic, flattened fruits. Resembles fennel, but is shorter and has a subtler, less strongly aniseed flavour.

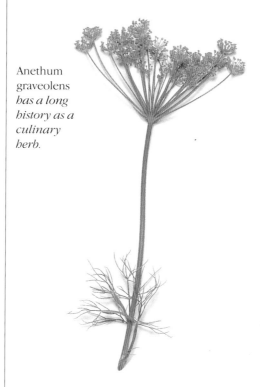

Anethum graveolens *has a long history as a culinary herb.*

Related species Indian dill is known as sowa. It is usually classified as *A. sowa,* but this is either a subspecies of *A. graveolens* or very closely related.

Habitat/distribution Originated in southern Europe and Asia, now widely grown in herb gardens worldwide.

Growth Plant dill in well-drained but nutrient-rich soil, in full sun. Requires adequate moisture as it bolts (runs quickly to seed) in poor, dry soil. Best propagated from seed sown in spring, straight into the ground where it is to grow, as it does not take well to being transplanted. Should not be grown near fennel as the two plants crosspollinate.

Parts used Leaves, seeds.

USES Medicinal A cooling, soothing herb which aids digestion, prevents constipation and is an ingredient of "gripe water" given to babies for indigestion. In Indian herbal medicine dill and fenugreek seeds are included in preparations for diarrhoea and dysentery. Poultices of the leaves are applied to boils and to reduce swelling and joint pains. Seeds are chewed to cure bad breath.

Culinary Leaves and seeds add a caraway-like flavour to fish, seafood and egg dishes and go well with bland-tasting vegetables, especially cucumber and potatoes. Widely used in Scandinavian cuisine. In Indian cookery, it is added to curries, rice dishes, soups, pickles and chutneys.

UMBELLIFERAE/APIACEAE
Angelica archangelica
Angelica

History and traditions According to legend, this herb took its name from the angel who revealed its virtues to a monk during a plague epidemic. It was widely thought to give protection from infection and, during the Great Plague of 1664–5, people were recommended to "bite and chaw" on its roots. It is also variously connected with the archangel Gabriel who is said to have appeared to the Virgin Mary at the Annunciation, celebrated at the end of March, and the archangel Michael, whose feast day is in May. In all northern European folklore it has an ancient reputation for its powers against witchcraft and evil spirits. In Lapland poets wore crowns of angelica, supposedly to gain inspiration from its scent. John Parkinson in his *Theatre of Plants*, 1640, wrote of it: "The whole plante, both leafe, roote and seede, is of an excellent comfortable scent, savour and taste."

Description Angelica is a statuesque biennial, though it often lives for three years. The whole plant is subtly aromatic. Standing 1.2 m–2.4 m (4–8 ft) high, it has hollow stems, large, deeply divided pale-green leaves and globular umbels of green flowers in early summer, followed by flat, oval seeds.

Related species *A. atropurpurea*, American angelica, has red stems. *A. sylvestris* is the wild European angelica.

Habitat/distribution Native to Europe and parts of Asia. Introduced in other parts of the world.

Growth Prefers a rich, damp soil but tolerates most conditions, provided it is not too dry. Plant in sun or partial shade. Self-seeds freely. Propagate by seed sown in autumn, in situ or in pots; seed remains viable for 6–12 months.

Parts used Leaves, stems, roots, seeds.

USES Medicinal Has anti-inflammatory properties, lowers fevers and acts as an expectorant. Infusions of the root are used to aid digestive disorders and bowel complaints. A poultice of the leaves has been known to soothe sunburn, but should be used with caution.

Culinary In Europe young stems are candied, cooked with rhubarb, tart fruits and berries to reduce acidity. It can be added to jams or marmalade (ginger and angelica make a good combination), seeds are added to biscuits (cookies). Seeds and roots are constituents of Benedictine, Chartreuse and other liqueurs.

Aromatic Leaves and seeds are dried and added to pot-pourri.

CAUTION Furocoumarin content increases skin photosensitivity and may cause skin irritation in susceptible people.

Far left Angelica atropurpurea *is a North American species.*
Left *A seed head of angelica.*

Culinary angelica

Angelica and rhubarb
Angelica has a pleasantly aromatic, slightly sweet taste, which enhances the flavour of rhubarb and reduces its acidity, so that less sugar is necessary. Only the very young leaf stems should be used, as older ones are coarse and stringy. Allow two or three 15 cm (6 in) pieces for each 450 g (1 lb) of rhubarb sticks. Cut them into small pieces and add to your favourite rhubarb pie or crumble recipe. Angelica is also excellent puréed with rhubarb to make a mousse or fool.

Candied angelica
Old recipe books contain instructions for candying leaves and roots, as well as stems of angelica. "Boil the stalks of Angelica in water till they are tender; then peel them and cover with other warm water. Let them stand over a gentle fire till they become very green; then lay them on a cloth to dry; take their weight in fine sugar with a little Rose-water and boil it to a Candy height. Then put in your Angelica and boil them up quick; then take them out and dry them for use."

UMBELLIFERAE/APIACEAE

Anthriscus cerefolium

Chervil

History and traditions The Romans were very fond of chervil and it is listed in 15th-century manuscripts as an essential kitchen herb. Confusion sometimes arises, however, as at that time both *A. cerefolium* and sweet cicely, *Myrrhis odorata*, were known as "chervil", sometimes distinguished as "sweet chervil" and "common chervil". John Parkinson, who wrote during the 17th-century in England, indicates: "Common chervil is much used of the French and Dutch people to bee boiled or stewed in a pipkin either by itself or with other herbs, whereof they make a Loblolly and so eate it. Sweete chervil gathered while it is young and put among other herbs for a sallet addeth a marvellous good relish to all the reste."

Description A hardy annual, 30–60 cm (1–2 ft) high, with bright green, finely divided feathery leaves and flat umbels of small white flowers in early summer.

Habitat/distribution Native to the Middle East and southern Russia. Widely cultivated elsewhere in warm and temperate climates.

Growth Chervil prefers light, moist soil and a sunny situation. Propagate from seed sown successionally for a continuous supply. It does not transplant well and runs to seed quickly, but can be sown where it is to grow, or cropped straight from the seed tray.

Parts used Leaves, preferably fresh, cut just before flowering.

USES Medicinal Although it has mild digestive properties, and is sometimes taken as a tea for this purpose, its chief use is culinary.

Culinary The delicate taste, which is more distinctive than parsley, complements most dishes. It brings out the flavour of other herbs and is an essential ingredient, along with parsley, tarragon and chives, of the classic French combination, *fines herbes*. It is best used raw or in a very short cooking process, if the subtle flavour is to be retained.

Chervil's light aniseed flavour makes it a culinary herb of distinction.

ROSACEAE

Aphanes arvensis

Parsley piert

History and traditions The common name comes from this herb's vague resemblance to parsley and from the French name for it, *perce-pierre*, meaning to pierce or break a stone. Breakstone is an alternative country name in English also and refers to its traditional use in treating kidney stones. Culpeper lists as its chief use that "it provokes urine, and breaks the stone", and it is still used for the treatment of kidney stones in herbal medicine today.

Description A prostrate annual with small fan-shaped leaves and inconspicuous green flowers in summer.

Habitat/distribution Found in dry places and wastelands, it is native to Britain and widely distributed throughout the world.

Growth As a wild plant, it grows best in well-drained soil, in sun or partial shade, and tolerates gravelly, stony soils. Propagated by seed sown in spring.

Parts used Leaves.

USES Medicinal A diuretic which also soothes irritated and inflamed tissues. It is used for painful urination and in the treatment of kidney and bladder stones.

Culinary It was a popular salad herb during the 16th century, but the taste is uninteresting and it is seldom eaten today.

UMBELLIFERAE/APIACEAE
Apium graveolens
Wild celery

History and traditions Remains of this plant were found in Egyptian tombs, including that of Tutankhamun, *c.* 14th century BC. Although rather bitter in flavour, it was the only celery known until the 17th century, when the cultivated variety we enjoy today, *A. g. var. dulce,* was developed in Italy.

Description An aromatic biennial with a bulbous, fleshy root. Grooved stems grow from 30–90 cm (1–3 ft) high in the second year. It has pointed, divided leaves (similar in shape to cultivated celery) and umbels of sparse, greenish-white flowers in late summer, followed by small, ridged seeds.

Habitat/distribution Found in marshy, often salty ground in Europe, Asia, northern Africa, North and South America.

Growth It prefers rich, damp soil, sun or partial shade and tolerates saline conditions. Does best in a sheltered position, and bears flowers for seed production in warm climates. Propagated by seed sown in spring, but needs a minimum temperature of 13–16°C (55–61°F) to germinate.

Parts used Roots, stems, leaves, seeds.

USES Medicinal It has digestive, anti-inflammatory properties and is also a diuretic. Used in the treatment of arthritis and rheumatism and in Ayurvedic medicine as a nerve tonic.

Culinary The plant is seldom eaten today, and is toxic in large quantities. Seeds may be used for flavouring in small amounts.

COMPOSITAE/ASTERACEAE
Arctium lappa
Greater burdock

History and traditions This plant comes into the thistle group of the extended Compositae/Asteraceae family. Its names relate to the clinging nature of the burs which follow the flowers. *Arctium* comes from *arktos*, Greek for a bear (supposed to indicate the plant's roughness), and *lappa* from a word meaning to seize, though some authorities also connect the species name with the Celtic word for hand, *llap*. The English common name is a little more obvious in derivation, "bur" referring to the prickles and "dock" to the shape of the large leaves. Culpeper lists its popular names as "Personata", "Happy-Major" and "Clot-bur", adding that it is too well known to describe, "even by the little boys, who pull off the burs to throw at one another".

Description A biennial, or short-lived perennial, which grows to 1.5 m (5 ft) tall. It has long, ovate leaves covered in down and thick, hairy stems. Purple thistle-like flowers appear in mid to late summer, followed by fruits (seed heads) made up of hooked spines or burs.

Related species *A. minus,* lesser burdock, has similar properties. *A. lappa* 'Gobo' is a culinary cultivar grown in Japan.

Habitat/distribution Greater burdock is native to temperate regions of Asia and widely distributed throughout Europe and North America, found on roadsides, waste ground and in nitrogen-rich soil.

Growth It is usually collected from the wild, but a cultivated species is grown in Japan. Prefers a moist soil, sun or partial shade and it self-seeds quite freely.

Parts used Roots, stems, seeds, leaves (rarely).

USES Medicinal It has antibacterial and fungicidal properties and is used as a decoction or poultice for inflamed skin, sores, boils and disorders such as eczema and psoriasis. It is also taken for gastric ulcers and said to increase resistance to infection. Used in traditional Chinese medicine.

Culinary It is cultivated in Japan for the roots, which are eaten as a vegetable. The stalks, before flowering, can be chopped and added to salads, or cooked as a celery-like vegetable. In the past, they were sometimes candied, in the same way as angelica.

Cosmetic An infusion of the leaves, or decoction of the roots, makes a tonic skin freshener or hair rinse for dandruff.

Other names Lappa and beggar's buttons.

Arctium lappa

Right *Close up of leaf.*

ERICACEAE
Arctostaphylos uva-ursi
Bearberry

History and traditions The generic name from the Greek, *arcton staphyle*, and the specific, *uva-ursi*, from the Latin, both mean "bear's grapes", perhaps because bears enjoyed the fruit, or perhaps because the sour taste of this plant was only thought fit for consumption by bears. It is listed in 13th-century herbal manuscripts and was described in detail by the 16th-century Dutch botanist Clusius (Charles de L'Ecluse). In the 17th century John Josslyn discovered this herb growing in North America, where many of the Native American tribes made use of its medicinal properties and added it to smoking mixtures. He found it to be highly effective against scurvy. It was considered medicinally important in 18th-century Europe, and remained so into the 20th century, appearing in the British *Pharmacopoeia*.

Description A creeping, evergreen shrub, growing to 15 cm (6 in), with dark-green, leathery, small, oval leaves. Terminal clusters of tiny, white or pink, bell-shaped flowers appear in summer, followed by red fruit.

Habitat/distribution Found in rocky moorland and woodland, in northern Europe, Scandinavia and Russia, northern Asia, Japan, North America and cool, northern hemisphere regions.

Growth Needs moist, sandy or peaty soil. Ericaceous compost (soil mix) must be used if container-grown and for propagating, which can be done from seed, by layering in spring or from cuttings, taken with a heel, in summer.

Parts used Leaves – usually dried. For commercial use they are collected from the wild, mostly in Scandinavia and Russia, field cultivation having proved too costly.

USES Culinary Although the berries are edible, they taste extremely sharp, and are more suitable as "grouse feed", (a use given in one herbal). The leaves were at one time a popular tea in Russia.

Medicinal Constituents include arbutin and methylarbutin, which have been established as effectively antibacterial, especially against urinary infections, such as cystitis.

General The leaves have a high tannin content and have been used in the past in leather tanning and to produce a dark-grey dye.

Other names Mountain box and uva-ursi.

> CAUTION Bearberry should not be taken by women during pregnancy, by children, or where kidneys are diseased.

PALMAE/ARECACEAE
Areca catechu
Betel nut

History and traditions The Chinese discovered the medicinal properties of this tree by 140 BC, when they brought it back from their conquests of the Malayan archipelago. It is the main ingredient of paan or "betel nut", a mixture of areca nut, lime and spices, wrapped in betel leaf, *Piper betle*, and it is widely chewed throughout the Middle East and Asia. It induces mild euphoria and is supposed to increase sexual virility.

Description A tall palm, reaching 20 m (65 ft) in height, with numerous feathery leaflets making up its 2 m (6 ft) long leaves. The pale yellow flowers appear when the tree is about 6–8 years old, followed by bunches of up to 100 round, orange fruits.

Habitat/distribution A native of Malaysia, and found throughout India, the Far East and eastern Africa, usually on coastal sites. Introduced in American tropical zones.

Parts used Fruit, rind, seeds.

USES Medicinal Stimulates the flow of saliva, and accelerates heart and perspiration rates. Chewed to sweeten breath, strengthen gums, improve digestion, and suppress intestinal worms – but permanently stains teeth red. Research is being carried out in America on this tree as a source of a potential anticancer drug. However, excessive chewing can lead to cancer of the mouth.

> CAUTION Toxic in large doses, excess causes vomiting and stupor. Legal restrictions are in force in some countries.

CRUCIFERAE/BRASSICACEAE

Armoracia rusticana
Horseradish

History and traditions Horseradish was valued in the Middle Ages for the medicinal properties of both leaves and root. The great English botanist and herbalist William Turner, writing in 1548, referred to it as 'Red Cole', and it was not commonly called horseradish until so named in Gerard's Herbal of 1597, (England). At that time it was used in Germany and Scandinavia to make the hot and spicy condiment we know today, but this did not become popular in Britain until well into the 17th century. John Parkinson, in 1640, describes its use as a sauce in Germany, adding, "and in our own land also", but he considered it "too strong for tender and gentle stomaches". In 1657, William Coles reiterated that it was the practice in Germany for "the root, sliced thin and mixed with vinegar (to be) eaten as a sauce with meat".

Description A perennial, with a deep, fleshy taproot and large bright-green, oblong to ovate leaves, with serrated margins, sprouting from the base to a height of 60 cm (2 ft). Racemes of tiny, white flowers on drooping stems, up to 1.2 m (4 ft) long, appear in summer.

Habitat/distribution In the wild it is found in dampish soils in Europe and western Asia. Now naturalized in many parts of the world.

Growth In theory it prefers a moist soil, but in practice flourishes in most conditions. It can be propagated by seed in spring, or by root cuttings in spring or autumn. It grows vigorously and,

once established, is nearly impossible to eradicate as it regenerates from the tiniest scrap of root left in the soil.

Parts used Leaves, roots.

USES Medicinal The root may be taken in the form of a syrup for bronchial infections, catarrh and coughs and as a general tonic for debility. The sliced root is applied externally to boils, or in a poultice to relieve rheumatic pains (but see CAUTION below).

Culinary The young, fresh leaves have a milder flavour than the pungent root and can be added to salads or chopped into smoked-fish pâtés. The fresh root is shredded to make a strong-flavoured, creamy-textured sauce, traditionally served with beef, but also excellent as an accompaniment to cold, especially smoked, meat and fish, hard-boiled eggs and stuffed aubergines (eggplant). For a milder flavour, grated apple, sprinkled with lemon juice and vinegar, can be mixed with horseradish.

To make horseradish sauce

2–3 pieces of fresh horseradish root
2 tbs cider vinegar
115 g/4oz fromage frais
salt, pepper and a pinch of sugar
2 tsp fresh, chopped dill

Scrub the horseradish root, grate it finely, and cover with the vinegar. Or, for a smoother texture, mix the horseradish and vinegar in an electric blender till pulped. Mix in the fromage frais, season with salt, pepper, sugar and chopped dill.

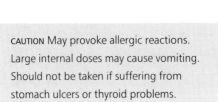

CAUTION May provoke allergic reactions. Large internal doses may cause vomiting. Should not be taken if suffering from stomach ulcers or thyroid problems.

Above *Digging up roots of established plants to make horseradish sauce.*

Above *Leaving some behind will ensure an ongoing supply of material.*

Above *Home-grown horseradish roots make a pungent sauce.*

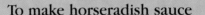

COMPOSITAE/ASTERACEAE

Arnica montana

Arnica

History and traditions Pier Andrea Mattioli, a household name in herbs in the 16th century, and physician at the Court of the Holy Roman Emperor Ferdinand I, in Prague, rated arnica highly. It became fashionable when he wrote about it in his standard work, *Commentarii*, a version of which appeared in Venice in 1544. It was widely used in the folk medicine of other European countries, principally Germany and Austria, where it has remained an important medicinal herb to this day. Arnica was used by Native Americans to treat muscular injury and back pain.

Description An alpine perennial with a creeping rootstock, it has a basal rosette of small, ovate, downy leaves and flowering stems growing to 30–60 cm (1–2 ft). The daisy-like flowers are golden yellow and borne in midsummer.

Related species *A. fulgens* is a North American species said to be even more medically powerful.

Habitat/distribution Found in mountainous regions of central and northern Europe and North America. *A. montana* is becoming rare in the wild and is protected in many countries.

Growth It prefers a sandy soil, enriched with humus, and a sunny position. As an alpine plant it needs a cool climate, and does not thrive in wet, waterlogged soil – grow arnica in containers or raised beds if necessary.

Parts used Flowers – dried, for use in pharmaceutical preparations.

USES Medicinal Recent research has established both the therapeutic value of this herb and its toxicity. It has a stimulating effect on the heart muscle and the circulatory system, but effects are rapid and correct doses crucial, with a high risk of overdose. It has antiseptic, anti-inflammatory properties when applied externally and is available as a pharmaceutical ointment for bruises. It is also used in homeopathy, for a range of conditions, including sprains, aching muscles, sore throats and sea sickness. In Germany it is widely available; in Britain it is legal only for external use and in the United States it is considered unsafe.

Other names Leopard's bane, mountain arnica, mountain daisy and mountain tobacco.

CAUTION Highly toxic and should not be taken internally, except in homeopathic remedies when the dosage is very small. It may cause dermatitis when used externally – do not apply to broken skin. Legally restricted in some countries. Use with advice from qualified medical practitioners.

Above *Flowers of* Arnica montana.

Right *Golden arnica flowers and pink* Mimulus lewisii *cover a hillside in bloom in Glacier National Park, United States.*

COMPOSITAE/ASTERACEAE

Artemisia

This genus of some 300 species, containing many garden ornamentals, supplies four of the best-known herbs. These include one of the most popular culinary herbs, tarragon, which is the exception of the four in character and uses.

Artemisia abrotanum
Southernwood

History and traditions A native of southern Europe, southernwood was introduced to Britain in about 1548, where the popular name, southernwood, directly described its origins as a woody plant from the south. It soon became established as a cottage garden favourite, attracting new names and associations. Lad's love and old man came about because smearing its ashes in an ointment base was supposed to make pimply youths sprout virile beards and bring new growth to bald heads. Other authorities claim that boys in love wore it in their hats, or gave sprigs as love tokens to the objects of their affections. The French name "*garde-robe*" refers to the habit of including this herb in sachets to protect clothes from insect infestation. It was also thought to protect from infection and was included in nosegays carried for the purpose.

Description A shrubby semi-evergreen (it loses foliage in winter in cold climates and as the plants age), it grows to 1 m (3 ft) tall and has feathery, grey-green leaves with a clean, lemony scent. It seldom flowers in northern climates, but in warmer southern regions small yellow flowers appear in summer.

Habitat/distribution Southernwood is native to southern Europe and parts of Asia, introduced and widespread in temperate zones and naturalized in North America.

Growth Prefers a light soil, full sun and tolerates drought. It is easy to propagate from softwood cuttings throughout summer, or heeled cuttings from old wood in autumn. Needs clipping back hard in late spring to prevent straggly, woody growth. Plants are best replaced after 6–8 years.

Parts used Leaves.

USES Medicinal Southernwood tea is said to stimulate the appetite and digestion. It is also prescribed for menstrual problems. At one time it was given to children to rid them of their threadworms.

Culinary Although there is some evidence of its use in southern European cookery, it is really far too bitter for the purpose.

Aromatic Its insect repellent properties and pleasant smell when dried make it a first choice herb for sachets to keep moths and insects at bay, or to include in pot-pourri.

Other names Lad's love and old man.

Artemisia abrotanum is easy to propagate from cuttings.

CAUTION Taken internally, southernwood stimulates the uterus and should never be given to pregnant women.

Artemisia absinthium
Wormwood

History and traditions Known since antiquity, this bitter herb was highly valued medicinally, with a reputation for overcoming bodily weakness. As a 15th-century manuscript declares: "Water of wormwood is gode – Grete Lords among the Saracens usen to drinke hitt." And Sir John Hill, in his *Virtues of British Herbs* (1772), alleging that the Germans have a tendency to overeat, says this is made possible by a habit of washing down each mouthful with a decoction of wormwood.

Description A perennial subshrub, 1 m (3 ft) in height, leaves are silvery-grey, downy and finely divided. Flowers are yellowish-green, tiny and ball-shaped, borne on bracts in late summer.

Habitat/distribution Found wild in temperate regions of Europe, North and South America, Asia and South Africa. Widely introduced as a garden plant.

Parts used Leaves, flowering tops.

USES Medicinal Has anti-inflammatory properties, expels intestinal worms and stimulates the uterus. Sometimes recommended for digestive problems, poor appetite and general debility, but there are more modern and safer ways to deal with these conditions.

Aromatic Strongly insect-repellent, it is dried for inclusion in sachets against moths, fleas and other insects, or made into tinctures and infusions to deter them.

CAUTION As a medicinal preparation, should not be given to children or pregnant women. Taken habitually, or in excess, can cause vomiting, convulsions and delirium.

Artemisia vulgaris
Mugwort

History and traditions Ascribed magical properties by cultures in Europe, China and Asia, this plant has accumulated many legends and superstitions. It was one of the nine herbs in the Anglo-Saxon charm against flying venom and evil spirits, when it was held to be "Mighty against loathed ones / That through the land rove" (Anglo-Saxon Ms, Harleian Collection). Roman soldiers are said to have put it in their shoes to prevent aching feet on long marches, a claim updated by William Coles in The Art of Simpling, 1656, with his assertion, "If a Footman take mugwort and put it into his shoes in the morning, he may goe forty miles before Noon and not be weary." In Europe it is connected with St John the Baptist.

Description A tall straggly perennial, 1–1.5 m (3–5 ft) in height. The leaves are grey-green with white undersides and slightly downy. Panicles of inconspicuous grey-green flowers appear in the summer.

Habitat/distribution A wild plant growing in a variety of soils, in wastelands, hedgerows, field margins, by streams and rivers in Europe, Asia and North America.

Parts used Leaves.

USES Medicinal As with some of the other artemisias, it is said to have digestive properties, stimulate appetite and act as a nerve tonic. It is a diuretic and used in regulating menstruation. Used in Chinese medicine for rheumatism.

Culinary At one time it was included in stuffings and sauces for meat and poultry such as duck and goose – but the slightly bitter, unpalatable taste makes it hardly recommendable.

Aromatic Has insect-repellent properties.

Artemisia dracunculus
French tarragon

History and traditions The species' name, *dracunculus*, is from the Latin meaning "a little dragon" after its supposed ability to cure the bites of serpents and mad dogs. A native of southern Europe, it was first introduced to the royal gardens of Britain in Tudor times. John Evelyn in his *Acetaria*, 1699, recommended it as "highly cordial and friendly to the head, heart, and liver" and advised that it "must never be excluded from sallets".

Description A perennial 1 m (3 ft) high, with branched erect stems, and slim, pointed leaves. Flowers are inconspicuous and greyish-green but appear only on some plants grown in warm climates – it does not flower at all in cool northern climates. Not to be confused with the subspecies, known as Russian tarragon, a larger, more vigorous plant, with coarser leaves and practically no discernible aroma.

Habitat/distribution A native of southern Europe and Asia, widely distributed in temperate zones worldwide.

Growth It prefers a fairly moist, but well-drained soil and full sun. Tarragon needs protection in winter in colder climates, especially in areas where frost is prolonged or where the ground becomes waterlogged. Propagate by division of

French tarragon is a superbly flavoured culinary herb.

roots in spring or autumn. It cannot be propagated from seed.

Parts used Fresh or dried leaf.

USES Culinary One of the top culinary herbs for distinction of flavour, it is used in salads, savoury pâté, cooked meat, fish and egg dishes. Well known for its affinity with chicken, it also enhances the flavour of root vegetables such as carrots and parsnips. Vinegar flavoured with tarragon is a classic condiment and it is a main ingredient of sauces and stuffings.

Feathery foliage of
Asparagus officinalis.

LEGUMINOSAE/PAPILIONACEAE
Aspalathus linearis
Rooibos

History and traditions A traditional tea plant of native South Africans of the Cape, it was adopted by European travellers and colonists in the late 18th century. It has gained popularity in the 20th century for its soothing, medicinal properties and because it makes a pleasant-tasting tea with a similar flavour to ordinary, Asian tea.

Description A small shrub up to 2 m (6 ft) in height, with bright-green, thin, linear leaves, bearing short, leafy shoots in their axils. Small yellow pea flowers are followed by long pods. The leaves turn a reddish-brown during processing which gives the tea its name.

Habitat/distribution Native to dry, mountainous areas of Cape Province, South Africa.

Growth A frost-hardy bush – it cannot tolerate temperatures below −5°C (23°F), or prolonged severe weather. Requires dry, sandy soil and full sun. Propagated by seed sown in spring. Pinch out shoots, as it grows, to encourage bushiness. Commercially cultivated in South Africa.

Parts used Leaves and shoots – sun-dried and fermented to make tea.

USES Medicinal High in vitamin C and mineral salts, it is taken internally for digestive disorders and to relieve allergies and eczema and applied externally for skin irritations.

Culinary It has a refreshing flavour, is low in tannins and makes a caffeine-free substitute for Asian tea. It is sometimes used as a flavouring herb in sauces and soft drinks and as an ingredient of a local alcoholic liquor.

Other name Red bush tea.

ASPARAGACEAE/LILIACEAE
Asparagus officinalis
Asparagus

History and traditions Appreciated as a delicacy by the ancient Greeks and Romans and mentioned by Pliny in his *Natural History*. The name is originally from a Greek word, the medieval Latin for which was "sparagus", leading to the popular derivation of sparrow-grass. This was once so widely used that a commentator remarked in 1791, "The corruption of the word into *sparrow-grass* is so general that *asparagus* has an air of stiffness and pedantry about it." Gerard recommended its culinary virtues and Culpeper stressed the medicinal properties. His assertion that it clears the sight and eases toothache no longer holds sway, but he also recommended it for sciatica as do herbalists today.

Description A perennial whose fleshy shoots are eaten as a delicacy. If left uncut it develops feathery leaves to a height of 1–1.5 m (3–5 ft) with small greeny-white flowers followed by red berries.

Habitat/distribution Native to coastal, sandy areas and woodlands of Europe and Asia, now widely cultivated throughout the world.

Growth It requires rich, well-drained loam and a sunny position. Plants may be propagated from seed, but beds are usually established from bought one-year-old crowns. It takes three years to produce the vegetable, beds then last 10–12 years.

Parts used Young shoots.

USES Medicinal Asparagus has cleansing, restorative properties, combats acidity and is taken for rheumatism, sciatica and gout, as either a food or an infusion. It also has diuretic and laxative properties, and is taken for urinary infections, but it should be avoided where there is kidney disease. An important medicinal herb in India, where it is considered to be a good aphrodisiac, helpful in treating impotence and sold for this purpose as *Safed musli*.

Culinary High in vitamins A and C and minerals, including calcium, phosphorus and iron. Young shoots, lightly steamed, are served as a vegetable with melted butter or a vinaigrette sauce, or puréed to make soup.

Other name Sparrow-grass.

Above *An asparagus shoot emerging from soil.*

CAUTION Not to be taken by anyone with kidney disease.

CHENOPODIACEAE
Atriplex hortensis
Orache

History and traditions This herb was eaten as a spinach-like vegetable by Native American tribes, and introduced to Britain in 1548. Sixteenth-century herbalists considered it to be effective against gout when applied as a poultice with honey, vinegar and salt. John Evelyn in his *Acetaria,* 1719, refers to its "cooling properties" and recommends it as a salad herb or vegetable, advising that, like lettuce, it should be boiled in its own moisture. Culpeper agreed that it could be eaten as a salad but thought its real virtue lay in the seeds, which he claimed made an effective laxative in the form of an alcohol tincture.

Above Atriplex hortensis *var. 'Rubra', red orache, makes a spectacular plant in the border, and the leaves add colour to salads.*

Description An upright annual, growing to 1.2 m (4 ft), it has spear-shaped green to purple leaves, slightly downy when young, and a mass of yellow-green, sorrel-like flowers, borne on tall spikes, in summer.

Related species *A. hortensis* var. 'Rubra', or red orache (above) is a more attractive cultivar, with purple-red foliage and flowers, followed by spectacular seed heads sought after by flower arrangers.

Habitat/distribution Occurs in Asia, North America and Europe, often in coastal areas. It is widely cultivated in temperate and warm regions worldwide.

Growth Flourishes in any soil, tolerates dry conditions but growth is more luxuriant in moister, more fertile soil. Prefers an open, sunny position. Propagated by seed sown *in situ* in spring. Self-seeds prolifically.

Parts used Leaves.

USES Culinary Leaves of red orache add colour and interest to salads, but, despite some recommendations, neither red nor green make very succulent spinach substitutes when cooked as vegetables.

Other name Mountain spinach.

Left *Leaves of* Atriplex hortensis *var. 'Rubra'.*

SOLANACEAE
Atropa belladonna
Deadly nightshade

History and traditions In 16th-century Venice this plant was known as *herba bella donna*, and used to dilate the pupils of their eyes by women who sought to beautify themselves. Its potential to cause fatalities was well understood at the time, the apothecaries' name for it being *solatrum mortale*, which translates as "deadly nightshade". Writing at the end of the 16th century, Gerard pontificates on its dangers, advising that a plant "so furious and deadly" should be banished from "your gardens".

Description A bushy perennial, 1–1.5 m (3–5 ft) tall, it has ovate, dull-green leaves, bearing single, purple-brown, bell-shaped flowers in the axils in summer, followed by shiny black berries.

Related species Not to be confused with the *Solanum* genus, many of which are poisonous also and include other nightshades – as well as potatoes, aubergines (eggplant) and climbers.

Habitat/distribution Native to Europe and Asia, introduced and naturalized elsewhere.

Growth Grown as a commercial crop (for the pharmaceutical industry) in well-drained, moist soil and full sun – warm, dry conditions increase the alkaloid content.

Parts used Whole plant – dried and processed.

USES Medicinal It contains the alkaloid, atropine, which dilates the pupils of the eye and gives the plant its toxic, sedative properties. A constituent of pharmaceutical drugs, used as premedication before surgery and in eyedrops for ophthalmic treatment.

CAUTION Highly poisonous. Subject to legal restrictions in most countries. For use by qualified medical practitioners only.

MELIACEAE
Azadirachta indica
Neem tree

History and traditions A common tree of southern Asia, it has played an important role in Ayurvedic medicine, and in agriculture and domestic life as an insect repellent since earliest times. The first part of the botanical name is from a Persian word meaning "noble tree", reflecting its many useful properties, which remain valid to this day. The Neem Foundation, Bombay, dedicated to its study, was established in 1993 and the tree's potential as a source of a low-cost, environmentally-friendly pesticide for field crops in developing countries is currently being investigated.

Description A large, evergreen tree, 12–15 m (40–50 ft) tall, it has dense pinnate leaves. Clusters of small white flowers appear in spring to be followed by long greeny-yellow fruits each containing a seed. The wood secretes resin, and *margosa* or *neem* oil is made from the seeds.

Habitat/distribution Occurs in India, Sri Lanka, Myanmar, southeast Asia and tropical regions of Australia and Africa. Widely planted as shade trees to line the roads.

Growth It will not grow in temperatures below 15°C (59°F). It requires sun and tolerates poor, dry soil.

Parts used Leaves, bark, seeds, oil, resin.

USES Medicinal Neem has anti-inflammatory and insecticidal properties, reduces fever, and acts as a tonic and detoxicant, increasing vitality. It is used in the treatment of malaria and has been found to have some effect against leprosy. Also used externally for skin disorders and irritations, especially boils and ulcers, and in eye and ear complaints. Twigs can be used to clean teeth, prevent breath odour and protect from infection.

Cosmetic Reputed to prevent hair loss if a decoction of the leaves is applied as a rinse. The oil is used in hair and skin lotions, toothpaste and soap.

General Makes an effective mosquito and insect repellent, and insecticide for crops. In its countries of origin the dried leaves are used to protect stored clothes or books from insect damage. Although it has been found to be safe and efficient as a sheep dip, this use has not been developed commercially.

Other name Margosa.

Above *Neem leaves have excellent insecticidal properties.*

BERBERIDACEAE
Berberis vulgaris
Barberry

History and traditions Barberry has been grown since medieval times for medicinal and culinary use and as a dye plant, producing a yellow colour. It was said to be excellent for "hot agues" and all manner of burnings and scaldings. It had a reputation for blighting wheat, now justified, as it is a known host of the disease, wheat rust.

Description A shrub which grows to 2 m (6 ft), with sharp spines on the stems and small oval leaves. Clusters of yellow flowers in late spring are followed by the shiny red fruits (berries).

Habitat/distribution Found in hedges and woodland in Europe, also in Asia, the Americas and northern Africa.

Growth A wild plant, it grows on any soil in sun or partial shade. It is propagated by layering or by taking cuttings in early autumn and can also be grown from seed sown in spring or autumn.

Parts used Leaves, bark, roots, fruit.

USES Medicinal It contains an anti-bacterial alkaloid, berberine, and is used in the treatment of tropical diseases, including dysentery and malaria. It has also been found to contain anti-cancer compounds and is included in chemotherapy drugs. Used in Ayurvedic medicine for liver complaints and as an anti-inflammatory.

Culinary The berries are very bitter, but high in vitamin C. At one time they were made into jams, jellies, preserves and tarts.

CAUTION Restrictions on the cultivation of barberry exist in some countries.

BORAGINACEAE
Borago officinalis
Borage

History and traditions There are various historical references to the ability of this herb to bring comfort and cheer. Gerard mentions references to it in this context by Pliny and Dioscorides, along with the Latin tag: *"Ego Borago, gaudia semper ago"*, which he translates as "I, Borage, bring alwaies courage". He goes on to advise adding the flowers to salads to "exhilerate and make the mind glad", the leaves to wine to "drive away all sadnesse, dulnesse and melancholy", making a syrup of the flowers to calm a "phrenticke or lunaticke person" or, for even greater force and effect, candying them with sugar. According to John Parkinson, their attractive colour and form made the flowers a favourite motif in women's needlework.

Description A short-lived hardy annual, 60–90 cm (2–3 ft) high, with a sprawling habit of growth, hollow, hairy stems, downy leaves and blue (sometimes pink) star-shaped flowers with black centres. It is very attractive to bees.

Related species *B. officinalis* 'Alba' is a white-flowered variety.

Habitat/distribution Native to the Mediterranean region from Spain to Turkey. Now naturalized in most of Europe and in many other parts of the world.

Growth Grows in any soil, even if poor and dry, but it makes a lusher, healthier plant, less prone to mildew, given better soil and more moisture. Prefers a sunny position. It is easy to propagate from seed sown in spring or autumn, and despite common advice to the contrary, the seedlings may be successfully transplanted when young, if they are well watered until established. It also self-seeds.

Parts used Leaves, flowers, oil from the seeds.

USES Medicinal A cooling, anti-inflammatory herb with diuretic properties. It is also said to be mildly antidepressant. Used externally to soothe inflamed skin and in mouthwashes and gargles. The seeds contain gamma-linolenic acid, and oil extracted from them is used as an alternative to evening primrose oil for hormonal problems and skin complaints. Borage is grown as a commercial crop for its oil, which is used in pharmaceutical drugs and cosmetic products.

Culinary The leaves have a faint flavour of cucumbers and are added to soft drinks and wine cups. The flowers make a pretty garnish for salads, and are candied or dried as decorations for sweet dishes and cakes.

CAUTION Borage may cause allergic reactions in some people. The leaves, but not the oil, have been found to contain very small amounts of an alkaloid that may cause liver disease. The plant, but not oil extracted from the seeds, is legally restricted in some countries. Use with advice from qualified medical practitioners.

Top left *Borage is grown as a commercial crop for the pharmaceutical and cosmetic industries.*

Top Borago officinalis *'Alba'.*

Above *Borage flowers make a pretty garnish for salads.*

BURSERACEAE
Boswellia sacra syn. *B. carteri*
Frankincense

History and traditions Since ancient times, frankincense has been an ingredient of incense, used in the religious ceremonies of the Egyptians, Babylonians, Assyrians, Hebrews, Greeks and Romans, and is still used in religious ritual to this day. It was highly valued by early civilizations as an item of trade, considered as precious as gold, and was one of the gifts said to have been given to Jesus Christ at his birth by the wise men from the east (Matt. 2:11). It is also thought to have been used by Cleopatra as a cosmetic for smoothing skin. In charred form it made *kohl*, the black eyeliner worn by eastern women. Ancient medicinal uses include Pliny's claim that it provided an antidote to hemlock poisoning and Avicenna's recommendations that it should be prescribed for tumours, ulcers, vomiting, dysentery and fevers. There is also some evidence that at one time it was used in China for leprosy.

Description A small deciduous tree, 2–5 m (6–16 ft) in height, with papery bark, pinnate leaves and racemes of small greenish-white flowers. The gum is secreted in the wood.

Related species Several species of *Boswellia* produce frankincense – formerly it was mostly derived from *B. sacra* and *B. papyrifera*. Today, *B. carteri* and *B. frereana* are usual sources. *B. serrata* (from India) is grown for timber.

Habitat/distribution *B. sacra* comes from Somalia and southern Arabia, *B. papyrifera* from Nigeria and Ethiopia, *B. carteri* and *B. frereana* from Somalia across to eastern Africa, found in desert scrubland. Many *Boswellia* species are threatened with extinction in the wild, due to over-exploitation and over-grazing.

Growth Grows wild, in shallow, rocky soil.

Parts used Gum resin – obtained by incising the trunk to produce a milky sap, which hardens into yellowish globules. Available in the form of grains or powder.

USES Medicinal The resin has antiseptic properties and has many uses in both Chinese and Ayurvedic medicine. The essential oil is used in aromatherapy to counteract anxiety (often by heating the essential oil in a vaporizer).

Aromatic Its chief use is as an ingredient of incenses and fragrant preparations. Also added to commercial cosmetics and is a constituent of an antiwrinkle face cream.

Other name Olibanum.

CRUCIFERAE/BRASSICACEAE
Brassica nigra
Mustard

History and traditions Mustard has a long history both as a medicinal and as a flavouring herb. The ancient Greeks thought highly of it and Hippocrates recommended that it be taken internally, or as a poultice, for a variety of ailments. It probably came to Britain with the Romans, who mixed the seeds with wine as a condiment and ate the leaves as a vegetable. Gerard describes pounding the seeds with vinegar to make an "excellent sauce" for serving with meat as a digestive and appetite stimulant.

Description An erect annual, 1–1.2 m (3–4 ft) high, with narrow, lobed leaves and racemes of bright yellow flowers, followed by pods containing reddish-brown seeds.

Related species *B. juncea*, or brown mustard, being easier to harvest mechanically, though less pungent, has largely replaced the medicinal *B. nigra*. White mustard (*Synapsis alba*, syn. *Brassica alba*) is also grown for commercial production. It is used to make American mustard and is the species that was sown with cress as a salad.

Growth Requires rich, well-dressed soil and full sun and is propagated by seed sown in spring.

Parts used Leaves, seeds – seedpods are picked before they are fully ripe and dried.

USES Medicinal Mustard has warming and antibiotic properties and is applied externally in poultices, baths or footbaths for rheumatism, aching muscles and chilblains. A mustard foot-bath is a traditional British remedy for colds.

Culinary The ground seeds, mixed into a paste, make the familiar "hot-flavoured" condiment to serve with a range of dishes. The whole seeds are added to curries, soups, stews, pickles and sauces. Young leaves are eaten with cress, or added to salads.

Description Common box is an evergreen shrub, or small tree, growing to about 4.5 m (14 ft), with glossy green, ovate leaves and a strange, rather acrid scent.

Related species There are over 70 species, ranging from tender to hardy. *B. sempervirens* 'Suffruticosa' is a dwarf form – for edging and low hedges: *B. sempervirens* 'Elegantissima' is slow-growing with variegated cream and silver-green foliage; *B. sempervirens* 'Latifolia Maculata' has gold leaves; and *B. microphylla* makes low-growing mounds of dark green.

Habitat/distribution Occurs in Europe, Asia, Africa, North and Central America.

Growth Requires well-drained, but not poor, soil, sun or shade. Although hardy, *B. sempervirens* does not thrive in very cold winters and new growth is damaged by frosts – clip after frosts to avoid encouraging vulnerable new shoots. Propagated by semi-ripe cuttings, in late summer.

Parts used Leaves, bark, wood.

USES Medicinal Said to be effective against malaria, but contains toxic alkaloids, and is little used in herbal medicine today. It is currently being researched for its potential as treatments for cancer, HIV and AIDS.

> CAUTION Poisonous, can be fatal if taken internally. May cause skin irritations.

BUXACEAE
Buxus sempervirens
Box

History and traditions The gardens of ancient Rome featured formally clipped box hedges and topiary, a fashion which was enthusiastically revived in Renaissance Europe, when knot gardens and elaborate parterres dominated garden design. Box foliage has been used to decorate the house for American Thanksgiving and at Christmas time in Europe, when it was made into "kissing boughs" or "Advent crowns" (depending on inclination and piety) – sprigs were tied on to frames and decorated with ribbons, candles and shiny red apples. Sometimes known as "boxwood" for its hard, durable wood, traditionally used to make engraving blocks, wooden tools, musical instruments and fine furniture.

Above Buxus sempervirens, *common box.*

Below left to right *Clipped dwarf box,* Buxus sempervirens *'Suffruticosa', the variagated leaves of* B. sempervirens *'Elegantissima' and the compact and very hardy* B. microphylla *var.* Koreana.

LABIATAE/LAMIACEAE
Calamintha nepeta
Calamint

History and traditions Now regarded as an ornamental, calamint was once an important medicinal herb, considered to be effective for "hysterical complaints" and "afflictions of the brain", as well as for a range of ailments from leprosy to indigestion. It had a reputation for hindering conception and as an abortifacient.

Description A small, bushy perennial, 30–60 cm (1–2 ft) high, it has small, ovate leaves and a mass of tubular pinky-mauve flowers in summer.

Related species The medicinal calamint of the apothecaries was *C. officinalis*, now classified as *C. sylvatica*, but *C. nepeta* seems to have been used interchangeably. *C. grandiflora* has larger flowers and *C. grandiflora* 'Variegata' is a cultivar with cream and green variegated foliage.

Habitat/distribution Native to Europe, found in grassland, woodland and chalky uplands of central Asia and northern temperate zones.

Growth Prefers well-drained, not-too-rich soil and a sunny position. The easiest method of propagation is by division in spring.

Parts used Leaves or flowering tops.

USES Medicinal It is taken as a tonic, or for indigestion, in the form of an infusion.

Culinary The young leaves and flowers, fresh or dried, may be infused to make a lightly mint-scented tea or added to salads.

> CAUTION It is not advisable for pregnant women, as one of its constituents is pulegone (also found in pennyroyal, *Mentha pulegium),* which stimulates the uterus.

COMPOSITAE/ASTERACEAE
Calendula officinalis
Pot marigold

History and traditions This cheerful, familiar flower was valued for its medicinal, culinary and cosmetic properties in early civilizations of both east and west. Calendula is the diminutive of the Latin *calendulae* and thus "a little calendar or little clock" (*Oxford English Dictionary*). This ties in neatly with its habit of closing its petals when there is no sun as described by Shakespeare in *A Winter's Tale*:

The Marigold that goes to bed wi' the sun
And with him rises weeping.

In medieval England the usual name was simply "golds" – Chaucer refers to a garland of "yellow golds" as an emblem for jealousy and it was only later dubbed "marigold" in honour of the Virgin Mary. Its brightness inspired claims of exceptional virtues from an ability to draw "wicked humours" out of the head (*Macer's Herbal*, 15th century), which makes some sense of a fantastical tale in the *Book of Secrets of Albertus Magnus,* 1560, of how an amulet of marigold petals, a bay leaf and a wolf's tooth will ensure that only words of peace will be spoken to the wearer. In Tudor times the petals were dried in huge quantities and sold in grocers' shops to flavour winter stews. They were made into conserves and syrups and also added to salads.

Description A low-growing annual – to 50 cm (20 in) – with hairy, slightly sticky leaves and large orange-yellow daisy-like flowers throughout summer into early autumn.

Related species There are a number of hybrids and ornamental cultivars that do not necessarily have the same medicinal value, but may be used for culinary and cosmetic purposes and to add to pot-pourri. The *Tagetes* genus of marigolds are not related. Many are toxic and should not be used for the same purposes as *Calendula*.

Growth Easy to grow in any soil. Propagate from seed sown in autumn or spring. Regular dead-heading ensures a good supply of blooms over a long period. Self-seeds prolifically.

Parts used Flowers – petals can be used fresh or dried.

USES Medicinal Pot marigold or calendula has anti-inflammatory, antiseptic properties and is also antibacterial and antifungal. It makes an excellent ointment for soothing irritated, chapped skin, eczema, insect bites and sunburn. It may also be made into an infused oil, for the same purpose, by steeping petals in warm vegetable oil.

Culinary Once known as "poor man's saffron", the fresh or dried petals add rich colour to rice dishes and salads and may be sprinkled over sweet dishes or baked in buns and biscuits.

Cosmetic Petals are added to face and hand creams, or made into an infusion as a lotion for spotty or oily skins.

Aromatic Whole dried flowers, or petals lend colour to a fragrant pot-pourri.

> CAUTION Not to be confused with inedible marigold (tagetes).

Pot marigold skin salve

300 ml/^{1}/2 pint/1 ^{1}/4 cups boiling water
15 g/^{1}/2 oz dried pot marigold petals or
*   30 g/1 oz fresh petals*
60 ml/4 tbs emulsifying ointment
15 ml/1 tbs glycerine
4 drops tincture of benzoin
4–5 drops infused calendula oil (optional)

First make a strong marigold infusion by pouring the boiling water over the marigold petals in a jug or bowl. Cover and leave until cool before straining.

Put the emulsifying ointment and glycerine in a bowl set over a pan of gently simmering water and stir until melted – which will take about 10 minutes.

Remove from the heat and mix in 150 ml/^{1}/4 pint/ ^{2}/3 cup of the marigold infusion, with the tincture of benzoin and calendula oil. Stir the mixture until it has cooled and reached a consistency similar to double (heavy) cream. Pour into a small jar before it sets.

• Emulsifying ointment, tincture of benzoin and calendula oil are available from specialist herbal suppliers.

CANNABACEAE

Cannabis sativa
Cannabis

History and traditions Cannabis has a long history as a medicinal plant, being mentioned in ancient Chinese and Indian texts dating from the 10th century BC. Herodotus reports that the Scythians (nomadic people of Iranian origin, living between the 7th and 2nd centuries BC) "crept into their huts and threw the seeds onto hot stones". Pliny thought very highly of this plant's medicinal values. Hildegarde of Bingen, AD 1150, refers to it as a relief for headaches and it is mentioned in all the great Renaissance herbals – though its narcotic effects were well understood and it was known as "The Leaf of Delusion". As hemp, it has been grown for its fibre since ancient times, and it provided rope for the hangman in 16th-century Britain (old names are "gallowgrass" and "neckeweed"). The word "assassin" comes from the Arabic for hashish-taker.

Description An annual which grows to 5 m (16 ft) in height, on erect stems with narrow, toothed leaves and panicles of inconspicuous green flowers.

Habitat/distribution Cannabis is native to northern India, southern Siberia, western and central Asia; it can be grown throughout temperate and tropical regions.

Parts used Leaves, flowering tops – processed in various forms, under various names, such as "marijuana", "pot", "dagga", "kif", "ganja", "charas" or "churras", and "bhang".

USES Medicinal Cannabis is widely used as an illegal narcotic drug. It can be addictive, and is weakening and harmful in excess, but there is some evidence of its therapeutic value for diseases such as cancer, multiple sclerosis, cerebral palsy and glaucoma.

General Rope is made from the fibre. Seeds are the source of hempseed oil used in varnishes, foods and cosmetics. Hemp *per se* does not contain appreciable amounts of THC and is a legal crop in some places – as a weed it grows with abandon and great success in Iowa.

Other name Hemp.

CAUTION It is illegal in most countries.

CRUCIFERAE/BRASSICACEAE

Capsella bursa-pastoris
Shepherd's purse

History and traditions Most of its names in English, Latin and other European languages refer to the resemblance of the seeds to purses or little pouches. It is of ancient origin, seeds were found at Catal Huyuk, a site dating from 5950 BC, and in the stomach of Tollund Man. Following a visit to America, John Josselyn listed it in his herbal, 1672, as one of the plants unknown to the New World before the Pilgrims went there. Despite being a common weed, it has proved a valid medicinal plant in this century – extracts were used during World War I to treat wounds.

Description An annual, or more usually biennial, plant with a flower stem rising to 50 cm (20 in) from a basal rosette of oval, dentate leaves. It has tiny white flowers, followed by triangular seedpods.

Habitat/distribution Grows worldwide in temperate zones in fields and waysides on gravelly, sandy and nitrogen-rich soils.

Growth A wild plant, it tolerates poor soil. It can be propagated from seed. Self-seeds freely.

Parts used Leaves – fresh, or dried for use in infusions and extracts.

USES Medicinal Contains a glycoside, diosmin, which has blood-clotting effects and is reputed to stop internal haemorrhages and reduce heavy menstruation when taken as an infusion of the dried leaf. Also taken for cystitis and applied externally for eczema and skin complaints.

Culinary The leaves are rich in vitamins A, B and C and, although not very tasty, make a healthy addition to salads.

SOLANACEAE

Capsicum

History and traditions Capsicums were first brought to Europe and the West from Mexico following Columbus's voyage of 1492, when the doctor who accompanied him noted their uses by the Native Americans as pain relievers, toothache remedies and for flavouring food. The Portuguese were responsible for their spread to India and Africa.

Habitat/distribution They are now grown in tropical and subtropical regions worldwide, and under glass in temperate zones. They can be grown outside in many areas of North America and in the southern states are a major commercial crop.

Description *Capsicum annuum* var. *annuum* are annuals, sometimes short-lived perennials, and most grow into small bushy plants 60–90 cm (2–3 ft) high; a few may reach 1.5 m (5 ft). They have glossy lance-shaped to ovate leaves and small white flowers followed by conical, or spherical, green, ripening to red, fruits.

Species Most cultivated peppers are of the species *C. annuum* var. *annuum*. There are over 1,000 cultivars grown across the world, with fruit in a wide range of shapes, sizes and degrees of pungency, divided into five main groups:

1. **Cerasiforme Group (cherry peppers)** – with small, very pungent fruits.

2. **Conoides Group (cone peppers)** – with erect, conical fruits.

3. **Fasciculatum Group (red cone peppers)** – slender, red, very pungent fruits.

4. **Grossum Group (bell peppers, sweet peppers, pimento)** – these have large, sweet, bell-shaped fruit, green, then ripening to red or yellow. Rich in vitamin C, they lack the medicinal properties of the hot, pungent peppers.

5. **Longum Group (cayenne peppers, chilli peppers)** – fruits are usually drooping, very pungent and the source of chilli powder, cayenne pepper and hot paprika. *C. frutescens* is a name often used for varieties of *C. annuum* whose fruits are used in Tabasco sauce.

Growth Frost-tender plants, which must be grown under glass in cool temperate climates. Plant in loam-based (John Innes) growing medium (soil mix), water freely, feed with a liquid fertilizer once a week and mist flowers with water daily to ensure that fruit sets. Propagation is from seed, at a temperature of 21°C (70°F) in early spring. Outside, they are grown in well-drained, nutrient-rich soil.

Parts used Fruits – are eaten ripe or unripe; or dried (ripe only) for powders.

USES Medicinal It is the bitter alkaloid, capsaicin, which gives peppers their hot taste and has been established by modern research as an effective painkiller – it works by depleting the nerve cells of the chemical neurotransmitter which sends pain messages to the brain.

Peppers are antibacterial and also contain vitamins A, C, and mineral salts. Pungent varieties increase blood flow, encourage sweating, stimulate the appetite and help digestion. In tropical countries they are useful food preservatives and help prevent gastric upsets. Taken internally or used as gargles (infusions of the powder) for colds, fevers and sore throats; applied externally (in massage oil or compresses) for rheumatism, arthritis, aching joints and muscles. A pharmaceutical analgesic cream, with capsaicin as active ingredient, has recently been developed for reducing rheumatic pain.

Culinary Sweet red or green peppers make delicious cooked vegetables or raw salad ingredients. Hot chilli peppers are added to pickles and chutneys; dried to make cayenne pepper, chilli powder or paprika (from milder-tasting fruits); added to dishes in Indian, Mexican, Thai and other worldwide cuisines.

Other names Peppers and chilli peppers.

Top centre Capsicum frutescens, *a hot chilli pepper.*

Top right Capsicum annuum *var.* annuum, *Grossum Group, a sweet, bell pepper.*

CAUTION Hot chilli peppers may cause inflammation and irritation to skin and eyes, so wear gloves when handling them. If taken internally to excess, they may cause digestive disorders.

CARICACEAE
Carica papaya
Papaya

History and traditions Originally from South and Central America and the West Indies, this tree with its fragrant, fleshy fruit was unknown in Europe before the end of the 17th century. The Spanish took it to Manila and, with the expansion of trade and travel at the beginning of the 18th century, it made its way to Asia and Africa and is now grown in tropical countries around the globe.

Description A small, evergreen tree, up to 6 m (20 ft) in height with deeply cut, palmate leaves, forming an umbrella-shaped crown. The large, ovoid fruits have dark-green, leathery skin, ripening to yellow, containing sweet orange-yellow flesh and numerous tiny black seeds surrounding a central cavity.

Habitat/distribution Native to South and Central America, occurs widely in tropical zones.

Growth A tender, tropical plant it will not grow in temperatures below 13°C (55°F). Requires rich, moist soil, and a sunny, humid climate.

Parts used Fruit, seeds, leaves – fresh. Sap, known as "papain", is extracted from the unripe fruits by scarification, and produced in dried or liquid form.

USES Medicinal The fruit is one of the best natural digestives, containing enzymes similar to pepsin. Juice is applied externally to destroy warts and for skin eruptions and irritations. Seeds and papain are used in preparations to expel intestinal worms.

Culinary Fruit is high in vitamin C and minerals, and is eaten fresh, canned or made into ice creams, desserts and soft drinks. Papain is used commercially as a meat tenderizer, and, on a domestic level, the inside of the skin of the fruit and leaves are wrapped round meat for the same purpose. Seeds have a pungent flavour and are sometimes eaten, or used as food flavouring, in countries where it is grown.

Cosmetic Juice smooths skin, removes freckles and reduces sun damage. Papain is included in commercial cosmetic products.

General Papain is used as an insecticide against termites, as an ingredient of chewing gum, to reduce cloudiness in beer and to make woollen and silk fabrics shrinkproof.

Above *Papaya leaves tenderize meat.*

Papaya fruit has excellent digestive properties.

COMPOSITAE/ASTERACEAE
Carlina acaulis
Carline thistle

History and traditions In medieval times this thistle was thought to be an antidote to poison and the root was sometimes chewed to relieve toothache. It is said to be named after the Emperor Charlemagne following a dream that it would cure the plague.

Description A low-growing, short-lived perennial, 5–10 cm (2–4 in) high, with a deep tap root, it has basal rosettes of spiny leaves and large stemless flowers with silvery-white bracts surrounding a brown disc-shaped centre.

Habitat/distribution Native to Europe and Asia, it is found in fields, grasslands and waste ground on poor dry soils in sunny positions.

Growth It grows best in a poor, dry soil. If kept too wet it will rot, and if the soil is too rich it becomes lax, overgrown and loses its neat, stemless habit. Propagated from seed sown in autumn and overwintered in a cold frame.

Parts used Roots – dried for use in decoctions, liquid extracts and tinctures.

USES Medicinal It has antibacterial and diuretic properties. A decoction of the roots is used externally as a gargle for sore throats, for skin complaints and to clean wounds. It is taken internally for urine retention.

Culinary Claims have been made for the flower centres as substitute artichoke hearts.

CAUTION Large doses taken internally are purgative and emetic.

COMPOSITAE/ASTERACEAE

Carthamus tinctorius
Safflower

History and traditions Cultivated in Egypt, China and India since ancient times, safflower was a valued dye plant – producing several colours, including a pink dye, used for the original "red tape" of Indian bureaucracy. It was introduced to Europe from the Middle East during the mid-16th century, for its medicinal properties, and is now cultivated for the oil extracted from the seeds.

Description A hardy annual, growing to 1 m (3 ft) high, with finely toothed, long, ovate leaves and shaggy, thistle-like, yellow flower heads set in spiny bracts.

Habitat/distribution Native to Asia and Mediterranean regions, widely cultivated for its seeds in many countries, including Asia, India, Africa and Australia.

Growth Grows in any light, well-drained soil and tolerates dry conditions. Propagated by seed, sown in spring.

Parts used Flowers, seeds, oil.

USES Medicinal Tea, infused from fresh or dry flowers, is taken to induce perspiration and reduce fevers and is mildly laxative. Infusions are also applied externally for bruises, skin irritations and inflammations.

Culinary Oil extracted from the seeds is low in cholesterol and has a delicate flavour. The flower petals, which are slightly bitter, have been used as a substitute for saffron in colouring food.

Household Flowers produce a yellow dye with water and red dye with alcohol. They are dried for adding to pot-pourri and as "everlasting" flowers for dried arrangements.

UMBELLIFERAE/APIACEAE

Carum carvi
Caraway

History and traditions Caraway seeds have been found during archaeological excavations at Neolithic sites in Europe and the plant was well known to the Egyptians, Greeks and Romans. The seeds were a popular culinary flavouring in Tudor England, cooked with fruit and baked in bread and cakes. They were made into sugared "comfits", and frequently served as a side dish with baked apples, as in Shakespeare's *Henry IV* when Falstaff is invited to take "a pippin [apple] and a dish of carraways". This custom is said to have continued into the early 20th century at formal dinners of London livery companies. There is also an old superstition that caraway has retentive powers, and, if sprinkled about, is capable of preventing people and personal belongings from straying.

Description A biennial 45–60 cm (18 in–2 ft) tall, it has feathery leaves, with umbels of white flowers appearing in its second year, followed by ridged fruits (popularly known as seeds).

Habitat/distribution Native to Asia and central Europe in meadowlands and waste grounds. Introduced and cultivated elsewhere.

Growth Prefers well-drained soil and a sunny position. Propagated from seed sown in spring, preferably *in situ* as it does not transplant well.

Above *Young, tender caraway leaves add flavour to salads.*

Parts used Leaves, seeds, essential oil from the seeds.

USES Medicinal The seeds are taken as an infusion or decoction for digestive disorders and to relieve flatulence. Seeds may be chewed as breath sweeteners.

Culinary Seeds are used to flavour cakes, biscuits, bread, cheese, stewed fruit, baked apples, cabbage and meat dishes. Also as a pickling spice and to flavour the liqueur, Kümmel. Young leaves make a garnish and are added to salads.

Aromatic Essential oil (containing over 50% carvone, which gives it its aromatic scent) is used as a flavouring in the food industry and in perfumes and cosmetics.

FAGACEAE
Castanea sativa
Sweet chestnut

History and traditions Sweet chestnut trees were grown in ancient Greece and Rome. The Greek physician, Theophrastus, wrote of their medicinal virtues and the Romans enjoyed eating them. They were probably introduced to Britain by the Romans and there are records of chestnuts grown in the Forest of Dean being paid as tithes, during the reign of Henry II, 1154–1189. Writing in the mid-17th century Culpeper considered the "inner skin" of the chestnut would "stop any flux whatsoever" and that the ground, dried leaves made into an electuary with honey made "an admirable remedy for the cough and spitting of blood". Their culinary diversity was praised by the 17th-century diarist and gourmet, John Evelyn, as "delicacies for princes and a lusty and masculine food for rusticks", while he regretted that all too often they were mere animal fodder.

Description A deciduous tree, growing to 15 m (50 ft) with dark grey, furrowed bark, and narrow, glossy, serrated-edged leaves. The small white flowers, appearing in spring, are followed by clusters of prickly green spherical fruits, containing 1–3 edible brown nuts. Trees grown in cool, northerly regions do not produce the same quality of large, succulent fruits as those grown in warmer, Mediterranean climates.

Habitat/distribution Occurs in woodlands of southern Europe, Asia, North America and northern Africa.

Growth Grows best in well-drained loam in sun or partial shade. Propagated by seed sown in autumn.

Parts used Leaves, seeds (nuts).

USES Medicinal Infusions of the leaves are taken for coughs and colds and used as a gargle for sore throats. Also said to be helpful for rheumatism.

Culinary Chestnuts are equally suited to savoury and sweet dishes. They are the classic stuffing ingredient for turkey, other poultry and game, make excellent soups, pâtés, and accompaniments to vegetable and meat dishes. Sweetened purée forms the basis of desserts, especially in France, where chestnuts are also crystallized as "marrons glacés".

Other name Spanish chestnut.

Sweet chestnuts.

Left *Spiky fruits contain the edible nuts.*

BERBERIDACEAE
Caulophyllum thalictroides
Blue cohosh

History and traditions A herb used in the traditional medicine of the Native Americans to facilitate childbirth. Its value being appreciated by the wider population, it was listed at the end of the 19th century as an official medicinal herb in the United States pharmacopoeia. The name "cohosh" is from a local tribal language.

Description A perennial which grows on a rhizomatous rootstock. The palmate leaves develop with, or just after, the yellow-brown flowers. Fruits split open to reveal spherical seeds, which turn from green to deep blue as they ripen.

Habitat/distribution Occurs in moist woodlands in North America.

Growth Requires moist, rich soil, in partial or deep shade. Divide plants in spring. Propagation from seed is slow and germination may often be erratic.

Parts used Rhizomes and roots are dried for inclusion in powders, liquid extracts and other medicinal preparations.

USES Medicinal A herb which stimulates the uterus and is taken internally, as a decoction or infusion to facilitate contractions during labour and for other conditions connected with childbirth. It also has anti-inflammatory and diuretic properties and is used to treat inflammation of the pelvis and endometriosis.

Other names Squaw root and papoose root.

> CAUTION Not to be used without the advice of a qualified medical practitioner.

LABIATAE/LAMIACEAE

Cedronella canariensis syn
C. triphylla

Balm of Gilead

History and traditions This upstart from the Canary Islands is something of a fraud, sniffily dismissed by Mrs Grieve as being "called Balm of Gilead for no better reason than that its leaves are fragrant". But it has largely taken over from ancient, more worthy contenders for the name, because it has a similar musky, balsam scent, though not, apparently, any worthwhile medicinal uses. The original Balm of Gilead is usually taken to be *Commiphora opobalsamum*, a now rare and protected desert shrub, once greatly valued for its balsam-scented resin. Another source of Balm of Gilead is the balsam poplar, *Populus balsamifera*.

Description A half-hardy shrubby perennial, up to 1 m (3 ft) in height, it has lightly serrated, trifoliate leaves and pink flower clusters, made up of tubular, two-lipped florets.

Habitat/distribution A native of the Canary Islands, where it is found on sunny, rocky slopes. Introduced elsewhere.

Growth Requires well-drained soil and full sun. It does not withstand frost and although it may be grown outside in a sheltered position, in cool climates it needs winter protection. Propagation is easiest from softwood cuttings taken in late spring. Germination from seed is erratic and requires heat.

Parts used Leaves, flowers.

USES Culinary Fresh or dry leaves may be infused to make an invigorating tea.

Aromatic Leaves and flowers are dried for adding to pot-pourri.

PINACEAE

Cedrus libani

Cedar of Lebanon

History and traditions The ancient Egyptians used oil of cedar for embalming and in their religious rituals. These beautiful, wide-spreading trees, with their head-clearing pine scent, were much prized in biblical times and celebrated in the Song of Solomon ("His countenance is as Lebanon, excellent as the cedars"). And in the Canticles, that evocative Hebrew love poem, also attributed to Solomon, the beloved is compared to many plant fragrances, and told, "The smell of thy garments is like the smell of Lebanon." King Solomon is also alleged to have denuded Lebanon of its cedars to build his massive temple.

Description A tall, 30–40 m (100–130 ft) coniferous tree, with a dark-brown or grey, deeply ridged trunk and wide branches bearing whorls of needle-like leaves. It carries both male and female cones, the latter being the larger. They are green at first, turning brown as they ripen over a two-year period, when they break up to release the seeds. Cedars often reach a great age, living for several hundred years.

Related species There are only four species of conifers which are true cedars, all rich in aromatic essential oil. As well as *C. libani*, there is *C. atlantica* (Atlas cedar) and *C. brevifolia* (Cyprus cedar), both classified by some authorities as subspecies of *C. libani*, and *C. deodara*, the Indian cedar.

Habitat/distribution Native to forests of the Mediterranean region from Lebanon to Turkey (*C. libani*), the Atlas Mountains in North Africa (*C. atlantica*), Cyprus (*C. brevifolia*) and the western Himalayas (*C. deodara*).

Growth Fully hardy trees, they grow in any well-drained soil and a sunny position.

Parts used Wood, essential oil.

USES Medicinal The essential oil has antiseptic, fungicide and insect-repellent properties. It is used as a steam inhalation for bronchial and respiratory complaints, to soothe skin irritations, for alopecia, dandruff and other scalp problems. It also has a calming effect for states of anxiety.

Aromatic The oil is added to perfumery, soaps and cosmetics. The wood is used to make furniture and storage chests which, due to its aromatic properties, helps to deter moths and insects.

BOMBACACEAE
Ceiba pentandra
Cotton tree

History and traditions The Ceiba is the national tree of Guatemala and was held sacred by the ancient Mayans of Central America. They believed it grew through the centre of the universe, with its roots in the nine levels of the underworld, its trunk in the thirteen levels of the upperworld and its branches in heaven. The myth still prevails in the area, that this graceful tree is the home of the temptress, Ixtobai, recognizable by her backward-facing feet, who lures unfaithful husbands to disappear with her into the underworld through the trunk.

Description A deciduous, or semi-evergreen, tree growing to 40 m (130 ft) with wide-spreading branches and palmate leaves. The flowers are followed by large pods, containing seeds protected by white, fluffy, silky-textured padding, collected to make kapok.

Habitat/distribution Occurs in rainforests and other damp, wooded areas in tropical North, South and Central America, Africa and Asia.

Growth Requires a temperature of 15°C (59°F). Grown in fertile, moist, but well-drained soil and full sun. Usually propagated by cuttings.

Parts used Leaves, bark, seeds, seed-pod fibre.

USES Medicinal The bark and leaves are made into decoctions, taken internally, for bronchial and respiratory infections, or applied externally in the form of baths. The leaves are boiled in sugar to make cough syrup and applied as a compress for headaches, fevers and sprains.

Culinary The seeds are toxic, but an edible, non-toxic oil is extracted from them which is used locally for cooking.

COMPOSITAE/ASTERACEAE
Centaurea cyanus
Cornflower

History and traditions These pretty blue flowers were once a common sight in cornfields, as their name suggests, but have largely been ousted by the techniques of modern agriculture. In his *Herbal* of 1597, Gerard reports that the Italian name for the cornflower is a reference to blunting sickles, "because it hindereth and annoyeth the reapers, dulling and turning the edges of their sickles" and he includes "hurt-sickle" among its English names of blew-bottle, blew-blow and corne-floure. Although Culpeper found many uses for these flowers, Gerard's view was that there is "no use of them in physic", although they are recommended by some for inflammation of the eye.

Description An annual which grows from 20–80 cm (8–32 in) tall, with grey-green lanceolate leaves and bright-blue shaggy flower heads. Cultivated kinds also have pink, purple or white flowers.

Related species *C. montana* is a perennial species, found mainly in mountainous areas of Europe. The wild plant, *C. scabiosa*, is often called knapweed.

Habitat/distribution Native to Europe and the Mediterranean region, naturalized in North America, also found in Asia and Australia. Becoming less common in the wild, widely cultivated and grown in gardens.

Above *Cornflowers, once a common weed, are frequently cultivated in gardens for their striking colour and form.*

Growth A hardy annual, it is easy to grow from seed sown in spring *in situ*, as it resents being transplanted. May be given an early start by sowing in autumn or very early spring, in plugs, or biodegradable pots, to minimize root disturbance. Plant in well-drained soil and a sunny position.

Parts used Flowers.

USES Medicinal Traditionally used in the past to make eyewashes for tired or strained eyes, but seems to have little place in herbal medicine as practised today.

Aromatic Flowers are dried for pot-pourris.

Other names Bluebottle and batchelor's button.

COMPOSITAE/ASTERACEAE
Chamaemelum nobile
Chamomile

History and traditions "Thys herbe was consecrated by the wyse men of Egypt unto the Sonne and was rekened to be the only remedy for all agues", says William Turner in his *Newe Herball*, 1551, in reference to the veneration of chamomile by the ancient Egyptians. The Greeks called it "earth apple", from which its generic name is derived (*kamai*, meaning "on the ground" and *melon*, apple), and in modern Spanish chamomile is called *"manzanilla"*, meaning "little apple". It does indeed have an apple-like fragrance, especially noticeable after rain or when the plant is lightly crushed. To the Anglo-Saxons it was *"maythen"* and was one of the sacred herbs of Woden, featuring in the Nine Herbs Lay, a charm against the effects of "flying venom" and "loathed things that over land rove", from the *Lacnunga* in the Harleian manuscript collection, British Museum. Over the centuries chamomile has been celebrated for its soothing properties and its fragrance heads the list in an antistress prescription from *Ram's Little Dodoen*, 1606: "To comfort the braine smel to camomill, eate sage … wash measurably, sleep reasonably, delight to heare melody and singing".

Description An evergreen perennial with finely divided, feathery leaves growing to 15 cm (6 in). The white daisy-like flowers, with yellow disc centres, are borne singly on long stems rising to 30 cm (1 ft).

Related species *C. nobile* 'Flore Pleno' is a cultivar with creamy-coloured double flowers. The whole plant is more compact than the species, about 10 cm (4 in) tall, including flower stems, and makes a good edging plant. *C. nobile* 'Treneague' is a non-flowering cultivar which forms a dense carpet useful for lawns and seats and grows to about 6 cm (2 1/2 in).

Habitat/distribution Indigenous to Europe, it is widely grown in North America and many other countries. It is found in the wild on sandy soils in grasslands and waste ground.

Growth Prefers light, sandy soil and a sunny position. It is possible to propagate *C. nobile* from seed sown in spring, but the easier and more usual method is by division of runners or "offsets". *C. n.* 'Flore Pleno' and *C. n.* 'Treneague' must be vegetatively propagated.

Parts used Flowers, essential oil.

USES Medicinal Chamomile has an antiseptic, anti-inflammatory action and is soothing and sedative. It is taken as a tea for nausea and indigestion and to help promote sound sleep, and may also be helpful in relieving painful menstruation. It is made into ointments or lotions for skin irritations and insect bites. The true essential oil is very expensive and contains azulene, which gives it a deep-blue colour. It is frequently used for skin complaints and eczema (diluted in witch hazel or a pure, mild vegetable oil) and as a steam inhalation for asthma, sinusitis or catarrh.

Cosmetic An infusion of the flowers makes a rinse to give a shine to fair hair, or a skin freshener for sensitive skins. Essential oil or infusions are added to face or hand creams and fresh flowers floated in hot water make a deep-cleansing facial steam treatment.

Aromatic The dried flowers are added to sleep pillows and sachets or put into pot-pourri.

Other name Roman chamomile.

Chamaemelum nobile
'Flore Pleno'.

Top *The double flowers of the dwarf edging plant* C. nobile *'Flore Pleno'.*

CAUTION Despite being such a benevolent herb (when recommended doses and guidelines are followed), if taken internally to excess it may cause vomiting and vertigo. The plant may cause contact dermatitis.

Related species

COMPOSITAE/ASTERACEAE

Matricaria recutita
Wild chamomile

History and traditions The name *matricaria* comes from its early gynaecological uses in herbal medicine.

Description *M. recutita* syn. *M. chamomilla* is a tall hardy annual which grows to 60 cm (2 ft). Although from a different genus (due to botanical differences), flowers, feathery foliage and scent are similar in appearance to that of *Chamaemelum nobile.* Not to be confused with the scentless mayweeds, or false chamomiles *Matricaria inodora* and *Tripleurosperum maritimum,* or the almost scentless corn chamomile (*Anthemis arvensis*).

Habitat/distribution Occurs all over Europe, Western Asia and India.

Growth Propagated from seed, sown *in situ* in early spring, it grows easily in any dry, light soil.

Parts used Flowers – they have similar properties to those of *Chamaemelum nobile.*

USES As for *C. nobile.*
Other names German chamomile and scented mayweed.

Matricaria chamomilla

To make oyle of chamomile

Take oyle a pint and halfe, and three ounces of camomile flowers dryed one day after they be gathered. Then put the oyle and the flowers in a glasse and stop the mouth close and set it into the sun by the space of forty days.

The Good Housewife's Handbook, 1588

A chamomile lawn

Chamomile has been popular since medieval times for scented lawns, paths or places to sit, all of which still make delightful features in the herb garden.

A chamomile lawn
The main problem is that it requires regular hand weeding to keep it looking good and does not take heavy wear. The trick is to think small – grow it as a scaled-down version of a lawn, plant it round a fountain or sundial, or as a mini-lawn between paving stones.
• Use rooted cuttings or offsets of non-flowering *Chamaemelum nobile* 'Treneague', edged (or for a "flowery-mead" effect, interspersed) with *C. n.* 'Flore Pleno'.
• Choose an area with light, preferably sandy soil, prepare it well, eliminating weeds and removing stones. Rake in a little peat to hold water and help the plants settle in quickly.
• Set plants 10 cm (4 in) apart, water them in and keep lightly moist until established.
• To maintain the lawn, weed regularly and fill in any gaps that appear with new plants.

Above *A lawn of* C.n. *'Treneague'.*   Above *A brick-built chamomile seat.*

A chamomile seat

These are always attractive and have the added advantage that the area of chamomile is small enough to make maintenance simple. It is also a good way to grow chamomile in a garden with heavy or clay soil, as the seat forms a raised bed to provide a free-draining environment.

• The base of the seat may be constructed with brick, stone or timber, filled with rubble and a good layer of topsoil for planting.
• It is best to keep to *C. n.* 'Treneague' only for this, as flowers sticking out of a bench spoil the effect. Plant as for the lawn.
• If back and arm rests are required, they could be of the same material as the base. Clipped box also looks very effective.

CHENOPODIACEAE

Chenopodium ambrosioides
American wormseed

History and traditions American wormseed was introduced to Europe in the 17th century from Mexico, where it was taken as a tea and used in traditional medicine.

Description An annual, 60 cm–1.2 m (2–4 ft) high, it has longer, more lanceolate leaves than those of *C. bonus-henricus* and a strong acrid scent. The tiny, green flowers are followed by small nutlike, one-seeded fruits.

Habitat/distribution Native to tropical Central America, naturalized throughout much of North America and grown in other countries also.

Growth Frost-hardy (to -5°C/23°F), American wormseed grows in any well-drained soil. Propagated by seed sown in spring; in warm climates it often self-seeds freely.

Parts used Flowering stems, essential oil.

USES Medicinal Its chief use has always been to expel intestinal worms. It has also been recommended for nervous disorders, asthma and problems with menstruation. The volatile oil of chenopodium is a powerful insecticide as well as a vermifuge, but should never be administered in this concentrated form as it is highly toxic.

Other name Mexican tea.

CAUTION Poisonous in large doses, it should be taken only under medical supervision and is legally restricted in some countries.

CHENOPODIACEAE

Chenopodium bonus-henricus
Good King Henry

History and traditions According to the 16th-century physician and botanist, Rembert Dodoens, of the Netherlands, this plant was dubbed *bonus henricus*, "good Henry", to distinguish it from a poisonous plant *malus henricus*, "bad Henry". There is some uncertainty as to who "Henry" was, but one source claims it is a generic term for mischievous elves. "King" appears to have been spin-doctored into the English popular name to give this rather unattractive plant a spurious connection with King Henry VIII, "Good King Hal". The Latin name *Chenopodium* is derived from the Greek for "goose foot", an eloquent reference to the shape of the leaves.

Description A perennial which grows 60 cm (2 ft) tall and spreads indefinitely, it has fleshy, downy stems, dark-green, arrow-shaped leaves and greenish-yellow spikes of sorrel-like flowers in early summer.

Related species *Chenopodium album*, White Goosefoot – also known as allgood and fat hen (because it does a good job of fattening poultry) – as well as pigweed, mutton tops and lamb's quarters. It has long been a staple food of both animals and people. The Iron Age Dane, Tollund Man, made a last meal of it before he was hanged, seeds being found in his stomach.

Habitat/distribution Native to Europe but found worldwide on waste ground and previously cultivated land.

Growth This is an invasive plant which needs no cultivation and thrives in any soil. Said to be of "superior quality" if grown in rich soil, but little difference in taste or texture will be noticed. Tough taproots can make it difficult to eradicate if no longer wanted. Easily propagated from seed, or division, in spring.

Parts used Leaves, stems.

USES Medicinal Once made into ointments and poultices for skin complaints (an old name was "smearwort") but has no known medicinal value currently, apart from being mildly laxative.

Culinary Extravagant claims have been made for this plant as being a spinach-like vegetable (leaves) and asparagus substitute (young stems). Although edible if picked when young and tender, the leaves develop a fibrous texture with age which makes them less palatable. John Evelyn (*Acetaria* 1719) was right when in reference to one of its names, "blite", from the Greek for insipid, he commented that "it is well-named, being insipid enough". It is rich in vitamins C, B¹, iron and calcium – so it may be a case of "eating up your greens" for the sake of your health.

Other names Goosefoot, allgood, fat hen, English mercury and Lincolnshire asparagus.

The leaves of Chenopodium bonus-henricus *were thought to resemble goose feet.*

COMPOSITAE/ASTERACEAE
Cichorium intybus
Chicory

History and traditions This herb was cultivated in Egypt over 2,000 years ago, and known to the ancient Greeks and Romans, who used it as a salad ingredient and vegetable. Its use as a coffee substitute is thought to date from 1806 when Napoleon's Continental blockade prevented imports of coffee. It was widely used for the same purpose during the World Wars.

Description A tall, hardy perennial, growing to 1.5 m (5 ft). It has a deep taproot and thick stem which exudes a milky sap when cut. It has toothed, oval to lanceolate leaves and pale blue flowers appear in summer.

Habitat/distribution Native of the Mediterranean region, western Asia and North Africa, introduced and established worldwide.

Growth For best results grow in rich, but well-drained soil. Propagate from seed sown in spring. Sometimes self-seeds, especially on dry soils.

Parts used Leaves, roots.

USES Medicinal A bitter tonic herb, the dried, crushed root is made into infusions or decoctions for digestive upsets and to improve appetite. It is also a mild stimulant and laxative.

Culinary There are various cultivars whose leaves are added to salads, including red, broad-leafed radicchio types. Blanched heads, or chicons, eaten in salads and cooked as vegetables, are produced by lifting the roots, packing them in boxes in a growing medium, cutting off the leaves and keeping them in complete darkness until white, elongated shoots have sprouted.

RANUNCULACEAE
Cimicifuga racemosa
Black cohosh

History and traditions The root of this herb was used in the traditional medicine of Native Americans for female complaints and it was supposed to be an antidote to poison and to rattlesnake venom. Hence two of its popular names, "squaw root" (which it shares with blue cohosh) and "black snakeroot", after the colour of the rhizome and to differentiate it from another plant known as "snakeroot" (*Aristolochia serpentaria*). The generic name comes from the Latin *cimex,* a bug, and *fugere*, to run, in reference to its insect-repellent properties.

Description A tall, clump-forming, aromatic perennial, with a rather unpleasant smell. But it makes an attractive plant for the border with spires of creamy-white, bottle-brush flowers, rising to 1.5 m (5 ft) above the three-lobed basal leaves (40 cm (16 in) high).

Habitat/distribution Native to North America, it is grown in northern temperate regions and occurs in moist grassland or woodland.

Growth Fully hardy, it requires moist, fertile soil with plenty of humus and partial shade. It can be propagated by division of roots or by seed, sown in pots in autumn for overwintering in a cold frame for germination the following spring.

Parts used Rhizomes – dried for use in decoctions, tinctures and extracts.

USES Medicinal For arthritis, rheumatism and menstrual and menopausal problems.

CAUTION Large doses may cause abortion. Legal restrictions apply in some countries.

RUBIACEAE
Cinchona officinalis
Cinchona

History and traditions Said to be named after the Countess of Chinchon, wife of the Viceroy of Peru, after she had been cured of a fever (probably malaria)with a cinchona bark medicine in about 1638.

Description Cinchona species are tender, evergreen trees varying in height, according to species and habitat, from 10–25 m (30–80 ft). The oval leaves are often red-veined and small, crimson flowers are borne in panicles.

Related species There are several species of *Cinchona* of medicinal value, all closely related, including *C. calisaya* and *C. pubescens*.

Habitat/distribution Native to mountainous regions of South America, widely introduced and cultivated in tropical regions worldwide.

Growth In the wild, trees occur in dense, wet forest. Commercial plantations provide well-drained, moist soil and high humidity. Propagated by cuttings.

Parts used Bark – dried and powdered or as a liquid extract.

USES Medicinal Cinchona bark contains the antimalarial alkaloid, quinine, as well as quinidine, which slows the heart rate. It was the major treatment for malaria from the mid-17th century until recently, now largely replaced for this purpose by synthetic drugs. It is still an ingredient of many pharmaceutical preparations for colds and influenza, and of tonic water.

CAUTION Excess doses cause convulsions and may lead to deafness and blindness.

LAURACEAE
Cinnamomum zeylanicum
Cinnamon

History and traditions An important aromatic spice since biblical times, cinnamon was an ingredient of the holy ointment made by Moses. It is also cited as amongst the costly merchandise and luxury items available in Babylon, when the fall of that misguided city is predicted in the biblical book, Revelation. The Portuguese occupied Sri Lanka for its cinnamon in 1536. By the 18th century, cinnamon had become such a valuable commodity in Europe, that the Dutch took control of the island and set up a trading monopoly in the spice.

Description A medium-sized evergreen tree, it grows to about 9 m (30 ft) and has brown, papery bark and ovate, leathery green leaves. Creamy-white flowers are borne in short panicles, followed by olive-shaped dark-blue fruits.

Habitat/distribution Native to forest areas of Sri Lanka, southern India and Malaysia and widely cultivated in India, the Seychelles, Brazil, the Caribbean and tropical zones.

Growth Cinnamon grows in sandy soils, and needs plenty of rain, sun and a minimum temperature of 15°C (59°F). Young trees are cut to within 30 cm (1 ft) of the ground, stumps covered in mulch to encourage sprouting for re-harvesting within 2–3 years. It is also propagated by seed.

Parts used Inner bark of young stems – dried and wrapped round thin rods to form quills. Essential oil.

USES Medicinal It has digestive properties, dispels nausea, and is taken for colds, sore throats and rheumatic conditions. The essential oil is antibacterial and antifungal, helps deaden the nerve where there is toothache and is added to steam inhalations for colds and upper respiratory tract infections.

Culinary A popular spice for savoury and sweet dishes. It adds flavour to curries, baked goods, stews and meat dishes, savoury and sweet rice and is a traditional ingredient of Christmas puddings, mince pies, mulled wine and hot spiced drinks.

Aromatic Ingredient of pot-pourri (powdered or whole pieces) and clove-and-orange pomanders. The essential oil is used in perfumery.

Cinnamon sticks are formed from the rolled bark.

CISTACEAE
Cistus ladanifer
Cistus

History and traditions In his *Relation d'un voyage du Levant*, 1717, French botanist, Pitton de Tournefort, gives an eloquent description of collecting ladanum, a fragrant resin exuded by several species of cistus, by means of dragging a leather-thonged rake (a *ladisteron*) across the plants. He also refers to a method in use since Dioscorides' day, of combing it from the beards of goats allowed to browse on the sticky foliage. It has a perfume reminiscent of ambergris and was one of the main ingredients in the solid, resin-based pomanders popular in the Middle Ages for repelling infection.

Description A hardy evergreen shrub, growing to 2 m (6 ft), with lanceolate, sticky, dark-green leaves. The papery, saucer-shaped white flowers bloom for only one day.

Related species *C. creticus* syn. *C. incanus* subsp. *creticus*, the Cretan rock rose, and also a source of ladanum, is a more compact shrub, growing to 1 m (3 ft) with purplish-pink flowers and yellow stamens.

Habitat/distribution Found in Crete, southern Europe, Turkey, northern Africa and the Canary Islands, on dry, stony soils and sunny hillsides. Introduced and widely grown elsewhere.

Growth Prefers a light, well-drained soil and sheltered site in full sun. It is propagated from seed, sown in containers, in late summer or from softwood cuttings in early summer.

Parts used Dried leaves, oleo-resin – collected from young stems and leaves.

USES Aromatic Used as a fixative in perfumery, and in pot-pourri and home fragrance products.

RUTACEAE
Citrus

History and traditions The citrus species were unknown to Greek and Roman writers, but they have been cultivated for so long that their origins are hazy. Both oranges and lemons are probably natives of northern India, certainly China, and are thought to have been brought to the West by Arab traders via North Africa, Arabia and Syria, thence to Spain and Sicily. *C. limon*, found in the valleys of Kumaon and Sikkim, in the foothills of the Himalayas, has the Hindustani name *limu* or *nimbu*, which was taken into Arabic as *limun*. *C. aurantium*, the bitter Seville orange, is the species mentioned in a medicinal context by the Arabian physician, Avicenna, 980–1037, practising at Salerno, and was the orange tree planted in Rome by St Dominic in AD 1200. These must also have been the oranges which Edward I's Queen, Eleanor of Castille, is purported to have bought from a Spanish ship which called at Portsmouth in 1290 – sweet oranges were not known in the West before the mid-15th century, introduced from the East by the Portuguese. The custom of wearing orange blossom at weddings is said to have originated with the Saracens, who considered it an emblem of fecundity, and the practice was introduced to Europe by returning Crusaders. Essential oil distilled from the flowers of the bitter orange was said to have an "exquisite fragrance" by the Italian Giambattista Porta in his herbal of 1588. It became known as "oil of Neroli" from 1680, because it was favoured by the wife of the Count of Neroli for perfuming gloves.

Habitat/distribution Originated in Asia, cultivated in the Mediterranean region, in southern parts of North America and other countries.

Growth Orange and lemon trees are tender, and must be protected from frost, but they prefer cool rather than hot conditions. If grown in northern climates, with cold, frosty winters, they should be kept outside in summer and in a temperate conservatory or greenhouse in winter. They need a well-drained, not too acid compost – the correct pH value is crucial, 6–6.5 for lemons and 6.5–7 for oranges. *C. aurantium* and *C. limon* may be grown from seed, or from semi-ripe cuttings – but cultivars do not come true from seed.

Citrus limon
Lemon

Description A small evergreen tree, 2–6 m (6–19 ft) tall, with light-green, oval leaves and thorny stems. Clusters of white flowers, opening from pink-tinted buds, are followed by ovoid, bitter-tasting yellow fruits.
Parts used Fruits, essential oil, expressed from the peel.

USES Medicinal Rich in vitamin C and once used by British seamen to prevent scurvy (limes were also used). Lemons have anti-inflammatory properties and are used in home remedies for colds, frequently in conjunction with honey, which is antiseptic. Applied externally for insect bites and skin irritations.
Culinary The juice and rind are widely used as a flavouring in cooking, and in soft drinks, sauces, pickles, preserves and marinades.
Aromatic The peel is dried for pot-pourri and home fragrance preparations. The oil is used commercially in perfumery, and to scent soaps and household cleaning products.

Citrus aurantium
Bitter orange

Description An evergreen tree, growing to 8 m (26 ft) high, with shiny, ovate leaves and fragrant white flowers, followed by bitter, orange fruits.
Parts used Leaves, fruits, flowers. Essential oil of neroli, distilled from flowers; essential oil of petitgrain, distilled from leaves and twigs; distilled orange-flower water; oil of orange, expressed from the rind.

USES Medicinal Rich in vitamins A, B and C, and has energizing tonic properties. Infusions of leaves and flowers are used for digestive disorders. The essential oil of neroli is an anti-depressant and calming. It may also be helpful for insomnia.
Culinary The fruits are used to make Seville orange marmalade and a bitter sauce to complement fatty poultry such as duck and goose. Orange-flower water has a delicate fragrance, ideal for flavouring sweet dishes. Oil of orange is a flavouring in commercial food products.
Aromatic Essential oils of neroli and petitgrain are used in perfumery.
Cosmetic Orange rind pounded, mixed with rainwater and applied as a poultice is a traditional Indian remedy for acne. Oil of neroli is soothing for dry, sensitive skins as an ingredient of creams and lotions. Also used in many citrus-based cleaning products.
Other name Seville orange.

Left Citrus limon *'Jambhiri'.*

ASTERACEAE

Cnicus benedictus syn. *Carduus benedictus*
Holy thistle

History and traditions It is known as Holy or Blessed Thistle for much the same reasons as the Carline Thistle (*Carlina acaulis*) is named after Charlemagne – it was all down to visions of this plant as a cure for plague. Considering that it does have antiseptic and antibiotic properties, this may not be as far-fetched as it sounds. One writer of a dissertation on treating plague with this thistle said, "I counsell all that have gardens to nourish it, that they may have it always to their own use, and the use of their neighbours that lacke it."

Description The only plant in the *Cnicus* genus, sometimes classified as *Carduus benedictus*. It is an annual with hairy, branched stems, spiny grey-green leaves and solitary yellow flowers set in prickly bracts.

Habitat/distribution A Mediterranean native, it is widely naturalized throughout Europe and North America.

Growth A wild plant, it grows in any ordinary soil, is easily propagated by seed, and self-seeds. Cultivated commercially in Europe for the pharmaceutical industry.

Parts used Whole plant – leaves and flower tops.

USES Medicinal A very bitter herb with anti-septic, antibiotic properties. Taken in the form of an infusion as a tonic and to stimulate the appetite. It was traditionally used for fevers and is said to be helpful for nursing mothers to improve the supply of milk.

Culinary All parts of the plant are edible and have been eaten cooked or in salads.

BURSERACEAE

Commiphora myrrha syn. *C. molmol*
Myrrh

History and traditions Myrrh has long been valued for its medicinal properties and as an ingredient of incense, perfumes and ointments. A symbol of suffering, myrrh was used in embalming from the Egyptian period, and the name comes from an ancient Hebrew and Arabic word, *mur,* meaning bitter. It was one of the gifts of the wise men to Jesus Christ at his birth and was used, along with aloes and spices, to embalm his body following his crucifixion.

Description A small tree or shrub, growing to about 3 m (10 ft) tall, with spiny branches and sparse trifoliate leaves, made up of small oval leaflets. The gum exudes from the bark naturally, and after incisions have been made, when it flows out as a pale-yellow liquid and quickly hardens to a reddish-brown resin.

Habitat/distribution Native to Arabia, Somalia and Ethiopia, where it grows in desert scrub.

Growth Grows wild.

Parts used Oleo-gum resin – known as *bdellium.*

USES Medicinal Myrrh has antiseptic, anti-inflammatory properties and encourages healing when applied to wounds, ulcers, boils and bleeding gums. Sometimes added to tooth powders. A preparation is made from the bark for treating skin diseases. In parts of Africa some species are chewed as a source of moisture and used for cleaning teeth.

Aromatic An ingredient of incense. It has fixative properties when used in perfumery, and is added to pot-pourri, in granule or powdered form, to "fix" the scent.

UMBELLIFERAE/APIACEAE

Conium maculatum
Hemlock

History and traditions Poisoning by hemlock was the official method of state execution in ancient Athens. The philosopher Socrates was its best-known victim. It was also used as a medicinal herb in the classical world, mainly for external application. Dioscorides and Pliny, echoed by Avicenna, recommended it for the treatment of skin diseases and cancerous tumours. It appeared in Anglo-Saxon herbals and an old English myth associated the splotches on the stems with the mark of Cain.

Description A tall, unpleasant-smelling biennial, 1.5–2.4 m (5–8 ft) in height, with purplish-red speckles towards the base of the stems, finely divided, feathery leaves and large umbels of white flowers in midsummer.

Habitat/distribution Indigenous to Europe and parts of Asia, widely distributed in temperate parts of the world and found in damp, weedy places, waste grounds and waysides.

Growth A wild plant in Australia and other countries, cultivation is legally restricted.

Parts used Leaves, seeds.

USES Medicinal Hemlock contains the highly toxic alkaloid, coniine, in all parts, but especially in the seeds. At one time it was used as a sedative and powerful pain-reliever – but its toxicity made this a risky business and it is seldom used in herbal medicine today.

CAUTION All parts of the plant are highly poisonous, and may also cause skin irritations on contact.

LILIACEAE/CONVALLARIACEAE
Convallaria majalis
Lily-of-the-valley

History and traditions This pretty cottage-garden plant was known to the Anglo-Saxons for its medicinal properties and appeared in early manuscript herbals, including one attributed to Apuleius, AD 400 (written in Latin). Many of the 16th- and 17th-century herbalists, from Dodoens to Culpeper, took the line that a distillation of the flowers in wine was good for strengthening the memory and comforting the heart. The specific name is a reference to the month of May, when the flowers bloom – or to Maia, Roman goddess of fertility, if you prefer.

Description A hardy perennial with ribbed ovate to lance-shaped leaves and racemes of fragrant white flowers, hanging like little bells, followed by fruits which are round, red berries.

Habitat/distribution Native to Europe, Asia and North America and found in woodlands and alpine meadows.

Growth Prefers humus-rich, moist soil and partial shade. Propagation is easiest by division of the rhizomes in autumn – keep well watered until established and apply a leaf-mould mulch.

Parts used Leaves, flowers.

USES Medicinal It contains glycosides similar to those of foxgloves (*Digitalis* spp.), which affect the action of the heart. It is considered safer than *Digitalis* by some herbal experts and as having less of a cumulative effect.

> CAUTION A poisonous plant which should not be eaten. It should be stressed that it is for use by qualified practitioners only.

UMBELLIFERAE/APIACEAE
Coriandrum sativum
Coriander

History and traditions Seeds of this herb were found in Tutankhamun's tomb of 1325 BC. It was known to the Greeks and Romans and features in many medieval herbals – though the authorities were not always in agreement as to its properties. Galen said it was "warm", Dioscorides and Avicenna took it to be "cold". The *Herbarius Latinus,* printed in Mainz in 1484 by Peter Schoeffer, has much to say on the subject. There are recommendations for mixing the juice with houseleek (*Sempervivum tectorum)* and warm vinegar to put on abscesses, for taking it with vinegar soon after dining heavily to "prohibit vapours from rising to the head", and for mixing it with violets for a hangover. If smelled, sniffed or blown up the nostrils, it is claimed, it will restrain a nosebleed, and is effective against St Anthony's fire (erysipelas) and "in tremors of the heart when its powder is given with borage water". William Turner took the strange line that "Coriander taken out of season doth trouble a man's wit with great jeopardy of madness" (*A Newe Herbal,* 1551). From Tudor times until the beginning of this century coriander seeds coated in sugar (comfits) were a popular sweet.

Description An annual 30–60 cm (1–2 ft) tall, with pungent finely divided leaves – the basal ones are pinnatifid and wider than the upper ones, which are linear and feathery. Small umbels of white to mauvish flowers are followed by ridged, spherical, pale-brown fruits (seeds). There are related species and numerous cultivars, some developed for leaf quality, others for their seeds. A variety with smaller seeds is grown in temperate zones, and one with larger seeds in warmer climates.

Habitat/distribution Originating in northern Africa and the Mediterranean region, it is widely grown in southwest Asia, North and South America and in temperate regions.

Growth A hardy annual, it is propagated from seed sown in spring, preferably *in situ* as it does not transplant well. It succeeds best grown in a well-drained, fertile soil, with ample water in the early stages followed by warmth and sunshine. Young plants quickly run to seed if attempts are made to transplant them in hot, dry spells.

Parts used Leaves, fruits (seeds), essential oil.

Above *The lower leaves are used in cookery.*

USES Medicinal The leaves and seeds have digestive properties and stimulate appetite. The essential oil has fungicidal, antibacterial properties. In traditional Indian medicine decoctions of the seeds were taken as a small-pox preventive. They are still considered helpful in lowering blood cholesterol levels.

Culinary The leaves have a stronger, spicier taste than the seeds, which are milder and sweeter. Both are used in curries, pickles and chutneys and in Middle Eastern, Indian, southeast Asian and South American cuisines. Leaves are added to salads, seeds used in sweet dishes, breads, cakes and to flavour liqueurs.

Aromatic The crushed seeds are added to scented sachets and pot-pourri. The essential oil has fixative properties.

Commercial The essential oil is used in the pharmaceutical, cosmetic and food industries.

Other name Cilantro.

IRIDACEAE
Crocus sativus
Saffron crocus

History and traditions The Greeks called it *krokos*, the Romans *korkum*, and its common name is derived from the Arabic for yellow, *zafran*. In the classical world saffron was appreciated for its scent, flavour, medicinal properties and above all as a luminous yellow dye. In Greece it was a royal colour and in eastern cultures, too, it was reserved for dyeing the clothing of those of high rank or caste. Originating in Persia it spread to northern India and the Mediterranean by the 10th century. Its popularity in Europe followed the Crusades and it became a valuable trading commodity. So valuable indeed that adulteration was always a temptation – but penalties were high. Regular saffron inspections were held in Nuremberg in the 15th century and records reveal that at least one man was burned in the market place and three others buried alive for tampering with their saffron. Gerard certainly thought highly of its powers: "For those at death's doore," he wrote, "and almost past breathing, saffron bringeth breath again" (*The Herball*, 1597).
Description A perennial, it has linear leaves, growing from the rounded corm. Fragrant, lilac flowers, with deeper purple veins and yellow anthers, appear in autumn. The saffron spice is produced from the three-branched red style.
Habitat/distribution Occurs in southern Europe, northern Africa, the Middle East and India, with major centres of commercial cultivation in Spain and Kashmir, northern India.
Growth Needs well-drained soil, sun and warm summers in order to flower. Plants are sterile and can be propagated only by offsets.

ROSACEAE
Crataegus laevigata
Hawthorn

History and traditions Many superstitions surround this tree, often known as "may", or "mayblossom", for its time of flowering, associations with May Day celebrations and the return of summer. (It usually flowers later than 1 May owing to the revision of the British calendar in 1752.) It was considered an omen of both ill and good fortune – unlucky to bring into the house, yet tied outside as a protection from witches, storms and lightning or to stop milk going sour. The strange perfume, with its overtones of decay, contributed to its reputation as an emblem of death and the plague.
Description A deciduous shrub or small tree, growing to 8 m (26 ft), with thorny branches and small dark-green, lobed, ovate leaves. It is densely covered with clusters of white scented flowers with red anthers in spring, followed by red globe-shaped fruit in autumn.
Related species *C. monogyna* is very similar and hybridizes with *C. laevigata*. There are also many ornamental cultivars, some with pink or red flowers, but they lack therapeutic properties.
Habitat/distribution Native to Europe, northern Africa and western Asia, introduced in temperate regions elsewhere. Occurs in hedges and woodland.
Growth A traditional hedging plant, which grows in any soil in sun or partial shade. Propagated from seed, sown in early spring – stratification is necessary for germination.
Parts used Flowers, leaves, fruits.

USES Medicinal An important medicinal herb in Europe, it acts on the circulatory system, strengthens the heart, regulates its rhythm and lowers blood pressure. It is said to be gradual in effect and well tolerated by the body.
Culinary Leaves, sometimes berries, were once eaten in sandwiches by country people (especially children), and young shoots cooked in savoury, suet puddings. The fresh flowers add an interesting scented flavour to syllabubs and creamy desserts.
Other names May, Mayblossom, quickset and quickthorn.

Parts used Flower pistils – dried. It takes over 4,000 flowers to produce 25g (1 oz) of dried saffron. Cheap or powdered product is often adulterated – the genuine herb is always expensive and should be a dark reddish-yellow in colour.

USES Medicinal Saffron is known to have digestive properties, improves circulation and helps to reduce high blood pressure – its high consumption in Spain has been put forward as an explanation for the low incidence of cardio-vascular disease there. It is also the richest known source of Vitamin B^2. Externally it is applied as a paste for inflamed skin and sores.

Culinary It is widely used as a flavouring and colourant in Middle Eastern and northern Indian cookery, in rice dishes, such as the classic Spanish paella, and fish soups including bouilla-baisse from France. It is also used in sweets and cakes – especially in eastern cuisine, and the traditional saffron cakes and loaves of Cornwall in England.

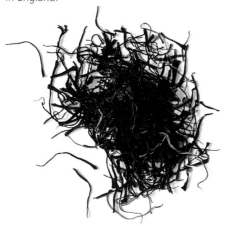

Top Saffron crocus *corms*.

Above *The dried threads have medicinal and culinary uses.*

CUCURBITACEAE
Cucumis sativus
Cucumber

History and traditions The cucumber is thought to have originated in northern India, where it has been cultivated for at least 3,000 years. It must have been known in ancient Egypt, as it was one of the luxuries missed by the Israelites after they left Egypt to wander in the desert. It was enjoyed by the Greeks and Romans – the Emperor Tiberius ate it every day, according to Pliny. In Britain it was known from the beginning of the 14th century, but not widely grown there before the 16th century. It features in herbals of the period as being help-ful in urinary disorders and was recognized for soothing and cleansing the skin. Gerard believed in its cooling properties and advised eating a cucumber pottage daily for three weeks to "perfectly cure all manner of … copper faces, red and shining fierie noses (as red as Roses) with pimples, pumples rubies, and such like …" (*The Herball*, 1597).

Description A trailing annual (of the same family as marrows, melons and the creeping wayside plant, bryony, *Bryonia alba*), it has lobed triangular leaves and yellow flowers, followed by the familiar cylindrical fruit with its thick green skin, watery, white flesh and white ovate seeds.

Habitat/distribution Cultivated worldwide.

Growth A tender plant, it must be grown under glass in cool, temperate climates. It is propagated from seed and needs rich, well-drained soil, ample moisture and humidity, with a minimum temperature of 10°C (50°F).

Parts used Fruit, seeds.

USES Medicinal Cucumber is a natural diuretic and laxative and has digestive properties. The seeds are high in potassium and beneficial for diseases associated with excess uric acid, such as arthritis and gout. In traditional Indian medicine, juice from the leaf is combined with coconut milk to restore the electrolyte balance when the body is dehydrated following diarrhoea. When applied externally, the flesh of the cucumber has soothing properties for skin irritations and sunburn.

Culinary The vitamins and minerals (vitamin C, small amounts of vitamin B complex, calcium, phosphorus, iron) which cucumber contains are concentrated in or near the skin, so it should not be peeled. It is also best eaten raw, as cooking destroys the potassium and phosphorus content. A popular salad ingredi-ent, and added to yoghurt-basedcondiments such as the Indian *raita,* Greek *tsatsiki* and Turkish *cacik*.

Cosmetic Soothing and refreshing to the skin, a cucumber face mask helps prevent spots and blackheads. Slices of cucumber, placed over closed eyelids, revive tired eyes.

Cucumber face mask

This recipe doubles up as a lotion to relieve sunburn

$1/2$ *a cucumber, chopped*
  (but not peeled)
1 tbs liquid honey
1 tbs rosewater
1 tbs ground almonds

Pound all the ingredients to a pulp, or put in a liquidizer, smooth over the face and leave for 15–20 minutes, before wiping off with damp cotton wool.

UMBELLIFERAE/APIACEAE
Cuminum cyminum
Cumin

History and traditions Cumin was grown in Arabia, India and China from earliest times. There are descriptions of how it was cultivated in the Bible (Isaiah 28:25–27) and the practice of paying it in tithes (a church tax) is referred to in the New Testament. It is mentioned by the Greek physicians, Hippocrates and Dioscorides, and Pliny reports that the ground seed was taken with bread and water or wine as a remedy for "squeamishness". Cumin was a very popular spice in Britain and Europe during the Middle Ages for its strong taste.

Description A half-hardy annual with finely divided, feathery leaves and umbels of very small white flowers. The fruits (seeds) are yellowish-brown and ovoid in shape with a distinctive, warm and spicy lingering aroma. The plant is a little like caraway (*Carum carvi*) in appearance, and occasionally confused with it, but quite different in taste.

Habitat/distribution Indigenous to Egypt and the Mediterranean, it is widely grown in tropical and subtropical regions, including northern Africa, India and North and South America.

Growth Grow in a well-drained to sandy soil. Propagated from seed and should be sown under glass in cool temperate regions and transplanted after all frosts. Although it may flower, it is unlikely that fruits will ripen in cool climates.

Parts used Seeds, essential oil.

USES Medicinal Decoctions or infusions of the seeds are taken for digestive disorders, diarrhoea, colds and feverish illnesses. In Ayurvedic medicine it is also used to treat piles and for renal colic. The essential oil has antiseptic and antibacterial properties and is applied externally (diluted) for boils and insect bites.

Culinary Widely used in Indian and Middle Eastern cookery to flavour curries, soups, meat and vegetable dishes, bread, biscuits and cheese; and as an ingredient of spice mixtures, pickles and chutneys. There are several species of cumin which produce seeds of varying colour and strength of flavour.

White cumin seeds.

Black cumin seeds.

ZINGIBERACEAE
Curcuma longa syn. *domestica*
Turmeric

History and traditions Turmeric is an ancient herb of India – mentioned in Sanskrit writings and used in Ayurvedic and Unani traditional medicine. A native of southeast Asia, it spread across the Pacific, taken by the Polynesians as far as Hawaii and Easter Island. Used as a dye and food flavouring in the manner of saffron (though it does not have the same subtlety of colour or flavour), the generic name is from the word used in ancient Rome for saffron, *korkum*.

Description A perennial, up to 1.2 m (4 ft) tall, it has shiny, lanceolate leaves and dense spikes of pale-yellow flowers, enclosed in a sheathing petiole. Of the same family as ginger, turmeric grows on a tuberous rhizome.

Growth A tender, tropical plant, it requires well-drained but moist soil, a humid atmosphere and minimum temperatures of 15–18°C (59–64°F). It is propagated by division of the rhizomes.

Parts used Rhizomes – boiled, skinned, dried and ground into bright-yellow powder.

USES Medicinal Turmeric has antiseptic properties and is applied, in the form of a paste made with water, to boils, cuts and wounds. It is taken internally, as an infusion in milk or water, for intestinal disorders and diarrhoea, for colds, coughs and sore throats. Rich in iron, it is helpful in counteracting anaemia.

Culinary An ingredient of Worcestershire sauce and curry powder, adding colour and a musky flavour to meat, vegetable and savoury dishes.

Cosmetic It makes an excellent skin softener and facial conditioner.

GRAMINEAE/POACEAE
Cymbopogon citratus
Lemon grass

History and traditions Lemon grass did not come to the attention of the west as a medicinal or culinary plant until the modern era. It is now extensively cultivated, in various tropical countries, mainly for distillation of the essential oil, which is used in commercial products. It has also risen in popularity as a culinary herb.

Description A tall, clump-forming perennial, growing to 1.5 m (5 ft) in height, it has linear, grasslike leaves, strongly scented with lemon.

Habitat/distribution Indigenous to southern India and Sri Lanka, found wild and cultivated in tropical and subtropical zones of Asia, Africa, North and South America.

Growth A tender plant, which is grown in fertile, well-drained soil, but needs plenty of moisture and minimum temperatures of 7–10°C (45–50°F). In cool temperate climates it must be grown as a conservatory or warm greenhouse plant, and moved outside in the summer.

Parts used Leaves, young stems, essential oil.

USES Medicinal The essential oil has antiseptic properties and is used externally for rheumatic aches and pains, ringworm and scabies. Internally (in doses of a few drops) it is sometimes taken for indigestion and gastric upsets.

Culinary The young white stem and leaf base are chopped and used in stir-fry dishes and in Thai, Malaysian and southeast Asian cookery. Leaves may also be infused to make tea.

Aromatic The essential oil is used in home fragrance preparations, in commercial perfumery, soaps and cosmetics and as a flavouring in the food and liquor industries.

COMPOSITAE/ASTERACEAE
Cynara cardunculus Scolymus Group
Globe artichoke

History and traditions The globe artichoke occurs only in cultivation and was probably developed, by selective breeding in the distant past, from the closely related cardoon (*Cynara cardunculus*). Both were grown as vegetables by the Greeks and Romans. Medieval Arabian physicians, including Avicenna, knew of its medicinal properties (the common name comes from the Arabic *alkharshuf)*, but it does not seem to have been widely grown in Europe before the 16th century, when it was introduced to Britain as a culinary delicacy and ornamental plant. Books of the period abound in recipes for boiling, frying, stewing or potting artichokes and making them into a variety of fancy dishes. Sir Hugh Platt (*Delights for Ladies*, 1594) gives instructions for preserving the stalks in a liquid decoction and for storing the heads (known as apples) throughout the winter.

Description A large perennial, growing to 2 m (6 ft), with long, greeny-grey, deeply cut leaves, downy on the undersides, ridged stems and large thistle-like flower heads with purple florets and a fleshy receptacle (the heart).

Above *The flower heads are a delicacy.*

Habitat/distribution Native to the Mediterranean and northern Africa, found on light, dry soils. Introduced and widely grown in other parts of the world.

Growth Tolerates some frost, but does not grow well in cold climates, where temperatures are regularly less than -15°C (5°F), or on heavy, waterlogged soil. Needs humus-rich, well-drained soil and a sunny position. Propagate from seed sown in spring, or by division of sideshoots in spring or autumn.

Parts used Leaves – fresh or dry (medicinal), unopened flowerheads (culinary).

USES Medicinal Recent research has shown that a major constituent of the leaves, cynarin, has a beneficial effect on gall bladder and liver function, stimulating its detoxifying action, and lowers blood cholesterol levels. It is also thought to counteract the undesirable side effects of treatments with antibiotic drugs.

Culinary The unopened flower heads are boiled and the tips of the scales eaten, dipped in melted butter or sauce. Hearts are eaten cold with vinaigrette, baked or fried. In Greek, Middle Eastern and Indian cuisines, hearts are eaten raw with lemon juice and pepper.

LEGUMINOSAE/PAPILIONACEAE

Cytisus scoparius

Broom

History and traditions Known in medieval times as *planta genista,* common broom gave its name to the Plantagenet royal line. It was the adopted emblem of the father of King Henry II of England, Count Geoffrey of Anjou, who wore a sprig in his helmet when going into battle. Broom is mentioned in Anglo-Saxon writings and the earliest printed herbals make much of its medicinal powers. Pickled broom-buds were a popular ingredient of Tudor salads.

Description An upright, deciduous shrub, growing to 1.5 m (5 ft), it has arching, twiggy branches, small trifoliate leaves and is covered in a mass of bright-yellow pea flowers in spring.

Related species There are many hybrids and cultivars that are not suitable for medicinal use.

Habitat/distribution A native of Europe and western Asia, found in heathlands, woods and scrublands. Introduced elsewhere.

Growth Grows in any well-drained soil in a sunny position. Propagation is by seed or semi-ripe cuttings, but seedlings do not transplant as well as established container-grown plants.

Parts used Leaves, flowers.

USES Medicinal A narcotic herb containing alkaloids similar to those in poisonous strych-nine, which affect respiration and heart action.

CAUTION The whole plant is toxic and if eaten leads to respiratory failure. Subject to legal restrictions in some countries. For use by qualified practitioners only. Under statutory control as a weed in Australia.

SOLANACEAE

Datura stramonium

Datura

History and traditions A native of North and South America, this plant was brought to Europe by the Spaniards in the 16th century. It was named "devil's apple" after European settlers in America discovered its narcotic effects, and "Jimson Weed" after Jamestown, Virginia, where they first found it growing. Also indigenous to India, datura appears in ancient Hindu literature of the Vedic period, when its intoxicant and healing powers were well understood and the seeds were smoked as a treatment for asthma.

Description A tall, bushy annual, 2 m (6 ft) tall, it has strong-smelling, triangular, lobed leaves and large white, or violet-tinged, trumpet-shaped flowers.

Habitat/distribution Indigenous to the Americas and temperate, hilly regions of India, now widely grown in other countries.

Growth A half-hardy annual, it does not tolerate frost. Grows in any light soil and is propagated by seed sown in spring.

Parts used Leaves, flowers, seeds.

USES Medicinal Of the same family as *Atropa belladonna,* it contains similar poisonous alkaloids, including atropine. It has been found useful in mitigating the symptoms of Parkinson's disease and for treating asthma.

CAUTION All parts of the plant are highly poisonous. Subject to legal restrictions in some countries. For use by qualified practitioners only.

CARYOPHYLLACEAE

Dianthus

History and traditions Pinks are of ancient origin; one species is thought to be represented in the murals at Knossos in Crete and there are records that *D. caryophyllus* were cultivated by the Moors in Valencia in 1460. The Elizabethan name for the pink was gillyflower (or "gillofloure"). This included wild and alpine species and the much-prized clove gillyflower, which seems to have covered any clove-scented pinks. By the 17th century there were many cultivated garden varieties, as featured by Parkinson in his *Paradisi,* 1629, with delightful names like 'Master Tuggie's Princesse', 'Fair Maid of Kent' and 'Lusty Gallant'. Some were known as sops-in-wine after the practice of soaking them in wine to flavour it. Herbals and stillroom books are full of recipes for making

Top Dianthus *'Pink Jewel'.*

Above *An old-fashioned pink* D. *'Mrs Sinkins'.*

syrups and conserves of gillyflowers, pickled and candied gillyflowers and wine. According to Gerard, a conserve of clove gillyflowers and sugar "is exceedingly cordiall, and wonderfully above measure doth comfort the heart, being eaten now and then" (*The Herball*, 1597).

Description The leaves of all *Dianthus* are linear, lance-shaped and blue-grey or grey-green in colour, with a waxy texture. The flowers are pink, white or purple (some bicoloured) with short tubular bases and flat heads with double or single layers of petals, some with toothed or fringed margins. Old-fashioned varieties often have fragrant, clove-scented blooms but only one flowering period in early summer. (Modern varieties repeat-flower.) Garden pinks are 25–45 cm (10–18 in) high, and alpine species a more compact 8–10 cm (3–4 in) high. All are fully hardy.

Habitat/distribution Found in mountains and meadows of Europe, Asia and South Africa.

Species There are about 300 species, with over 30,000 hybrids and cultivars recorded. Pinks traditionally grown in the herb garden include *D. deltoides* (Maiden Pink) with cerise, single flowers with toothed petals (to 20 cm (8 in) high) or the more compact *D. gratianopolitanus* syn. *D. caesius*, which has very fragrant single pink flowers (to 15cm (6 in) high) or any of the fragrant old-fashioned pinks such as *D. 'Mrs Sinkins'*, with its highly scented double white flowers and fringed petals. There are also numerous modern pinks, with an old-fashioned look, to choose from, such as *D. 'Gran's Favourite'* or the laced *D. 'London Delight'*.

Growth Pinks need a very well-drained neutral to alkaline soil and full sun. In gardens with heavy, clay soils, they can be grown in raised beds to provide sharp drainage. Easily propagated from cuttings of non-flowering shoots in summer or by division in spring or autumn.

Parts used Flowers – fresh or dried.

USES Medicinal At one time thought to have tonic properties, but they are little used today for medicinal purposes.

Culinary Fresh flowers may be added to salads, floated in drinks or crystallized for garnishing cakes and desserts. Before culinary use remove the bitter petal base.

Aromatic Flowers are dried for inclusion in pot-pourri and scented sachets. Flowers should be cut when just fully out, the heads twisted off the stems and dried whole.

Gillyflower vinegar

"Gilliflowers infused in Vinegar and set in the Sun for certaine dayes, as we do for Rose Vinegar do make a very pleasant and comfortable vinegar, good to be used in time of contagious sickness, and very profitable at all times for such as have feeble spirits."

John Evelyn, *Acetaria*, 1719.

Other names Pinks, gillyflower, clove gillyflower and sops-in-wine.

Top left D. gratianopolitanus, *known as the Cheddar pink.*

Top centre D. deltoides, *often called the maiden pink.*

Above *A pink-flowering cultivar of* D. *'Mrs Sinkins'.*

Below *Garden pinks, raised from several wild species of dianthus, are a mainstay of the traditional garden. They thrive on an alkaline soil and dislike damp conditions.*

RUTACEAE
Dictamnus albus
Dittany

History and traditions It is called "burning bush" because the whole plant is rich in volatile oil, which can allegedly be set alight as it evaporates, leaving the foliage intact and undamaged. It has a similar lemony, balsamic scent to that of *Origanum dictamnus*, or dittany of Crete, and both plants are probably named after Mount Dicte in Crete. According to Mrs Grieve (*A Modern Herbal*, 1931), *Dictamnus albus* was an ingredient of a number of exotic pharmaceutical preparations available in the early decades of the 20th century, including "Solomon's Opiate", "Guttète Powder", "Balm of Fioraventi" and "Hyacinth Mixture".

Description A clump-forming, aromatic perennial, 40–90 cm (16–36 in) tall, with pinnate leaves, made up of lance-shaped leaflets, and tall racemes of white flowers.

Related species *D. albus* var. *purpureus* has pale-pink flowers, striped with darker pink, and is more commonly grown in gardens than the species, but shares its characteristics.

Habitat/distribution Found from central and southern Europe across to China and Korea in dry grasslands and woodlands.

Growth Dittany grows in any well-drained to dry soil in full sun or partial shade. Propagated by seed sown in late summer, in containers and over-wintered in a cold frame. It does not transplant well and is not easy to establish from division.

Parts used Root – dried and powdered.

USES Medicinal It was once prescribed for nervous complaints and feverish illnesses, but does not seem to be widely used in Western herbal medicine today. The root bark of a similar species is used in Chinese medicine for its cooling, antibacterial properties.

Horticultural The chief use of this herb today is as an aromatic ornamental in the border or herb garden.

Other name Burning bush.

Above Dictamnus albus *var.* purpureus.

SCROPHULARIACEAE
Digitalis purpurea
Foxglove

History and traditions The foxglove was given its Latin name by the German botanist, Leonard Fuchs, in 1542 (it does not appear in any classical texts). He called it *digitalis,* for its supposed resemblance to fingers (*digit* = finger), and the common name in German, as in several other European languages, is connected with thimbles. Various ingenious explanations have been put forward for what it has to do with foxes: that they wore the flowers on their feet to muffle their tread when on night-time prowls; that it is really from "folksglove" for the "fairy folk"; or from an Anglo-Saxon word *"foxes-glew"* meaning fox-music, for its resemblance to an ancient musical instrument – you can take your pick. Once used in folk medicine for a variety of disorders (despite occasional fatalities), it was its effectiveness as a diuretic against dropsy which led to the discovery of its action on the heart by a Dr Withering, who published his findings in 1785.

Description A biennial or short-lived perennial, reaching 2 m (6 ft) in height. The plant has a rosette of large, downy leaves and spectacular one-sided flower spikes of purple or pink

tubular flowers, with crimson on the inside.

Related species *D. purpurea* f. *albiflora* is a white-flowering form and *D. lanata* has fawn-coloured flowers with purplish-brown veins. Both *D. purpurea* and *D. lanata* contain the active principles, though *D. lanata* is most commonly grown in Europe for the pharmaceutical industry.

Habitat/distribution Occurs throughout Europe, northern Africa and western Asia, mostly on acid soil in grassland and woodland.

Growth Although it will grow in most conditions, it prefers moist, well-drained soil in partial shade, with a mulch of leaf mould. Propagate from seed sown in autumn and over-winter in a cold frame. Self-seeds.

Parts used Leaves – from which the active principles digitoxin and digoxin are extracted.

USES Medicinal The foxglove contains glycosides which affect the heartbeat and is used in orthodox medicine as a heart stimulant. It should never be used for home treatments.

CAUTION Foxgloves are poisonous and should not be eaten or used in any way for self-medication. A prescription drug only. Legal restrictions apply.

COMPOSITAE/ASTERACEAE

Echinacea purpurea
Purple coneflower

History and traditions Coneflowers were used by Native Americans as wound-herbs, to treat snakebite and as a general cure-all. The early settlers took to them as home remedies for coughs, colds and a variety of infections. In recent years their medicinal properties have been established by modern research.

Description A tall, hardy perennial, 1.2 m (4 ft) high, with a rhizomatous rootstock and ovate-lanceolate leaves. The purplish-pink daisy-like flowers have raised conical centres, made up of prickly brown scales, reminiscent of hedgehogs (*Echinacea* is from the Greek word for hedge-hog). There are also white-flowered cultivars.

Related species *E. angustifolia* and *E. pallida* are species with similar properties, which were also used by the Native Americans.

Habitat/distribution Native to Central and eastern North America, found in dry prairies and open woodlands. Introduced and grown in other temperate regions of the world.

Growth It prefers well-drained, humus-rich soil and a sunny position or partial shade. Cut back the stems as the flowers fade to encourage a second blooming. Propagate by seed sown in spring, under glass at a temperature of 13°C (55°F), or by division of roots in late spring or autumn.

Parts used Roots, rhizomes – dried, powdered or made into capsules.

USES Medicinal Recent research has shown that echinacea has a beneficial effect on the immune system and stimulates the production of white blood cells – and has been used in treating AIDS. It has antiviral, antifungal and antibacterial properties and is taken internally in the form of capsules or tinctures, for respiratory tract infections, kidney infections, skin diseases, boils, abscesses and slow-healing wounds. A decoction of the roots is applied externally as a wash for infected wounds and skin complaints.

Echinacea purpurea *boosts the immune system.*

BORAGINACEAE
Echium vulgare
Viper's bugloss

History and traditions Early herbalists thought that the stems, speckled with pustules, looked like snakeskin, the fruits like snakes' heads and the flower stamens like snakes' tongues. So, in line with the medieval Doctrine of Signatures (whereby the appearance of a plant indicates what it can cure) *E. vulgare* was considered an antidote to the bite of an adder and by extension to anything else that was poisonous. In the words of William Coles, "a most singular remedy against poyson and the sting of scorpions" (*The Art of Simpling*). It was also widely dispensed against "swooning, sadness and melancholy" (Parkinson). A native of Europe, this attractive but invasive plant spread around the world, and became known as a tiresome weed in many countries, notably Australia and North America – where it is known as "blue devil".

Description A bushy, bristly biennial, 60–90 cm (2–3 ft) tall, with narrow lance-shaped leaves, spotted, hairy stems and dense spires of bell-shaped, violet-blue flowers in summer, opening from pinkish buds.

Habitat/distribution Native to Europe and Asia, it occurs on poor, stony soils and semi-dry grassland. Introduced to, and widespread in, many countries worldwide.

Growth Grows in any well-drained soil, in full sun. Propagated from seed sown in spring or early autumn.

Parts used Leaves, flowers and seeds (formerly).

USES Medicinal Once widely respected as an antidote to poison, its medicinal properties are now doubtful.

Horticultural Traditionally grown in herb gardens for its historical associations.

Other names Blue weed and blue devil.

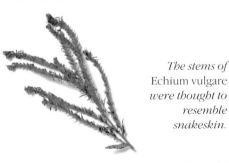

The stems of Echium vulgare were thought to resemble snakeskin.

CAUTION May cause stomach upsets if ingested and irritate skin on contact. For use by qualified practitioners only.

ZINGIBERACEAE
Elettaria cardamomum
Cardamom

History and traditions This pungent spice was known to the Greeks and Romans and mentioned by Theophrastus, Dioscorides and other classical writers. It features in Chinese medical texts, dating from AD 270, and has long been used in Ayurvedic medicine as a treatment for impotency. Cardamom is a traditional ingredient of eastern aphrodisiacs and mentioned in this context in the *Arabian Nights* stories. *Elettaria* is taken from an Indian name for this plant, *elaichi*.

Description A large perennial, 2–2.4 m (6–8 ft) tall, with a clump of long lanceolate leaves, growing from a fleshy rhizome. Flowers arise from the base of the plant, followed by pale-green capsules, which dry to a pale yellow, containing many small, pungent black seeds.

Related species There are various species, including black cardamom, a taller plant with large, dark-brown seed capsules, containing small black seeds with a strong eucalyptus aroma.

Habitat/distribution Native to southern India and Sri Lanka, it is also grown in Thailand, Central and tropical South America.

Above *Green cardamom seed pods.*

Growth It needs a minimum temperature of 18°C (64°F), well-drained, rich soil, partial shade, plenty of rain and high humidity. Propagated by seed or division of the rhizomes.
Parts used Seeds, essential oil.

USES Medicinal A warm, stimulating herb, it acts as a tonic and has antidepressant properties. It is also used as a digestive, and an infusion of the seeds is said to relieve hiccups. Seeds are chewed to freshen the breath.
Culinary A major curry spice, the seeds are also used to flavour hot wine punches, sweet, milky rice puddings and egg custard.
Aromatic The pleasant-smelling essential oil is used in perfumery and pharmaceutical products.

Above *Black cardamom.*

EQUISETACEAE
Equisetum arvense
Horsetail

History and traditions The Latin generic name comes from *equus*, a horse, and *seta*, a bristle. In former times this strange-looking, bottle-brush plant was used to clean pewter vessels and scour wooden kitchen utensils – the stems contain silica, which has a polishing action, as well as being a healing agent. In northern counties of England until the 19th century horsetail was commonly employed by milkmaids for cleaning out their pails. The Swedish botanist, Carl Linnaeus, claims that in his country it was eaten by both cattle and reindeer, though inclined to provoke diarrhoea. There are no records as to whether poor Romans, who were reputed to have eaten it (as an ubiquitous asparagus substitute), were similarly affected. Rich Romans, presumably, did not have to put it to the test. Culpeper lists many medicinal uses for horsetail, and declares that "it solders together the tops of green wounds and cures all ruptures in children".
Description A relic from prehistory, closely related to the vegetation which decayed to form modern coal seams, it is a perennial, which grows on a creeping rhizome to about 50 cm (20 in) in height. Brown stems, topped by cones, release spores and then wither, the method of reproduction of this plant being very similar to that of ferns. The mass of branched green stems, with black-toothed sheaths, are sterile.
Habitat/distribution Occurs throughout Europe from the arctic region to the south, also in Asia and China, and is found in moist waste ground. In some countries, where it has been introduced, it is regarded as a pernicious weed.
Growth A hardy plant, it grows in most conditions, although it prefers moist soil and sun or partial shade. It is propagated by division, but is invasive – and it would be wise to take this into account before introducing it into the garden.
Parts used Stems – fresh or dried.

USES Medicinal It has astringent, diuretic properties and is said to be helpful for prostate problems, cystitis and urinary infections, but it can be an irritant and self-medication is not advised. It is also said to be beneficial, when applied externally, for haemorrhages and ruptured ligaments.
Other names Bottle-brush and paddock pipes.

CRUCIFERAE/BRASSICACEAE

Eruca vesicaria subsp. *sativa*
Rocket (Arugula)

History and traditions Rocket (arugula) has
been a salad herb since Roman times. Its strong,
mustard-like taste is indicated by the generic
Latin name, which comes from *urere,* to burn.
Various claims were made for it in the past as a
painkiller. William Turner said the seed was
effective "against the bitings of the shrew-
mouse and other venemous beasts". Gerard
made the claim that "whosoever taketh the
seed of Rocket before he be whipt, shall be so
hardened that he shall easily endure the paines"
(*The Herball,* 1597). Culpeper declared it to be
"celebrated against diseases of the lungs" and
that "the juice is excellent in asthmas … as also
against inveterate coughs". But none of this has
stood the test of time and salad rocket (arugula)
is no longer used medicinally.

Description A frost-hardy
annual, 60–100 cm (2–3 ft)
tall, with dentate, deeply
divided leaves. Small, four-
petalled, white flowers,
streaked at the centre of each
petal with violet, appear in late
winter to early summer. Originally a
wild plant, rocket (arugula) has been
cultivated for so long that it is now classified
as a subspecies.

Habitat/distribution Native to the
Mediterranean and Asia, introduced and widely
grown elsewhere.
Growth Propagate from seed, sown
successionally, *in situ,* from late winter to early
summer. When grown on poor, dry soil, with
plenty of sun, it has a more pungent taste than
if grown on moist soil in cooler conditions.
Parts used Leaves.

USES Culinary A pungent herb that lends
interest to lettuce and other bland-tasting
leaves as a salad ingredient.
Other name Salad rocket.

*Peppery rocket
(arugula) leaves
add interest to
salads.*

PAPAVERACEAE

Eschscholzia californica
Californian poppy

History and traditions This bright-yellow
poppy is the state flower of California. It has
similar properties to those of the opium poppy
– but milder – and was used by Native
Americans as a gentle narcotic and pain reliever,
especially against toothache.

Description A hardy annual up to 60 cm (2 ft)
tall, with finely divided, feathery leaves. A mass
of shallow-cupped flowers in orange, yellow,
red and occasionally white appear in early
summer, followed by long curved seedpods.
There is also a wide range of cultivars.

Habitat/distribution Native to western North
America, introduced and widely grown in many
other countries.

Growth Grow this plant in well-drained to poor
soil and full sun, for the best-quality flowers.
Propagated by seed sown *in situ* in spring or
autumn. Sow successionally for a continuous
show of flowers.

Parts used Whole plant – dried as an
ingredient for infusions and tinctures.

USES Medicinal The Californian poppy is a
sedative herb that relieves pain and it is taken
internally as an infusion, for anxiety, nervous
tension and insomnia. It also has diuretic
properties and promotes perspiration.

MYRTACEAE
Eucalyptus spp.
Gum tree

History and traditions Eucalyptus trees are native to Australia and were used by the Aborigines in their traditional medicine. They have been widely adopted by other countries, including Africa, the Americas, India and southern Europe, as timber and shade trees, for planting in marshy ground to dry out malaria-inducing swamps, and for their volatile (essential) oil content. Commercial production of eucalyptus essential oils began in Australia in the second half of the 19th century, coinciding with their introduction to the West by a German botanist and director of the Melbourne Botanical Gardens.

Description Large, fast-growing evergreen trees which grow to considerable heights in warm climates, averaging 70 m (230 ft), with varying estimates for the record, dating from 1872 between 97 m (318 ft) and 132.5 m (434 ft). Many have distinctive, rounded juvenile foliage, adult leaves of *E. globulus* and *E. gunnii* are lanceolate, blue-grey and studded with oil-bearing glands. Clusters of fluffy cream-coloured flowers appear in summer, followed by globe-shaped fruits.

Species There are over 500 species and all contain antiseptic essential oils, though constituents and properties vary. *E. globulus*

(blue gum) has been most widely cultivated around the world and has attractive, juvenile leaves much sought after in floristry. *E. gunnii* is one of the hardiest and most suited to growing in cool temperate regions.

Habitat/distribution: Native to Australia, *E. globulus* is found in moist valleys of New South Wales and Tasmania, *E. gunnii* in Tasmania. All are native to Australia and have been introduced elsewhere.

Growth *Eucalyptus* spp. vary from tender to fully hardy – but none will stand prolonged low temperatures, especially when immature. *E. globulus* is half-hardy, -5°C (23°F), and *E. gunnii* is frost-hardy, -15°C (5°F). Grow in well-drained soil and full sun. Propagate from seed, sow under cover in spring or autumn.

Parts used Leaves, essential oil.

USES Medicinal Eucalyptus has decongestant, expectorant properties and helps to lower fever. The essential oil is highly antiseptic. Leaf or oil is used in steam inhalations and vapour rubs to ease the symptoms of colds, catarrh, sinusitis and respiratory-tract infections. Essential oil is used in massage oils and compresses for inflammations, rheumatism and painful joints.

Above left *Eucalyptus trees are rich in volatile oils.*

Above *Immature foliage of* Eucalyptus gunnii, *syn.* E. divaricata, *Tasmanian Blue Gum.*

Lavender and eucalyptus vapour rub

50 g/2 oz petroleum jelly
15 ml/1 tbs dried lavender
6 drops eucalyptus essential oil

Melt the petroleum jelly in a bowl over a pan of simmering water. Stir in the lavender and heat for 30 minutes.

Strain the liquid jelly through muslin, leave to cool slightly, then add the eucalyptus oil. Pour into a clean jar and leave to set.

• Use as a soothing decongestant rub for throat, chest and back.

COMPOSITAE/ASTERACEAE
Eupatorium

Eupatorium cannabinum
Hemp agrimony

History and traditions The Latin specific name
and common name are taken from the words
cannabis and *hemp*, because of a similarity in
the shape of the leaves. Hemp being used for
rope fibre, by extension *E. cannabinum* gained
the name "holy rope" – a plant with beneficent
characteristics was often arbitrarily associated
with holiness. But it was never in fact a source
of rope and shares none of the properties of
Cannabis sativa. It has a history of medicinal use
as a diuretic, purgative, cure for dropsy, general
spring tonic and antiscorbutic. Seventeenth-
century herbalists also recommended it for
healing "fomenting ulcers" and "putrid sores".
Description A woody-based, hardy perennial,
up to 1.2 m (4 ft) tall, leaves are opposite and
mostly subdivided into 3–5 leaflets. A froth of
pinky-white flowers, borne in corymbs, appear
in mid-summer – giving rise to another of the
herb's country names, "raspberries and cream".

Habitat/distribution Indigenous to Europe,
found in damp, rich soils, marshy places and fens.
Growth Grow in moist soil, in full sun or partial
shade. Propagate by division in spring or sow
seed in containers in spring.
Parts used The whole plant – the flowering
tops are dried for use in infusions, extracts and
other preparations.

USES Medicinal It has long been known for its
diuretic properties, as a tonic for debility and a
treatment for influenza-like illnesses, but the
wider medicinal action of this herb is complex,
even contradictory. Recent research suggests
that it contains compounds that are capable of
stimulating the immune system and combating
tumours, but it also contains alkaloids that are
potentially dangerous to the liver and in large
enough doses could cause liver damage.
Externally, it is applied, as in previous times,
to ulcers and sores.
Other names Holy rope, St John's herb and
ague weed.

Eupatorium perfoliatum
Boneset

History and traditions Boneset was an
important herb in the traditional medicine of
native Americans, used for fevers, digestive
disorders, rheumatism and as a powerful emetic
and laxative. It also had magical protective
properties assigned to it – infusions were
sprinkled to keep evil spirits away. The name
has nothing to do with its ability to mend bone
fractures, but refers to its efficacy in treating
"break bone fever", a virulent flu-like illness,
from which the early settlers suffered. It was
listed in Dr Griffith's *Universal Formulary,* 1859,
to be administered in combination with sage
and cascarilla bark "for a hectic fever".
Description A tall, hardy perennial, growing to
1.5 m (5 ft), with lanceolate, rough-textured
leaves surrounding the stems (perfoliate), and
large clusters of white flowers in late summer.
Habitat/distribution A native of North
America in open, marshy regions – introduced
in other countries.
Growth Grow in moist soil in full sun or partial
shade. Propagate by seed sown in containers in
spring or by division in spring or autumn.
Parts used Whole plant – dried for use in
infusions, extracts and tinctures.

Boneset in flower.

USES Medicinal A herb which lowers fevers
and relieves congestion, it is taken internally for
colds, influenza and bronchitis. It is also
thought to stimulate the immune system, as is
E. cannabinum.
Other names Feverwort, ague weed,
thoroughwort, Indian sage, sweating plant.

Eupatorium purpureum
Joe Pye weed

History and traditions Joe Pye is said to have been a traditional healer from New England, with a reputation for successful cures, who swore by *E. purpureum*, using it in his remedies. The name gravel root pertains to the herb's ability to clear urinary stones, for which it is still used today, and Queen of the meadows is because the massed plants, when in flower, are a truly splendid sight.

Description A handsome hardy perennial which grows to at least 2.1 m (7 ft) tall, with purplish stems, whorls of slender, finely toothed, ovate leaves and dense, domed corymbs of purple-pink flowers in late summer to autumn. (It makes a magnificent plant for the border and is often sold as an ornamental.)

Habitat/distribution A North American native, found in woodland and grassland on moist or dry soils.

Growth Grows best in moist, well-drained soil in partial shade or sun. Propagated by seed sown in containers in spring, or by division when dormant.

Parts used Rhizomes, roots – dried for use in decoctions and tinctures.

USES Medicinal It has a restorative, cleansing action, mainly used in modern herbal medicine for kidney and urinary disorders, including stone, cystitis and prostate problems. Also used for painful menstruation, rheumatism and gout.

Other name Gravel root.

SCROPHULARIACEAE
Euphrasia officinalis
Eyebright

History and traditions The botanical name of this plant comes from the Greek for gladness, presumably for the cheer experienced when an eye problem is resolved. It was unknown to the classical writers and first introduced as an "eye" herb by Hildegard of Bingen, in her *Physica*, compiled *c.* 1150. In the 16th century, Fuchs and Dodoens also promoted it as a specific for eye complaints. The Doctrine of Signatures had a considerable bearing on the matter, as the markings on the little white flower were supposed to resemble a bloodshot eye.

Description An annual semi-parasitic herb, 5–30 cm (2–12 in) in height, it attaches itself to the roots and stems of grasses, absorbing mineral substances from them. Leaves are rounded, toothed and small – 1 cm ($^1/_2$ in) long – and the tiny white flowers are double-lipped with yellow throats and dark-purple veins.

Habitat/distribution Native to northern Europe, found also in Siberia and the Himalayas in meadowland and pastures on poor soil.

Growth A wild plant that is difficult to cultivate because of its semi-parasitic habit. If propagation is to be attempted, seeds should be sown near to potential host grasses.

Parts used Whole plant – dried for use in infusions and herbal preparations.

USES Medicinal A herb which reduces inflammation and is said to be helpful, taken as an infusion, for hayfever, allergic rhinitis, catarrh and sinusitis. For external use it is made into washes for sore, itchy eyes and conjunctivitis, or for skin irritations and eczema.

UMBELLIFERAE/APIACEAE
Ferula asa-foetida
Asafoetida

History and traditions The specific name refers to the strong, fetid smell of the gum resin obtained from the roots of this plant. It was valued throughout the Middle Ages as a prophylactic against plague and disease, and a piece was sometimes hung around the neck for this purpose. Asafoetida is still popular in India today as a flavouring and condiment and for its medicinal properties.

Description A herbaceous perennial, growing to 2.3 m (7 ft), it has a thick, fleshy taproot, finely divided, feathery leaves and yellow flower umbels in summer – and looks like giant fennel.

Habitat/distribution Occurs in western Asia from Iran to Afghanistan and Kashmir, on rocky hillsides and open ground.

Growth It is frost-hardy, withstanding temperatures to -5°C (23°F) and should be grown in well-drained, reasonably rich soil. Propagated by seed sown in autumn as soon as it is ripe.

Parts used Gum resin – produced from the base of the stems and root crown when the plant is cut down, drying as reddish tears. Sold whole, in powdered form, or as a tincture.

USES Medicinal It has a long tradition of use in Ayurvedic medicine for many complaints, including digestive disorders, respiratory diseases, impotence, painful menstruation, and problems following childbirth, and is said to counteract the effects of opium.

Culinary Despite its strong, sulphurous aroma, when added in small quantities, this herb enhances the flavour of curries and spicy food. The green parts are used as a vegetable.

MORACEAE
Ficus carica
Fig

History and traditions Figs originally came from Caria, a region of modern Turkey, which is the source of the species name. They were widely cultivated in ancient Greece and Rome and there are many references to them in classical writings from Homer to Theophrastus, Dioscorides and Pliny. Greek athletes ate figs to improve their strength and performance and the Romans fed them to their slaves (presumably for similar reasons). In Roman mythology the fig was dedicated to Bacchus and renowned as the tree which gave shelter to the wolf who suckled Romulus and Remus. Figs have been grown in the rest of Europe since they were popularized by the Emperor Charlemagne in the 9th century.

Description A deciduous tree, growing to 10 m (33 ft) with deeply lobed, palmate leaves. The flowers are completely concealed within fleshy receptacles and are followed by small green, pear-shaped fruits, ripening to dark purple, when the flesh surrounding the seeds becomes sweet and juicy.

Habitat/distribution Native to Turkey and southwest Asia, naturalized throughout the Mediterranean region and grown in many warm temperate zones worldwide.

Growth Although fig trees will withstand temperatures to -5°C (23°F), they need some protection from prolonged frost and cold. Warm, sunny summers are necessary to produce good fruit. Grow in well-drained, rich soil in a sunny position, and provide a sheltered place in cool areas. Propagated from semi-ripe cuttings in summer.

Parts used Fruits – fresh or dried.

USES Medicinal Well known for their laxative properties – syrup of figs is a traditional remedy for constipation – they are also highly nutritious, containing vitamins A, C and minerals, including calcium, phosphorus and iron, and are considered restorative and strengthening to the system. The milky juice, or sap, from green figs helps to soften corns and calluses on the skin.

Culinary The fruits are delicious raw, or as a cooked ingredient of sweet pies, pastries, desserts and conserves. Dried figs are stewed, or eaten as they are.

Related species

MORACEAE
Ficus religiosa
Peepal

Ficus religiosa is a large, spreading tree with distinctive, broad oval leaves, each tapering to a point. It was while meditating beneath a peepal tree that the Buddha achieved enlightenment, and it is revered by both Hindus and Buddhists. In Ayurvedic medicine it is used to treat various diseases, including dysentery and skin disorders.

ROSACEAE
Filipendula ulmaria
Meadowsweet

History and traditions The Dutch named this herb *"reinette"* (little queen) and it is known in several European languages as queen of the meadows. It features in the poetry of Ben Jonson as "meadow's queen" and John Clare celebrates its beauty in his poem "To Summer". It is said to have been Queen Elizabeth I's favourite strewing herb.

Description A herbaceous perennial, on a stout rootstock, 1–1.2 m (3–4 ft) tall, with irregularly pinnate, inversely lance-shaped leaves and dense corymbs of fluffy, creamy flowers in summer. Leaves have a more pleasant, aromatic scent than the sickly, hawthorn-like smell of the flowers.

Habitat/distribution Native to Europe and Asia, introduced and naturalized in North America. Widely grown in northern temperate regions, in marshlands and meadows, by ponds and streams.

Growth Grow in moist to boggy soil, or by a pond margin, in sun or partial shade – dislikes acid soil. Propagated by seed sown in spring or in autumn and overwintered in a cold frame, or by division in autumn or spring.

Parts used Leaves, flowers – fresh or dried.

USES Medicinal A traditional remedy, taken as an infusion, for heartburn, excess acidity and gastric ulcers. Also said to be helpful for rheumatism, arthritis and urinary infections.

Culinary The leaves may be used to flavour soups and stews.

Aromatic Leaves and flowers, dried, are added to pot-pourri – the scent of the flowers improves with keeping.

UMBELLIFERAE/APIACEAE

Foeniculum vulgare

Fennel

History and traditions The Romans enjoyed fennel both as a culinary plant, eating the stems as a vegetable, and for its medicinal properties – Pliny listed it as a remedy for no fewer than 22 complaints. It appears in early Anglo-Saxon texts and European records of the 10th century and was associated with magic and spells, being hung up at doors on Midsummer's Eve to deter witches. It was also used as a slimming aid and to deaden the pangs of hunger. William Coles wrote that it was "much used in drinks and broths for those that are grown fat, to abate their unwieldiness and cause them to grow more gaunt and lank" (*Nature's Paradise*, 1650). A use which is still valid today, it may be relevant that the chemical structure of fennel bears certain similarities to that of amphetamines.

Description A graceful aromatic perennial, up to 2 m (6 ft) tall, with erect, hollow stems and mid-green, feathery foliage – the leaves are pinnate, with threadlike leaflets. Umbels of yellow flowers are borne in summer, followed by ovoid, ridged, yellow-green seeds. The whole plant is strongly scented with aniseed.

Related species *F. v.* 'Purpureum' has bronze foliage and makes an attractive ornamental. *F. v.* var. *dulce* (Florence fennel, sweet fennel, finocchio) is cultivated for its bulbous, white stem bases.

Habitat/distribution Native to Asia and the Mediterranean, and occurs in much of Europe on wasteland, on dry sunny sites and in coastal areas. Widely naturalized in other countries.

Growth Grow *F. vulgare* and *F. v.* 'Purpureum' in well-drained to sandy soil in a sunny position. Does not always survive severely cold or wet winters, especially if grown on heavy soil. *F. v.* var. *dulce* needs a richer but well-drained soil, and plenty of water to produce the requisite swollen stems, which are blanched by earthing up around them. Propagation is from seed sown in spring.

Parts used Leaves, stems, roots, seeds, essential oil.

USES Medicinal An infusion of the seeds soothes the digestive system, and is said to increase the production of breast milk in nursing mothers as well as being settling for the baby. Also used as a mouthwash for gum disorders and a gargle for sore throats.

Culinary Leaves and seeds go well with fish, especially oily fish, such as mackerel. Seeds lend savour to stir-fry and rice dishes. The bulbous stems of Florence fennel are eaten raw in salads or cooked as a vegetable.

Aromatic The essential oil is used in perfumery, to scent soaps and household products, and as a flavouring in the food industry.

CAUTION Not suitable for pregnant women as in large doses fennel is a uterine stimulant.

Above *F. v.* var dulce, *florence fennel.*

Above centre *Fennel foliage.*

Fennel tea

Drinking fennel tea can have a good effect when on a slimming regime. Try taking a cup before meals to reduce appetite, or at any time instead of tea or coffee laced with milk and sugar.

250 ml/^{1}/2 pt/1 cup of boiling water
1 tsp of fennel seeds
^{1}/2 thin slice of fresh orange/or fresh shredded rind

Put the fennel seeds in a cup or pot, crush them lightly and pour over the boiling water. Cover and leave to infuse for 5 minutes.

Strain before pouring and add a slice of orange, or shred of curled orange rind, for extra flavour.

Wild strawberry leaves are included in blended herbal teas.

ROSACEAE
Fragaria vesca
Wild strawberry

History and traditions The large garden strawberry was not developed until the end of the 18th century by cross-breeding with American species. Until then, wild strawberries were the only kind known, although they were cultivated – when "by diligence of the gardener" the fruits were "as big as the berries of the Bramble in the hedge", as Thomas Hill puts it in *The Gardener's Labyrinth*,1590. Hill recommended eating them with cream and sugar, or, preferably in his view, with sugar and wine. Old stillroom books give recipes for strawberry teas and cordials, and for beauty aids, such as a face wash of strawberries, tansy and new milk. Culpeper had great faith in the powers of this plant to counteract all manner of disorders from cooling the liver, blood and spleen, refreshing and comforting fainting spirits and quenching thirst, to washing foul ulcers, fastening loose teeth and healing spongy gums.

Description A low-growing perennial, 25 cm (10 in) tall, which spreads by sending out rooting runners. It has shiny, trifoliate leaves, made up of ovate, toothed leaflets, and small white, yellow-centred flowers, followed by red ovoid fruits with tiny yellow seeds embedded in the surface.

Related species Alpine strawberries are cultivars of the species, *F. vesca*, and have smaller, but more distinctively aromatic fruits.
Habitat/distribution Found in Europe, Asia and North America, in grassland and woodland. Widely grown in temperate and subtropical regions.
Growth Grow in fertile, well-drained soil (on the alkaline side), in sun or partial shade. Propagate by separating and replanting runners – or by seed sown in containers at a temperature of 13–18°C (55–64°F).
Parts used Leaves, roots, fruits.

USES Medicinal Infusions or decoctions of the leaves and root are traditionally recommended for gout, are also taken for digestive disorders and used as a mouthwash to freshen breath. (Leaves of large, garden varieties do not have medicinal properties.) Leaves are diuretic, fruits mildly laxative. Preparations made with the fruits can be applied externally for skin inflammations, irritations and sunburn.
Culinary Rich in vitamin C, fruits are eaten fresh or made into desserts, conserves and juices. Dried leaves are included in blended herbal teas to improve taste and aroma.
Cosmetic The wild strawberry fruits have a cleansing, astringent action on the skin and are often added to face masks, skin toners and cleansing lotions.

Strawberry cleansing milk

A soothing lotion suitable for oily, spotty or blemished skins.

225 g/8 oz fresh, ripe strawberries
150 ml/¼ pt/⅔ cup milk

Mash the strawberries to a pulp and mix with the milk – or blend the ingredients in a blender. Pour into a clean bottle and keep in the refrigerator. Apply to the face on pads of cotton wool (cotton balls). (Lotion does not keep and should be used within two days.)

PAPAVERACEAE
Fumaria officinalis
Fumitory

History and traditions Shakespeare had no high opinion of this plant, referring to it twice as "rank fumitory" – it was one of the "idle weeds" with which King Lear crowned himself when mad, and a plant which grew in "fallow leas", left uncultivated because of war (*Henry V*). *Fumaria* is from the Latin for smoke, *fumus*. Various explanations have been put forward for its application to this plant – from the leaves having a "smoky appearance" to smoke from the plant when burnt, dispatching evil spirits; or the view, attributed to Pliny, that putting the juice in the eyes makes the tears run to such an extent that it's like being blinded by smoke.

Description An annual herb, 15–30 cm (6–12 in) tall, with trailing stems, small, finely divided grey-green leaves and racemes of tubular, pink flowers, in midsummer to autumn.

Habitat/distribution A European native, also found in western Asia and naturalized in North America, occurs on weedy ground, in fields and gardens (once a common cornfield weed).

Growth A wild plant, it will grow in any light soil, in sun or shade. Propagated from seed sown in spring, it also self-seeds readily.

Parts used Whole plant; cut in flower and dried..

USES Medicinal Contains small amounts of similar alkaloids to those found in poppies. Formerly used internally for digestive complaints and externally for eczema, skin disorders and conjunctivitis, but is little used today.

CAUTION Mildly toxic – not for self-medication.

LEGUMINOSAE/PAPILIONACEAE
Galega officinalis
Goat's rue

History and traditions The generic Latin name is said to come from the Greek for milk, *ghala*. The reputation of this herb for increasing the milk supply of cattle and other animals who eat it was established at the end of the 19th century by studies carried out in France. It was, at one time, thought to be helpful in cases of plague and was a favourite choice for fevers.

Culpeper advised that "a bath made of it is very refreshing to the feet of persons tired of over-walking". The common name "goat's rue" is possibly because the crushed leaves have a rank smell.

Description A bushy, hardy perennial, up to 1.5 m (5 ft) tall, with lax stems, pinnately divided leaves and racemes of mauve, white or bicoloured flowers borne throughout the summer – it makes an attractive plant for the border or herb garden.

Related species *G. offinalis* 'Alba' is a white-flowering cultivar.

Habitat/distribution Native to Europe and western Asia, introduced in other countries, found in moist meadows and pasturelands.

Growth Goat's rue will grow in most soils, but prefers moist conditions, thrives and spreads rapidly in rich, fertile soil. Plant in full sun or partial shade. Propagated from seed sown in spring (soaking seeds overnight, or scarifying them, encourages germination).

Parts used Flowering tops – dried.

USES Medicinal An infusion of the herb is supposed to improve lactation for humans, just as eating the plant does for animals. It also has digestive properties and is said to lower blood-sugar levels, making it helpful for late-onset diabetes.

General High in nitrogen, it makes a useful "green manure" when ploughed into the soil.

Other name French lilac.

Below Galega officinalis *'Alba'*.

Galium aparine
Goosegrass

RUBIACEAE
Galium

Galium odoratum syn.
Asperula odorata
Sweet woodruff

History and traditions A strewing herb since medieval times, it is one of many species containing compounds which release coumarin, with its characteristic scent of new-mown hay, as the plant dries. Thomas Tusser called it "sweet grass" and recommended it for making a water to improve the complexion as well as for strewing. Gerard recommended it as a kind of air conditioning: "The flowers are of a very sweet smell as is the rest of the herb, which, being made up into garlands or bundles, and hanged up in houses in the heat of summer, doth very well attemper the air, cool and make fresh the place" *(The Herball,* 1597). The dried leaves were put into sachet mixtures to deter moths, used to stuff pillows and mattresses and placed between the pages of books.

Description A spreading perennial, growing on a creeping rhizome, about 40 cm (16 in) tall, it has four-angled stems, whorls of rough-textured, lanceolate leaves and a mass of tubular, star-shaped, scented, white flowers in summer.

Habitat/distribution Native to Europe and Asia, also found in northern Africa and naturalized in North America. Found on loamy, nutrient-rich soils in mixed woodland.

Growth Grow in humus-rich soil in partial shade. Propagation is easiest by division of runners in spring or autumn. Can also be grown from seed, sown as soon as ripe in late summer.

Parts used Whole plant – cut when in flower and dried.

USES Medicinal Coumarin gives it sedative properties and infusions are taken for nervous irritability and insomnia. Modern research has found that two of its coumarin molecules join to produce dicoumarol, which prevents blood-clotting and strengthens capillaries, and it is taken internally for varicose veins and thrombophlebitis. It is a diuretic and said to improve liver function and have a tonic effect on the system.

Aromatic The coumarin smell intensifies and improves with keeping, so the dried herb is added to pot-pourri or sachets for the linen cupboard – it helps repel insects.

Galium verum
Ladies' bedstraw

This member of the *galium* species has the characteristic four-angled stems and whorls of clinging, bristled leaves, but the flowers are bright-yellow and smell of honey. It too emits the sweet, coumarin scent when dry and was much used in the past as a mattress stuffing – hence its popular name. Dioscorides wrote about it as a "milk" plant and it was used in his time and for centuries afterwards as an agent for curdling cheese and colouring it yellow – it does in fact contain a rennin enzyme.

This familiar, creeping, clinging plant may look like a tiresome weed (and all too often behave like one) but is not without its uses. It is a traditional springtime tonic in central Europe, taken as an infusion of the fresh green parts, or as a pulped juice, and is said to help eliminate toxins from the system. Some herbalists recommend it for debilitating conditions such as myalgic encephalomyelitis (ME) and glandular fever. It may also be eaten, as a lightly cooked vegetable, as they do in China apparently, and the seeds have even been recommended as a coffee substitute. Gerard's comment was "Women do usually make pottage of cleavers … to cause lanknesse and keepe them from fatnes."

Other name Cleavers.

Above *Ladies' bedstraw.*

ERICACEAE
Gaultheria procumbens
Wintergreen

History and traditions This shrub is the source of the original wintergreen, later extracted from a species of birch, *Betula lenta*, and nowadays mostly produced synthetically. It was used as a tea and medicinally by Canadian Indians for aching muscles and joints. Its Latin name comes from Dr Jean-Francois Gaulthier, who worked in Quebec in the mid-1700s. The leaves were officially in the United States *Pharmacopoeia* until towards the end of the 19th century and wintergreen oil is still listed.

Description A prostrate shrub, 15 cm (6 in) high, it has dark-green, glossy, oval leaves and clusters of small, white, drooping, bell-shaped flowers in summer, followed by scarlet berries.

Habitat/distribution A North American native, found in woodlands and mountainous areas.

Growth Grow in a moist soil, on the acid side of neutral, in partial shade. Dividing the rooted suckers is the easiest way to propagate this plant. Semi-ripe cuttings can be taken in summer, or seeds can be sown in containers and overwintered in a cold frame.

Parts used Leaves, essential oil – obtained by distillation of the leaves.

USES Medicinal The leaves contain methyl salicylate, an anti-inflammatory with similar properties to aspirin. The essential oil has anti-septic properties and is used for massaging aches and pains, for rheumatism and arthritis. Infusions of the leaves are used as gargles.

CAUTION The oil is toxic in excess.

GENTIANACEAE
Gentiana lutea
Yellow gentian

History and traditions Gentians are said to be named after a King Gentius of Illyria (an ancient country of the East Adriatic), who was credited by Pliny and Dioscorides as having been the first to recognize its medicinal properties. In the Middle Ages it was popular as a counter-poison and the German physician and botanist Hieronymus Bock in his *Neue Kraüter Buch*, 1539, refers to the use of the roots in dilating wounds. Nicholas Culpeper, inventive as ever, recommends it as a healing decoction for cows unlucky enough to be bitten on the udder by venomous beasts. It is not certain which species were used in former times, but *G. lutea* has proved to be the most important from a medicinal point of view. In former times gentian wine was taken as an aperitif.

Description A hardy herbaceous perennial, it grows on a thick taproot, to a height of 1–2 m (3–6 ft). Erect stems have fleshy, ribbed leaves in pairs, joined at the base, and bright-yellow flowers, with short, tubular petals, borne in clusters in the leaf axils. It usually flowers about three years after planting.

Habitat/distribution Native to Europe and western Asia. Found in mountainous pastures and woodlands.

Growth Grow in well-drained, humus-rich soil, in sun or partial shade, and keep fairly moist – heavy, waterlogged soil is likely to induce root rot. Propagated by division or offshoots in spring, or by seed sown in autumn.

Parts used Roots, rhizomes – dried for use in decoctions, tinctures and other preparations.

USES Medicinal The most bitter of herbs, yellow gentian has been used in tonic medicines for centuries. It is said to be anti-inflammatory and to reduce fevers and is taken internally for digestive complaints and loss of appetite. Said to stimulate production of blood corpuscles and to reduce anaemia.

General An ingredient of commercially produced tonics and bitter aperitifs.

CAUTION It should not be used without advice from a qualified practitioner, as it could have adverse effects on some gastric disorders. Not to be taken by anyone with high blood pressure, nor by pregnant women.

GERANIACEAE

Geranium maculatum
Cranesbill

History and traditions The common name refers to the beak-like shape of the fruit, and the generic name is from the Greek word for a crane, a stork-like bird with a long bill. The leaves become distinctively speckled as they age, and the specific name *maculatum* means spotted. Traditionally used in the folk medicine of Native Americans, it was at one time listed in the United States *Pharmacopoeia*.

Description A hardy, clump-forming perennial, it grows to 75 cm (30 in) and has deeply divided palmate leaves. Large, round, purple-pink flowers appear in the axils in late spring to early summer, followed by the beak-shaped fruits.

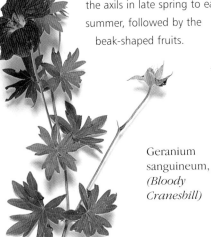

Geranium
sanguineum,
*(Bloody
Cranesbill)*

Related species *G. robertianum* (herb Robert) is a common wild plant, growing to 50 cm (20 in), with a creeping decumbent habit and soft, downy, reddish stems. Leaves have three pinnately-lobed leaflets and small five-petalled, rose-pink flowers, striped in white. It gives off an unpleasant smell when crushed. It was formerly associated with magic and widely used in folk medicine for inflammations of the skin and mouth and for diarrhoea.

Habitat/distribution *G. maculatum,* native to North America, and found in a variety of habitats. Widely grown in temperate regions elsewhere. *G. robertianum* is native to Europe, North America, Asia and northern Africa in poor, dry soils.

Growth *G. maculatum* prefers moist soil and a sunny position or partial shade. Most easily propagated by division in early spring or late winter, seeds may be sown in spring or autumn. *G. robertianum* is a wild plant and grows best in poor, dry soil.

Parts used *G. maculatum* – whole plant, roots – dried for use in infusions, powders, tinctures and other preparations.

USES Medicinal *G. maculatum* is an astringent herb, which is said to control bleeding and discharges. It was formerly used in the treatment of diarrhoea, dysentery and cholera. Externally it is applied to wounds and used as a gargle for sore throats and mouth ulcers.

Other names American cranesbill and spotted cranesbill.

Above Geranium robertianum.

ROSACEAE

Geum urbanum
Wood avens

History and traditions The medieval name was *herba benedicta*, or the blessed herb, for its supposed ability to repel evil spirits – and the second part of one of its common names, herb bennet, is a contraction of *benedicta*. The three-part leaf and the five petals of the flower supposedly represented the Holy Trinity and five wounds of Christ, and it appears as a carved decoration in 13th-century churches. As a medicinal herb there were rules laid down as to the time and season for digging up the root for maximum efficacy and it was included in cordials to be taken as a plague preventative.

Description A rather undistinguished, hardy perennial plant, growing from 20–60 cm (8–24 in), with downy stems, three-lobed leaves and tiny, yellow, five-petalled flowers in summer, followed by fruits with brown, hooked bristles.

Habitat/distribution Native to Europe and found in wasteland, hedgerows and woodlands on moist, high-nitrogen soils.

Growth A wild plant, it grows best on rich, moist soils and self-seeds freely.

Parts used Whole plant, roots – the flowering tops are dried for use in infusions, roots used fresh or dried in decoctions.

USES Medicinal An antiseptic, anti-inflammatory herb with tonic properties, taken internally for digestive upsets, applied externally to wounds, or used as a gargle for sore gums and mouth inflammations.

Culinary The roots were formerly used for their supposed clove-flavouring in soups and ale.

Other name Herb bennet.

ROSACEAE
Gillenia trifoliata
Indian physic

History and traditions A medicinal plant of Native Americans with emetic, purgative properties. Also known as "bowman's root", for its wound-healing effects, and "American ipecacuanha". The early colonists adopted it and it was formerly listed in the United States *Pharmacopoeia*.

Description A graceful hardy perennial, growing to 1 m (3 ft), with red-tinged, wiry stems, bronze-green, three-palmate leaves and irregularly star-shaped flowers, with narrow white petals and red-tinted calyces.

Habitat/distribution Native to eastern North America, found in moist woodlands, introduced and widely grown as a garden plant in Europe and temperate regions.

Growth Grow in humus-rich, moist soil in partial shade. Propagated by division in spring or autumn, or by seed sown in autumn in containers and overwintered in a cold frame.

Parts used Root bark – dried for use in decoctions and powders.

USES Medicinal It is used as a purgative and expectorant.

Right Gillenia trifoliata.

GINKGOACEAE
Ginkgo biloba
Ginkgo

History and traditions Identical in appearance to tree fossils 200 million years old, ginkgo has always been a sacred tree in China – it was grown for centuries in temples, some specimens reaching a great age, with circumferences up to 9 m (29 ft). It has been cultivated in Europe since the early 18th century with seeds brought from China or Japan. The seeds have long been used in traditional Chinese medicine, and modern research has discovered constituents in the leaves of potential therapeutic importance, unknown in any other plant species.

Description There is only one species in the genus. A deciduous tree growing to 40 m (130 ft), it has lobed, fan-shaped leaves (similar in appearance to maidenhair fern foliage, but larger), which turn yellow in autumn. Flowering takes place after 20 years, with male and female flowers and fruits borne on separate trees. Male trees have an earlier leaf-fall and less spreading form; female fruits have a rancid smell when fallen. Ginkgo is a very robust tree and suffers from few pests, tolerates pollution well and a salty atmosphere.

Habitat/distribution Originating in China and Japan, it is no longer found in the wild, but is cultivated as specimen and shade trees, and now widely grown in other countries.

Growth Fully hardy, it does best in well-drained but fertile soil and a sunny position. Propagated from seed sown in containers in autumn or from cuttings taken in summer. It should not be pruned as this leads to die-back.

Parts used Leaves – picked in autumn and dried. Seeds – used in decoctions.

USES Medicinal The leaves have recently been discovered to contain compounds called ginkgolides, which promote blood flow, inhibit allergic reactions and have been found helpful for Parkinson's disease. The seeds have anti-fungal and antibacterial properties, and are used in Chinese medicine for asthma and coughs.

Culinary Ginkgo nuts (the female fruits with the outer unpleasant layer removed) are roasted and sometimes served with bird's-nest soup in Chinese cuisine.

General Seeds produce oil, which may cause dermatitis in sensitive people, and leaves contain insecticidal compounds.

LEGUMINOSAE/PAPILIONACEAE

Glycyrrhiza glabra
Liquorice

History and traditions Liquorice has been valued for thousands of years for the sweetness of its root (it contains glycosides, including glycyrrhizin, that are 50 times sweeter than sugar) and for its medicinal powers. The generic name is from the Greek *glykys* (sweet) and *rhiza* (a root). This became corrupted to *"gliquiricia"* and thence to "liquorice". The Egyptians put it into funeral jars and some was found in the burial chamber of Tutankhamun. The Chinese believed it was rejuvenating and gave them long life and strength. Roman legionaries chewed it on the battlefield – a habit taken up by Napoleon, who believed it had a calming effect on the nerves. It did not reach Europe until the 15th century, when it soon became established as a remedy for many ailments, including coughs, chest infections and digestive disorders. In 1760 a Pontefract apothecary, George Dunhill, thought of adding sugar and flour to the liquorice essence to produce the well-known confectionery. Liquorice confectionery is still made from the plant and it is an ingredient of

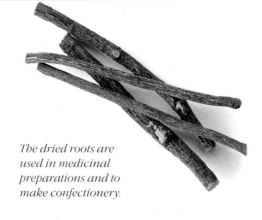

The dried roots are used in medicinal preparations and to make confectionery.

many pharmaceutical products with principal centres of commercial cultivation in Russia, Spain and the Middle East.

Description A hardy perennial, growing up to 1.2 m (4 ft), the leaves are pinnate, divided into 9–17 oval leaflets; the violet, pealike flowers are borne in short racemes, followed by long seed pods.

Related species *G. lepidota* is a North American wild species of liquorice, used by Indian tribes to ease childbirth.

Habitat/distribution Originally from the Middle East, Asia and China, it is now cultivated in temperate regions worldwide, including parts of Australia, North and South America.

Growth It requires a deep, rich, moisture-retentive soil and a sunny position. Propagated by division of roots in autumn or spring. Germination from seed is slow. To encourage strong root growth, remove flower heads.

Parts used Roots – lifted in autumn, when plant is 3–4 years old, and dried for use in decoctions, liquid extracts and powders. Roots are boiled to extract the essence used in confectionery.

USES Medicinal An important herb in Ayurvedic medicine for stomach disorders, sore throats, respiratory infections and as first aid for snake or scorpion bites. In Chinese herbal medicine, it is used for sore throats and food poisoning. It has soothing anti-inflammatory properties and is added to proprietary cough mixtures, lozenges and laxatives. Liquorice root should not be used for self-medication.

General As well as being used in confectionery production, liquorice is used to flavour beers and tobacco, and is employed in the manufacture of shoe polish, plastics and fibreboard.

CAUTION For use by qualified practitioners only. May increase fluid retention, blood pressure and blood potassium levels. It should not be given to pregnant women, or anyone with high blood pressure, kidney disease or on digitalis drugs.

HAMAMELIDACEAE
Hamamelis virginiana
Witch hazel

History and traditions Native American tribes used decoctions of the bark to reduce swellings and bruises. Colonists took note and it was listed in the United States *Pharmacopoeia* from 1860 onwards. It was also thought to have supernatural properties and the forked branches were used as divining rods in the search for water and gold.

Description A deciduous tree or shrub, up to 5 m (16 ft) in height, it has smooth brown bark and obovate leaves. Clusters of fragrant, yellow flowers appear in late autumn to early winter.

Habitat/distribution Native to North America, now widely cultivated in other countries as a garden ornamental.

Growth A hardy shrub, it requires moderately fertile, moist but well-drained soil and a sunny or partially shady position. Propagation is from seed sown in containers in autumn.

Parts used Twigs – cut after flowering, to make the distilled extract. Bark – used in tinctures and extracts. Leaves – dried for use in powders, liquid extracts, ointments.

USES Medicinal Distilled witch hazel is available for external use on bruises and sprains. The tincture is much stronger and should be used only under the guidance of a qualified practitioner. Witch hazel extract is a constituent of proprietary haemorrhoid ointments and other pharmaceutical preparations.

COMPOSITAE/ASTERACEAE
Helianthus annuus
Sunflower

History and traditions The sunflower originated in the Americas, probably Mexico. There is evidence that before 1000 BC it was grown there, for its seeds. It was among the many plants introduced to Europe from the New World in the 16th century, but did not become a major food plant and source of oil until large-scale cultivation began in Russia two centuries later (by the 1970s it was second only to soya bean as an oil crop). At some point it gained a reputation for being antimalarial and was used in Russian folk medicine for reducing fevers. The common name is a translation of the generic term, which is taken from the Greek for sun, *helios,* and flower, *anthos* – both for its sunlike appearance and because it turns its head to follow the sun's direct rays.

Description A tall, impressive annual, up to 3 m (10 ft) in height, with erect stems and oval, hairy leaves. The showy daisy-shaped flower heads, up to 30 cm (1 ft) across, have bright yellow ray florets, and brown disc florets at the centre, followed by the striped black and white seeds, about 1,000 per head.

Habitat/distribution Native to Central, North and South America, introduced and widely grown in Europe and other countries in open sunny sites.

Growth A hardy annual which tolerates most soils, as long as reasonably well-drained. Propagate by seed sown in spring.

Parts used Whole plant – cut when flowering begins for use in extracts and tinctures. Seeds are collected when ripe in autumn, and used fresh or pressed to produce a fatty oil.

USES Medicinal Sunflower seeds and oil are a good source of vitamin E, which has anti-oxidant properties, and are high in poly-unsaturates, especially linoleic acid, needed for the maintenance of cell membranes – they also help lower blood cholesterol levels. Formerly, preparations made from the seeds were used for treating coughs and bronchial infections, applied externally to bruises and for easing rheumatic pains.

Culinary Seeds are eaten fresh or roasted in salads, bread and bakery products. Oil is used for cooking and in salad dressings. Also a constituent of margarine.

Above Helianthus annuus *'Velvet Queen' is an attractive cultivar.*

ones are in small inconspicuous clusters, the female in conelike, pale-green inflorescences, which are the hops used in beer making.

Related species *H. lupulus* 'Aureus' has golden-green foliage and it makes an attractive and vigorous ornamental climber for the herb garden.

Habitat/distribution Its country of origin is not certain, but it is found in Europe, western Asia and North America and widely distributed in northern temperate zones. Naturalized in woodland and hedgerows.

Growth Prefers moist, fertile, well-drained soil and a sunny position or partial shade, but is a vigorous plant that grows under most conditions. Propagated by softwood cuttings in spring.

Parts used Female flowers (strobiles) – dried; oil distilled from flowers; fresh young shoots.

USES Medicinal Has sedative and antibacterial properties and is taken internally in infusions or tinctures for insomnia, nervous tension and anxiety; applied externally for skin complaints.

Culinary Young shoots can be cooked and eaten like asparagus.

Aromatic Dried flowers are added to sleep pillows, distilled oil used in perfumes. Active principles are thought to help prevent ageing of skin and brittleness of hair. Flowers or essential oil are included in rejuvenating baths and hair treatments.

General Flowers (hops) used to flavour beers and ales, distilled oil and extracts used in the food industry.

COMPOSITAE/ASTERACEAE
Helichrysum italicum syn. *H. angustifolium*
Curry plant

History and traditions A native of southern Europe, it seems to have crept into modern herb gardens, where it is now firmly established, because of the popular name, curry plant, relating to its strong smell. But it is not a culinary plant and has nothing to do with curry – or curry leaves (see *Murraya koenigii*). It is one of the "everlasting" flowers (most of which have a papery texture and retain form and colour when dried). It justifies its position as a herb because it is included in pot-pourri and has insect-repellent properties.

Description An evergreen subshrub, 60 cm (2 ft) in height, it has linear, silver-grey leaves and clusters of yellow button-shaped flowers in summer.

Habitat/distribution Native to the Mediterranean and grown throughout Europe, other species occur in Africa and Asia.

Growth Although frost hardy, it does not tolerate prolonged cold, wet winters. Grow in light, well-drained soil in full sun. Propagated by semi-ripe or heel cuttings in summer.

Parts used Leaves, flowers.

USES Aromatic Dried flowers and foliage may be added to pot-pourri and insect-repellent sachet mixtures. The essential oil is said to be antiviral, but it is not confirmed.

CANNABACEAE
Humulus lupulus
Hops

History and traditions The hop plant was described by Pliny, who named it "*lupus salictarius*", or "willow wolf", for its habit of twining round willow stems and strangling them "as a wolf does a lamb". The Romans ate the young shoots as vegetables, as did country folk in Britain into the 20th century. Its major importance was that it changed the character of beer, acting as an efficient preservative (it has bacteriostatic properties) and giving it a bitter flavour. It was first used for this in Flanders in the 14th century, but there was great opposition to it in Britain, where it was thought to "spoil" the traditional ales, so it was not in general use there before the 17th century. Even then John Evelyn wrote, "Hops transmuted our wholesome ale into beer. This one ingredient … preserves the drink indeed, but repays the pleasure in tormenting diseases and a shorter life" (*Pomona*, 1670). But it did become established as a medicinal plant and Culpeper's view was that a "decoction of the tops cleanses the blood, cures the venereal disease, and all kinds of scabs, itch, and other breakings out of the body; as also tetters, ringworms, spreading sores, the morphew, and all discolourings of the skin".

Description A hardy, twining, herbaceous climber, it has clinging hairy stems and 3–7 lobed palmate leaves. Male and female flowers are borne on different plants – the male

Above Humulus lupulus *'Aureus', golden hops.*

RANUNCULACEAE
Hydrastis canadensis
Golden seal

History and traditions This was once a very common herb in North America, its orange root being variously used to make a yellow dye, in medicinal remedies for digestive problems, bruises and swellings and also as an insect repellent. Early settlers were impressed by its properties and it was listed in the United States *Pharmacopoeia* from 1831 to 1936. Its continued popularity has led to overexploitation: it is now rare in the wild, from which all trade supplies come (cultivation is difficult).

Description A hardy perennial, 20–30 cm (8–12 in) in height, it has a thick, knotted, yellow rhizome, palmate, deeply lobed leaves, and single greenish-white flowers, with no petals, in late spring to early summer. Fruits are red and raspberry-like, but inedible.

Habitat/distribution Native to north-eastern North America, found in damp forests.

Growth It requires moist, humus-rich soil and a shady position. Propagation is by seed sown in autumn, though germination is slow and erratic, or by division in early spring or late autumn. Plants do not establish easily.

Parts used Rhizome – dried for use in tinctures, decoctions and pharmaceutical preparations.

USES Medicinal It has anti-inflammatory properties, helps to check bleeding, is also antibacterial, decongestant and mildly laxative. Popular in North America for boosting the immune system, taken as a tea in combination with other herbs, such as *Echinacea purpurea*.

CAUTION Poisonous in large doses. Not to be given to pregnant women or anyone with high blood pressure.

SOLANACEAE
Hyoscyamus niger
Henbane

History and traditions This is a poisonous herb with a long history. It appears in the works of Dioscorides, Pliny and other classical writers as a sleep-inducing and pain-relieving drug and is mentioned in Anglo-Saxon herbals under the name of "Henbell". In Greek mythology the dead, consigned to the underworld kingdom of Hades, were crowned with wreaths of henbane. Its narcotic properties, inducing giddiness and stupor, made it a sought-after herb for witches' brews and sorcerers' spells. It is thought to have provided the "leprous distillment" poured into the ear of Hamlet's father as he lay sleeping. Seventeenth-century herbals recognized its deadly nature, recommending it for external use only, and dental practitioners of the time burned seeds of henbane in chafing dishes to produce analgesic fumes as they treated their patients.

Description An annual or biennial, growing to 60–90 cm (2–3 ft), it has a rank, unpleasant smell and coarsely toothed, grey-green, sticky leaves. Bell-shaped, creamy-yellow flowers, veined with purple, grow from the leaf axils and appear throughout the summer, followed by fruit capsules containing many seeds.

Habitat/distribution Probably originated in the Mediterranean region, now widely distributed in Europe and Asia, found in sandy waste ground and coastal sites.

Growth Grow in poor, stony or sandy soils. Propagated from seed sown *in situ* in spring, often self-seeds.

Parts used Leaves, flowering tops – dried for use by the pharmaceutical industry.

USES Medicinal It contains toxic alkaloids hyoscyamine, hyoscine and atropine (as in *Atropa bella-donna*) which affect the central nervous system. These constituents are included in some pharmaceutical drugs for asthma and nervous disorders. Also for muscle spasms and tremors as suffered in senility and diseases associated with old age.

Other name Hogbean.

CAUTION All parts are highly poisonous. Henbane is for use by qualified practitioners only and should never be used for self medication. Legally restricted in some countries.

GUTTIFERAE/CLUSIACEAE

Hypericum perforatum
St John's wort

History and traditions This is a herb that has attracted a wealth of folklore over the centuries and been ascribed many magical and mystical properties. It is named after St John the Baptist, the red pigment, hypericin, which exudes from the crushed flowers signifying his blood. It is in full flower on St John's Day, 24 June, which also coincides with northern hemisphere midsummer rituals, and it was ascribed the power to drive away ghosts and witches and protect from thunderbolts and lightning. Many superstitions surrounded it, including gathering it on St John's Eve with the dew still on it in order to find a husband, or as a childless wife, gathering it naked to ensure a speedy conception. Despite all this, it has been discovered recently to be an effective antidepressant, without the side effects of conventional drugs. In Germany it has a medical licence and has been widely prescribed for depressive states, outselling Prozac eight times over. But as with many beneficial plants, there are contra-indications which should be taken into account (see **CAUTION**).

Description It is a hardy perennial, about 30–60 cm (1–2 ft) in height, the stems are erect, woody at the base, with small linear-oval leaves, dotted with glands, which can be seen as little pinpricks when held up to the light. The flowers have five petals, edged with glands.

Habitat/distribution A native of Europe and temperate Asia, found in woodlands, and in hedgerows on semi-dry soils. Naturalized in America and Australia.

Growth Grow in well-drained, dryish soil in full sun or partial shade. Propagation by division is the easiest method; it can also be grown from seed sown in spring or autumn, and spreads rapidly once established.

Parts used Flowering tops – fresh or dried for use in infusions, creams, oils, and as liquid extracts for use in pharmaceutical preparations.

USES Medicinal It is said to have calming properties. Infusions are taken for anxiety and nervous tension. It also has antiseptic and anti-inflammatory properties and promotes healing; creams and infused oils are applied to burns, muscular pain, neuralgia and sciatica. Prescribed in Germany as an antidepressant (Jarsin), a lower-dose product is available in Britain (Kira).

Above *The flowers of* Hypericum perforatum *contain the active principle hypericin.*

St John's wort oil

To make an infused massage oil:
*25 g/1 oz fresh flowering tops of
St John's wort
600 ml/1 pint/2 ½ cups sunflower oil*

Put the flowering tops into a bowl and crush them lightly. Pour in the oil. Stand the bowl over a pan of barely simmering water and heat very gently for about 1 hour.

Strain off the herb by pouring it through muslin or a jelly bag (cheese-cloth) fixed over a jug, then transfer to a clean, airtight bottle.

CAUTION Harmful if eaten, and poisonous to livestock – this herb is statutorily controlled in some countries (including Australia). It is also a skin allergen in sunlight.

LABIATAE/LAMIACEAE
Hyssopus officinalis
Hyssop

History and traditions The name is an ancient one – it is virtually the same in all European languages and comes from the Greek, *hyssopos*. In Hebrew it is *ezob*, meaning a "holy herb", though it is not certain whether the hyssop we know is the plant referred to in the Bible. Hippocrates and Dioscorides rated it highly as a medicinal herb, recommending it for respiratory disorders – as it is still used in herbal medicine today. Its strong, aromatic smell meant it was suitable for strewing in rooms in the house – and is included for this purpose in Thomas Tusser's list (*Five Hundred Points of Good Husbandry*, 1580). It frequently featured in designs for knot gardens of the 17th century, was a popular culinary herb used in "pottages" (soups) and salads, and was taken as a tea, or made into syrups and cordials for coughs and colds. It was one of the original ingredients of the liqueur, Chartreuse.

Description Classed as a semi-evergreen, because it loses some foliage in winter, mainly if weather is severe. It is a bushy perennial, about 60–90 cm (2–3 ft) high. The stems are woody at the base with small, dark-green, linear leaves and dense spikes of deep-blue flowers in late summer, which are very attractive to bees. There are also forms with pink and white flowers.

Habitat/distribution Native to the Mediterranean region and western Asia, found on dry, rocky soils. Introduced and widely grown throughout Europe and North America.

Growth Grow in well-drained to dry soil in a sunny position. Propagated by seed sown in spring, or by cuttings taken in summer. Prune back hard in spring to prevent it becoming straggly (it will regenerate from the old wood).

Parts used Leaves, flowers – fresh or dried.

Above left *Hyssop flowers add colour to the garden in mid to late summer.*

Above *The leaves have a pungent flavour and were popular in culinary dishes during the Elizabethan era.*

USES Medicinal Hyssop has expectorant properties, promotes sweating and is anti-catarrhal and antibacterial. Infusions are taken for coughs, colds and chest infections.

Culinary The leaves have a strong, slightly bitter flavour and may be added to soups and cooked meat and vegetable dishes with discretion. The attractive blue flowers make a pretty garnish for salads.

Old recipes for hyssop

- A Water to Cause an Excellent Colour and Complexion
  Drink six spoonfuls of the juice of Hyssop in warm Ale in a Morning and fasting.
  From *The Receipt Book of John Nott*, cook to the Duke of Bolton, 1723.

- To Make Syrup of Hysop for Colds
  Take an handful of Hysop, of Figs, Raysins, Dates, of each an ounce, French Barley one ounce, boyl therein three pintes of fair water to a quart, strain it and clarifie it with two Whites of Eggs, then put in two pound of fine Sugar and boyl it to a Syrup.
  The Queen's Closet Opened, W. M., cook to Queen Henrietta Maria, 1655.

COMPOSITAE/ASTERACEAE
Inula helenium
Elecampane

History and traditions It is said to be named after Helen of Troy, who was gathering this herb when abducted by Paris, or, according to another version, it grew from her tears on the same occasion. In any case it is an ancient herb, well known to the Greeks and Romans, who ate it as a bitter vegetable and digestive after a heavy meal. They also appreciated its medicinal properties – Galen recommended it for sciatica and Pliny thought that the root "being chewed fasting, doth fasten teeth". It appears frequently in Anglo-Saxon medical texts and in the writings of the Welsh physicians of Myddfai of the 13th century. It remained popular in folk medicine as a cough and asthma remedy over the centuries, and was grown in cottage gardens. The roots were often candied and old herbals contain many recipes for conserves, cough remedies and tonics made of this plant. John Lindley in his *Flora Medica*, 1838, remarks, "The plant is generally kept in rustic gardens, on account of many traditional virtues."

Description A hardy perennial, with tall, erect, softly hairy stems, to 2 m (6 ft) in height, it has ovate, pointed leaves, toothed at the edges, and terminal yellow flower heads, shaped like shaggy daisies, in late summer.

Habitat/distribution Native to southern Europe and western Asia, naturalized in North America, introduced elsewhere in warm and temperate zones. Found on damp soils, near ruins, in woodland and field edges.

Conserve of elecampane root

Cleanse and scrape the root. Cut them into thin round slices, letting them soke in water over the hot embers for a long space, and boil them till all the liquor be wasted. Beat them in a stone mortar, very fine. Boyle the whole with a like weighte of honey or sugar two or three times over.

All other roots may in like manner be candied and made into Conserve, but far pleasanter in the eating if to the confection a quantity of cinnamon be added. Candy the roots in October.

From *The Gardener's Labyrinth*, by Thomas Hill, 1577.

Growth Grow in rich, moist soil in a sunny position. Propagated by division of roots in spring or autumn, or by seed, which may be slow to germinate.

Parts used Roots, flowers – fresh or dried.

USES Medicinal The constituents of this herb include up to 40 per cent insulin and it is sometimes recommended as a sweetener for diabetics. But its chief use in herbal medicine is for coughs, hay fever, asthma, catarrh and respiratory infections, taken as infusions or decoctions (these must be filtered to exclude irritant fibres). Elecampane is also said to have a beneficial effect on the digestion when taken internally. Applied externally it is said to relieve many skin inflammations and irritations and has sometimes been recommended as an embrocation, or rub, for the relief of sciatica and neuralgia.

IRIDACEAE
Iris germanica var. *florentina*
Orris

History and traditions Orris, taken directly from the Greek *iris*, is the name for the powdered rhizome of the Florentine iris, which has been valued since ancient Egyptian times for its faint violet scent and fixative properties in perfumery and pot-pourri. During the 18th century it was incorporated in many cosmetic powders for wigs, hair and teeth. This variety of iris has been associated with Florence, in Italy, since the 13th century, when it was first cultivated there on a large scale, and can still be seen on the city's coat of arms.

Description A hardy perennial, growing on a stout rhizome, 60–90 cm (2–3 ft) tall, with narrow, sword-shaped leaves. Flowers are white, with outer petals mauve-tinged and yellow-bearded, or occasionally pure white.

Habitat/distribution Native to southern Europe, naturalized in central Europe, the Middle East and northern India, introduced elsewhere. Found in sunny, stony, hilly locations.

Growth Grow in well-drained soil in full sun. Propagated by division of rhizomes and offsets in late summer to early autumn.

Parts used Rhizomes – dried and powdered.

USES Aromatic An indispensable ingredient for making pot-pourri and scented sachet mixtures. It enhances the scent of the other ingredients and gives the whole preparation a more lasting quality. Also used in commercial pot-pourri products and perfumery.

Cosmetic Occasionally seen as an ingredient of home-made toothpowders. A constituent of commercial dental preparations and scented dusting powders.

Other name Florentine iris.

Above *The rhizome of the Florentine iris is dried to make orris root powder.*

CAUTION All parts of the plant are harmful if eaten – the powdered root causes vomiting. May cause skin irritations.

CRUCIFERAE/BRASSICACEAE
Isatis tinctoria
Woad

History and traditions Woad was the source of the blue body paint of the ancient Britons, described by Pliny and other Roman writers. Although largely replaced by indigo, from the subtropical *indigofera* species, in the 1630s and then by synthetics at the end of the 19th century, a factory producing dye from woad existed in England until the 1930s.

Description A hardy biennial (or short-lived perennial if flower heads are cut before seeding), it grows on a taproot, from 50 cm –1.2 m (20 in–4 ft) tall. In the first year it produces a rosette of ovate leaves, from which branching stems with lanceolate leaves topped by racemes of yellow flowers grow in summer, followed by pendulous black seeds.

Habitat/distribution Indigenous to Europe and western Asia, introduced elsewhere. Found on chalky (alkaline) soils in sunny, open sites.

Growth Grow in humus-rich, moist but well-drained soil, in full sun. Propagated by seed sown in containers in spring, maintaining a temperature of 13–18°C (55–64°F) or in autumn for overwintering in a cold frame. Does not flourish in the same ground for more than a few years.

Parts used Leaves – dried, fermented and also powdered for use as a dye. Leaves and roots – dried for Chinese herbal preparations.

USES Medicinal Traditionally a wound-healing herb, as well as a dye, it has long been used in Chinese herbal medicine and recently discovered to have antiviral properties.

General The leaves yield a very fast blue dye.

JUGLANDACEAE
Juglans regia
Walnut

History and traditions The walnut tree has been valued since ancient Greek times for its medicinal properties and many uses. It was known to the Romans as a fertility symbol and Pliny was the first to give directions for making it into a dye for restoring grey hair to brown – a use which lasted into the 20th century.

Description A variable deciduous tree, growing to about 30m (99ft), it has pinnate leaves, with 7–9 ovate leaflets. Male catkins and female flowers are followed by dark green fruits, each containing a wrinkled brown nut.

Habitat/distribution Native to south eastern Europe, Asia, China and the Himalayas, widely introduced elsewhere.

Growth Walnut trees require deep, rich soil and a sunny position.

Parts used Leaves, bark, fruit, oil.

USES Medicinal Infusions of the leaves are taken internally as a digestive tonic and applied externally for cuts, grazes and skin disorders, such as eczema. Decoctions of the inner bark are used for constipation and of the outer nut rind for diarrhoea.

Culinary The nuts are included in many dishes. Oil from the seeds is popular for salads, especially in France.

Cosmetic An infusion of the nut rind is said to make a hair restorer.

CUPRESSACEAE
Juniperus communis
Juniper

History and traditions From biblical times juniper has symbolized protection, and there are many references to people using it for shelter. "Elijah went a day's journey into the wilderness and came and sat down under a juniper tree" (I Kings 19:4). In medieval Europe a fire of juniper wood was burned to discourage evil spirits and protect from plague – and it was thought that felling a tree would bring a death in the family within a year. Its medicinal properties were recorded by the ancient Greek and Roman physicians. Culpeper recommended it, among many other uses, as "a counter-poison, resister of the pestilence and excellent against the biting of venomous beasts". It is famous as a flavouring ingredient of gin – the English word being an abbreviation of "Holland's Geneva" as gin was first known, from the Dutch word for juniper, *jenever*.

Description A hardy, coniferous, evergreen shrub or small tree, 2–4 m (6–13 ft) tall, of upright or prostrate form with needle-like leaves. The small, spherical fruits, borne on the female plants, are green at first, and take two years to ripen to blue-black.

Related species Various junipers were used medicinally by Native Americans, including *J. virginiana*, which produces the extremely toxic red cedar oil. *J. sabina* has poisonous berries and should not be confused with those of *J. communis*.

Habitat/distribution Widely distributed in the northern hemisphere of Europe, Asia and North America on heaths, moors and mountain slopes. Those grown in warmer regions, with longer,

Above *Unripened juniper berries.*

sunnier summers, such as the Mediterranean, have sweeter more aromatic berries.

Growth Tolerant of most soils. For berry production grow female plants in a sunny position. Propagated by heel cuttings in late summer, or by seed sown in containers under cover in spring or autumn.

Parts used Fruits – collected from wild plants by beating them from the bushes on to ground-sheets, for use fresh, dried or for distillation of the volatile oil.

USES Medicinal The berries have antiseptic, anti-inflammatory and digestive properties and are thought to be helpful for rheumatism, gout, arthritis and colic.

Culinary Juniper is added to pickles, chutneys, sauces, marinades, meat and game dishes, pâtés and sauerkraut.

General Used to flavour gin. Oil is used in cosmetics and perfumery.

CAUTION The berries are not given to patients with kidney disease, or to pregnant women, as they are a uterine stimulant.

LAURACEAE

Laurus nobilis

Bay

History and traditions This is the plant from which the victor's crown of laurels was made – the Latin name is from *laurus* (praise) and *nobilis* (renowned or noble). It was dedicated to Apollo, Greek god of music, healing, light and truth, and many superstitions arose as to its powers. In the writings of Theophrastus there is a reference to the custom of keeping a bay leaf in the mouth to prevent misfortune and by Roman times it had gained a reputation for preventing lightning strikes – the emperor Tiberius always wore a laurel wreath on his head during thunderstorms as a precaution. Bay trees were also thought to purify the air where they grew. During a plague epidemic, the Roman emperor Claudius moved his court to Laurentium, named after the bay trees that grew there, because of the protection they would provide. Introduced to Britain from the Mediterranean, the sweet bay tree brought its

reputation with it. Writing in the 17th century, Culpeper said of it, "Neither witch nor devil, thunder nor lightning will hurt a man where a bay tree is." A wreath of bay leaves was the traditional garnish for the boar's head, centrepiece of the Yuletide feast.

Description An evergreen shrub, or small tree, 3–15 m (10–50 ft) tall, it has aromatic dark-green, glossy ovate leaves. Clusters of small creamy-yellow flowers, opening from tight round buds, appear in spring, followed by purple-black berries.

Related species *L. n.* 'Aurea' is an attractive cultivar with golden-yellow foliage.

Habitat/distribution Native to southern Europe, the Mediterranean and North Africa, introduced and widely grown in other warm temperate regions.

Growth Grow in fertile, reasonably moist but well-drained soil in a sheltered, sunny position. Although frost-hardy, it needs winter protection when immature; and foliage is sometimes damaged by severe frosts and cold winds. Propagated by semi-ripe cuttings in summer.

Parts used Leaves – fresh or dried. Essential oil.

USES Medicinal Bay is not widely used in modern herbal medicine. But studies carried out in the late 1980s on the ability of herbs to inhibit bacterial growth showed bay to be one of the most effective.

Culinary A first-rate culinary herb, a bay leaf is always included in a *bouquet garni,* and adds flavour to marinades, casseroles, stews, soups and dishes requiring a long cooking time. Also used to flavour sweet sauces and as a garnish for citrus sorbets.

Above *Bay leaves for culinary use have a more agreeable, less bitter flavour when dried.*

Below *A standard bay tree in a pot.*

Decorative bay

The Romans embellished their houses with branches of bay for the festival of Saturnalia, celebrated between 17–23 December, to coincide with the winter solstice. With Christianity, bay became a symbol of eternal life, as did other evergreens, and was once widely used as a decoration for homes and churches during the Christmas season. The aromatic, dark-green leaves make it ideal for festive decorations today:

- Bay leaves make an impressive and welcoming wreath for the front door. Push them into a base of floral foam, in a circular holder, and decorate with sprays of golden cupressus, fir cones, shiny red apples and ribbon.
- A glass bowl filled with floating candles surrounded by bay leaves makes a spectacular, fragrant table-centre.
- A mophead bay (tree-form standard), studded with baubles, makes an attractive alternative to a fir Christmas tree.

LABIATAE/LAMIACEAE

Lavandula

History and traditions The Romans are said to have scented their bathwater with lavender (the Latin name is from *lavare,* to wash) and its inimitable fragrance has ensured its lasting popularity. But its medicinal and insecticidal properties were recognized early and have been largely vindicated since. In 1387 at the court of Charles VI of France all the cushions were stuffed with lavender both for its pleasant scent and to deter insects. It was an essential ingredient of "Four Thieves' Vinegar", which is supposed to have given immunity to those who robbed the bodies of plague victims, and William Turner had the idea "that the flowers of Lavender quilted in a cap and dayly worne are good for all diseases of the head that come of a cold cause and that they comfort the braine very well" (*A New Herball,* 1551). In the early years of this century, René Gattefosse, one of the founders of aromatherapy, discovered the powers of lavender when his badly burned hand was healed after it had been immersed in neat essential oil of lavender. And since then, modern scientific research has established the antiseptic, antibacterial properties of this herb.

Description and species Lavender has been cultivated for so long that accurate identification is not always easy, and most of those grown in gardens are hybrids or cultivars. There are three important groups of lavenders (but this by no means provides a definitive list or complete explanation of lavender nomenclature):

1. *L. angustifolia* (common lavender, English lavender) – Has small purple flowers, grows to 60–90 cm (2–3 ft), and is said to be effective for medicinal purposes. It has many attractive cultivars, which may not have the same degree of medicinal qualities, but are probably more suitable for fragrant, culinary and decorative purposes. These include *L. a.* 'Hidcote' – with a neat, erect habit and strongly scented, deep violet flowers, 30–60 cm (1–2 ft). *L. a.* 'Munstead' is more compact, 30–45 cm (12–18 in), with paler, purple flowers. *L. a.* 'Alba Nana' is a dwarf, white-flowered cultivar, 15–30 cm (6–12 in). There are also some pink-flowered cultivars, such as *L. a.* 'Rosea'.
2. *L.* x *intermedia* are hybrids of *L. angustifolia* and *L. latifolia* and include *L.* x *intermedia* 'Grappenhall', which has long spikes of lavender-blue flowers, and *L.* x *intermedia* 'Twickel Purple', with shorter, bushier flowers.
3. *L. stoechas* (French or Spanish Lavender) – This is a species that is also considered to have medicinal value – and was probably the type of

lavender known to the Greeks and Romans. It has short, fat spikes of dark-purple flowers, topped by butterfly wing bracts, and grows from 30–90 cm (1–3 ft).

Habitat/distribution Lavender is native to the Mediterranean and Middle East, introduced and widely grown elsewhere.

Growth Requires a very well-drained soil and plenty of sun. Lavenders hybridize easily; most do not come true from seed and they are best propagated from heel cuttings taken in mid- to late summer. *L. angustifolia* and cultivars are hardy, so are *L.* x *intermedia* and cultivars. *L. stoechas* is frost-hardy. (Some other species of lavender are tender or half-hardy).

Parts used Flowers – fresh or dried, and the essential oil.

USES Medicinal Infusions of the flowers may be applied as a compress to ease headaches, and are sometimes taken internally (made weak) for anxiety and nervous exhaustion. As an embrocation an external stimulant and antiseptic.

Above left Lavandula angustifolia *'Hidcote'.*

Above right Lavandula angustifolia *'Munstead'.*

Lavandula stoechas

Essential oil (diluted in a carrier oil) is applied to sunburn, burns and scalds, or used as a massage oil for tension headaches, migraine and muscular aches and pains. Inhaling the fragrance of flowers or oil can be very calming, anti-depressive and may help relieve insomnia. The oil is applied to prevent and relieve insect bites and discourages head lice when applied to the comb.

Culinary Flowers are used to flavour sugar for making cakes, biscuits, meringues, ice-creams and desserts. They can be added to vinegar, marmalade or jam, or cooked (tied in a muslin bag) with blackcurrants or soft fruit mixtures.

Cosmetic Infusions of fresh flowers make a fragrant hair rinse, or they can be tied in bags to scent bathwater. Drops of essential oil are also added to baths or included in home-made beauty preparations. Lavender oil is widely used in commercial perfumery.

Aromatic Flowers are dried for pot-pourri and scented sachets.

Above *Dried lavender is a traditional filling for scented sachets.*

Top left Lavandula x intermedia *'Twickle Purple'.*

Top right Lavandula stoechas *subsp.* pedunculata *with purple sage in the background.*

Centre right Lavandula angustifolia *'Rosea'.*

Lavender sachets

The flowers have been used for centuries to scent clothes and deter moths and insects.

• **To make them from your own lavender:**
First dry the flowers by cutting them, with long stalks, as soon as they are fully open, on a dry day. Tie with raffia or string, in small bunches and hang up in a warm, dry place, with the heads suspended in paper bags – to keep off dust and catch petals as they fall. When fully dry – this will take about a week, depending on humidity and air temperature – rub the petals off the heads.

• **To make the sachets:**
Cut circles of muslin, or any fine see-through fabric, put a small handful of dried lavender in the centre, gather up to form a bundle and fasten at the neck with an elastic band. Finish with a ribbon.

LABIATAE/LAMIACEAE
Leonurus cardiaca
Motherwort

History and traditions In ancient Greece, this herb was first given to pregnant women to calm their anxieties, which is the origin of its common name. The generic name, *Leonurus,* refers to the plant's supposed resemblance to a lion's tail, but the specific name, *cardiaca,* comes directly from the Greek word for heart because of its widespread use in former times for treating heart palpitations and afflictions. *Macer's Herbal*, 1530 goes further, giving it supernatural powers against wicked spirits.

Description A tall, hardy, strong-smelling perennial, growing to 1.2 m (4 ft), it has square, hollow stems, with deeply lobed, prominently veined leaves, set opposite each other. The mauve-pink, double-lipped flowers appear in the upper leaf axils throughout summer. Widely grown in herb gardens for its attractive foliage.

Habitat/distribution Indigenous to Europe and western Asia. Introduced elsewhere. Found on roadsides and waste grounds on light, calcareous soils.

Growth Grow in moist but well-drained soil in a sunny position. Propagated by seed sown in spring, or by division in spring or autumn.

Parts used Flowering tops – dried for use in infusions, liquid extracts and tinctures.

USES Medicinal Research has shown that this herb does have a beneficial and calming effect on the heart, and is mildly sedative. It also has antibacterial and antifungal properties – but despite its original usage, origins and name, it is not to be given to pregnant women in modern herbal medicine.

UMBELLIFERAE/APIACEAE
Levisticum officinale
Lovage

History and traditions Lovage has been cultivated since the time of Pliny as a seasoning and digestive herb, but has somehow failed to capture popular imagination, and has attracted neither stories nor superstitions. The Greeks and Romans chewed the seed to aid digestion, a practice followed by Benedictine monks of the Middle Ages, and Parkinson refers to its "hot, sharpe, biting taste" and culinary usage: "The Germans and other Nations in times past used both the roote and seede instead of Pepper to season their meates and brothes and found them as comfortable and warming" (*Paradisi,* 1629). An earlier writer mentions lovage as a bath herb for its aromatic scent: "This herbe for hys sweete savoure is used in bathe" (*The Gardener's Labyrinth,* 1577). Its former medicinal uses, referred to by many herbalists, included "expelling stone of the kidneys and bladder". All of which remains broadly valid today, though the leaves are used in preference to seeds and roots for culinary purposes.

Description A hardy herbaceous perennial, growing on deep fleshy roots to 2 m (6 ft) in height, it has glossy, deeply divided leaves with a spicy, celery-like scent, and umbels of undistinguished, dull-yellow flowers in summer, followed by small seeds.

Habitat/distribution Lovage probably originated in Europe, but has long been widely cultivated throughout the world. Rarely found in the wild, except as a garden escape.

Growth A vigorous, spreading plant, it will grow in most soils (except heavy clay), but thrives best in well-manured, moist but well-drained soil, in sun or partial shade. Propagated from seed sown in spring or by division of the roots in spring or autumn.

Parts used Leaves – fresh or dried for culinary use and infusions; stems – fresh; roots, seeds – dried for use in decoctions and other medicinal preparations; essential oil – distilled from leaves and roots.

USES Medicinal It is taken internally for digestive disorders, colic and flatulence, also for cystitis and kidney stones. Lovage tea was formerly taken for rheumatism.

Culinary Leaves are used to flavour soups, stews, meat, fish or vegetable dishes; young shoots and stems are eaten as a vegetable (like braised celery) and may be candied like angelica; seeds are added to biscuits and bread. Lovage cordial used to be a popular drink.

Aromatic Essential oil is used in perfumery, and as a flavouring in the food and drink industry.

Above *The flawless white blooms of* Lilium candidum *were considered a symbol of purity and innocence from earliest times and were closely associated with the Madonna.*

LILIACEAE

Lilium candidum

Madonna lily

History and traditions *L. candidum* appears in Cretan frescoes dating to 3000 BC and has been cultivated since at least 1500BC for its scent and its medicinal properties. The flawless white flowers ensured its place as a symbol of purity and its association with the Virgin Mary and it is frequently featured in religious paintings. Shakespeare makes endless references to the whiteness of the "unsullied lily", the "sweetest and the fairest", and Gerard records that the white lily was known as "Juno's Rose" because it grew from her milk, which had fallen to the ground (*The Herball,* 1597). He also writes of using the bulbs of the white lily, mixed with honey, to heal wounds, but makes it clear that a variety of lilies were used for medicinal purposes. He ascribes many virtues to the "red lily", including its ability to remove facial wrinkles, and reveals that Pliny recommended it as a corn remover. *L. candidum* is little used in modern herbalism, but the flowers are cultivated commercially in some countries for their perfumed essence, and it remains a traditional herb garden ornamental.

Description A perennial, growing from a scaly bulb to 1–1.5 m (3–5 ft) in height, it has stiff, erect stems with small, lance-shaped leaves and racemes of 5–20 fragrant, trumpet-shaped, white flowers, tinged inside with yellow, and with bright-yellow anthers. It is the only lily to have overwintering basal leaves.

Habitat/distribution A Mediterranean native, widely cultivated in other countries.

Growth Can be difficult to grow and requires conditions that suit it exactly before it will flourish. All lilies dislike heavy, clay soils.

Parts used Roots, flowers – juice is used fresh in ointments and herbal preparations.

USES Medicinal It has soothing, healing properties and is used externally (but only rarely) for burns, skin inflammations and disorders.

Growing Madonna lilies

Lilium candidum is one of the oldest flowering plants in cultivation and the flowers are strongly fragrant. These beautiful white lilies can be unpredictable to grow, but the following guidelines will help to ensure success:

- Plant bulbs immediately they arrive. If there is a delay, keep it as short as possible, and meanwhile store bulbs in peat in a dark place – if exposed to light, they soften and deteriorate quickly.
- Good drainage is essential. Prepare soil thoroughly. Dig out to two spades' depth, put in a layer of coarse gravel, then replace the top soil, mixing it with sand and leaf mould. Alternatively, plant in containers, putting in a layer of coarse gravel, topped by a gritty, open compost (soil mix).
- Plant in early autumn (preferably at the beginning of September, no later than October, in the northern hemisphere).
- Bulbs should be only just covered – unlike other lilies, which require deeper planting.
- Once planted and established, do not disturb – Madonna lilies resent being moved.

LINACEAE

Linum usitatissimum
Flax

History and traditions Flax has been an important economic crop since 5000 BC, valued for its fibre in making linen and for its oil-producing seeds. The Bible has many references to linen woven from flax, and both seeds and cloth have been found in Egyptian tombs. In medieval Europe it was promoted by the Emperor Charlemagne for the health-giving properties of the seeds and there are detailed descriptions in old herbals of the process of turning flax stems into fibre for making clothing, sheets, sails, fishing nets, thread, rope, sacks, bags and purses. Many superstitions have arisen, especially concerning its cultivation: sitting on the seed bag three times and facing east before planting, ringing church bells on Ascension Day and jumping over midsummer fires were all thought to ensure a good crop – and of course the seeds provided protection from witchcraft. It has also been a valued medicinal herb since Hippocrates recommended it for colds and is still used in herbal medicine.

Description A hardy, slender annual, about 90 cm–1.2 m (3–4 ft) in height. It has narrow, lanceolate, greeny-grey leaves and simple, five-petalled, pale-blue flowers borne in summer, followed by spherical seed capsules, rich in oil.

Related species *L. usitatissimum* is thought to be a cultivar of *L. bienne* in the distant past. Tall cultivars have been developed for textiles, and shorter ones for the production of seeds for linseed oil. *L. perenne,* grown in Europe and North America, is a perennial species. *L. catharticum* (purging flax) is a white-flowered annual with oval leaves; used homeopathically to treat bronchitis and piles.

Habitat/distribution Probably of Middle Eastern origin, it is widely distributed in temperate and subtropical regions of the world and found as a cultivated escape on sunny waste ground and waysides.

Growth Grow in dry, sandy soil in full sun. Propagated from seed sown *in situ* – does not respond well to transplantation. Sow in late spring or early summer.

Parts used Whole plant – used fresh in infusions, cut after flowering for fibre; seeds – collected when ripe – dried for use whole, in infusions and other preparations, or extracted for linseed oil.

USES Medicinal Seeds are used as laxatives, in infusions and macerations for coughs, sore throats and gastric disorders, in poultices for boils and abscesses. Linseed oil contains linolenic essential fatty acids, necessary for many bodily functions, as well as vitamins A, B, D, E, minerals and amino acids. It is said to be helpful for many disorders, including rheumatoid arthritis, menstrual problems and skin complaints.

General Stem varieties are soaked ('retted') in water to release fibres for making linen cloth. Linseed oil from seed varieties is one of the most important commercial drying oils, used in paints, varnishes and putty.

Other name Linseed.

CAUTION Contains traces of prussic acid, but this plant is not thought to be harmful unless taken in very large doses. Some *Linum* species have been suspected of poisoning stock in Australia. Artists' linseed oil should not be taken medicinally.

CAMPANULACEAE

Lobelia inflata
Indian tobacco

History and traditions This North American plant gained its common name from the local tradition of smoking it to relieve chest infections and asthma. It was enthusiastically adopted by early settlers as a cure-all for a wide variety of complaints and promoted in the early 19th century by the herbalist Samuel Thomson, who was charged with murder after one of his patients died from its effects. The generic name *Lobelia* (there are over 350 species) is named after the Flemish botanist Matthias de L'Obel (1538–1616). The specific name is a reference to the inflation of the seed capsule as it ripens.

Description A hardy annual, 20–60 cm (8–24 in), it has hairy stems and ovate leaves, toothed at the edges. Inconspicuous flowers borne in terminal racemes are pale violet, tinged with pink, followed by two-celled, oval capsules.

Habitat/distribution Native to North America.

Growth Grow in rich, moist soil in full sun or partial shade. Propagated by seed.

Parts used Whole plant – cut when flowering.

USES Medicinal It contains alkaloids that increase the rate of respiration and induce vomiting. It is also an expectorant and emetic. In small doses it dilates the bronchioles and is used for conditions such as bronchitis, asthma and pleurisy, but is for use by qualified practitioners only. Used in proprietary cough medicines.

CAUTION Poisonous and can cause fatalities.

CAPRIFOLIACEAE
Lonicera

History and traditions Various species of honeysuckle have been used since ancient Greek times for their medicinal properties. Dioscorides is quoted by Gerard as recommending the seeds for "removing weariness" and "helping the shortness and difficulty of breathing" and a syrup of the flowers for diseases of lung and spleen. Little used medicinally today, honeysuckle keeps its place in the herb garden as a fragrant climber, memorably described by Shakespeare as the "lush woodbine" and "sweet honeysuckle" which "over-canopied" Titania's bower (*A Midsummer Night's Dream*). The name honeysuckle comes from the old practice of sucking the sweet nectar from the flowers.

Description and species The two species that were most often recommended for medicinal purposes are *L. periclymenum* (woodbine, wild or common honeysuckle) – Has whorls of very fragrant, creamy-white to yellow, tubular two-lipped flowers, followed by red berries. *L. capri-folium* (Italian, Dutch or perfoliate honey-suckle) – Has upper leaves surrounding the stem and creamy-white to pink flowers. Both are fully hardy, *L. periclymenum* grows to 7 m (23 ft), *L. caprifolium* to 6 m (19 ft). *L. japonica* (Japanese honeysuckle) – Often has violet-tinged white flowers, which are followed by black berries.

Habitat/distribution Widely distributed in the northern hemisphere, in woodlands, hedgerows and rocky hillsides.

Growth Grow in fertile, well-drained soil in full sun or partial shade. Propagated by seed sown in late summer to autumn in containers and overwintered in a cold frame, or by semi-ripe cuttings taken in summer. Prune out straggly or overgrown branches.

Parts used Flowering stems.

USES Medicinal *L. caprifolium* and *L. periclymenum* were formerly used for their expectorant, laxative properties. *L. japonica* (*jin yin hua*) is used in traditional Chinese medicine for clearing toxins from the system.

CAUTION Honeysuckle berries are poisonous.

Top right *A cultivar of* Lonicera periclymenum.

Above *Honeysuckle flowers contain sweet-tasting nectar.*

Growth It grows best in moist to wet soil in sun or partial shade and is propagated by seed or division in autumn or spring. It often self-seeds and spreads rapidly. It is classed as a noxious weed in some countries and imports of the plants and seeds are forbidden.

Parts used The whole flowering plant – it is used fresh or dried in infusions, decoctions and ointments.

USES Medicinal It has been found in modern research to have antibacterial properties and is still recommended by modern herbalists for diarrhoea and dysentery as well as for haemorrhages and excessive menstrual flow. It is said to be soothing, when applied externally, to sores, ulcers, skin irritations and eczema.

LABIATAE/LAMIACEAE
Lycopus europaeus
Gipsyweed

History and traditions This herb is said to have gained its name because gipsies used it to stain their skins darker. It was also effective in dyeing fabrics and at one time was a valuable medicinal plant.

Description A perennial, mint-like herb, but with no aroma, it grows on a creeping root-stock to about 60cm (2ft) in height. It has single stems with opposite, deeply-toothed, pointed leaves and whorls of small, pale-mauve flowers in the leaf axils in late summer.

Related species *L. virginicus* (Virginia bugle weed) also known sometimes as gipsyweed is native to North America. It is a very similar plant to *L. europaeus* and shares the same properties.

Habitat/distribution *L. europaeus* is a native of Europe and western Asia.

Parts used Whole flowering plant – it can be used fresh or dried.

USES Medicinal Gipsyweed is reputed to have sedative properties. It was used in the past for the control of internal haemorrhages, including excessive menstrual bleeding; and it was also thought to be effective for other conditions such as an overactive thyroid.

General It produces a black or dark-grey dye on woollen and linen fabrics.

LYTHRACEAE
Lythrum salicaria
Purple loosestrife

History and traditions The name loosestrife is connected to this herb's old reputation for soothing ill-behaved animals. Gerard, in his *Herball* of 1597, writes of it "appeasing the strife and unruliness which falleth out among oxen at the plough, if it is put about their yokes". As it was also supposed to drive away flies and gnats, perhaps this was the reason for its calming influence. The generic name is from the Greek, *luthron*, meaning blood, a reference to the colour of the flowers, and it was considered by herbalists of old to be effective against internal haemorrhages, excessive menstruation and nosebleeds. John Lindley, in *Flora Medica*, 1838, refers to it as "an astringent, which has been recommended in inveterate cases of diarrhoea," and it was often used in his day to treat outbreaks of cholera.

Description Purple loosestrife is a perennial which grows on a creeping rhizome with erect stems reaching 60cm–1.5 m (2–5 ft) in height. It has long, lanceolate leaves and crimson-purple flowers borne on whorled spikes in mid to late summer.

Habitat/distribution A European native, it occurs widely in Asia, northern Africa, Australia and North America. It is usually found in wet and marshy places.

Lythrum salicaria

MALVACEAE
Malva sylvestris
Mallow

History and traditions The common mallow was cultivated by the Romans as a medicinal and culinary herb, the leaves being cooked as a vegetable and seeds added to salads and sauces. By the 16th century it had gained a reputation as a cure-all, commended for its gentle purgative action, a process that was thought to rid the body of disease. But its culinary uses remained paramount, and herbals and household books of the period are full of recipes for cooking the leaves with butter and vinegar, making "suckets" (candy) of the stalks, and, even more imaginatively, cutting and rolling them into balls and passing them off as green peas (*Receipt Book of John Nott*, 1723). The generic name, *Malva*, meaning soft, refers to the downy leaves and soothing properties of the plant.

Description A perennial, growing from 45–90 cm (18 in–3 ft), it has much-branched erect or trailing stems, with 5–7-lobed leaves, and pink, five-petalled flowers, streaked with darker veins, borne throughout summer.

Related species *M. moschata* (musk mallow) grows to 90 cm (3 ft) and has purple-spotted stems, heart-shaped basal leaves and narrowly divided upper leaves, both scented faintly with musk. Solitary pale pink flowers are borne in the leaf axils. It is weaker in effect than *M. sylvestris*, but with the same uses. The closely related plant *Althaea officinalis* (marsh mallow) is considered more medicinally effective than either of the *Malva*.

Habitat/distribution Native to Europe, western Asia and North America. Found at field edges, embankments and on waste ground, in porous soils and sunny situations.

Growth Grow in well-drained to dry soil, in a sunny position. Propagated by seed sown in the spring or by division of the roots in late autumn or early spring.

Parts used Leaves, flowers – used fresh or dried. Fruits (seed capsules) – picked unripe and used fresh.

USES Medicinal Mallow contains a high proportion of an emollient mucilage, reduces inflammation and calms irritated tissues. Infusions are taken internally for coughs, sore throats and bronchitis. The leaves are applied externally as a poultice for skin complaints, eczema and insect bites. It is also an expectorant herb and large doses can have a laxative effect.

Culinary Young leaves and shoots contain vitamins A, B^1, B^2 and C and can be eaten raw in salads or cooked as vegetables. Unripe fruits are sometimes added to salads.

Other name Common mallow.

Above *A flower of the musk mallow,* Malva moschata.

Malva moschata *f.* alba

SOLANACEAE
Mandragora officinarum
Mandrake

History and traditions Mandrake has attracted more stories and superstitions than almost any other herb – perhaps because of its hallucinogenic properties, coupled with its strange appearance and forked roots, fancifully thought to resemble the human form. Closely related to *Atropa belladonna* and *Hyoscyamus niger* (henbane), it contains the toxic alkaloids atropine and hyoscyamine and has been used since the ancient Greek and Roman period as a powerful sedative, when it was first found to deaden the pain of surgery. An early introduction to Britain, it features in many Anglo-Saxon medicinal texts and was mentioned by Turner in 1551 for its anaesthetic properties. Just holding the fruit (mandrake apple) in the hand was said to be a cure for insomnia. At the end of the 19th century it became an official hom-eopathic preparation but is rarely used today and retains its place as a "herb" because of its historical interest.

Description A low growing perennial, 15 cm (6 in) in height, it has a basal rosette of broad, oval, veined and rough-textured leaves, with wavy margins, which start erect and spread flat as they grow. Clusters of bell-shaped, greenish-white flowers, flushed with purple, arise from the base and are followed by large, spherical green fruits ripening to yellow.

Habitat/distribution Originated in the Himalayas and southeast Mediterranean, introduced into western Europe, Britain and other countries. Found on sunny sites, in poor, sandy soil.

Above *Mandrake fruits, sometimes known as the devil's apples.*

Growth Although hardy to -10°C (14°F), mandrake needs protection from prolonged cold and wet weather in winter. Grow it in a sheltered, sunny spot such as at the base of a wall, or in a rockery, in well-drained, reasonably fertile soil. It resents disturbance once properly established and is propagated by seed in autumn, root cuttings in winter.

Parts used Roots.

USES Medicinal Formerly used as a sedative and painkiller.

Other name Devil's apples.

CAUTION A dangerously poisonous plant, which should not be used internally or externally. Can be fatal. Subject to legal restrictions in some countries.

Mandrake myths

One of the most popular superstitions about mandrake was that its unearthly shrieks, when pulled up, sent people mad if it did not kill them. As Shakespeare records: "And shrieks like mandrakes torn out of the earth/That living mortals hearing them run mad" (*Romeo and Juliet*) or "Would curses kill as doth the mandrakes groan" (*Henry VI*, Part 2).

An ingenious way to avoid death on digging up the plant was to tie it to a hungry dog, with a dish of meat just out of reach, so that he would die instead as he pulled the root from the ground. Once dug up it could be handled with impunity.

The fancied resemblance of the roots to people meant they were sought after as amulets to protect from witchcraft and bring prosperity. This led to a lucrative scam (scathingly described by Turner in his *New Herbal*, 1551) of false mandrake manikins being sculpted out of bryony roots and sold to the gullible at high prices. The sensible Gerard, too, dismissed the mandrake myths with these words: "There have been many ridiculous tales brought up of this plant, whether of old wives or runnegate surgeons, or phisick mongers, I know not, all which dreames and old wives tales you shall from henceforth cast out your bookes of memorie" (*The Herball,* 1597).

LABIATAE/LAMIACEAE

Marrubium vulgare

Horehound

History and traditions This herb has been known since Egyptian times, and is thought to be one of the bitter herbs which the Jews consumed at the Feast of the Passover. The generic name *Marrubium* comes from the Hebrew word *marrob* – a bitter juice. Its reputation as a remedy for coughs and colds goes back to at least Pliny's time. Several 16th-century herbalists, including Gerard, use almost the same words to recommend a syrup of the fresh leaves in sugar as a "most singular remedie against the cough and wheezing of the lungs." Horehound candy was still being made to the old recipes well into the 20th century.

Description A hardy perennial growing to 60 cm (2 ft), with erect, branched stems and greeny-grey, soft, downy, ovate leaves, bluntly toothed, arranged opposite. Whorls of small, white, tubular flowers appear in the leaf axils in summer.

Related species *Ballota nigra*, although from a different genus, is known as black horehound, and was once used for similar purposes. However, it has an unpleasant smell and is considered less effective and has been superseded by *M. vulgare*.

Habitat/distribution Native to Europe, northern Africa and Asia, introduced elsewhere. Found on dry grassland, pastures and field edges.

Growth Grows in any soil and prefers a sunny situation. Propagated from seed sown in spring, but can be slow to germinate, or by division of roots in spring. (It is under statutory control as a weed in Australia and New Zealand.)

Parts used Flowering stems – fresh or dried.

USES Medicinal Taken as an infusion for coughs, colds and chest infections. Combined with hyssop, sage or thyme to make a gargle for sore throats. Made into cough candy.

Above Marrubium vulgare, *or white horehound.*

Top right and right Ballota nigra, *or black horehound, is considered inferior as a medicinal plant.*

Horehound recipes

• Horehound and ginger tea – for a cold
15 g/1/2 oz fresh horehound leaves
1 tsp powdered ginger
600 ml/1 pint/ 2 1/2 cups boiling water
honey to taste
Put the roughly chopped leaves into a pot or jug with the ginger, pour in the boiling water, cover and leave to infuse for 5–7 minutes. Strain off the leaves and sweeten with honey to taste before drinking.

• A Recipe for horehound candy from *The Family Herbal* (1810)
Boil some horehound till the juice is extracted. Boil up some sugar to a feather height, add your juice to the sugar, and let it boil till it is again the same height. Stir it till it begins to grow thick, then pour it on to a dish and dust it with sugar and when fairly cool cut into squares. Excellent sweetmeat for colds and coughs.

MYRTACEAE
Melaleuca alternifolia
Tea-tree

History and traditions Tea-tree was named by Captain Cook's crew when, following local custom, they drank it as a tea substitute. The Australian Aborigines used it medicinally and in World War II tea tree oil, distilled from *M. alternifolia,* was used in Australia as a powerful germicide. It has since gained ground in herbal medicine for its remarkable healing properties.

Description Melaleucas are half-hardy to tender evergreen trees, 15–40 m (50–130 ft), with thin, peeling, corky bark, narrow, pointed, leathery leaves and bottle-brush-shaped flowers.

Related species Several species of melaleuca are used medicinally. *M. leucadendron* produces distilled cajuput oil, which has similar uses to eucalyptus oil. *M. viridiflora* is the source of niaouli oil used in perfumery.

Habitat/distribution Native to Australia and Malaysia, introduced in other tropical regions. Often found in swampy areas.

Growth *M. alternifolia* is half-hardy, *M. leucadendron* is tender. Grow in moisture-retentive to wet soil, in full sun. They must be grown as conservatory plants in cool, temperate regions. Propagated by seed or by semi-ripe cuttings.

Parts used Essential oil.

USES Medicinal Strongly antiseptic, antibacterial and antifungal, tea-tree oil is used diluted in a carrier oil and applied externally for healing cuts, burns, stings, insect bites, acne, and athlete's foot. It is also said to be effective against warts, verrucas and head lice eggs when used undiluted.

General A constituent of many pharmaceutical and cosmetic industry products.

LEGUMINOSAE/PAPILIONACEAE
Melilotus officinalis
Melilot

History and traditions Once popular as a strewing herb for the haylike scent it develops when drying, due to the coumarin content, the name of the genus means "honey-lotus" for the sweet smell of its nectar and it is very attractive to bees. It was used in the Greek physician Galen's time, AD 130–201, as an ingredient of ointments for reducing swellings, tumours and inflammations, and appears in later European herbals for similar purposes. Culpeper adds that "the head often washed with the distilled water of the herb and flowers is good for those who swoon, also to strengthen the memory".

Description An erect, straggly biennial, 60 cm–1.2 m (2–4 ft) high, it has ridged, branched stems with trifoliate leaves and narrow ovate leaflets. The yellow, honey-scented flowers are borne in slender axillary racemes, from midsummer to autumn.

Habitat/distribution Native to Europe and Asia, naturalized in North America. Found in dry, chalky embankments, wastelands and roadsides.

Growth Grow in well-drained to dry soil, in a sunny situation. Propagated by seed sown in spring or autumn.

Parts used: Flowering stems – dried for use in herbal preparations.

USES Medicinal An aromatic herb with sedative, anti-inflammatory properties, it was formerly

Melilotus officinalis

taken as an infusion or tincture for insomnia, tension headaches and painful menstruation, and applied externally to wounds and skin inflammations. It also has a reputation for helping to prevent thrombosis and has been used for bronchial complaints and catarrh.

Aromatic It has insect-repellent properties and the dried herb is sometimes included in scented sachets for the wardrobe.

Other names Yellow melilot and yellow sweet clover.

CAUTION Dicoumarol, a powerful anticlotting factor, is sometimes produced if fermentation takes place during the drying process; it is poisonous in excess and harmful to sheep and cattle.

LABIATAE/LAMIACEAE
Melissa officinalis
Lemon balm

History and traditions Lemon balm has been cultivated as a bee plant for over 2000 years, bunches being put into empty hives to attract swarms. It is thought that that the leaves contain the same terpenoids as found in glands of honey bees. The Arab physicians of the 1st and 2nd centuries are credited with introducing it as an antidepressant medicinal herb. John Parkinson wrote that "the herb without question is an excellent help to comfort the heart" (*Paradisi*, 1629) and many of the old herbalists refer to it as driving away "all melancholy and sadnesse". It has been taken as a calming tea, for its gently sedative effects ever since. Unsubstantiated stories of regular drinkers of balm tea living into their hundreds have been perpetuated by modern herbal writers.

Description A vigorous, bushy perennial, 30–80 cm (12–32 in) in height, it has strongly lemon-scented, rough-textured, ovate, toothed leaves. Inconspicuous clusters of pale-yellow flowers appear in the leaf axils in late summer.

Related species *M. officinalis* 'Aurea' is a cultivar with bright gold and green variegated leaves. It is inclined to revert as the plant matures, so cut back after flowering to encourage new variegated growth. *M. officinalis* 'All Gold' has bright-yellow foliage, but should be planted in partial shade, as it is inclined to scorch in a position where it receives full sun.

Habitat/distribution Native to southern and central Europe, introduced and widely distributed in northern temperate zones. Often found as a garden escape.

Growth Grows in any soil in sun or partial shade. Spreads and self-seeds freely. The easiest method of propagation is by division in spring. The species can be grown from seed, but cultivars must be vegetatively propagated.

Parts used Leaves – best used fresh, as scent and therapeutic properties are lost when dried and stored; essential oil – distilled from leaves.

USES Medicinal Lemon balm has sedative, relaxing, digestive properties and infusions are taken internally for nervous anxiety, depression, tension headaches and indigestion. It also has insect-repellent properties, is antiviral and antibacterial and is applied externally, in infusions, poultices or ointments, for sores, skin irritations, insect bites and stings. The essential oil is used in aromatherapy for anxiety states.

Culinary Fresh leaves add lemon flavour to salads, soups, sauces, stuffings, poultry game and fish dishes, desserts, cordials, liqueurs and wine cups.

Above centre Melissa officinalis *'All Gold'*.

Above Melissa officinalis *'Aurea'*.

Recipes for lemon balm

- **Chicken lemon balm**
  Use handfuls of the fresh leaves to stuff the body cavity of a chicken, and sit it on a further bed of leaves before roasting it, to keep flesh moist and impart a subtle lemon flavour.

- **Orange and lemon balm salad**
  Snip fresh lemon balm over peeled, thinly sliced oranges, sprinkled with a mixture of fresh orange and lemon juice, sweetened with honey.

- **Carmelite cordial**
  Lemon balm was one of the chief ingredients of Carmelite water, which also included lemon peel, nutmeg and angelica root – said to be the favourite tipple of the Holy Roman Emperor, Charles V (1500–1558).

LABIATAE/LAMIACEAE

Mentha

History and traditions The Romans made great use of mint for its clean, fresh scent, putting it in their bathwater and making it into perfumes. The poet Ovid describes scouring the boards with "green mint" before setting out food for the gods, and Pliny has been attributed with the view that the smell of mint stirs up the taste buds "to a greedy desire of meat". This conflicts with a modern study, carried out in the United States in 1994, which found that the smell of mint helped alleviate hunger pangs of subjects on diets. The Romans introduced spearmint to Britain, where it soon became established and is mentioned in medieval texts and plant lists. In the late 16th century, Gerard talks of its popularity as a strewing herb "in chambers and places of recreation". It is now one of the most popular herbs worldwide.

Habitat/distribution Mints are widely distributed in Europe, Asia and Africa, introduced and naturalized elsewhere, often found in damp or wet soils. Cultivated as a crop in many countries including Europe, North America, the Middle East and Asia.

Species There are 25 species of mint in all, but they are often variable and individual plants can be difficult to identify because mints hybridize readily both in the wild and under cultivation. The following hardy perennials are top favourites for the herb garden. Most are vigorous, the variegated ones less so, and spread rapidly on creeping rootstocks.

M. x *gracilis* 'Variegata' (gingermint) – Has gold and green variegated, smooth, ovate leaves, scented with a hint of ginger, and grows 30 cm–1 m (1–3 ft) tall. Tiny, pale lilac flowers are borne in whorls in the leaf axils in mid- to late summer.

M. x *piperita* (peppermint) – Has dark-green (often tinged with purple) lanceolate to ovate, toothed leaves and whorls of pale pink flowers in summer. It grows to 30–90 cm (1–3 ft) tall. Peppermint is a variable hybrid of *M. spicata* and *M. aquatica*, sometimes assigned two different forms as black peppermint, *M.* x *piperita* f. *rubescens*, and white peppermint, *M.* x *piperita* f. *pallescens*. It is rich in menthol, which gives it the characteristic cooling, slightly numbing, peppermint taste, but is too dominant for general cookery and is used to flavour sweet foods.

M. x *piperita citrata* (eau-de-Cologne mint) (Bergamot, Lemon or Orange Mint) – A cultivar with large, toothed, ovate leaves, 30–90 cm

(1–3 ft) tall. The scent is reminiscent of lavender water with citrus overtones.

M. pulegium (pennyroyal) – There are creeping (to 10 cm/4 in) and upright (to 40 cm/16 in) varieties. Both have small, elliptic to ovate, usually smooth-edged leaves, and prolific, distinctive whorls of mauve flowers in the leaf axils. The high concentration of pulegone gives it a pleasantly antiseptic smell, but it is toxic in very large doses and abortifacient.

Mentha requienii (Corsican mint) – A creeping, mat-forming mint, 2.5–10 cm (1–4 in), with very small, smooth and shiny, rounded leaves and tiny, mauve flowers in summer. It makes a good ground cover herb for a damp, shady situation.

M. spicata (spearmint) – This has bright-green, wrinkled, finely toothed leaves, with a fresh, uncomplicated, not too overpowering mint scent. White or pale-mauve flowers are borne in terminal spikes in mid- to late summer. A popular culinary mint, used since the time of the Romans; 30–90 cm (1–3 ft) tall.

M. suaveolens 'Variegata' (variegated applemint also known as pineapple mint) – This has soft, downy, cream and white variegated leaves and a sweet, apple scent. 30–90 cm (1–3 ft) tall. Pineapple mint makes a very attractive ornamental and container plant.

M x villosa f. *alopecuroides* (Bowles' Mint) – Formerly known as *M. rotundifolia* var. 'Bowles', it is in fact a variety of a sterile hybrid between *M. spicata* and *M. suaveolens*. The rounded, ovate, toothed leaves are greyish-green; soft and downy, lilac-pink flowers are borne in terminal, branched spikes. It is popular for culinary use, the clean mint flavour has overtones of apple.

Growth Mints grow best in rich, damp soil and partial shade. Most do not come true from seed or are sterile hybrids. They are easily propagated by division or by taking root cuttings from early spring, throughout the growing season.

Parts used Peppermint, spearmint – leaves, essential oil; pennyroyal, gingermint, Bowles' mint, eau-de-Cologne mint – leaves.

USES Medicinal Peppermint can be taken as a tea for colds and to aid digestion. The essential oil has decongestant, antiseptic, mildly anaesthetic effects and is used externally, often as an inhalant to relieve colds, chest infections, catarrh and asthma. It also has insect-repellent properties. Excess use may cause allergic reactions. Pennyroyal is taken internally as an infusion for indigestion and colic. Stimulates the uterus and is not given to pregnant women. Toxic in large doses. An insect-repellent plant,

used to deter ants when planted in the garden. Spearmint can be taken as a tea for digestive disorders; it is less pungent than peppermint and a non-irritant.

Culinary Spearmint and Bowles' mint are used in sauces, mint jelly, to flavour yoghurt as a savoury dip or side dish, in salads, rice dishes, meat, fish or vegetable dishes, as a garnish, to flavour herb teas and drinks. Peppermint is used to flavour sweets and chocolates, icings, cakes, desserts, ice creams, cordials and as a tea. Gingermint leaves may be floated in fruit cups and summer drinks. Pennyroyal is traditionally used to flavour black pudding (an old name is pudding grass).

Aromatic Any of the fragrant mints, dried or as essential oils, may be added to pot-pourri, fresh leaves or essential oils are added to baths, cosmetics and fragrant household preparations.

General Essential oils are used in food, pharmaceutical and cosmetic industries.

Top, from left to right Mentha x gracilis *(gingermint)*; M. x piperita *f.* rubescens *(black peppermint)*; M. x piperita *f.* citrata *(eau-de-Cologne mint)*; M. pulegium *(pennyroyal)*; M. requienii *(Corsican mint)*; M. spicata *(spearmint)*.

Above right M. suaveolens *'Variegata' (variegated applemint)*.

Above Mentha suaveolens, *or apple mint.*

LABIATAE/LAMIACEAE
Monarda didyma
Bergamot

History and traditions The Monarda or horse-mint genus is named after Nicholas Monardes, author of *Joyfull Newes Out of the Newe Found Worlde,* 1577. Native Americans used several monarda species medicinally. *M. didyma* became known as "Oswego tea" after the Oswego river, near Lake Ontario, where it was found growing by European settlers and its refreshing taste made it a good tea substitute. The scent of both flowers and leaves is similar to the Bergamot orange, which is how it gained its popular name.

Description An aromatic, hardy perennial, 40–90 cm. (16 in–3 ft) in height, it has soft, downy, greyish-green, ovate leaves, with serrated edges, and red or mauve flowers in solitary terminal whorls in late summer.

Related species: *M. fistulosa* (wild bergamot) is closely related and has purple flowers – also called "Oswego tea". There are many attractive hybrids including 'Cambridge Scarlet' (above) and 'Croftway Pink'.

Habitat/distribution Native of eastern North America, found in damp woodlands, introduced and widely grown elsewhere.

Growth Grow in humus-rich, damp soil. Prefers partial shade, but tolerates full sun if kept moist. Prone to mildew in dry conditions. Propagated by division or by seed sown in spring.

Parts used Leaves, flowers – fresh or dried.

USES Medicinal Taken as a digestive tea.

Culinary Fresh leaves are added to wine cups, fruit drinks and to oriental tea to give it an "Earl Grey" flavour.

Aromatic Flowers are dried for pot-pourri.

RUTACEAE
Murraya koenigii
Curry leaves

History and traditions The Indian name for the leaves of this shrub is "curry patta" and they have long been used in southern India and Sri Lanka in local dishes as well as for their medicinal properties. Curry leaves are not widely used in the West because much of the flavour is lost on drying – but they are imported fresh by wholesalers for use in the food industry.

Description An aromatic, more or less deciduous shrub, growing to 6 m (20 ft) in height, it has bright-green pinnate leaves, with smooth, ovate leaflets. Clusters of small white flowers are followed by edible berries, which turn from green to purple as they ripen.

Habitat/distribution Native to southern India and Sri Lanka, introduced and grown in all tropical zones, found in rich soils.

Growth A tender, tropical shrub, it is grown in humus-rich, moist but well-drained soil in sun or partial shade. Propagated by seed or cuttings.

Parts used Leaves – picked and used fresh; seeds; essential oil – distilled from leaves.

USES Medicinal Contains alkaloids with anti-fungal activity. The juice of the leaves contains vitamin C and minerals, including calcium, phosphorus and iron and is used as a herbal tonic for digestive disorders. Eating the fresh leaves is reputed by some to help prevent the onset of diabetes and to encourage weight loss. Juice of the crushed berries, mixed with lime juice, is applied to insect bites and stings.

Culinary Used in Indian cookery to flavour a variety of dishes, including curries and chutneys.

General Essential oil used in the soap industry.

MYRICACEAE
Myrica gale
Bog myrtle

History and traditions This was once an indispensable plant in much of northern Europe for its many household uses. It was used as a hops substitute to flavour beer and improve its foaming; the fruits were boiled to produce wax for making candles; it made a yellow dye; and its insect-repellent properties meant it was often put into mattress stuffings, which gave it the former name "flea wood".

Description Hardy, deciduous shrub, growing to 1.5 m (5 ft), it has narrow, bright-green, oval to lanceolate leaves and yellowish-green flowers, borne in dense catkins in late spring to early summer, followed by flattened yellow-brown fruits.

Habitat/distribution Native to North America, northwest Europe and northeast Siberia, found in wet heathlands.

Growth Prefers a damp, acid soil (tolerates boggy conditions) and partial shade, but can be grown in full sun. Propagated by separating suckers, by cuttings, or by seed sown in spring or autumn.

Parts used Leaves – dried.

USES Aromatic Strongly insecticidal. Dried leaves can be added to insect-repellent mixtures and sachets.

Other name Sweet gale.

MYRISTICACEAE
Myristica fragrans
Nutmeg / Mace

History and traditions Nutmeg and mace are different parts of the same fruit of the nutmeg tree. The scent of the nutmeg has variously been compared with myrrh and musk. The common name comes from "nut" and the Latin, *muscus,* or old French, *mugue,* meaning musk. Nutmegs were probably introduced to Europe in about the 6th century by Arab or Indian traders, who brought them to the Mediterranean from the Far East. The Portuguese set up a trade monopoly in this valuable spice at the beginning of the 16th century after taking possession of the Moluccan islands where the trees grew. This was taken over by the Dutch, who limited cultivation of nutmeg to the Moluccas and continued the monopoly into the 19th century. Today nutmeg is widely grown in tropical regions, with Indonesia and the West Indies as leading world producers. It has been used over the centuries as a medicinal tonic and culinary spice, its hallucinogenic properties have long been recognized and it acquired a reputation as an effective aphrodisiac.

Description An evergreen dioecious tree, usually 9–12 m (29–39 ft) but occasionally up to 15–20 m (49–65 ft) tall, with glossy, pointed oval leaves and inconspicuous pale yellow flowers, male in clusters with numerous fused stamens, the female solitary or in groups. Brownish-yellow globular fruits each containing an ovoid brown seed (nutmeg), surrounded by a shredded crimson aril (mace), do not appear before the tree is 9–10 years old.

Habitat Indigenous to Molucca (Maluku) and Banda islands, now widely grown in Indonesia, Sri Lanka, India, the West Indies, Brazil and elsewhere in tropical zones, frequently on volcanic soils in areas of high humidity.

Growth A tender, tropical tree, grown in sandy, humus-rich soil. Prefers shade or partial shade. Propagated by seed or cuttings. May be grown as a conservatory or hothouse plant in temperate regions, with a minimum temperature of 18°C (64°F) and a humid atmosphere.

Parts used Seed (nutmeg), aril (mace) – dried and used whole or powdered; volatile oil distilled from fruits; fatty oil compressed from mace (nutmeg butter, mace oil).

USES Medicinal Nutmeg is taken internally, in small doses, for digestive disorders, nausea and insomnia. Applied externally for toothache and rheumatic aches and pains.

CAUTION Nutmeg should always be used sparingly. It contains a toxic compound, myristicin, whose chemical structure has similarities with mescaline, and can cause hallucinations and convulsions even in moderate doses.

Above *The outer shell splits to reveal the nutmeg seed, enclosed in a red aril.*

Above left *Whole nutmeg fruits on the tree.*

Culinary Both nutmeg and mace are ground or grated and used in a wide range of sweet and savoury dishes, but mace is less pungent. Added to soups, sauces, milk and cheese dishes, meat and vegetable dishes, biscuits, fruit cakes, puddings and drinks.

General Volatile oil and fatty oil (nutmeg butter) are used in the pharmaceutical and perfumery industries.

Top *Nutmegs with outer covering of mace (dried aril).*

Centre *Ground nutmeg.*

Right *Dried nutmeg seeds.*

UMBELLIFERAE/APIACEAE

Myrrhis odorata

Sweet cicely

History and traditions The Latin name refers
to the sweet aniseed smell of this herb, said to
resemble myrrh – *Myrrhis* comes from the Greek
word for fragrance. It is probable that the "wild
chervil", or "sweet chervil", referred to in old
herbals is the same plant. *The Leech Book of
Bald*, c. AD 950, gives a salve of wild chervil
for the treatment of tumours. It was used as
a medieval strewing herb, and the roots and
leaves were cooked as a pot-herb. Recent
scientific research has found that compounds
isolated from *M. odorata* are related in chemical
structure to podophyllotoxin, the highly
poisonous active ingredient of *Podophyllum
peltatum* (American may-apple). However, this
does not mean that *M. odorata* as a whole
plant, or the isolated compounds, have the
same high level of toxicity as *Podophyllum
peltatum*, and it is not thought to be harmful
as a culinary herb.

Description A vigorous, hardy, herbaceous
perennial, with a strong taproot, grows 90
cm–1.2 m (3–4 ft) tall, with hollow stems and
soft, downy fernlike leaves. Compound umbels
of white flowers appear in late spring, followed
by large, distinctively beaked and ridged brown
fruit. The whole plant is pleasantly scented.

Habitat/distribution Native to Europe,
introduced and naturalized in other temperate
regions, found in hedgerows and field edges
often in shady positions.

Growth Grows under any conditions, in sun or
shade, but said to prefer moist, humus-rich soil.

Myrrhis odorata

An invasive plant which self-seeds and spreads
rapidly and is virtually impossible to eradicate
once established. Propagated by seed, after
vernalization, or by division of roots in spring.

Parts used Leaves – fresh.

USES Culinary Traditionally used as a
sweetening agent and flavouring for stewed
soft fruits and rhubarb. Leaves also make a
pretty garnish for sweet and savoury dishes.

MYRTACEAE

Myrtus communis

Myrtle

History and traditions This sweet-smelling
shrub from the Mediterranean was dedicated to
Venus, goddess of love. Myrtle has long been
associated with weddings and included in bridal
bouquets. After the ceremony, sprigs were often
planted as cuttings in the garden of the marital
home or beside the front door, to ensure peace
and love within, which happy states would be
lost if the plants died or were dug up.

Description An evergreen shrub, to 3 m
(10 ft) tall, with glossy ovate to lanceolate
leaves, dotted with oil glands. Fragrant white
five-petalled flowers, which appear in early
summer, are followed by blue-black berries.

Related species *M. communis* subsp. *tarentina*
is a compact variant, 90 cm–1.5 m (3–5 ft) tall.

Habitat/description Native to the
Mediterranean region and western Asia,
introduced and widely grown elsewhere.

Growth Frost-hardy, but does not tolerate
prolonged cold spells and waterlogged soils.
Propagated by semi-ripe cuttings in late summer.

Parts used Leaves – fresh for culinary use, dried
for infusions; fruits – fresh or dried; volatile oil.

USES Medicinal Myrtle has antiseptic, decongestant properties and it is taken internally, in
infusions, for colds, chest infections, sinusitis
and for urinary infections.

Culinary The leaves and fruits are used in
Middle Eastern cookery with lamb and game.

General The essential oil is used in perfumery,
cosmetic and soap industries.

VALERIANACEAE

Nardostachys grandiflora
Spikenard

History and traditions This plant was an ingredient of the expensive perfumed unguents of the Romans and ancient Eastern nations, prized for the durability of its scent. It was the "very costly" ointment of spikenard with which Mary wiped the feet of Jesus (John 12:3–5). The Indian name *jatamansi* refers to the bearded appearance of the fibrous rhizomes, or "spikes", which were supposed to resemble ears of corn.

Description An erect perennial, 25–30 cm (10–12 in) in height, with a fibrous rootstock, crowned by nearly basal lanceolate leaves and from which stems bearing pale-pink flowers in terminal clusters arise.

Habitat/distribution Native to the Himalayas from Kumaon to Sikkim and Bhutan, at altitudes of 3,000–5,000 m (9,800–16,400 ft), where the atmosphere is cool and moist, on poor, stony soil and rocky ledges.

Growth Fully hardy; grow in gritty, well-drained, poorish soil, in a rockery or similar situation, but provide midday or partial shade and plenty of moisture to keep roots cool.

Parts used Roots – dried for use in decoctions; volatile oil distilled from roots.

USES Medicinal: An important herb in Ayurvedic medicine for over 3,000 years, the root has antiseptic, bitter tonic properties and is soothing to the nervous system. It is used for insomnia and as a gentle tranquillizer, for menopausal problems, respiratory disorders and in the treatment of intestinal worms.

LABIATAE/LAMIACEAE

Nepeta cataria
Catmint

History and traditions This herb often proves irresistible to cats. It is mildly hallucinogenic, which could be the attraction, but another theory is that the plant has overtones of tomcats' urine and is associated with courtship behaviour. It is also said to be hated by rats. Chewing the root is reputed to make humans aggressive, and one old British story recalls that a reluctant hangman used it to give him courage to carry out his duties. There are references to its medicinal properties in old herbals, it was occasionally used for flavouring, and found its way into herbal tobaccos, but it does not seem to be widely used today, except perhaps to make toys for cats.

Description A hardy perennial, 30–90 cm (1–3 ft) tall, it has coarse-textured, ovate, grey-green leaves, with serrated edges. Pale-mauve flowers in terminal or axillary whorls are borne from midsummer to autumn. The whole plant has a strong, antiseptic, mintlike odour, similar to pennyroyal.

Related species The hybrid *N*. x *faassenii*, commonly known as *N. mussinii*, is a more attractive plant, frequently grown in herb gardens for its prolific, soft-blue flowers, which bloom over a long period. It has no medicinal virtues – but cats have been observed rolling in it.

Habitat/distribution Occurs in Europe, Asia and Africa, introduced and naturalized in North America and temperate zones. Found in moist, calcareous soils, on roadsides, in hedgerows and field edges.

Above Nepeta x faassenii.

Growth Catmint prefers moist soil and a sunny position. Propagated by root division in spring or autumn or by cuttings in summer.

Parts used Leaves and flowering stems – dried or fresh.

USES Medicinal Catmint lowers fever, increases perspiration and is mildly sedative. It is sometimes taken as an infusion for feverish colds, influenza, nervous tension, anxiety and gastric upsets, or applied externally to cuts and bruises.

Culinary It makes a stimulating, minty tea.

Household The dried herb is used to stuff toys for cats.

Other names Catnip and catnep.

Nepeta cataria 'Citriodora', a lemon-scented cultivar.

Nepeta cataria

LABIATAE/LAMIACEAE

Ocimum basilicum

Basil

History and traditions A native of India, basil first came to Europe in the 16th century. In India, where it is known as *tulsi,* it is sacred to the god Vishnu, thought to protect from misfortune and is planted in temple gardens and offered at Hindu shrines. A basil leaf was traditionally placed on the chest of a corpse, after the head had been washed in basil water, and in other Eastern cultures it became a funeral herb, planted or scattered on graves. But basil has a mass of conflicting associations. As Culpeper remarked, "This is the herb which all authors are together by the ears about and rail at one another (like lawyers)" (*The English Physician*, 1653). The Greeks and Romans thought it represented hate and misfortune, and that shouting abuse at it encouraged it to grow. In some later European cultures it represented sympathy and the acceptance of love. In Crete, it stood for love washed with tears, taking a middle line. There was no agreement on its properties either, in former times. Some said it was poisonous, others that it was health-inducing. In 16th-century Britain it

was appreciated for its scent. Thomas Tusser listed it as a strewing herb and John Parkinson wrote, "The ordinary Basil is in a manner wholly spent to make sweete or washing waters among other sweete herbs, yet sometimes it is put into nosegays" (*Paradisi*, 1629). Today it is among the most popular and widely grown of culinary herbs.

Description A much-branched half-hardy annual, to 20–60 cm (8–24 in) tall, with soft, ovate, bright-green leaves and whorls of small white flowers, borne in terminal racemes in mid to late summer.

Related species Basils are extremely variable. Even within the same species, the pungency and flavour vary considerably, according to the composition of their volatile oils, which depends on soil, climate and growing conditions. They also hybridize easily under cultivation and many that are sold commercially are not recognized as distinct varieties or cultivars by botanists. *O. b.* 'Dark Opal' is a reliable cultivar with purple leaves and bright cerise-pink flowers. *O. b.* 'Purple Ruffles' has large crinkled, purplish leaves with curly edges and makes a vigorous bush. *O. b.* var. *crispum* (curly basil) has coarse, curled, dark-green leaves, and is sometimes known as "Neapolitana". *O. b.*

'Genovese' has soft but broader leaves than the species, is strongly aromatic, and frequently offered as a culinary variety – popular in pesto sauce. *O. b.* var. *minimum* (bush basil, Greek basil) is very compact and bushy, growing 15–30 cm (6–12 in) tall, and has small, but pungent leaves and tiny white flowers. *O. sanctum* (holy basil, tulsi) is a shrubby perennial, 45–60 cm (18–24 in), with green, slightly hairy, ovate leaves and thin white to pale-mauve flower spikes. Other cultivars with interesting flavours include *O. b.* 'Thai', often used in oriental cuisines; and *O. b.* 'Cinnamon', which is from Mexico, about 30–60cm (12–24in) high, with pink flowers and a distinctive cinnamon scent.

Habitat/distribution Native to India and the Middle East, naturalized in parts of Africa and other tropical and subtropical regions, introduced and widely grown elsewhere.

Growth Basil requires well-drained, moist, medium-rich soil and full sun. It is propagated from seed, which must be sown after any danger of frost in cool regions. In cold, wet, northern summers it may need to be grown on under glass, but flourishes as a container plant and should be kept outside in hot, dry spells to develop the best flavour.

Parts used Leaves – fresh, essential oil.

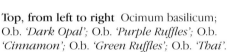

Top, from left to right Ocimum basilicum; O.b. *'Dark Opal';* O.b. *'Purple Ruffles';* O.b. *'Cinnamon';* O.b. *'Green Ruffles';* O.b. *'Thai'.*

Right Ocimum basilicum *var.* minimum.

Below right Ocimum sanctum.

USES Medicinal Has antidepressant, antiseptic, soothing properties. The fresh leaves are rubbed on insect bites and stings to relieve itching, made into cough syrups with honey and taken as an infusion for colds. The leaves or essential oil are used in steam inhalations as a decon-gestant for colds; diluted essential oil makes an insect repellent or massage oil for depression and anxiety.

Culinary The leaves do not retain their flavour well when dried and are better used fresh in a wide range of Mediterranean dishes. They have an affinity with tomatoes and aubergines (eggplant), and add a distinctive fragrance to ratatouille, pasta sauces, pesto sauce and pizza toppings. Fresh basil should be added towards the end of the cooking process so that its fragrance is not lost. Basil is a good choice for planting in a kitchen herb garden.

Aromatic The essential oil is used in aromatherapy and as a perfumery ingredient.

Other name Sweet basil.

Pesto sauce

The traditional way of making this sauce was to pound the ingredients with a pestle and mortar – the name is from the Italian *pestare* (to pound or crush), but it is much easier to make in a food processor or blender.

Serves 4
50 g/2 oz fresh basil leaves
25 g/1 oz fresh parsley
2–3 cloves of garlic
8 tbs extra virgin olive oil
25g/1 oz grated Parmesan cheese
salt and freshly ground black pepper,
 to taste

Put all the ingredients, except the cheese and seasoning, into a liquidizer (food processor or blender) and blend until smooth. Pour the mixture into a bowl, stir in the grated Parmesan and season to taste with salt and pepper. Keep refrigerated for up to a couple of weeks.

CAUTION Essential oil should not be used during pregnancy.

ONAGRACEAE
Oenothera biennis
Evening primrose

History and traditions An American native, the evening primrose was introduced to Europe in 1619, when seeds were brought to the Padua Botanic Garden in Italy. Although it had some place in the folk medicine of Native Americans, in Europe it was used more as a culinary than a medicinal herb – leaves were put into salads and roots cooked as vegetables. It came to prominence after modern research in the 1980s established that oil from the seeds contains GLA, or gamma-linolenic acid, an unsaturated fatty acid which assists the production of prostaglandins, hormone-like substances, which act as chemical messengers and regulate hormonal systems. It is not related to the primrose, but takes its name because it opens in the evening.

Description An erect biennial, up to 1.5 m (5 ft) tall, with a thick, yellowish taproot and a rosette of basal leaves from which the flowering stems arise. These have alternate, lanceolate to ovate leaves, and are topped by bright, yellow flowers, which open at night to release their fragrance and are pollinated by moths. Downy pods follow, containing tiny seeds.

Habitat/distribution Originated in North America, introduced and naturalized throughout Europe and in temperate zones. Found on poor, sandy soils, waste ground and embankments, as a garden escape.

Growth Grow in open, sandy soil in a warm sunny position. This plant self-seeds freely once established. Propagated from seed sown in autumn or spring.

Parts used Seeds – pressed to produce oil.

USES Medicinal The oil is thought to benefit the immune system and regulate hormones. It is taken internally for premenstrual tension, menopausal problems, allergies, skin complaints, such as eczema and acne, and to counteract the effects of excess alcohol. It may also be helpful for high blood pressure, arthritis and multiple sclerosis.

Cosmetic The fresh flowers are often made into face masks to improve skin tone. The oil is an ingredient in commercial cosmetics and pharmaceutical products.

OLEACEAE
Olea europaea
Olive

History and traditions There is evidence that the olive tree has been cultivated north of the Dead Sea since 3700–3600 BC. Known to the Egyptians, it was always prized for the quality of the oil from the fruits. The Romans called the tree "*olea*", from *oleum,* meaning oil, the Greek word being *elaio*. The olive branch has been a symbol of peace and reconciliation since the biblical story of the dove returning with a sprig of olive in its beak to Noah's Ark after the flood had subsided.

Description An evergreen tree, 9–12 m (29–40 ft) tall, it has pale-grey bark and pendulous branches, with smooth, leathery, grey-green, lanceolate to oblong leaves. Creamy-white flowers are borne in short panicles in summer, followed by green, ripening to dark-purple fruits, known as drupes.

Habitat/distribution Native to the Mediterranean region, introduced in warm temperate regions of Africa and Asia.

Growth Requires well-drained to dry soil and full sun. Although frost-hardy, it can be grown outside successfully only in Mediterranean climates. Propagated by seed sown in autumn or by semi-ripe cuttings in summer.

Parts used Leaves – dried for use in infusions and other herbal preparations; fruits – harvested in autumn and winter, by beating them from

ASTERACEAE/COMPOSITAE
Onopordum acanthium
Scotch thistle

History and traditions This is thought to be the thistle that is the national emblem of Scotland, dating from the time of James III of Scotland (d. 1488). It is also the emblem of the ancient, knightly Order of the Thistle, inaugurated by James V of Scotland, 1513–1542. Some bizarre claims were made for the properties of this plant. Pliny recommended it for baldness . and Dioscorides as "a remedy for those that have their bodies drawne backwards".

Description A hardy biennial, growing on a strong taproot, the spiny, toothed, dark-green leaves have a striking cobweb-effect pattern of white veins, with purple thistle-head flowers rising on long stems to 1.5 m (5 ft).

Habitat/distribution Occurs in the Mediterranean, Europe and Asia, introduced and naturalized in other countries.

Growth Grows in most conditions, but flourishes in reasonably fertile, well-drained soil and a sunny position. Propagated by seed sown in autumn or spring.

Parts used Leaves, stems, flowers.

USES Medicinal Scotch thistle is rarely used medicinally currently.

Culinary The whole plant is edible if not very palatable. Young stems can be boiled as a vegetable; flower receptacles are said to be substitutes for artichoke hearts.

Horticultural It is widely grown as a herb garden ornamental.

Other names Cotton thistle and woolly thistle.

the trees on to groundsheets; oil – pressed from the fruit. Extra-virgin, cold-pressed oil, extracted without heat or chemical solvents, has the best flavour and properties.

USES Medicinal The oil is monounsaturated and its consumption is thought to help lower cholesterol levels and blood pressure, reducing risk of circulatory diseases. Leaves are antiseptic and astringent, taken internally in infusions for nervous tension and high blood pressure and applied externally to cuts and abrasions. The oil

Top *The olive tree is slow growing and often attains a great age, revealed by the girth of the trunk.*

Above *An olive grove in Extremadura, Spain.*

is thought to be helpful when taken internally for constipation and peptic ulcers.

Culinary The fruits of the olive tree are eaten as appetizers, made into *tapenade* spread, added to salads, sauces, bread, pizzas, pasta and many other dishes. The oil is used in salad dressings, sauces, mayonnaise and as a general cooking oil.

LABIATAE/LAMIACEAE

Origanum

Origanum majorana
Sweet marjoram

Description A half-hardy perennial, often grown as an annual, 60 cm (2 ft) tall, with elliptic pale greyish-green leaves, arranged opposite. The small, white, sometimes pinkish, flowers grow in distinctive knotlike clusters, surrounding the stems, giving it the once popular name "knotted marjoram".

Habitat/distribution *O. majorana* originated in the Mediterranean and Turkey and is widely naturalized in northern Africa, western Asia, parts of India and introduced to many places elsewhere. Found on dryish but often nutrient-rich soils in sunny positions.

Growth Requires well-drained, but not too dry, fertile soil and full sun. Propagated by seed sown in spring, after danger of frost in cool temperate regions.

Parts used Leaves, flowering stems – fresh or dry; essential oil distilled from leaves.

USES Medicinal A warming, relaxing herb with antiseptic properties, taken internally as an infusion for nervous anxiety, insomnia, tension headaches, colds and bronchial complaints, digestive complaints and painful menstruation. Dilute oil is applied externally for muscular aches and pains, sprains and stiff joints.

Culinary It is said to have the most delicate flavour of the marjorams and is widely used in Italian, Greek and Mediterranean cookery, especially in pasta sauces, pizza toppings, tomato sauces, vegetable dishes, and to flavour bread, oil and vinegar.

Aromatic Dried flowering stems add fragrance to pot-pourri. Essential oil is used in food and cosmetic industries.

History and traditions *Origanum* means "joy of the mountains" from the Greek *oros*, a mountain, and *ganos*, brightness or joy. According to legend, Aphrodite, Greek goddess of love, found this herb in the depths of the ocean and took it to the top of a mountain where it would be close to the sun's rays. Ever since it has been associated with the return of sunshine and warmth, with love and the banishing of sorrow. It found a place at both weddings and funerals, being used to crown newly married couples and to provide comfort to mourners. The tradition arose that planting origanum on a grave ensured a happy afterlife for the deceased and Gerard recommends it for those "given to over much sighing" (*The Herball*, 1597). It is one of the most versatile herbs, variable in form, and valued through the centuries for its fragrant, medicinal and culinary properties alike.

Species and nomenclature There is often confusion about the difference between oregano and marjoram. Marjoram is the common English name for the *Origanum* species, but *O. vulgare*, or 'wild marjoram', is widely known as 'oregano' and *O. onites* is sometimes called 'Greek oregano'. To complicate

Above Origanum onites, *or pot marjoram, surrounded by Golden marjoram.*

Origanum vulgare, *popularly known as oregano, adds flavour to Mediterranean cookery.*

matters further, there are many hybrids among cultivated marjorams, which are difficult to identify and variously named.

Origanum onites
Pot marjoram

Description A hardy to frost-hardy perennial, 60 cm (2 ft) tall, with hairy stems, and ovate-elliptic, bright-green, downy leaves. White or purple flowers are borne in dense clusters in mid to late summer.

Habitat/distribution Native to the Mediterranean and the Middle East, introduced and widely grown in other countries. Grows on light, well-drained soils and open hillsides.

Growth Grow in well-drained soil in a sunny position. Propagated by division or by cuttings taken in summer.

Parts used Leaves, flowers – fresh or dried.

USES Culinary The flavour is less delicate than *O. majorana,* and not as pungent and aromatic as most *O. vulgare,* but it makes an acceptable alternative for similar culinary uses.

Aromatic Dried leaves and flowers are added to pot-pourri.

Origanum
onites

Origanum vulgare
Oregano

Description A variable, bushy, hardy perennial, to 60 cm (2 ft), with aromatic, ovate, dark-green leaves and panicles of pink to purple tubular flowers in summer. It usually has a higher proportion of thymol than *O. majorana,* giving it a more thyme-like scent. The composition of the essential oils and flavour of the plant varies according to soil, sun and general growing conditions. Oregano grown in cooler, wetter regions does not have the same intensity of flavour as that grown in a Mediterranean climate.

Related species There are many attractive, ornamental cultivars of *O. vulgare,* which are not suitable for culinary and medicinal use but are frequently grown in herb gardens, including *O. v.* 'Aureum', a golden marjoram, and *O. v.* 'Polyphant', a variegated marjoram.

Habitat/distribution Native to the Mediterranean, found in dry soils on sunny, open hillsides. Introduced and widely grown in other countries.

Growth Requires well-drained soil and a sunny position. *O. vulgare* is best propagated by division or by cuttings taken in summer – the cultivars must be vegetatively propagated.

Parts used Leaves, flowers – fresh or dried; essential oil distilled from the leaves.

Top Origanum vulgare *'Polyphant' is a variagated cultivar with white flowers.*

Below Origanum vulgare *'Aureum', or golden marjoram, an attractive ornamental.*

USES Medicinal Similar uses to *O. majorana.*
Culinary: Similar uses to *O. majorana.*
Other name Wild marjoram.

CAUTION Marjorams are not given to pregnant women in medicinal doses or in the form of essential oil, as they are uterine stimulants.

ARALIACEA
Panax ginseng
Ginseng

History and traditions Used as a tonic and "vital essence" in Chinese medicine for thousands of years. It was so highly prized for its medicinal properties that emperors set up monopolies and wars were fought over the rights to harvest ginseng. First introduced to Europe as early as the 9th century, it did not catch on until the 1950s when scientific studies discovered that its active principles have a "normalizing" effect on various bodily functions. The name *panax* comes from *pan*, all, and *akos*, a remedy. The Chinese name, from which the word ginseng is adapted, means man root, or like a man. *Panax ginseng* is probably extinct in the wild, but various *Panax* species are cultivated in Asia, China, Russia, Japan, the United States and Britain.

Description A hardy perennial, 70–80 cm (28–31 in) tall, it usually has a forked root, erect stems, with fleshy scales at the base and whorls of palmate leaves, with finely serrated leaflets. Insignificant greenish-yellow flowers are followed by bright red berries.

Related species There are several species of ginseng with similar medicinal properties, and as the plants look very alike they are often confused. These include *P. japonicus*, which grows wild in wooded areas of central Japan; *P. quinquefolius* (American ginseng); *Eleutherococcus senticosus* (Siberian ginseng), which has almost identical properties to the Panax species, but is stronger and considered very beneficial. *P. pseudoginseng* refers to several sub-species found in Asia, from the Himalayas to China.

Habitat/distribution The *Panax* species are native to China, Korea and Japan. Found in damp, cool, woodlands. *Eleutherococcus senticosus* is from Siberia.

Growth For successful cultivation well-drained, sandy loam, with added leaf-mould, is essential. Propagation is from seed, but germination is often erratic.

Parts used Roots – processed from 6–7-year-old plants for use in tablets, extracts, tea and medicinal preparations.

USES Medicinal Ginseng is said to stimulate the nervous and immune systems, improve and regulate hormonal secretion, increase general stamina and strength, lower blood-sugar and blood cholesterol levels. Modern research has not managed to isolate an active principle in this herb which relates to any one of the specific claims made for it. However, it has been found that the combined action of its many constituents has a general tonic effect on the whole body.

Top left Panax ginseng *roots.*

Top right Panax japonicus.

Centre right Eleutherococcus senticosus – *the berries are borne in single clusters at the ends of the stems.*

Right Panax quinquefolius.

CAUTION Should only be taken under qualified medical supervision for short periods. Excess or regular intake may cause headaches, giddiness, nausea, double vision, raised blood pressure and other side effects.

PAPAVERACEAE
Papaver somniferum
Opium poppy

History and traditions Opium, made by lancing the green seed capsule to extract the milky latex, has been used for medicinal purposes since earliest times and the Greek authorities, Theophrastus and Dioscorides, wrote of it in this context. It was probably introduced to Europe by early Arabian physicians, and a cough syrup made from the opium poppy, widely recommended by the Arabian, Mesue, in the 11th century, was adopted as a standard for many centuries following. But as a highly addictive, powerful narcotic, opium caused as many problems as it solved. Opium poppies are now cultivated on a large scale as the source of powerful pain-killing drugs, including morphine and codeine (two of the most important of its 25 alkaloids), as well as to produce the illegal drug, heroin (diamorphine). The flowers are frequently grown in herb gardens as ornamentals.

Description A hardy annual, up to 1.5 m (5 ft) tall, it has oblong, deeply lobed, blue-green leaves. Large, lilac, pink or white flowers, with papery petals, borne in early summer, are followed by blue-green seed pods.

Habitat/distribution Native to south-east Europe, the Middle East and Asia. Introduced elsewhere. Grows on shallow, chalky (alkaline) soils in sunny positions.

Growth Prefers well-drained soil and full sun. Propagated by seed sown in spring, often self-seeds once established.

Parts used Fruits, seeds.

USES Medicinal Proprietary drugs and pharmaceutical products are made from the fruits. Not for home remedies or self-treatment.

Culinary The seeds do not contain any of the alkaloids found in the capsules. They are dried for use whole or ground in breads, biscuits, bakery products and as a garnish. Commercially produced seed is from a subspecies of *P. somniferum*, developed for its seed production.

CAUTION Legal restrictions apply to this plant and its products in most countries.

PASSIFLORACEAE
Passiflora incarnata
Passion flower

History and traditions A plant of tropical and subtropical regions of the Americas, it was imaginatively dubbed "Calvary Lesson" by Roman Catholic missionaries in South America, taking the intricate form of its flower to represent Christ's crucifixion. The three styles are for the nails used on the cross; the five anthers for the five wounds; the corona is the crown of thorns; and the ten sepals are for ten of the twelve apostles – leaving out Peter and Judas Iscariot, who betrayed him. The lobed leaves and tendrils symbolize the hands and scourges of Christ's tormentors.

Description A hardy perennial, climbing plant on a woody stem, to 8 m (26 ft), it clings to its support with axillary tendrils and has deeply lobed leaves and attractive creamy-white to lavender flowers, with purple calyces.

Habitat/distribution Native to tropical regions of North and South America, occurs in Asia and Australia, introduced and grown elsewhere.

Growth Requires well-drained, sandy soil and a sunny position. Propagation is easiest from semi-ripe cuttings taken in summer. Seed requires heat to germinate and can be slow and erratic to grow.

Parts used The whole plant – cut when fruiting and dried for use in infusions and medicinal preparations.

USES Medicinal Has sedative, pain-relieving properties and is taken for nervous conditions and insomnia.

GERANIACEAE
Pelargonium

History and traditions Most scented pelargoniums, often familiarly known as "geraniums", come from South Africa and were introduced to Europe some time in the 17th century. The scented-leafed varieties were very popular in Britain with the Victorians, who grew them as house plants, and in France distilled oil from the "rose-scented" group became an important perfume ingredient in the mid-19th century.

Description and species There are numerous hybrids and cultivars with differing foliage, habits of growth and types of fragrance. It is the leaves that are scented. The flowers, appearing in summer, are virtually unperfumed, smaller and more insignificant than those of regal and zonal pelargoniums, grown as colourful bedding plants. These are some of the most popular scented-leafed pelargoniums:

P. 'Graveolens' – An upright shrubby plant, it grows 60–90 cm (2–3 ft) tall, and has deeply cut, triangular, rough-textured, bright-green leaves and small pink flowers. It grows vigorously and is slightly hardier than most of the others. This is the original "rose geranium", though the scent is much harsher and more spicy than a true rose fragrance, with strong overtones of lemon.

P. odoratissimum – A low-growing, species – 30 cm (1 ft) – with a trailing habit and little white flowers borne on long stems. The soft, rounded, bright-green leaves are wavy at the edges and apple-scented.

P. crispum – Has a neat, upright habit, and grows 60–70 cm (24–28 in) tall. It has pink flowers and clear green, three-lobed, crinkly leaves, which are coarse to the touch and pungently lemon-scented.

P. crispum 'Variegatum' – Is an attractive variegated cultivar, with crisply curled leaves, edged with creamy yellow and the same, strong lemon scent as the species.

P. tomentosum – Is a lovely trailing, or prostrate species, 90 cm–1.2 m (3–4 ft), which makes a good container plant, if grown on a stand and allowed to drape downward. It has small white flowers and soft, downy, grey-green leaves with a strong peppermint fragrance.

P. 'Fragrans' – A small, upright subshrub, 45 cm (18 in) tall, it has clusters of small, greyish-green, rounded leaves, with finely cut, crinkled edges and a smooth, silky texture.

The flowers are white and the foliage pleasantly pine-scented with overtones of nutmeg.

P. 'Lady Plymouth' – An attractive hybrid, 60 cm–1.5 m (2–5 ft) tall, it has triangular, deeply lobed, crisp-textured leaves, with a cream and green variegation, little pink flowers and a citrus fragrance with a hint of rose.

Habitat/distribution Most pelargoniums are natives of South Africa; a few come from tropical Africa, the eastern Mediterranean, the Middle East, India, western Asia and Australia. Cultivated in France, northern Africa and Réunion for essential-oil production.

Growth All are tender and must be grown as conservatory plants in cool, temperate regions, though they are best kept outside in the summer months. A few (including P. 'Graveolens' and P. 'Fragrans') may survive a mild winter in a cold greenhouse. They make good container plants and should be given a gritty, loam-based compost. Cut back in autumn and prune lightly in spring to maintain a neat, bushy habit. Pelargoniums grown outside need free-draining soil and a sunny position. They are easily propagated by softwood cuttings taken in summer.

Parts used Leaves, essential oil – distilled from the leaves.

USES Culinary The pungency of the leaves makes them suitable as flavouring agents, to be removed after cooking rather than being eaten themselves. Leaves of P. 'Graveolens' and P. odoratissimum are best for flavouring ice creams and cakes (put 2–3 leaves in the base of the cake tin before baking) and fruit punches.

Aromatic Dried leaves and essential oil are added to pot-pourri and their strong scents make them effective in insect repellent or anti-moth sachets. "Geranium oil" is used as a commercial flavouring and perfume ingredient and used in aromatherapy.

Other name Scented pelargonium.

Opposite page, far left and top right Pelargonium *'Graveolens'*; below right Pelargonium odoratissimum.

This page, clockwise from top to bottom Pelargonium tomentosum; Pelargonium *'Fragrans'*; Pelargonium *'Lady Plymouth'* Pelargonium crispum.

LABIATAE/LAMIACEAE
Perilla frutescens
Perilla

History and traditions In China, perilla has been a medicinal herb for centuries and it has long been cultivated in the East, from India to Japan, as a culinary herb and for its many economic uses. The leaves produce a sweet volatile oil, the seeds a pressed oil, which is used in similar ways to linseed oil. It has recently become increasingly popular in the West for its culinary uses and as an ornamental garden plant.

Description A half-hardy annual with broadly ovate, deeply-veined leaves, reddish stems and small spikes of white flowers in summer. There are both green and purple-leaved forms.

Related species *P. frutescens* 'Crispa' (pictured below) is a variety with curly-edged leaves.

Habitat/distribution Occurs from the Himalayas to East Asia, naturalized in parts of Europe and North America.

Growth Grows best in deep, rich, moist but well-drained soil, in sun or partial shade. Propagated by seed sown in spring, after frosts in cool temperate regions. Pinch out tips to encourage and maintain bushy plants.

Parts used Leaves – fresh for culinary use, dried for medicinal infusions and decoctions; seeds – dried for decoctions; volatile oil – from leaves; pressed oil – from seeds.

USES Medicinal Used in Chinese herbal medicine for colds and chest infections, nausea, stomach upsets and allergic reactions.

Culinary Leaves and seeds are a popular ingredient in Japanese cookery and add colour and an unusual spicy flavour to salads, seafood and stir-fry dishes.

General Volatile oil is added to commercial food, confectionery and dental products; oil from seeds is used to waterproof paper for umbrellas, in paints and printing inks.

Other names Beefsteak plant and shiso.

Above P. frutescens *'Crispa'*.

UMBELLIFERAE/APIACEAE
Petroselinum crispum
Parsley

History and traditions Petroselinum comes from the Greek name given to it by Dioscorides, *petros selinon*. In the Middle Ages this became corrupted to *petrocilium*, ending up in the anglicized version, by a process of "Chinese whispers" as parsley. The Greeks associated it with death and funerals and according to Homer fed it to their chariot horses, but it was the Romans who took to it as a major culinary herb. Pliny complained that every sauce and salad contained it, and it has remained ubiquitous as a sauce, salad and garnishing herb to this day. Parsley has attracted a mass of silly superstitions. Transplanting it, giving it away, picking it when in love and so on, all foretold disaster. Some said it flourished only where the "mistress is master", others that it would grow only for the wicked, or, conversely, for the honest. Its slowness to germinate when soil is cold led to tales that it had gone seven times to the devil and back, and should be sown on Good Friday to outwit him. *A Grete Herball*, 1539, has some ingenious ideas on how to ensure it is well "crisped" or curly: "Before the sowing of them, stuffe a tennis ball with the seedes and beat the same well against the ground, whereby the seedes may be a little bruised. Or when the

parcelye is well come up, go over the bed with a waighty roller whereby it may so presse the leaves down."

Description A frost-hardy biennial, growing on a short, stout taproot to 30–60 cm (1–2 ft), it has triangular, three-pinnate leaves, curled at the margin. Yellow-green flowers are borne in umbels in its second year.

Related species *Petroselinum crispum* 'Italian', also known as French or flat-leaved parsley, is a larger, hardier plant, growing to 80–90 cm (32 in–3 ft) and has smooth, uncurled three-pinnate leaves. *P. c.* var. *tuberosum*, Hamburg parsley, has small, flat leaves, with a celery-like flavour and is grown for its large roots, which are eaten as a vegetable.

Habitat/distribution
The genus is native to the Mediterranean region of Europe, found in fields and on rocky slopes.

Flat-leaved parsley.

P. crispum has been developed under cultivation and is widely grown as a crop in many countries.

Growth Parsley requires rich, moist but well-drained soil and a sunny position, or partial shade. As leaves coarsen in the second, flowering, year, it is often grown as an annual and is propagated by seed, sown in spring. If sown *in situ* before soil has warmed up, germination may be slow or erratic. For best results, sow in containers, maintaining a temperature of 18–21°C (64–70°F) until seedlings appear. The young plants can then be hardened off to grow outside at lower temperatures.

Parts used Leaves, stems – best fresh or frozen for culinary use as flavour is lost with drying; roots – of 'Hamburg' variety; essential oil – distilled from leaves and seeds.

Above left *Hamburg parsley.*

Above *'Italian' or flat-leaved parsley.*

USES Medicinal Parsley is rich in vitamin A and C, and acts as an antioxidant. It also contains a flavonoid, apigenin, which is an anti-allergen. Although used in herbal medicine for a variety of complaints, including menstrual problems, kidney stones, urinary infections, rheumatism and arthritis, it is not for self-treatment. Tea can be made from leaves or roots used to treat jaundice and coughs.

Culinary The leaves of this extremely popular herb are added to salads, sauces, salad dressings, savoury butter, stuffings, snipped into meat, fish and vegetable dishes and used as a garnish. The stalks, which have a stronger flavour than the leaves, are essential to a *bouquet garni* for flavouring casseroles and cooked dishes. The roots of *P. tuberosum* are cooked as a vegetable. The essential oil is used in commercial food products.

CAUTION Although parsley is perfectly safe, used whole in culinary dishes, it is toxic in excess, particularly in the form of essential oil. *Petroselinum*, especially the flat-leaved varieties, should not be confused with *Aethusa cynapium*, fool's parsley, a highly poisonous wild plant.

MONIMIACEAE
Peumus boldus
Boldo

History and traditions The medicinal properties of this small, shrubby tree from Chile were first investigated in Europe by a French doctor in 1869. It was discovered to be effective in stimulating the liver and expelling intestinal worms. In its country of origin it was formerly taken as a tonic tea and digestive, prescribed as a substitute for quinine and made into a powder to take as snuff.

Description An aromatic, dioecious, evergreen tree growing to 6–7 m (19–23 ft), it is the sole species of its genus. It has light to grey-green, leathery leaves, rich in a balsamic volatile oil. Greenish male and female flowers appear in late summer, borne on separate trees.

Habitat/distribution It is native to Chile, introduced elsewhere. Occurs on sunny slopes of the Andes mountains.

Growth It is frost-hardy, and grows best in sandy, acid soil in a sunny position. Propagated by semi-ripe cuttings in summer, may also be grown from seed sown in spring.

Parts used Leaves – dried for use in infusions and other medicinal preparations; bark – dried for extracts.

USES Medicinal It has mainly been used for liver complaints, urinary infections and to expel intestinal worms. Extracts are included in commercial and pharmaceutical products.

PHYTOLACCACEAE
Phytolacca americana
Pokeweed

History and traditions A poisonous plant, once used by Native Americans as a purgative and powerful treatment for various complaints. They knew it as *pocan*, which is where the name pokeweed comes from. It was adopted by European settlers as a treatment for venereal disease, and for its painkilling and anti-inflammatory properties. In modern times, its complex chemical structure has attracted much scientific interest. It contains compounds that affect cell division and it is currently being investigated as a potential source of drugs to combat AIDS-related diseases and cancers.

Description A large, frost-hardy perennial, 90 cm–1.5 m (3–5 ft) tall, with smooth, hollow, purplish stems and ovate to lanceolate leaves. It has racemes of white, sometimes pink-tinged flowers in late summer, followed by large drooping spikes of purple-black berries, which provide a dye to colour ink.

Habitat/distribution A North American native, it has been introduced elsewhere and widely grown in the Mediterranean region of Europe. Occurs in rich soils at field edges.

Growth Grow in rich, moist soil. Propagated by seed sown in spring or autumn or by division.

Parts used Roots and fruits (berries) – collected in autumn and dried for use in decoctions, tinctures and other medicinal preparations.

USES Medicinal Pokeweed has anti-inflammatory, antibacterial, antiviral, antifungal properties and is destructive to many parasitic disease-causing organisms. It is also capable of stimulating the immune and lymphatic systems. Used for many disorders, including autoimmune diseases, skin diseases, bronchitis and arthritis, but is for qualified practitioners only. Despite its toxicity, the leaves of this plant are sometimes boiled as a vegetable, the water being discarded.

CAUTION The whole plant is toxic if eaten, especially roots and berries.

PIPERACEAE
Piper nigrum
Black pepper

History and traditions Black pepper has been a valuable trading commodity since Alaric I, King of the Visigoths, demanded 3,000 lb of it as a ransom during his siege of Rome between 410–408 BC. Its high price during the Middle Ages was a major incentive for the Portuguese to find a sea route to India, where it came from, although the price fell following the discovery of a passage round the Cape of Good Hope in 1498. As cultivation was extended into Malaysia, the Portuguese retained a lucrative trading monopoly in pepper into the 18th century, and much of the wealth of Venice and Genoa depended on its trade. In Britain it was heavily taxed from the 17th to the 19th centuries. Pepper's virtues as a digestive were early recognized in the West and it has a long tradition of medicinal use in Ayurvedic and Chinese systems of healing.

Description A perennial climber, growing to 6 m (20 ft), with a strong, woody stem and ovate, prominently-veined, dark-green leaves. It has drooping spikes of inconspicuous white flowers, followed by long clusters of spherical green fruits or berries, which redden as they mature. Black pepper is produced from whole fruits, picked and dried just as they start to go red; white pepper is from ripe fruits, with the outer layer removed, and green pepper is from unripe fruits, pickled to prevent it turning dark.

Habitat/distribution Native to southern India and Sri Lanka, introduced and cultivated in Indonesia, Malaysia, Brazil and many tropical regions. In the wild it grows in humus-rich, moist soil. It is cultivated by training it up trees or horizontally along frames.

Growth Pepper requires deep, rich, manured soil, plenty of water, a humid atmosphere and a shady position. It is sometimes grown as a pot plant in temperate climates.

Parts used Fruits (peppercorns).

USES Medicinal A pungent, stimulating digestive, which relieves flatulence. It is used in Ayurvedic medicine for coughs and colds and as a nerve tonic. It also has a reputation as an aphrodisiac.

Culinary Its chief use is as a condiment and flavouring in a wide range of dishes in the cookery of most countries. It is currently the most widely consumed spice in the world.

Mixed peppercorns.

PLANTAGINACEAE
Plantago major
Plantain

History and traditions The Saxons called it *"waybroad"*, because it was so often found by the wayside. And the story goes that this plant was once a beautiful young girl, who was changed into plantain for refusing to leave the roadway where she expected her lover to appear. As a medicinal herb it was highly rated by Pliny, who attributed to it the ability to fuse together pieces of flesh cooking in a pot, and to cure the madness of dogs – or their bites. It was often recommended as an antidote to poison and in the US it was held to be a remedy for rattle-snake bite by native tribes.

Description A small, undistinguished perennial, 40 cm (16 in) high, it has a basal rosette of ovate leaves and cylindrical spikes of inconspicuous brownish-green flowers.

Habitat/distribution Native to Europe and introduced in other temperate zones worldwide. Occurs widely in cultivated land, garden paths and lawns, fields, wastelands and roadsides.

Growth Said to prefer moist soil, but tolerates any conditions in sun or shade. Self-seeds freely.

Parts used Leaves – fresh or dried.

USES Medicinal Plantain was thought to promote healing and to have antibacterial properties. Mainly used as a poultice or in ointments to be applied externally to wounds, sores, ulcers, bites and stings.

POLEMONIACEAE

Polemonium caeruleum
Jacob's ladder

History and traditions This is an ornamental plant, which retains its place in the herb garden through its ancient traditions and associations. Known to the Greeks, it was mentioned by Dioscorides, used for treating dysentery and thought to be effective against the bites of venomous beasts. It was still listed in various European pharmacopoeias into the 19th century. The whole flowering plant and roots were used and it was recommended for venereal disease and the bites of rabid dogs, but it is no longer considered to be of medicinal value. The name Jacob's ladder comes from the ladder-like arrangement of the leaves, and someone thought of associating it with the ladder to heaven of Jacob's dream in the biblical story (Genesis 28:12), with the sky represented by the blue flowers.

Description A hardy, clump-forming perennial, 30–90 cm (1–3 ft) tall, it grows on a creeping rootstock, with pinnate leaves divided into lance-shaped leaflets. The lavender-blue, bell-shaped flowers are borne on erect stems in drooping panicles.

Habitat/distribution Occurs widely in northern and central Europe, North America, and Asia in damp areas and shady woodlands.

Growth Requires rich, moisture-retentive soil and a shady or partially shady position. Propagated by seed sown in spring or by division in autumn.

USES Medicinal Rarely used today.

BERBERIDACEAE
Podophyllum peltatum
American mandrake

History and traditions A poisonous herb, *Podophyllum peltatum* was formerly used by Native Americans as a powerful purgative medicine, vermifuge and wart remover. They also made it into an insecticide for potato crops and reputedly took it to commit suicide. It was introduced to Western medicine in the 1780s by a German doctor involved in the American War of Independence and by 1820 was listed in the United States *Pharmacopoeia*. It is called may apple for the juicy fruits, which were sometimes eaten, despite their relative toxicity. The generic name comes from the Greek for *podos*, a foot, and *phyllon*, a leaf, for its supposed resemblance to a bird's webbed foot. The specific term, *peltatum*, means shield-shaped. Despite being called mandrake it is not related to *Mandragora*. In recent years, the active ingredient, podophyllotoxin, has been isolated for use in anti-cancer drugs.

Description A hardy perennial with a creeping rhizome, and usually unbranched stems, it is 30–45 cm (12–18 in) tall. The large leaves are deeply divided into 4–7 wedge-shaped segments, lobed at the tops. Small, drooping white flowers, with yellow centres, are followed by fleshy, lemon-shaped fruits. The whole plant has an unpleasant smell.

Related species *P. hexandrum* (Indian podophyllum) which grows in the Himalayas, has red fruits and is more poisonous, with a higher concentration of podophyllotoxin.

Habitat *P. peltatum* is native to North America, found in damp woods and meadows.

Growth Grow in humus-rich, moist soil in dappled shade. Propagated by division of runners.

Parts used Rhizomes – extracted for commercial drugs.

USES Medicinal It is a component of pharmaceutical drugs for treating certain cancers.

Other name May apple.

> CAUTION Although once used in herbal treatments, it is very poisonous and should never be used for self-medication. Subject to legal restrictions in most countries.

POLYGONACEAE

Polygonum bistorta

Bistort

History and traditions The generic name comes from the Greek *poly*, many, and *gonu*, knee, for the knotted shape of the stems, not unlike little joints, of many polygonum species. Bistort was not known as a medicinal plant until the 16th century, but soon gained a reputation as a wound-healing herb. It was cited in *The Universal Herbal*,1832, as a treatment for "intermittent fever", and considered helpful for diabetes into the early 20th century.

Description A hardy perennial with a stout, twisted rhizome, it has a clump of broad, ovate basal leaves, from which the pale-pink, cylindrical flower spikes arise on erect "jointed" stems to about 50 cm (20 in).

Habitat/distribution Occurs throughout Europe and Asia, frequently found near streams and waterways in damp meadows, mixed woodlands and on high slopes.

Growth Grows best in rich, moist soil, in sun or partial shade. Easily propagated by division, it is an invasive plant, but can make useful ground cover in damp areas.

Parts used Rhizomes – dried for powders, extracts, decoctions and other medicinal preparations.

USES Medicinal Said to reduce inflammation and promote healing, it is used as a gargle for gum disease, mouth ulcers and sore throats, applied externally to haemorrhoids, cuts and wounds and taken internally for diarrhoea.

PORTULACACEAE

Portulaca oleracea

Purslane

History and traditions A herb of ancient origin, purslane was known to the Egyptians, and grown in India and China for thousands of years. The Romans ate it as a vegetable and it was cultivated in Europe from at least the beginning of the 16th century, though not introduced to Britain until 1582. An important remedy for scurvy, it was one of the herbs that the early settlers thought indispensable and took with them to North America. Although it had some medicinal applications in former times, especially in China, it has always been chiefly valued for its culinary uses. It is still appreciated in France and commercially cultivated there for this purpose.

Description A half-hardy annual, with pink, prostrate, much-branched stems and rounded, fleshy, bright-green leaves, it grows to about 30 cm (12 in). It has very small, yellow flowers in late summer which soon fade to reveal the seed capsules with opening lids and filled with numerous black seeds.

Related species There is a golden-leafed variety, *P. oleracea* var. *aurea*, and the widely cultivated *P. oleracea* var. *sativa*.

Habitat/distribution Native to southern Europe, Asia and China, introduced elsewhere. Occurs on dry, sandy soils in sunny sites.

Growth Grow in light, well-drained soil, but provide plenty of water for good leaf development. Propagated from seed, sown after danger of frosts in cool temperate regions.

Parts used Leaves – fresh, picked before flowering for culinary use, fresh or dried for medicinal use.

USES Medicinal Recent scientific studies have found that *P. oleracea* contains omega-3 fatty acids, thought to be helpful in preventing heart disease and strengthening the immune system. The leaves are also a good source of Vitamin C and contain calcium, iron, carotene, thiamine, riboflavin and niacin. Purslane is also a diuretic and mildly laxative.

Culinary In 18th-century Britain it was a popular salad herb and is still eaten in the Middle East and India as a cooked vegetable and in salads. In France it is used in sorrel soup, helping to reduce the acidity of the sorrel.

Sorrel and purslane soup

Serves 4–6

1 tbs olive oil
1 medium onion, chopped
2 cloves garlic, crushed
225 g/8 oz sorrel leaves
50 g/2 oz purslane leaves
225 g/8 oz potatoes, peeled and diced
1.2 litres/2 pints/5 cups water
salt, pepper and a dash of grated
*   nutmeg*

Heat the oil in a large pan, add the onion and garlic and cook gently for 5 minutes, until soft but not browned.

Add the sorrel, purslane and potato and stir over a low heat for a further 2–3 minutes. Season with salt, pepper and a little grated nutmeg, pour in the water, bring to the boil then simmer for about 15 minutes until the potatoes are tender.

Cool slightly, then liquidize the soup in a blender or food processor, and reheat before serving.

PRIMULACEAE

Primula veris

Cowslip

History and traditions Cowslips were sometimes known as "keyflowers", suggested by the shape of the flower clusters, which look like a little bunch of keys. In Norse mythology they were dedicated to Freya, giving access to her palace, but in the Christian era became "St Peter's Keys" or the "Keys to Heaven". The generic name, *Primula*, comes from *primus*, first, in recognition that they are among the earliest flowers of spring. At one time, when they were plentiful, they were gathered in vast quantities to make spring tonics and the gently soporific, pale-yellow cowslip wine. Many medicinal uses were assigned to the flowers and distilled cowslip water was said to be good for the memory. The cosmetic applications were mentioned reprovingly by William Turner: "Some women we find, sprinkle ye floures of cowslip with whyte wine and after still it and wash their faces with that water to drive wrinkles away and to make them fayre in the eyes of the worlde rather than in the eyes of God, Whom they are not afrayd to offend" (*The New Herball*, 1551).

Description A perennial on a short rhizome with dense fibrous roots and a rosette of broadly ovate, rough-textured leaves. Flower stems rise above the basal leaves, 15–20 cm (6–8 in), and are topped by terminal umbels of fragrant, golden-yellow flowers, with tubular calyces.

Habitat/distribution Native to Europe and parts of Asia, introduced and sometimes naturalized elsewhere, found in meadows and pasture lands. A once common plant, it is now rare in the wild and a protected species in many European countries.

Growth Prefers deep, humus-rich, moist soil and partial shade. Propagated by seed sown in late summer in containers, left outside through the winter as a period of stratification, when they are exposed to frost, is necessary for germination. Easily propagated by division in autumn.

Parts used Flowers – fresh (but must not be picked from the wild, as they are quite rare).

USES Medicinal Cowslips have sedative, expectorant properties and contain salicylates (as in aspirin). They are taken as a tea for insomnia, anxiety, respiratory tract infections and rheumatic disorders.

Culinary Flowers may be added to salads.

CAUTION Should not be taken during pregnancy or if sensitive to aspirin. May cause allergic skin irritations.

PRIMULACEAE

Primula vulgaris

Primrose

History and traditions The medicinal properties of the primrose, *P. vulgaris*, are similar to those of the cowslip (*P. veris*) and have been listed in old herbals, since Pliny's time, for similar complaints. The primrose was made into salves and ointments and considered an important remedy for paralysis, rheumatic pain and gout. Its value as a sedative was well known and Gerard remarks that primrose tea, drunk in the month of May, "is famous for curing the phrensie". It was popular in cookery, and recipe books include instructions for making soup, pies, and a pudding based on rice, almonds, honey, saffron and ground primrose petals.

Description A low-growing perennial, to 15 cm (6 in), with a rosette of deeply veined, softly hairy, broad ovate leaves and clusters of saucer-shaped, pale-yellow, slightly fragrant flowers in early spring.

Habitat/distribution A European native, also found in northern Asia, introduced elsewhere, found on rich, damp soils in shady woodlands and hedgerows. Once common, now becoming rare in the wild, and a protected species in many countries.

Growth See *P. veris*.

Parts used Flowers (must not be picked from the wild, as they are becoming very rare).

USES Medicinal Primroses are taken as a tea to calm anxiety. It has similar properties to cowslips.

Culinary Flowers are added to salads and desserts or candied to decorate cakes.

BORAGINACEAE
Pulmonaria officinalis
Lungwort

History and traditions Both the Latin and common names of this herb point to its principal former use in treating lung complaints. The spotted leaves were thought to resemble lungs and it is often cited as an example of the application of the Doctrine of Signatures, an influential Renaissance philosophy, which held that the medicinal uses of plants were indicated by their correspondence in appearance to the part of the human body affected. It is often grown in herb gardens for its historical associations and attractive foliage and habit.

Description A hardy perennial, growing to 30 cm (12 in), it has hairy stems and dark green leaves, blotched with creamy-white spots. The tubular flowers, borne in spring, are pink at first, then turn blue.

Habitat/distribution Occurs in Europe, parts of Asia and North America, in woodlands.

Growth Grows best in humus-rich, moist soil and a shady position. Propagated by division, in late spring after flowering, or in autumn. Although it self-seeds in the garden, collected seed seldom germinates satisfactorily.

Parts used Leaves – dried for use in infusions and extracts.

USES Medicinal The herb contains a soothing mucilage and has expectorant properties. It is still sometimes used for bronchial infections and coughs, but it is now thought that it may mirror some of the toxicity discovered in *Symphytum*, to which it is closely related.

LABIATAE/LAMIACEAE
Prunella vulgaris
Selfheal

History and traditions A herb with an ancient history in Chinese herbalism, but apparently unknown to the ancient Greeks and Romans. *Prunella vulgaris* has featured in Chinese medical texts since the end of the previous millennium, where it is said to be mainly associated with "liver energy" disorders. In Europe its common names, "self-heal", "all-heal" and "hook-heal", all indicate its former use as a wound herb and activator of the body's defences, as explained by Culpeper: "Self-heal, whereby when you're hurt you heal yourself." It was held to be "a special remedy for inward and outward wounds" (Culpeper, *The English Physician*, 1653) and commonly taken to have the same virtues as *Ajuga reptans* (bugle). It was taken to North America by settlers, where it soon became established and known as "heart of the earth" and "blue curls". However, unlike *Ajuga* it still has a limited place in modern herbal medicine.

Description An aromatic perennial on a creeping rootstock, it is 50 cm (20 in) in height. Leaves are linear to ovate, and compact spikes of violet, two-lipped florets are borne in the leaf axils in midsummer to mid-autumn.

Habitat/distribution Native to Europe, northern Africa and Asia, naturalized in North America, found on sunny banks, in dry grassland and open woodland.

Growth Grow in light soil in sun or dappled shade; tolerates most conditions. Propagated by seed sown in spring or by division in spring. It is inclined to be invasive.

Parts used Flowering stems – dried for use in infusions and medicinal preparations.

USES Medicinal It has antibacterial properties and is used externally to soothe burns, skin inflammations, bites and bruises, sore throats and inflamed gums.

the leaf axils and followed by ovoid fruit, in little "cups" (acorns).

Related species The North American *Q. alba*, the white oak, also has a history of medicinal use, and was said to be effective against gangrene.

Habitat/distribution Native to Europe, occurs widely in the northern hemisphere in forests, open woodland and parkland, often found on clay soils.

Growth Grow in deep, fertile soil. May be propagated from seed, sown in containers in autumn. Very slow-growing.

Parts used Bark – stripped from mature trees and dried for use in decoctions and extracts.

USES Medicinal The oak has astringent, anti-inflammatory, antiseptic properties and is said to control bleeding. Applied externally to cuts, abrasions, ulcers, skin irritations, varicose veins and haemorrhoids. Sometimes recommended to be taken internally for haemorrhage, diarrhoea and gastric upsets. It was formerly used as a substitute for cinchona bark.

Other names Common oak and English oak.

FAGACEAE

Quercus robur

Oak

History and traditions Few plants have been invested with as much magic, mystery and symbolic importance in Britain and much of Europe as the common oak. It was used in Druid ceremonies and thought to protect from lightning strikes – especially if planted near buildings to attract lightning away from them. Carrying an acorn was said to preserve youth, and dew gathered from beneath an oak was a potent ingredient in beauty lotions. They are exceptionally long-lived trees, and individual oaks were attributed characters of their own, complete with their own canon of folklore. They were also greatly valued for the durability of the wood, used in furniture, buildings and ships. The medicinal properties of the bark were well recognized by herbalists in former times. Culpeper lists many uses for it, declaring that it will "assuage inflammation and stop all manner of fluxes in man or woman".

Description A large, monoecious, deciduous tree, growing up to 25 m (82 ft) in height. It has wide spreading branches, rugged grey-brown bark and small dark-green ovate leaves, with deep rounded lobes. Male flowers are thin catkins; female flowers are borne in spikes in

Top *An English oak,* Quercus robur, *growing in a park in Germany.*

Above *An oak tree in fresh, springtime growth.*

Left *The distinctive, lobed dark-green leaves of the oak tree feature in decorative carvings through the centuries, as family emblems and on heraldic shields.*

Left Rheum palmatum.

Above *A cultivar of garden rhubarb,*
R. rhabarbarum.

POLYGONACEAE

Rheum palmatum

Rhubarb

History and traditions Rhubarb has been an important medicinal herb in China for many centuries. It is mentioned in the *Shen Nong Canon of Herbs*, dating from 206 BC–AD 23, though claims exist that it has been recorded in much earlier Chinese texts, dating from 2700 BC. Several species of rhubarb (there are 50 in the genus) were used, but *R. palmatum* is thought to be the main source of Chinese medicinal rhubarb. The plant was first grown in Europe in 1763. *R. officinale*, also medicinal and of Chinese origin, came to Europe, as a plant, in 1867. However, rhubarb in dried or powdered form had been known for centuries before that in the West. It was imported to ancient Greece, where they called it *rha-barbarum* because it was brought by traders from the barbaric regions beyond the river Rha (Volga). It reached Europe in the 13th century and was in demand as a purgative drug, which lacked the side effects of other more toxic products, remaining popular into the 20th century. Rhubarb powder was a major constituent of the 19th-century proprietary medicine, Gregory powder, named after the Scottish doctor who patented it. And in an article in *The Lancet,* 1921, it is cited as a certain, even "magical", remedy for dysentery, when administered in small, strictly controlled amounts.

Description A large hardy perennial, to 2 m (6 ft), on a thick rhizome, with a basal clump of palmately lobed leaves. Spires of reddish-green flowers arise on long, hollow stems in summer.

Related species Edible garden rhubarb is from hybrids, developed during the 19th century, of *R. rhabarbarum* syn. *R. rhaponticum*, and there are now many cultivars. It is slightly laxative, but does not have medicinal properties.

Habitat/distribution Native to China and northeast Asia, found on deep, moist soils at altitudes of 3,000–4,000 m. Introduced elsewhere in temperate zones.

Growth Requires rich, moist soil and a sunny situation. It is possible to propagate from seed, but division of roots in spring or autumn is the preferable method. Cultivars must be propagated by division.

Parts used Rhizomes – dried for use in decoctions, powders and medicinal preparations.

A 13th-century wonder drug

Rhubarb's reputation as a wonder drug is said to have been established in the 13th century after an Armenian monk staked his life (and won) that rhubarb would cure a lady of the court of the Mongol chieftain Mangu, in the now ruined city of Karakorum. Medicinal dried rhubarb all came from China originally but was known by a variety of names after the route it took to reach its customers in Europe, or from the ports of entry.

"East India rhubarb" came down the Indus to the Persian Gulf, the Red Sea and Alexandria. "Turkey rhubarb" came overland, to the Turkish ports of Aleppo and Smyrna. "Chinese rhubarb" came via Moscow, and "Russian" or "Crown rhubarb" was the same product, so named once it had become a Russian monopoly, controlled from the early 18th century by the Kiachta Rhubarb Commission, set up on the Siberian/Mongolian border.

This organization maintained quality and price but prevented international trade until its eventual abolition in 1782. *R. rhabarbarum* (from which edible, garden rhubarb was later developed) comes from Siberia and was grown in the Padua Botanic Gardens from 1608. This was sometimes passed off as genuine "Turkey rhubarb" – its salesmen dressing up as Turks to give their product authenticity.

USES Medicinal Used in very small doses for diarrhoea and gastric upsets, and in larger doses for chronic constipation. Also given for liver and gall bladder complaints.

CAUTION As with all rhubarbs, leaves are toxic. Medicinal rhubarb should not be taken during pregnancy.

ROSACEAE

Rosa

History and traditions Roses have been cultivated for thousands of years and were once valued as much for their medicinal and culinary qualities as for their fragrance. Asian species of roses were used in ancient Chinese medicine and roses of Persian origin by the Greeks and Romans. The Greek poet Anacreon referred to their therapeutic value when he wrote, "The rose distils a healing balm, the beating pulse of pain to calm." And, in AD 77 the Roman writer Pliny listed over 30 disorders as responding to treatment with preparations of rose. Medieval herbals contain many entries on the healing and restorative power of the rose, and in *The English Physician*, 1653, Culpeper gives pages of rose

remedies for inflammation of the liver, venereal disease, sores in the mouth and throat, aching joints, "slippery bowels" and a host of other complaints. Red rose petals were listed in the British *Pharmacopoeia* as ingredients for pharmaceutical preparations until the 1930s. Their medicinal, culinary and fragrant uses are celebrated in all the old herbals and stillroom books with a huge range of recipes for ointments, lozenges, syrups, vinegars, conserves, cakes, candies and wafers. There are instructions for making rosewater, rose oil and cosmetic lotions. Sir Hugh Platt, in *Delights for Ladies*, 1594, has at least three lengthy entries on different methods of drying rose "leaves" (petals) to best effect.

Description and species

R. canina (**Dog rose**) – This is the wild rose of English hedgerows, known as the dog rose for its supposed ability, according to Pliny, to cure the bites of mad dogs. Its succulent, but acidic, red hips were made into tarts in the 17th century, and came to be greatly valued in the 20th century for their high vitamin C content. It is a hardy, deciduous climber, 3 m x 3 m (10 ft x 10 ft), with prickly stems and single flat, white, or pink-tinged flowers, followed by scarlet, ovoid hips.

R. eglanteria (**Sweet briar**, or **Eglantine**) – A vigorous semi-climber, 2.5 m x 2.5 m (8 ft x 8 ft), it has lovely apple-scented foliage

and numerous single pink flowers, followed by rounded ovoid red hips. This is the rose which appears in the works of Chaucer and is described by Shakespeare as adorning Titania's bower:

With sweet musk roses and with eglantine
There sleeps Titania, sometime of the night
Lull'd in these flowers with dances and delight.

R. gallica var. *officinalis* (**Apothecary's rose**) – Probably the oldest of garden roses, it was widely grown in medieval times for its medicinal properties (though *R. damascena*, the damask rose, said to have been brought to Europe by the Crusaders in the 11th century, was almost as popular). A hardy deciduous, bushy shrub, 1.2 m x 1.2 m (4 ft x 4 ft), it has large, very fragrant, semi-double, bright-pink blooms and distinctive golden stamens.

R. gallica versicolor, also known as Rosa Mundi, after the 'Fair Rosamund', mistress of King Henry IV of England, (1367–1413). A sport from *R. g. officinalis*, it has crimson-pink petals, splashed with cream.

Growth Fertile, moist soil and a sunny position are best for producing thriving rose plants with large flowers. However, *R. eglanteria* does quite well on a poor, dry soil. The most suitable method of propagation is by hardwood cuttings in the autumn.

Parts used Flowers of *R. gallica*, hips of *R. canina*, essential oil, distilled rosewater from various rose species.

USES Medicinal Rose essential oil is used in aromatherapy for depression and nervous anxiety. In its purest form it is said to be the least toxic of the essential oils, safe to use undiluted. But many are adulterated, synthetic or semi-synthetic, and of no therapeutic value. Both hips and flowers are still sometimes recommended by herbalists to be taken internally in various preparations for colds, bronchial infections and gastric upsets and applied externally for sores and skin irritations. Rose hips are used nutritionally for their vitamin C content.

Culinary Hips are used for making vinegar, syrups, preserves and wines. Flower petals are added to salads and desserts, crystallized, made into jellies, jams and conserves. Distilled rosewater is used to flavour confectionery and desserts, especially in Middle Eastern dishes.

Aromatic Dried petals and essential oil are added to pot-pourri, other fragrant articles for the home and beauty preparations, such as hand lotions and masks. Rosebuds and whole flowers are dried for decorative use. Dry roses in a warm, dry room but not in direct sunlight, which will bleach the petals.

Opposite page, clockwise from lower left Rosa eglanteria; Rosa canina; *and the superb double cultivar* Rosa 'Charles de Mills'.

This page, clockwise from top left Rosa gallica 'Versicolor'; *the nutritious hips of* Rosa canina; *a single flower of* Rosa gallica var. officinalis – *the famed Apothecary's rose; and the massed blooms of the Apothecary's rose on a bush.*

Rose-petal skin freshener

40 g/1¹/2 oz fresh rose petals (any fragrant red rose petals are suitable)
600 ml/1 pint/2¹/2 cups boiling distilled water
15 ml/1 tbs cider vinegar

Put the rose petals in a bowl, pour over the boiling water and add the vinegar. Cover and leave to stand for 2 hours, then strain into a clean bottle.

Apply to the face with cotton wool (cotton ball) to tone the skin. Keep chilled or in a refrigerator and use up within 2–3 days.

LABIATAE/LAMIACEAE
Rosmarinus officinalis
Rosemary

History and traditions Rosemary was well known in ancient Greece and Rome and the Latin generic name, *Rosmarinus*, means "dew of the sea", from its coastal habitat and the appearance of its flowers. It gained an early reputation for improving memory and uplifting the spirits, which is referred to in many herbals. *Bancke's Herbal*, 1525, includes a long list of remedies, practical suggestions and superstitions regarding rosemary, including putting it under the bed to "be delivered of all evill dreames", boiling it in wine as a cosmetic face wash, binding it round the legs against gout, and drinking it in wine for a cough or for lost appetite. It was also a major ingredient of Hungary Water, said to be invented by a hermit for Queen Elizabeth of Hungary, who was cured of paralysis after rubbing it on daily. A symbol of remembrance, it found a place at weddings, funerals and in Christmas decorations, when it was often gilded. In Spanish folklore rosemary is believed to give protection from the evil eye and to have sheltered the Virgin Mary, during the flight into Egypt, when the once white flowers took on the celestial blue of her cloak.

Description A variable evergreen shrub, to 2 m (6 ft), it has woody branches and strongly aromatic, needle-like foliage. A dense covering of small, tubular, two-lipped flowers, usually pale blue (but there are dark-blue and occasionally pink variants) appear in spring.

Habitat/distribution Native to the Mediterranean coast, found on sunny hillsides and in open situations. It is introduced and widely grown elsewhere.

Growth Thrives on sharply drained, stony soils and requires little moisture. Although *R. officinalis* is frost-hardy (not all species are), it needs a sunny, sheltered position and protection in cold winters and periods of prolonged frost. Easily propagated from semi-ripe cuttings taken in summer. It becomes straggly unless pruned hard in summer, after flowering, but must not be cut back to old wood.

Parts used The leaves and flowering tops are used fresh or dried for cookery and in medicinal preparations; essential oil distilled from leaves.

USES Medicinal A restorative, tonic herb, with antiseptic and antibacterial properties. It is taken internally as an infusion for colds, influenza, fatigue and headaches, or as a tincture for depression and nervous tension; and applied externally in massage oil for rheumatic and muscular pain. The essential oil is added to bath water for aching joints and tiredness.

Above left *Flowers of* Rosmarinus officinalis.

Above Rosmarinus officinalis '*Miss Jessopp's Upright*'.

Culinary A classic flavouring for roasted or broiled lamb, stews and casseroles, and added to marinades, vinegar, oil and dressings. Used sparingly, it adds spice and interest to cakes, biscuits, sorbets and baked or stewed apples.

Cosmetic Infusions are used as rinses for dry hair and dandruff and added to bath lotions and beauty preparations. Essential oil is used in perfumery and cosmetic industries.

Aromatic Dried leaves add fragrance to pot-pourri and insect-repellent sachets.

CAUTION Not suitable to be taken internally in medicinal doses when pregnant, especially in the form of essential oil, as excess may cause abortion. Safe for normal culinary use.

Rumex scutatus,
French sorrel.

Description A hardy perennial, growing up to 1.2 m (4 ft), with large, pale-green, oblong to lanceolate leaves, and large terminal spikes of small disc-shaped reddish-brown flowers on long stalks.

Related species *R. scutatus*, Buckler-leaved, or French Sorrel, is a lower-growing plant, with shield-shaped leaves and less acidity, and is favoured for culinary uses in France.

Habitat/distribution Occurs in Europe and North Asia in grasslands and is frequently found on nitrogen-rich soils.

Growth Grows best and runs to seed less quickly in rich, moist soil, in a sunny or partially shady position. Propagated by seed sown in spring or by division in spring or autumn.

Parts used Leaves – when fresh and young.

USES Culinary Sorrel adds a pleasant, lemony flavour to soups, sauces, salads, egg and cheese dishes. But it is acidic and not recommended for rheumatism and arthritis sufferers. The leaves have the best flavour and texture in spring, before they become coarse and fibrous.

POLYGONACEAE
Rumex acetosa
Sorrel

History and traditions Various species of sorrel were used medicinally from at least the 14th century, but it was always chiefly valued as a culinary herb, especially in France and Belgium, where it was even potted as a preserve for winter use. Recipe books of the 17th and 18th centuries reveal that sorrel was not just made into soup, but frequently served with eggs, put into a sweet tart with orange flowers and cinnamon, as well as being cooked as a spinach-like vegetable. John Evelyn considered that it should never be left out of a salad, lending it sharpness, as a useful substitute for lemons and oranges when they were scarce. He also wrote that it "sharpens appetite ... cools the liver and strengthens the heart" (*Acetaria*, 1719). Culpeper recommended it for many medicinal purposes, including the breaking of plague sores and boils.

Above left Rumex acetosa – *the leaves are high in vitamin C.*

Above *Sorrel in flower.*

CAUTION Sorrel contains oxalates, also found in spinach and rhubarb, which are toxic in excess.

Above Ruta graveolens 'Variegata'.

Left Ruta graveolens *in flower*.

RUTACEAE
Ruta graveolens
Rue

History and traditions Rue has a long tradition as an antidote to poison and defence against disease. The Greek physician Galen (c. AD 130–201) took rue and coriander (cilantro), mixed with oil and salt, as a protection against infection, and Dioscorides (c. AD 40–90) recommended it against every kind of venom. Most 17th-century herbalists continued the anti-venom theme, as illustrated by William Coles: "The weasell when she is to encounter the serpent arms herselfe with eating of rue" (*The Art of Simpling*, 1656). Rue was an ingredient of the celebrated anti-plague concoction, Four Thieves Vinegar, and always included in the judge's posy, placed in the courtroom to protect him from diseased prisoners and the dreaded jail-fever. The name "herb of grace" is said by some to originate from the practice of sprinkling holy water with a sprig of rue at Sunday mass. Its potent smell and protective attributes ensured its place as a powerful anti-witchcraft and spells herb. Although it is an attractive plant and widely grown in herb gardens, it has few herbal uses today. Far from being a protective, it is now recognized as a toxic irritant.

Description An evergreen, or semi-evergreen, shrubby perennial to 60 cm (2 ft), it has deeply divided blue-green leaves, with rounded spatulate leaf segments and a mass of small yellow, four-petalled flowers in midsummer.

Related species *R. graveolens* 'Jackman's Blue' is a widely grown cultivar with steel-blue foliage. There is also a variegated cultivar with cream and grey-green leaves.

Habitat/distribution Native to southern Europe on dry rocky soils, introduced and often naturalized throughout Europe, North America and Australia.

Growth Prefers light, well-drained soil and, although reasonably hardy, requires a sunny, sheltered position in cooler regions. Variegated cultivars are slightly less hardy. Propagated from seed (not cultivars) sown in spring, or from cuttings taken in spring (always wear gloves to handle). Prune in spring, or just after flowering in summer, to maintain a neat shape, but do not cut into old woody stems. It should not be planted at the front of a border where it can be brushed against.

Parts used Leaves.

USES Medicinal Although recommended by some herbalists for various complaints, including painful menstruation, it is a dangerous, toxic herb and there are safer alternative remedies for such conditions.

Aromatic It has insect-repellent properties and leaves may be dried for adding to pot-pourri.

CAUTION Rue is a skin irritant, especially when handled in full sun, and causes severe blistering. Gloves should be worn when handling. Toxic if taken internally in excess, it affects the central nervous system and may be fatal. It is also an abortifacient.

SALICACEAE
Salix alba
Willow

History and traditions The willow contains salicylic acid and is the origin of aspirin (acetylsalicylic acid), which was synthesized from it as early as 1853. The bark had been used in Europe for centuries to reduce pain and fever, and in Native American traditional medicine several willow species were used for the same purposes. Willow branches were popular church decorations in Britain and used as substitute palms (which were not readily available) on Palm Sunday. In Russia, the week leading up to Easter was often called "willow week". The tree was always an emblem of sadness (it was a willow beneath which the "children of Israel" sat down and wept) and garlands of it were worn by the forsaken in love.

Description A spreading, fast-growing deciduous tree, up to 25 m (82 ft), it has greyish, fissured bark, arching branches and silvery-green, slender lanceolate leaves. Stalkless, yellow male and female catkins are borne in spring.

Related species There are several species of willow with medicinal properties in this large genus, including the North American *S. myrsinifolia* or black willow.

Habitat/distribution *S. alba* occurs widely in Europe and Asia, most often near rivers, streams and waterways.

Growth Requires damp soil and even does well on heavy clay, but dislikes chalk. Propagated by greenwood cuttings in spring, or by hardwood cuttings in winter.

Parts used Bark – collected from 2–3-year-old trees and dried for use in decoctions and other preparations; leaves – are also occasionally used in infusions.

USES Medicinal The salicylic compounds it contains give willow fever-reducing, analgesic, anti-rheumatic properties. Although it has been completely replaced by synthetics in pharmaceutical preparations it is still sometimes used in herbal medicine for fevers and neuralgia (taken internally), in baths for rheumatic pain and in ointments and compresses for cuts, burns and skin complaints.

Above right Salix alba *(white willow).*

Right Salix alba *subsp.* vitellina *(golden willow), coppiced to maintain its ornamental stems.*

Salvia

Salvia officinalis
Sage

History and traditions The Latin name comes from *salvere*, to save or heal, and this herb has always been connected with good health and a long life – even immortality. An old Arabian proverb asks, "How can a man die who has sage in his garden?" and John Evelyn wrote, "Tis a plant, indeed, with so many and wonderful properties as that the assiduous use of it is said to render men immortal", (*Acetaria*, 1719). And Sir John Hill in *The Virtues of British Herbs*, 1772, has many anecdotes of people living to improbable ages through regular intake of sage. It is another plant, like rosemary, which is said to thrive where the woman rules the household: "If the sage tree thrives and grows/The master's not master and he knows."

Description An evergreen, highly aromatic, shrubby perennial, growing to 60 cm (2 ft), it has downy, rough-textured, grey-green, ovate leaves and spikes of tubular, violet-blue flowers in early summer. *S. officinalis* is one of the few hardy plants in this huge genus of around 900 species worldwide.

Related species *S. o.* 'Icterina' (golden sage) – Has gold and green variegated leaves. It

seldom flowers in cool climates, but in warmer regions sometimes has pale mauve blooms. Although it may be used as a culinary herb it does not have such a good flavour as the species, or as the purple sages. But it does add colour when used in salads. It is reliably variegated, not as prone to revert as many and makes an attractive contrasting foliage plant for the border. *S. o.* Purpurascens Group (purple sage, or red sage) – Has striking purple, grey and green foliage. Some of its variants produce blue flower spikes. It has a strong flavour, is often used as a culinary herb and widely cultivated for its ornamental value. *S. elegans*

(pineapple sage) – This is a half-hardy perennial with green, soft, ovate leaves, scented with pineapple, and scarlet, tubular flowers in winter.

Habitat/distribution Sage is native to southern Europe, found on dry, sunny slopes, introduced in cool temperate regions.

Growth Grow in light, well-drained soil in full sun. Although *S. officinalis* is hardy, it does not always withstand prolonged cold below -10°C (14°F), especially in wet conditions. The cultivars are slightly less hardy than the species. *S. officinalis* may be propagated from seed; cultivars must be propagated from cuttings or by layering. Prune sage in the spring to keep it

Above Salvia officinalis *Purpurascens Group.*

Above Salvia elegans *in flower.*

in good shape, or just after flowering, but do not cut into old wood. After a few years, sages can become straggly and need to be replaced. Pineapple sage must be protected from frost and kept under cover during the winter. Grow in moist soil and if container-grown keep the compost (soil mix) damp. It is very easy to propagate from softwood cuttings taken throughout the summer.

Parts used Leaves – fresh or dried, essential oil.

USES Medicinal An astringent, antiseptic, antibacterial herb, infusions of the leaves are used as a gargle or mouthwash for sore throats, mouth ulcers, gum disease, laryngitis and tonsillitis. Infusions are taken internally as tonics, to aid digestion and for menopausal problems and applied externally as compresses to help heal wounds.

Culinary Leaves are used to flavour Mediterranean dishes, cheese, sausages, goose, pork and other fatty meat. In Italy it is added to liver dishes. It is also made into stuffings, a classic combination is sage and onion. Leaves of pineapple sage may be floated in drinks.

Aromatic/cosmetic An infusion of the leaves makes a rinse for dark hair and to treat dandruff. The essential oil is used in the perfume and cosmetic industries.

Above Salvia officinalis *in flower.*

Opposite page, bottom left Salvia officinalis; **top left** *A flowering form of* S. o. *Purpurascens Group;* **top right** S. elegans *in leaf;*

This page, top left S. o. *'Icterina';* **top right** S. o. *'Tricolor'.*

CAUTION Sage, especially the essential oil, is toxic in excess doses, and should not be taken medicinally over long periods, by pregnant women or by epileptics (the thujone content may trigger fits). It is quite safe used in small amounts in cookery.

Salvia sclarea
Clary sage

History and traditions The specific name, *sclarea*, comes from *clarus*, meaning clear, and is also the origin of the common name clary, a corruption of "clear eye" which refers to an old use, mentioned in many herbals, of clary sage as a lotion for inflammations of the eye. It has long been a flavouring for alcoholic drinks – as it remains to this day – and clary wine is said to have been a 16th-century aphrodisiac. In the 19th century it was sometimes used as a hops substitute, to make beer more heady and intoxicating. In conjunction with elderflowers, it provided German wine producers with a way of adding a muscatel flavour to Rhenish wine.

Description A biennial, up to 1.2 m (4 ft) tall, it has a large basal clump of broadly ovate grey-green leaves, and in its second year a tall, branched, flower spike of silvery, lilac-blue and pink two-lipped florets. The whole plant has an unpleasantly overpowering scent, but it is showy and decorative in the border.

Habitat/distribution Native to southern Europe, found on dry, sandy soils.

Growth Grow in free-draining, but reasonably moist and fertile soil. Propagated by seed sown in spring or autumn. Often self-seeds.

Parts used Leaves – fresh or dried, essential oil.

USES Medicinal Infusions of the leaves are used as lotions for cuts and abrasions, and as a gargle for mouth ulcers. Sometimes recommended to be taken internally in small doses for promoting appetite.

Aromatic Essential oil is used to flavour vermouth and liqueurs, and widely used in commercial soaps, scents and eau-de-Cologne.

CAPRIFOLIACEAE
Sambucus nigra
Elder

History and traditions The elder has been associated since earliest times with myth and magic, witchcraft and spells. At the same time it was always valued for its many practical uses, medicinal, household, culinary and cosmetic. In Norse mythology, hauntings, deaths and harmed babies were the result of upsetting the Elder-Mother and guardian spirit, by not obtaining her permission before cutting down a tree to make furniture or cradles. Christian legends, referred to in English literature from the 14th-century *Piers the Plowman*, by William Langland, to Spenser and Shakespeare, included the story that Judas hanged himself on an elder tree, and that it was the wood used to make the cross of Calvary. From this it became a symbol of sorrow and death and was planted in graveyards. The idea that elders provided protection from witchcraft and evil spirits has ancient roots, and it is cited in Coles's *The Art of Simpling*, 1656, as being planted near cottages and fixed to doors and windows on the last day of April for this purpose. Some years earlier, in 1644, *The Anatomie of the Elder* was published, which celebrated its medicinal properties and asserted its capability of curing all known ills. Old herbals are full of culinary recipes, too, for the flowers, shoots, buds and berries, and the distilled water was said to ensure a fair complexion. The timber was valued for making fences, skewers, pegs and small household articles and the easily removable core of soft pith made elder prime material for pop-guns (as referred to by Culpeper), penny whistles and musical pipes, a use it has been put to since classical times. The generic name, *Sambucus*, is from the Greek for a musical instrument.

Description A small deciduous tree, up to 10 m (33 ft) tall, it has dull-green, pinnate leaves, divided into five elliptic leaflets. Flat umbels of creamy, musk-scented flowers in early summer are followed by pendulous clusters of spherical black fruits on red stalks in early autumn.

Related species There are a few ornamental cultivars which make attractive subjects for the garden but have no medicinal or culinary value.

Habitat/distribution Native to Europe, western Asia and northern Africa. Occurs widely in temperate and subtropical regions in hedgerows, woodlands and roadsides.

Growth Prefers moist but well-drained, humus-rich soil in sun or partial shade. Propagation by suckers or semi-ripe cuttings in summer are the easiest methods. The species, but not cultivars, can also be grown from seed. Elders often self-seed prolifically.

Parts used Leaves – fresh; flowers – fresh or dried; fruits – fresh.

USES Medicinal Has anticatarrhal and anti-inflammatory properties. Infusions of the flowers are taken for colds, sinusitis, influenza and feverish illnesses, and are said to be soothing for hayfever. The fruits (berries) are made into syrups, or "elderberry rob", also for colds.

Culinary Fresh flower heads in batter make elderflower fritters; fresh or dried flowers give a muscatel flavour to gooseberries and stewed fruits, and are added to desserts and sorbets. Flowers and berries are used to make vinegars, cordials and wines.

Cosmetic Fresh or dried flowers are used in skin toners, face creams and other home-made beauty preparations.

General The leaves have insecticidal properties and are boiled in water to make sprays against aphids and garden pests.

Elderflower

An old recipe
To take away the freckles in the face Wash your face, in the wane of the Moone, with a sponge, morning and evening, with the distilled water of Elder-leaves, letting the same dry into the skinne. Your water must be distilled in May. This from a Traveller, who hath cured himselfe thereby.

Delights for Ladies, 1659

Elderflower skin freshener

An infusion of elderflowers makes a soothing and refreshing lotion for sensitive or sunburned skin.

Pour 600ml/1 pint/2½ cups boiling distilled water over 25 g/1 oz dried elderflowers in a jug. Leave to cool, strain off the flowers and apply to the skin on cotton wool (cotton balls).

Keep the lotion cool and refrigerated and use within 2–3 days.

CAUTION Leaves contain toxic cyanogenic glycosides and should not be eaten. Berries are harmful if eaten raw.

Top left Sambucus nigra *in flower*.

Left *Elderberries*.

ROSACEAE
Sanguisorba minor
Salad burnet

History and traditions This is a traditional herb-garden plant recommended by Francis Bacon in his essay on the ideal garden (1625), to be planted in "alleys", or walks, along with thyme and water mints, for the pleasant perfume when crushed. The common name is a reference to the fact that this herb often lasted through the winter, providing welcome edible greenery when little else was available. It was also added to wine cups or ale for the cooling effect of the leaves. The generic name, *Sanguisorba*, comes from the Latin for *sanguis*, blood, and *sorbere*, to absorb, as it was formerly used medicinally as a wound herb interchangeably with *S. officinalis*, greater burnet.

Description A clump-forming perennial, 15–40 cm (6–16 in) in height, it has pinnate leaves with numerous pairs of oval, serrated-edged leaflets and long stalks topped by rounded crimson flower heads.

Habitat/distribution It is native to Europe and Asia, naturalized in North America. It is found on chalky soils in grassy meadows and roadsides.

Growth Thrives on chalk (alkaline). Requires reasonably rich, moist soil for good leaf production and a sunny or partially shady position. Propagated by seed sown in spring. Cut it back as soon as the flower buds appear in order to ensure a continuous supply of leaves.

Parts used Leaves – fresh.

USES Culinary The leaves have a mild, cucumber flavour, make a pleasant addition to salads and are floated in drinks or wine punch.

COMPOSITAE/ASTERACEAE
Santolina chamaecyparissus
Cotton lavender

History and traditions Cotton lavender is a native of southern Europe and was well known to the ancient Greeks and Romans and has long been valued as a vermifuge and for its insect-repellent properties. Culpeper recommended it also against poisonous bites and skin irritations (*The English Physician*, 1653). The neat, silvery foliage responds well to close clipping and it was introduced to Britain and northern Europe in the 16th century as hedging for knot gardens.

Description A small highly aromatic shrub, growing to about 60 cm (2 ft), it has silvery-grey, finely divided, woolly foliage and bright yellow, globular button-shaped flowers.

Related species *S. rosmarinifolia* subsp. *rosmarinifolia* syn. *S. viridis* has bright green foliage and makes an interesting contrast in knot-garden work.

Habitat/distribution Cotton lavender is native to the Mediterranean region, introduced and widely cultivated worldwide. Found in fields and wastelands on calcareous soil.

Growth Grow in light, sandy soil and a sunny position. Tolerates drought. Propagated by semiripe cuttings in summer. Prune hard in spring to maintain a neat, clipped shape. It will regenerate if cut back to old wood.

Parts used Leaves – dried.

USES Medicinal Formerly used to expel intestinal worms. It is said to have anti-inflammatory properties and is sometimes made into an infusion as a lotion for skin irritations and insect bites, but in general it is little used in herbal medicine today.

Aromatic Dried leaves are added to pot-pourri and insect-repellent sachets.

Other name Lavender cotton in the United States.

Below Santolina chamaecyparissus.

Bottom Santolina rosmarinifolia *subsp.* rosmarinifolia *syn.* S. viridis.

CARYOPHYLLACEAE

Saponaria officinalis

Soapwort

History and traditions Soapwort is indigenous to Europe and the Middle East and has been used there for its cleansing properties for many centuries. Some authorities claim that it was even known to the Assyrians around the 8th century BC. The name *Saponaria* comes from *sapo*, the Latin for soap, and, because of the high saponin content, soapwort roots produce a foamy lather when mixed with water. In Syria it was used for washing woollens, in Switzerland for washing sheep before shearing, and the medieval fullers, who "finished" cloth, used soapwort in the process. The common name, bouncing Bet, is a reference to the activity of plump washerwomen. It had its medicinal uses too. A decoction of the roots was formerly used for a variety of ailments from rheumatism to syphilis. Soapwort has been used until very recently by museums and by the National Trust in Britain, as it was found to be more suitable for cleaning delicate old tapestries and fabrics than most modern detergents.

Description A spreading, hardy perennial, on a creeping rhizomatous rootstock, 60–90 cm (2–3 ft) tall, it has bright-green, fleshy, ovate to elliptical leaves, and clusters of pale-pink flowers in mid- to late summer.

Habitat/distribution Native to Europe, the Middle East and western Asia, naturalized in North America and widely grown in temperate regions. Found near streams and in wastelands, often as an escape from gardens.

Growth Prefers moist, loamy soil, but tolerates most conditions and can become invasive. The easiest method of propagation is by division of the runners in spring. It can also be grown successfully from seed.

Parts used Roots, leafy stems – fresh or dried.

USES Medicinal It is seldom used in herbal medicine today.

Cosmetic An infusion or decoction of the roots and leafy stems makes shampoo – the addition of eau-de-cologne improves the slightly unpleasant smell.

Household Used for cleaning delicate fabrics.

Other name Bouncing Bet.

Above left Saponaria officinalis.

Above right *A decoction of the whole plant makes a gentle shampoo.*

Soapwort shampoo

If you are used to a detergent-based shampoo you will find this does not lather in the same way, although it will froth up if you whisk it. The gentle cleansing properties of soapwort shampoo are very beneficial if you suffer from an itchy scalp or dandruff.

25 g/1 oz fresh soapwort root, leaves and stem or 15 g/$^{1}/_{2}$ oz dried soapwort root
750 ml/1$^{1}/_{4}$ pints/3 cups water
lavender water or eau-de-Cologne

Break up the soapwort stems, roughly chop the root and put the whole lot into a pan with the water. Bring to the boil and simmer for 20 minutes.

Strain off the herbs and add a dash of lavender water or eau-de-Cologne, as soapwort has a slightly unpleasant scent.

Use like an ordinary shampoo, rubbing well into the scalp and rinsing.

CAUTION Soapwort should not be taken internally as it can be upsetting to the digestive system and is capable of destroying red blood cells if taken in large quantities.

LABIATAE/LAMIACEAE

Satureja

Satureja hortensis
Summer savory

History and traditions Both summer and winter savory are Mediterranean herbs that were appreciated by the Romans and commonly used in their cuisine. The poet Virgil, 70–19 BC, celebrated them as being among the most fragrant of plants suitable for growing near beehives. Shakespeare too, writes of the scent of savory and it is included in Perdita's herbal gift to Polixenes in *The Winter's Tale*. The savories were among the herbs listed by John Josselyn which were taken to North America by early settlers to remind them of their English gardens. Culpeper promotes both herbs to ease a range of ailments, including asthma, and for expelling "tough phlegm from the chest", with summer savory especially suitable for drying to make conserves and syrups. It has been established by modern scientific studies (carried out in the 1980s) that the savories do have strong antibacterial properties. However, the subtle, spicy flavour (like marjoram, with a hint of thyme) ensures that both summer and winter savory remain first and foremost culinary herbs.

Description A small, bushy, hardy annual, to 38 cm (15 in) high, it has woody, much-branched stems and small, leathery, dark-green, linear-lanceolate leaves. Tiny white or pale-lilac flowers appear in summer.

Habitat/distribution Mediterranean in origin, introduced and widely grown in warm and temperate regions elsewhere. Occurs on chalky soils (alkaline) and rocky hillsides.

Growth Grow in well-drained soil in full sun. Propagated from seed sown in containers, or *in situ,* in early spring. It may help reduce the incidence of blackfly when grown near beans.

Parts used Leaves, flowering tops – used fresh or dried.

USES Medicinal Has antiseptic, antibacterial properties and is said to improve digestion.

Culinary Summer savory has an affinity with beans and adds a spicy flavour to dried herb mixtures, stuffings, pulses, pâtés and meat dishes. Extracts and essential oil are used in commercial products in the food industry.

> CAUTION The savories stimulate the uterus and are not to be given to pregnant women in medicinal doses.

Below *The leaves have a mildly spicy flavour.*

Satureja montana
Winter savory

Description A clump-forming, hardy perennial, to 38 cm (15 in) tall, it is semi-evergreen (does not keep all its leaves in cool temperate regions through the winter, especially if frosts are prolonged). It has dark-green, linear-lanceolate, pointed leaves and dense whorls of small white flowers in summer. It has a stronger, coarser fragrance than summer savory, due to the higher proportion of thymol it contains.

Growth Grow in well-drained soil, in full sun. Propagated by seed, by division in spring, or by cuttings in summer. Prune lightly in early summer, after flowering, to maintain a neat shape.

USES It has the same uses as summer savory, but to most tastes has a less refined flavour for culinary purposes.

Satureja montana

SCROPHULARIACEAE

Scrophularia nodosa

Figwort

History and traditions This herb was used in the past to treat scrofula or "the king's evil", a disease which affected the lymph glands in the neck. It conformed to the Doctrine of Signatures theory because the knots on the rhizome were thought to resemble swollen glands. Culpeper, writing in 1653, called it "Throatwort", adding that "it taketh away all redness, spots and freckles in the face, as also the scurf and any foul deformity therein".

Description A strong-smelling perennial on a stout, knotted rhizome, 40–80 cm (16–32 in) in height, it has ovate to lanceolate leaves and terminal spikes of small, dull-pink flowers.

Habitat/distribution Native to Europe and temperate parts of Asia, naturalized in North America. Found in woods and hedgerows.

Growth Grow in very damp soil, in sun or partial shade. Propagated by division in spring, or by seed sown in spring or autumn.

Parts used Rhizomes – dried for use in decoctions and other medicinal preparations; leaves and flowering stems – fresh or dried.

USES Medicinal This has cleansing properties. Infusions of the leaves are taken internally or applied externally in washes or compresses for skin disorders and inflammations. Decoctions of the root are taken internally for throat infections, swollen glands and feverish illnesses.

CAUTION This herb has a stimulating effect on the heart and is not given to patients with heart diseases.

CRASSULACEAE

Sempervivum tectorum

Houseleek

History and traditions In the folklore of most European countries, houseleek is dedicated to Jupiter or Thor and was deemed to provide protection from lightning. It has been planted on thatched roofs or in the crevices of roof tiles ever since the Emperor Charlemagne, 747–814 AD, decreed to this effect. The second part of the common name, houseleek, is from the Anglo-Saxon word for plant, *leac*. Its Latin name refers to its ability to withstand any conditions, and comes from *semper*, always, and *vivum*, living or alive. The specific name *tectorum* is a reference to its roof habitat. This herb has been used since the time of Dioscorides and Pliny as a soothing agent for skin complaints. And Culpeper, writing in the 17th century, suggests a first-aid measure, which is equally valid today: "the leaves being gently rubbed on any place stung with nettles or bees, doth quickly take away the pain".

Description A mat-forming hardy succulent, it has blue-green, rounded leaves with pointed spiny tips, arranged in rosettes. Erect, hairy stems, to a height of 30 cm (12 in), bear pinkish-red star-shaped flowers in summer.

Habitat/distribution Native to southern Europe and western Asia, found on rocky slopes and in mountainous areas. Introduced and widely grown elsewhere.

Growth Thrives in gritty or stony, sharply drained soil and withstands drought. The easiest method of propagation is by separating and replanting offsets in spring.

Parts used Leaves – fresh.

USES Medicinal The leaves are made into infusions, compresses, lotions and ointments, or cut open to release the sap and applied directly to insect bites and stings, sunburn, skin irritations, warts and corns.

Above *A cultivar of* Sempervivum tectorum *with red suffused leaves.*

Below *Break open leaves to release the sap.*

COMPOSITAE/ASTERACEAE
Silybum marianum

Milk thistle

History and traditions It is called milk thistle for its milky-white veins, from which it earned its reputation, under the Doctrine of Signatures, as improving the milk supply of nursing mothers. The Latin specific name, *marianum*, associates it with the Virgin Mary, from the tradition that her milk once fell upon its leaves, and the genus name is a corruption of *silybon*, which was Dioscorides' term for this herb. Milk thistles were formerly frequently cultivated as a vegetable and it was decreed by Thomas Tryon (*The Good Housewife*, 1692) that "they are very wholesome and exceed all other greens in taste".

Description A tall annual or biennial, up to 1.2 m (4 ft) in height, it has large, deeply lobed, spiny leaves with white veins and purple thistle flowers in summer.

Habitat/distribution Native to Europe, introduced elsewhere and naturalized in North America and other countries. Found on dry, stony soils, in fields and roadsides.

Growth Grows in any well-drained soil in a sunny position. Propagation is by seed, sown in spring or autumn, and it self-seeds prolifically.

Parts used Leaves and flowering stems – dried for use in infusions or for extractions of the active principle silymarin.

USES Medicinal Taken as an infusion to stimulate appetite and for digestive disorders. Contains compounds, known as silymarin, which are said to be effective as an antidote to toxic substances that cause liver damage.

Other name Marian thistle.

SIMMONDSIACIAE
Simmondsia chinensis

Jojoba

History and traditions The oil from the seeds of this herb was used by Native Americans as a cosmetic and for softening garments made from animal skins. In the 1970s jojoba was discovered to be a valuable replacement for sperm whale oil and large commercial plantations have since been established in Arizona and across wide areas of semi-arid grassland in the United States.

Description A dioecious shrub, up to 2 m (6 ft) in height, with leathery, ovate leaves, it is the only species in the genus. Pale-yellow male flowers appear in axillary clusters, the greenish female flowers are usually solitary and followed by ovoid seed capsules.

Habitat/distribution It is native to southwestern North America and Mexico, and is widely grown as a crop in the United States and the Middle East.

Growth Tolerant of drought, it thrives in dry, gravelly soil. A half-hardy plant, it is propagated by seed sown in spring, or by heel cuttings taken in autumn.

Parts used Oil – expressed straight from the ripe seeds.

USES Medicinal Jojoba oil has exceptionally soothing and softening properties and is used in pharmaceutical ointments for dry skins, psoriasis and eczema.

Cosmetic It is also an important ingredient of moisturisers, body lotions and sunscreens.

General The oil is used as an engine lubricant. The shrubs are planted to prevent further encroachment of total desert in arid areas.

APIACEAE
Smyrnium olusatrum

Alexanders

History and traditions Alexanders was valued chiefly as a culinary herb from the days of the ancient Greeks until well into the 19th century. It is high in vitamin C and at one time was recognised as a useful antiscorbutic. It was also thought to have some medicinal properties, chiefly as a diuretic and stomachic. It was taken for asthma and to help menstrual flow, but it is no longer used in herbal medicine.

Description A large perennial, it grows up to 1.5 m (5 ft) tall, with thick ridged stems, dark-green, shiny leaves and domed umbels of greenish-yellow flowers, followed by black seeds. It is sometimes confused with angelica, of which it is taken to be a wild species.

Habitat/distribution Native to Europe and the Mediterranean, frequently found on coastal sites.

Growth It grows best in sandy, but moist and reasonably fertile soil, and is propagated by seed sown in spring.

Parts used Leaves, young stems, flower buds, seeds, roots.

USES Culinary The whole plant is edible. Leaves and young stems may be used like celery, the roots cooked as parsnips, the flower buds added to salads and the seeds lightly crushed or ground as a seasoning.

Other name Black lovage.

COMPOSITAE/ASTERACEAE
Solidago virgaurea
Golden rod

History and traditions Most of the nearly 100 species of *Solidago* came from North America, where a number of them were used in the traditional Native American medicine for healing wounds, sores, insect bites and stings. In the 17th century the dried herb was imported and sold on the London market for high prices as an exotic cure-all, until one day someone noticed golden rod growing wild on Hampstead Heath in London and the bottom dropped out of the market. As Thomas Fuller put it in his *History of the Worthies of England,* 1662, "When golden rod was brought at great expense from foreign countries, it was highly valued; but it was no sooner discovered to be a native plant, than it was discarded." However, by the 19th century it was firmly established as a popular ornamental in Britain, causing William Cobbett to complain in *The American Gardener,* 1816, "A yellow flower called the 'Plain-weed', which is the torment of the neighbouring farmer, has been above all the plants in this world, chosen as the most conspicuous ornament of the front of the King of England's grandest palace, that of Hampton Court."

Description A vigorous hardy perennial, growing to 1 m (3 ft) in height. It has branched stems, lanceolate, finely toothed leaves and terminal panicles of golden-yellow flowers in late summer. It is an invasive plant and spreads very rapidly.

Related species *S. canadensis*, native to Canada and North America, is a taller plant, growing to 1.5 m (5 ft), often seen in gardens, and also has medicinal properties. Most garden varieties of golden rod are hybrids.

Habitat/distribution *S. virgaurea* is the only native European species, and is found in woodland and grassland on acid and calcareous (alkaline) soils. Many closely-related species are native to North America.

Growth Prefers not too rich soil and an open, sunny position. Propagated by seed sown in spring, or by division in spring and autumn.

Parts used Leaves, flowering tops – dried for use in infusions, powders, ointments and other medicinal preparations.

USES Medicinal Golden rod has antifungal, anti-inflammatory and antiseptic properties. It is applied externally in lotions, ointments and poultices to help heal wounds, skin irritations, bites, stings and ulcers. Infusions are taken internally for urinary infections and chronic skin problems and to make gargles for sore throats.

Above left *A garden hybrid of* Solidago canadensis *and* S. virgaurea *in flower, and in bud (*above*).*

Golden rod superstitions

- Where golden rod grows, secret treasure is buried.
- When it springs up near the door of a house, it brings good fortune.

LABIATAE/LAMIACEAE
Stachys officinalis
Betony

History and traditions Betony was highly prized as a medicinal herb in Roman times, when Antonius Musa, physician to the Emperor Augustus, wrote a treatise on its virtues, assigning 47 remedies to it. It was of great importance to the Anglo-Saxons for its magical as well as its medicinal properties and is mentioned in the 10th-century manuscript herbal, the *Lacnunga*. It was made into amulets to be worn against evil spirits, planted in churchyards and held to be capable of driving away despair. *The Herbal of Apuleius* (c. AD 400) describes betony as "good for a man's soul or his body". Betony was much valued throughout Europe, and inspired the Italian proverb "sell your coat and buy betony". It was always associated with treatments for maladies of the head and said to be a certain cure for headaches – a use that it retains today in modern herbal practice. The name betony derives from *vettonica*, as the Romans knew it, which became *betonica* (as it was until recently classified). *Stachys* is from the Greek for a spike or ear of corn and refers to the shape of the flower cluster.

Description A mat-forming, hairy, hardy perennial, it has a basal rosette of wrinkled, ovate leaves with dentate margins. Flower stems rise to 60 cm (2 ft) with smaller opposite leaves and dense, terminal spikes of magenta-pink two-lipped flowers borne in summer.

Above S. byzantina *syn* S. lanata.

Related species *S. byzantina* syn. *S. lanata* is popularly known as "lambs' ears", "lambs' lugs", "lambs' tails" or "lambs' tongues" for its white, woolly foliage. It forms a mat of whitish-green, soft, downy, wrinkled leaves with short mauve flower spikes to 45 cm (18 in) tall. Although it has no medicinal or culinary properties it is grown as a herb garden ornamental.

Habitat/distribution Native to Europe, grows on sandy loam in open woods and grassland.

Growth Grow in ordinary, dry soil in sun or partial shade. Propagated by seed sown in spring or by division during dormancy.

Parts used Leaves, flowering stems – fresh or dried for infusions, ointments and lotions.

USES Medicinal Infusions are taken for headaches, especially if associated with anxiety and nervous tension, often combined with *Hypericum perforatum* and *Lavandula.* Made into lotions or ointments (often in combination with other herbs) for applying to cuts, abrasions and bruises.

Conserve of betony
(after the Italian way)

Betony new and tender one pound, the best sugar three pound, beat them very small in a stone mortar, let the sugar be boyled with two quarts of betony water to the consistency of a syrup, then mix them together by little and little over a small Fire, and so make it into a Conserve and keep it in Glasses [bottles].

The Queen's Closet Opened by W. M., cook to Queen Henrietta Maria, 1655.

CARYOPHYLLACEAE

Stellaria media
Chickweed

History and traditions The common name, chickweed, and the popular names in several other European languages refer to this herb's former usefulness as bird feed. It provided a source of fresh greens and seeds during the winter when other foods were scarce. For the same reason it was much valued as a culinary herb in broths and salads. Although it does not seem to have made its mark in the classical world, it appears in herbals from medieval times usually as an ingredient in a mixed green ointment based on lard, for rubbing on sores and swellings. The Latin name of the genus is from *stella*, a star, for the shape of the flowers.

Description A spreading, mat-forming annual, the much-branched stems grow up to 40 cm (16 in) long, but most are decumbent and creep along the ground. It has small ovate leaves and tiny, white, star-shaped flowers. It propagates quickly, reappearing throughout the year, and is often seen in the winter months.

Habitat/distribution Chickweed is native to Europe but naturalized in many countries throughout the world. Found on moist cultivated land and field edges.

Growth Grows in any reasonably moist soil in sun or partial shade. Self-seeds.

Parts used Leaves – fresh.

USES Medicinal It is rich in mineral salts, including calcium and potassium, and has anti-rheumatic properties when taken internally as a juice or infusion. Applied as a poultice or ointment for eczema, skin irritations and other skin complaints.

Culinary A pleasantly neutral-tasting herb for inclusion in salads or for cooking as a vegetable. It combines well with parsley to make a dip.

Chickweed and parsley dip

25 g/1 oz fresh chickweed
25 g/1 oz flat-leaved parsley
225 g/8 oz fromage frais
1 tbs mayonnaise
Salt and freshly ground black pepper,
* to taste*

Rinse and pick over the chickweed, and chop it finely with the parsley. Put this into a bowl with the other ingredients and mix well together.

Serve as a dip with raw vegetables, such as carrots, celery, cucumber and peppers.

BORAGINACEAE
Symphytum officinale
Comfrey

History and traditions Comfrey has been known since at least the Middle Ages as a healing agent for fractures. The generic name, *Symphytum*, is from the Greek, *sympho*, "growing together", and *phyton*, a plant. The common English name, comfrey, is derived from the medieval Latin, *confervia*, meaning to heal or "boil together". Gerard wrote that "a salve concocted from the fresh herb will certainly tend to promote the healing of bruised and broken parts" (*The Herball*, 1597), and he and other herbalists of his time advised taking it internally for "inward hurts" as well. The modern history of this herb is a chequered one. In about 1910 it was established that it contained allantoin, a cell-proliferant substance, which promotes healing of bone and bodily tissues. By the 1960s Russian comfrey, *S. x uplandicum*, was being promoted as a herbal wonder cure. But scientific studies of the late 1970s and 1980s, mostly carried out in Australia and Japan, revealed that comfrey also contains pyrrolizidine alkaloids (levels are higher in the roots than the leaves), shown to cause liver damage and tumours in laboratory animals when extracts were injected in large quantities. This has led to a ban on comfrey in many countries, including Australia, New Zealand, Canada and the United States.

Description A vigorous perennial, growing on thick taproots, 60 cm–1.2 m (2–4 ft) in height, it has oval, lanceolate leaves, with a rough, hairy texture. Pinkish-purple to violet, tubular flowers are borne in drooping clusters in early to midsummer.

Related species *S. x uplandicum* (Russian comfrey) is a larger – to 2 m (6 ft) – and more vigorous hybrid.

Habitat/distribution Native to Europe and the Mediterranean, and also from Siberia to Asia, introduced and naturalized elsewhere. Found in damp meadows, near rivers and streams.

Growth Although it favours damp soil in the wild, comfrey is a vigorous plant, which flourishes under any conditions and grows happily when planted in dry soil, in sun or partial shade. It is easily propagated by division of roots in spring, but is invasive and almost impossible to eradicate once established.

Parts used Leaves – fresh.

USES Medicinal The leaves are made into poultices, compresses and ointments and applied externally to bruises, varicose veins, inflamed muscles and tendons. While external use of the whole leaf is considered safe, it is inadvisable to take comfrey internally.

Horticultural The leaves are high in potash and make a good garden fertilizer, mulch and compost activator.

Other name Knitbone.

Top, from left to right *The flowers of* Symphytum officinale *are usually pink or blue, but there are forms with white or yellow flowers too.*

Below Symphytum x uplandicum *(Russian comfrey).*

CAUTION Comfrey is subject to legal restrictions in some countries.

by seed or cuttings. The cloves (the unopened flower buds) are harvested when the tree is 6–8 years old. The crop can be sporadic: one year heavy and the next light. Cloves are usually hand picked to avoid damage to the branches which would jeopardize subsequent crops.
Parts used Unripe flower buds – sun-dried; essential oil.

USES Medicinal Cloves have digestive properties, help relieve nausea, control vomiting and prevent intestinal worms and parasites. Oil of cloves is still used as a dental antiseptic and analgesic. A cotton bud soaked in oil of cloves and applied directly to the tooth will ease toothache.
Culinary Widely used as a spice in whole or ground form to add flavour to curries, pickles, preserves, chutneys and meat dishes – especially baked ham. It is also used in baked apples and apple pie, desserts and cakes, and for making mulled wine.
Aromatic Added whole or ground to pot-pourri and used to make pomanders. Essential oil is used in perfumery, and added to tooth-pastes, mouthwashes and gargles.

Whole cloves.

MYRTACEAE
Syzygium aromaticum
Clove tree

History and traditions The medicinal use of cloves is first mentioned in ancient Chinese texts, and it was a custom during the Han dynasty (266 BC–AD 220) to keep a clove in the mouth when addressing the emperor. Cloves originally came from the Molucca Islands, a group of islands in Indonesia, and were brought to the Mediterranean by Persian and Arab traders. They are mentioned in the writings of Pliny under the name *caryophyllon*, and were widely used in Europe by the 4th century, when their strong fragrance made them popular as ingredients of pomanders and as prevention against plague and infection. During the 17th century there was rivalry between the Dutch and the Portuguese over establishing a trading monopoly in this valuable spice. But by 1770 the French were growing their own crops in Mauritius and they were subsequently cultivated in Guiana, Brazil, the West Indies and Zanzibar. The name cloves comes from the French word for nail, *clou*, which they are supposed to resemble.
Description An evergreen tree, 20 m (65 ft) in height, it has soft, grey bark and dark-green, ovate leaves, with a shiny, leathery texture. At the beginning of the rainy season fragrant, green buds (cloves) appear at the ends of the branches. They gradually turn red and, if left unpicked, develop into pink or crimson flowers.
Habitat/distribution Native to the Moluccas, introduced and cultivated in other tropical zones.
Growth Tender, tropical trees, grown in fertile soil and requiring high humidity and minimum temperatures of 15–18°C (59–64°F). Propagated

Ground cloves.

COMPOSITAE/ASTERACEAE

Tanacetum

Tanacetum balsamita
Alecost

History and traditions Alecost came to
Europe from the Middle East during the 16th
century and soon became popular for its
pleasant balsam fragrance. As Culpeper wrote
a century later, "This is so frequently known to
be an inhabitant in almost every garden, that I
suppose it is needless to write a description
thereof." As its common name suggests, it
was used to flavour ale, the second syllable
"cost" is from a Greek word, *kostos*, meaning
fragrant or spicy. In the 17th century it was
taken to America by settlers, where it became
known as Bible-leaf from the custom of using it
as a Bible bookmark and sniffing its revivifying
scent during long sermons. As a medicinal herb
it was frequently recommended for disorders of
the stomach and head and Culpeper gives
instructions for making it into a salve with
olive oil, thickened with wax, rosin and
turpentine. But it is now little used as a
medicinal herb.

Description A hardy perennial, up to 1 m (3 ft)
tall, it has a creeping rhizome and oval, silvery-
green, soft-textured leaves, with a minty-
balsamic fragrance. Small, daisy-like flowers
are borne in mid- to late summer. Formerly
classified in the *Chrysanthemum* genus.

Habitat/distribution Native to western Asia,
naturalized in Europe and North America.

Growth Prefers a moisture-retentive but
well-drained soil and a sunny position.
Most easily propagated by division or
cuttings in spring, but can also be
grown from seed.

Parts used Leaves – fresh or dried.

USES Medicinal An infusion of the leaves
helps reduce the pain of insect bites and
stings, and a fresh leaf may be applied
directly to the spot as "first aid".

Culinary Fresh leaves may be added to fruit
cups and drinks; fresh or dried leaves make
an aromatic tea.

Aromatic The dried leaves are added to pot-
pourri and make fragrant bookmarks.

Other names Costmary and Bible-leaf.

The fresh leaves of
Tanacetum balsamita
*have a pleasant
minty fragrance.*

Tanacetum parthenium
Feverfew

History and traditions The medicinal
properties of feverfew have long been
recognized. The Greek philosopher, Plutarch,
writing in 1st-century Athens, says that the
plant was named *parthenium* after treatment
with feverfew saved the life of a workman who
fell from the Parthenon. The common name
comes from the Latin *febris*, fever, and *fugure*,
to chase away. In the centuries that followed,
herbalists recommended this herb, usually in a
mixture of honey or sweet wine to disguise its
bitterness, for a range of ills. *Bancke's Herbal*,
1525, advocates it for stomach disorders,
toothache and insect bites, Culpeper
recommends it for women's troubles and as
an antidote to a liberal intake of opium (*The
English Physician*, 1653). But others evidently
recognized its value for the relief of headaches
and migraine. Gerard wrote, "it is very good for
them that are giddie in the head, or which have
the turning called Vertigo, that is, swimming
and turning in the head" (*The Herball*, 1597).
And Sir John Hill, in his *Family Herbal*, 1772,
states clearly, "in the worst headaches, this herb
exceeds whatever else is known." Feverfew
came to prominence in modern times after a
Welsh doctor's wife found relief in 1974 from
both chronic migraine and rheumatism by

Tanacetum vulgare
Tansy

History and traditions Tansy is one of the essential strewing herbs, listed by Thomas Tusser in *One Hundred Points of Good Husbandry*, 1577, doubtless chosen for its insect-repellent properties. Despite the bitter flavour, there is plenty of evidence that it was widely used for culinary purposes in the past, with many recipes appearing in old household books. It was a popular ingredient of cakes and puddings, made with eggs and cream, traditionally served on Easter Day. William Coles, in *The Art of Simpling*, 1656, refers to the effect of tansy on the constitution after a Lenten diet of salt-fish. Tansy was also a popular substitute for mint in a sauce to accompany lamb. One authority refers to its cosmetic application. "I have heard that if maids will take wild Tansy and lay it to soake in Buttermilk for the space of nine days and wash their faces therewith, it will make them look very faire" (Jerome Braunschwyke, *The Virtuose Boke of Distyllacion*, 1527).

Description A spreading rhizomatous perennial, to 1.2 m (4 ft) in height, it has dark-green, feathery, pinnately-divided leaves, which are pungently aromatic, and terminal clusters of button-like bright yellow flowers in summer.

Related species *T. vulgare* var. *crispum* is a more compact plant, with attractive, curly, fern-like leaves.

Growth Grows well in dry, stony soil and prefers a sunny position. Propagated by seed, division or cuttings in spring.

Parts used Leaves.

USES Medicinal This herb is said to have been used in enemas for expelling intestinal worms, but is seldom used in herbal medicine today.

Culinary Despite the wealth of recipes in old books, tansy is not recommended as a pudding ingredient as it has an unpleasantly bitter taste, although the leaves used to be added to lamb dishes and spring puddings.

Horticultural Tansy is supposed to be an insect repellent and ward off aphids in companion planting.

CAUTION It is unsafe to take internally as a medicinal herb. The volatile oil is extremely toxic and should be avoided.

---

eating feverfew leaves. Since then this herb has undergone much scientific study and has been found to be a relatively effective and safe remedy for these complaints.

Description A bushy, hardy perennial, to 1 m (3 ft), with bright-green, pungently aromatic, pinnately-lobed leaves and a mass of white daisy-like flowers, with yellow centres, in early to midsummer.

Related species There are a number of cultivars, including some with golden foliage (as above), or double flowers, which make attractive ornamentals, but do not have the same medicinal properties.

Habitat/distribution It is native to southern Europe, widely introduced elsewhere. Found on dry, stony soils.

Growth Grows in any poor, free-draining soil and tolerates drought. Propagate by seed sown in spring, or by cuttings or division in spring. Self-seeds prolifically.

Parts used Leaves, flowering tops – for eating fresh, or dried for use in tablets and pharmaceutical products.

USES Medicinal Feverfew lowers fever and dilates blood vessels. Fresh leaves are sometimes eaten (usually sweetened with honey, as they are very bitter) to reduce the effects of migraine headaches. It is also taken in tablet form for migraine, rheumatism and menstrual problems.

Above *Golden feverfew does not have the medicinal properties of the species.*

CAUTION Feverfew may cause dermatitis or mouth ulcers if consumed to excess.

Above Tanacetum vulgare.

COMPOSITAE/ASTERACEAE

Taraxacum officinale

Dandelion

History and traditions Although known much earlier in Chinese medicine, the dandelion was first recognized in Europe in the 10th or 11th century, through the influence of the Arabian physicians, then prominent as medical authorities. The name, dandelion, comes from the French *dents de lion*, lion's tooth.

Description A perennial which grows on a stout taproot to 30 cm (1 ft) long, it has a basal rosette of leaves and yellow, solitary flowers followed by spherical, fluffy seed heads.

Habitat/distribution Native to Europe and Asia, and occurs widely in temperate regions of the world, often found on nitrogen-rich soils.

Growth Grows in profusion in the wild and self-seeds. Cultivated dandelions are grown in moist, fertile soil. Propagated from seed.

Parts used Leaves, flowers – fresh for culinary use, fresh or dried for medicinal preparations; roots – dried.

USES Medicinal An effective diuretic, it is taken internally for urinary infections and diseases of the liver and gall bladder. Considered beneficial for rheumatic complaints and gout. Also said to improve appetite and digestion. Of great benefit nutritionally, high in vitamins A and C and a rich source of iron, magnesium, potassium and calcium.

Culinary Young leaves of dandelions are added to salads, often blanched first to reduce bitterness, or cooked, like spinach, as a vegetable. Flowers are made into wine. The roasted root makes a palatable, soothing, caffeine-free substitute for coffee.

TAXACEAE

Taxus baccata

Yew

History and traditions Yews were sacred to the Druids and used in their ceremonies. They have also been grown in churchyards from the beginning of the Christian era. As evergreens and exceptionally long-lived trees (1,000–2,000 years), they were a life symbol and often used to decorate the church or to scatter in graves. *Taxus* is from the Greek word *taxon*, a bow, and the flexible, close-grained wood was the traditional material for longbows. Yew is from the Anglo-Saxon name for the tree. There are rare references to its former medicinal uses, in treating snakebite and rabies for example, but its poisonous nature was always recognized and it was known to kill cattle at a stroke. It has sometimes been used in homeopathy. In recent times yews have come to prominence as a source of taxol, used in the treatment of ovarian cancer.

Description *T. baccata* is a spreading, evergreen tree, growing to about 15 m (50 ft), with a rounded crown and reddish-brown scaly bark. The leaves are dark-green, flattened needles, arranged alternately. It is a dioecious tree, and the male flowers are small globular cones, which release clouds of pollen in very early spring; the female flower is a small green bud, followed by the fruit, a highly poisonous seed, partially enclosed in a fleshy, red, non-poisonous aril.

Related species *T. brevifolia*, the Pacific yew, has the highest taxol content, mostly in the bark, and is the main source of the drug. But six trees are needed to make one dose and wild stocks have been grossly over-exploited. *T. baccata*, the common yew, contains less significant levels of taxol-yielding compounds, found in the leaves, but is now used in taxol synthesis.

Above Taxus brevifolia.

Top Taxus baccata 'Fruco-luteo', a cultivar with yellow fruits.

Left Taxus baccata 'Fastigiata', the Irish yew.

Habitat/distribution *T. baccata* is native to Europe, Asia and northern Africa and *T. brevifolia* is found in north-western North America to the south-west of Canada.
Growth Yews will grow in any soil, including chalk. Propagated by seed, sown in early spring, or by cuttings in September. *T. baccata* responds well to close clipping and is frequently used as a hedge, or in topiary work.
Parts used Leaves, bark – for extraction of taxol.

USES Medicinal Extracts of yew are used in drugs for treatment of cancers, mainly ovarian, breast and lung.

> CAUTION All parts of yew are poisonous and it should never be used for self-medication.

LABIATAE/LAMIACEAE
Teucrium chamaedrys
Wall germander

History and traditions *T. chamaedrys* is said to be named after Teucer, son of Scamander, King of Troy, who, according to Greek mythology, was the first to recognize the medicinal properties of this herb. It is mentioned in the works of Dioscorides and developed a reputation over the centuries for being an effective treatment for gout. It was also taken in powdered form for catarrh and as a herbal snuff. Germander comes from the Latin form, *gamandrea*, of the Greek *khamaidrys*, and means "ground-oak", from *khamai*, on the ground, and *drus*, oak, a reference to the shape of the leaves.
Description A shrubby, evergreen perennial, 10–30 cm (4–12 in) in height, it has creeping roots and dark-green, glossy foliage, shaped like miniature oak leaves. Tubular, rose-purple flowers are borne in dense terminal spikes.
Habitat/distribution It is native to Europe and western Asia, widely introduced elsewhere and found in rocky areas, on old walls and in dry woodlands.
Growth Flourishes in light, dry, stony soils. Easily propagated by semi-ripe cuttings taken in early summer. Although the branches are erect to start with, it is inclined to sprawl, especially if allowed to flower. Clip hard in late spring or early autumn to maintain a neat shape.
Parts used Leaves, flowering stems.

USES Medicinal Although it is said to have some medicinal uses and digestive properties, it may cause liver damage and is best avoided.

LABIATAE/LAMIACEAE
Teucrium scorodonia
Wood sage

History and traditions A bitter-tasting herb, wood sage is one of the many plants said to have been used at one time for flavouring beer before hops became common for this purpose. One old story tells that hinds, wounded in the chase, sought it out for its healing properties. In past times it was used, like *Teucrium chamaedrys*, to treat gout and rheumatism and as a poultice or lotion for "moist ulcers and sores" (Culpeper). Its specific name, *scorodonia*, is from a Greek word for garlic, and if the leaves are crushed, it is possible with a little imagination, to detect a faint garlic odour.
Description: A hardy perennial, 30–60 cm (1–2 ft) tall, it has ovate to heart-shaped, pale-green, soft-textured leaves and inconspicuous greenish-yellow flowers in summer. *T. scorodonia* 'Crispum' has attractive, curly-edged foliage.
Habitat/distribution Native to Europe, naturalized in many northern temperate regions. Found in dry, shady woodland areas.
Growth It will grow in most conditions, but prefers a light, gravelly soil and partial shade.
Parts used Leaves (formerly).

USES Its herbal uses are now obsolete, but it makes an attractive traditional herb-garden plant – especially the curly-leaved form.

LABIATAE/LAMIACEAE

Thymus

History and traditions To the Greeks, thyme was an emblem of courage, to the Romans a remedy for melancholy, and appreciated by both for its scent. To tell someone they smelled of thyme was a compliment in ancient Greece, and Gerard refers to a description by the 3rd-century Roman writer, Aelianus, of the houses of a newly taken city being strewn with roses and thyme to sweeten them. *Thymus* is the original Greek name, used by Dioscorides. The scent of thyme is irresistible to bees, and the finest-flavoured honey comes from its nectar. The image of bees hovering over thyme was a frequent embroidery motif in former times. Its medicinal virtues were well known to the 16th- and 17th-century herbalists. Gerard recommended it to treat "the bitings of any venomous beast, either taken in drinke, or outwardly applied" and for Culpeper it was "a noble strengthener of the lungs". In modern times its antiseptic, antibacterial credentials have been fully established.

Description and species There are some 350 species of thyme, many hybrids and cultivars. The classification of them is complex and there are many synonyms and invalid names. For medicinal purposes, *T. vulgaris* and *T. serpyllum* are the main ones. For cookery, *T. vulgaris* and *T. x citriodorus* have the best flavour, though most of the others may also be used.

T. serpyllum (wild thyme) – Also sometimes called the "mother of thyme" and "creeping thyme", has a prostrate habit, growing to about 7.5 cm (3 in), and has tiny, ovate leaves and clusters of mauve to pink flowers in early summer, but is very variable in form. It is found throughout Europe and Asia on well-drained, stony or sandy soils and on sunny slopes.

T. vulgaris (common thyme) – Is a variable sub-shrub, 30–45 cm (12–18 in) tall, with gnarled, woody stems, dark-green to grey-green leaves and white, sometimes mauve, flowers. Native to southern Europe and the Mediterranean region, introduced elsewhere.

T. x citriodorus (lemon thyme) – A variable hybrid, 25–30 cm (10–12 in) tall, with bright-green, ovate to lanceolate, lemon-scented leaves and pale-mauve flowers in early summer. Cultivated worldwide.

T. x citriodorus 'Aureus' (golden lemon thyme) – Is a cultivar with golden foliage, which may be used interchangeably with *T. x citriodorus*.

Of the many ornamental thymes, these are some of the most attractive:

T. serpyllum, 'Pink Chintz' – Is a creeping thyme with grey-green woolly foliage and striking, bright-pink flowers. First selected as a cultivar, at the Royal Horticultural Society gardens at Wisley in 1939.

T. serpyllum var. *coccineus* – Is a favourite prostrate variety for the depth of colour of its crimson-pink flowers and the attractive form of dark-green foliage.

Above far left Thymus vulgaris *in flower with* T. x citriodorus; **above left** Thymus serpyllum.

Above Thymus serpyllum *'Pink Chintz'*.

Below Thymus serpyllum *var.* coccineus.

T. vulgaris, 'Silver Posie', and *T. x citriodorus*, 'Silver Queen' – Are grown for their variegated silver foliage, useful for giving contrast to an ornamental scheme.

T. pseudolanuginosus (woolly thyme) – Is a prostrate form with grey-green woolly leaves and pale-pink flowers.

Above Thymus x citriodorus *'Silver Queen'*.

Right A decorative thyme pot.

Below left Thymus pulegioides *'Broad-leafed thyme'*; below right Thymus pseudolanuginosus.

Growth All thymes require very free-draining, gritty soil and a sunny position. Though the ones mentioned are hardy to at least -10°C (14°F), in cool temperate climates they may need some protection in winter, as they are vulnerable to cold winds, especially if soil becomes too wet. Propagated by layering in spring, or by cuttings in summer. *T. vulgaris* and *T. serpyllum* can be propagated by seed sown in spring.
Parts used Leaves – fresh or dry for culinary use; leaves, flowering tops – fresh or dried for infusions and medicinal preparations; essential oil – distilled from leaves and flowering tops.

USES Medicinal A strongly antiseptic, antibacterial and antifungal herb. Infusions are taken for coughs, colds, chest infections and digestive upsets. Made into syrups for coughs, and gargles for sore throats. The essential oil is diluted in a vegetable oil (such as sunflower) as a rub for chest infections, or as a massage oil for rheumatic pain and aching joints.
Culinary Widely used as a culinary flavouring in marinades, meat, soups, stews and casseroles.

CAUTION Avoid medicinal doses of thyme, and especially of thyme oil during pregnancy, as it is a uterine stimulant.

Thyme and the ageing process

Research carried out by Dr Stanley Deans at the Scottish Agricultural College, Ayr, during the 1990s, in conjunction with Semmelweiss Medical University in Budapest, has found that laboratory animals fed with thyme oil aged much slower than animals that did not receive it. Thyme oil apparently delayed the onset of age-related conditions such as deterioration of the retina, loss of brain function and wasted muscles.

A key factor was the high level of antioxidants present in thyme oil, which helped prevent a decline in PUFAs (polyunsaturated fatty acids), important components of every living cell which help keep cell membranes fluid and strong.

TILIACEAE
Tilia cordata
Lime

History and traditions Linden tea, made from the flowers of *T. cordata*, has always been popular in Europe, especially in France, where it is called "tilleul" – as a soothing drink and for its medicinal properties. An infusion of the leaves as a complexion wash is an old prescription for a "fair" skin. The tree has been valued over the centuries for its many economic uses. The white, close-grained wood was used to make household articles, piano keys and carvings (notably by Grinling Gibbons, 1648–1721, at Windsor Castle and Chatsworth House, England). The inner bark produced fibre for matting and baskets; the sap provided a sweetener and the foliage animal fodder.

Description A hardy, deciduous tree, to 25 m (82 ft) in height, with a large rounded crown, it has smooth, silver-grey bark and heart-shaped leaves, dark green above and greyish below. The five-petalled, fluffy, pale-yellow flowers have a honey scent and appear in clusters in midsummer, followed by globe-shaped fruits.

Related species *T. cordata* is the small-leaved lime. Flowers of *T. platyphyllos*, the large-leaved lime, and of hybrids, such as *T. x europaea*, are also collected for tea. *T. tomentosa* (silver lime)

and *T. americana* (American lime) do not have the same concentrations of active principles.

Habitat/distribution *T. cordata* occurs in Europe and western Asia.

Growth Prefers moist, well-drained soil in full sun or partial shade. Propagated from seed, which needs a long period of stratification (at least three months) to germinate.

Parts used Flowers – collected when they first open and dried for teas.

USES Medicinal A soothing herb, which increases perspiration and is said to help lower blood pressure, the flowers are taken as an infusion, often sweetened with honey and flavoured with lemon, for colds, catarrh and feverish illnesses, for anxiety and as a digestive.

Other name Linden.

Above *The flowers of* Tilia cordata, *the small-leaved lime, are collected for tea.*

LEGUMINOSAE/PAPILIONACEAE
Trifolium pratense
Red clover

History and traditions Red clover has been an important agricultural and animal fodder crop since ancient times. But it was seldom used medicinally until its early introduction to the United States, where the Native Americans of the Unami and Ani-Stotini tribes discovered its therapeutic properties. They used it to treat cancerous tumours and skin complaints, took it during pregnancy and childbirth and as a general purification for bodily systems. As a result it was adopted by early settlers and found its way into British herbal medicine sometime during the 19th century.

Description A short-lived perennial, it is decumbent to erect, 20–60 cm (8 in–2 ft) in height. The leaves are trifoliate and the flowers rose-purple to white.

Habitat/distribution It is native to Europe, found across Asia to Afghanistan, and naturalized in North America and Australia, growing both wild and as a field crop.

Growth It requires moist, well-drained soil and is propagated from seed.

Parts used Flowering tops.

USES Medicinal Red clover blossoms are taken internally for skin complaints such as eczema and psoriasis, and applied externally for ulcers, sores and burns. Infusions were at one time thought to be helpful for bronchial complaints and the herb is also said to be effective in balancing blood sugar levels.

Red clover

LEGUMINOSAE/PAPILIONACEAE

Trigonella foenum-graecum

Fenugreek

History and traditions A herb with an ancient history, fenugreek has been cultivated since the time of the Assyrians and its seeds were found in Tutankhamun's tomb, c.1325 BC. In Europe it was one of the many herbs promoted by the Emperor Charlemagne, c. AD 742–814, and the seeds were sold for medicinal uses by the 16th- and 17th-century druggists and apothecaries. In Chinese medicine they have a history as a tonic and in Ayurvedic medicine are renowned for their exceptional ability to cleanse the system of impurities. They also have a reputation as an aphrodisiac. *Trigonella*, meaning triangle, refers to the leaf shape and the specific name, *foenum-graecum*, translates as "Greek hay", a reference to its long use as horse fodder. In recent times it has aroused interest for components of the seeds: the alkaloid, trigonelline, for its anti-cancer potential and a steroidal saponin diosgenin for its contraceptive effects.

Description A hardy annual, 60 cm (2 ft) tall, it has an erect, branched stem and trifoliate leaves. Pale-yellow pea-flowers appear in the upper leaf axils in summer followed by the fruit, a curved pod with a pointed "beak", containing up to 20 light-brown, aromatic seeds.

Habitat/distribution Native to southern Europe and Asia, widely cultivated in the Middle East, India and northern Africa.

Growth Grow fenugreek in well-drained, fertile soil in a sunny position. Propagated by seed, sown in spring.

Parts used Leaves – fresh for culinary use; seeds – dried for cookery or for making infusions, decoctions, powders or extracts.

USES Medicinal The seeds are rich in a softening mucilage and are used in compresses or ointments to ease swellings, inflammations, ulcers and boils. They are taken in infusions to reduce fevers, have digestive properties and are said to rid the body of toxins, dispelling bad breath and body odour. Fenugreek is also thought to control blood sugar levels in cases of diabetes.

Culinary Leaves, which have a high vitamin, mineral and iron content, are cooked as vegetables, mainly in India. Seeds are sprouted as salad vegetables, and used as a flavouring and condiment in northern African, Ethiopian, Middle Eastern, Egyptian and Indian cookery.

Fresh fenugreek leaves.

LILIACEAE/TRILLIACEAE

Trillium erectum

Bethroot

History and traditions Bethroot – the name is a corruption of birthroot – was traditionally used by Native Americans to control bleeding after childbirth and for soothing the sore nipples of nursing mothers. It was taken up by the Shaker community for the same purposes, for easing excessive menstruation and for haemorrhages in general. Sniffing the un- pleasant smell of the flowers, which has been likened to rotting meat, was said to stop a nosebleed. The generic name comes from the triple arrangement of all its parts.

Description A variable perennial, 25–38 cm (10–15 in) tall, it has broadly rhomboid three- sectioned leaves and solitary three-petalled flowers, ranging from crimson-purple to white.

Habitat/distribution Native to north-eastern North America and the Himalayan region of Asia and found in damp, shady woodland.

Growth Trilliums require moist, humus-rich soil and partial shade. Propagation by division in the dormant period is the easiest method, as growing from seed is slow and erratic.

Parts used Rhizomes – dried for use in decoctions and extracts.

USES Medicinal An antiseptic, astringent herb, it is said to be helpful to the female repro- ductive system and to control bleeding. Poultices are applied for skin diseases and the roots were at one time boiled in milk to be taken for diarrhoea and dysentery.

TROPAEOLACEAE

Tropaeolum majus

Nasturtium

History and traditions The garden nasturtium comes from South America. It was introduced to Spain, from Peru, in the 16th century and originally known as *Nasturtium indicum*, or Indian cress, for the spicy flavour of its leaves. Leaves and flowers were popular 17th-century salad ingredients. As nasturtiums are high in vitamin C, they were useful for preventing scurvy. The generic name *Tropaeolum* comes from *tropalon*, the Greek word for a trophy, as the round leaves were thought to resemble the trophy-bearing shields of the classical world.

Description In South America it is a perennial, but in Europe and cool temperate regions it is a half-hardy annual. It has trailing stems, to about 3 m (10 ft), and circular leaves with a radiating pattern of veins. The yellow or orange flowers grow on stalks arising singly from the leaf axils, and have prominently spurred calyces. They are followed by the globular fruits. There are many low-growing and climbing cultivars.

Habitat/distribution Native to South America, now widely grown throughout the world.

Growth Grow in relatively poor soil for the best production of flowers, but supply plenty of moisture. Easily propagated from seed sown in containers, or *in situ*, in spring.

Parts used Leaves, flowers, seeds – used fresh.

USES Medicinal The seeds have antiseptic, antibacterial properties and are taken in infusions for urinary and upper respiratory tract infections.

Culinary The leaves are added to salads for their peppery taste and the flowers for their colour. Flowers are also used as a flavouring for vinegar. Seeds, when still green, are pickled as a substitute for capers.

Other name Indian cress.

Above *The flowers and leaves make colourful and nutritious additions to a summer salad.*

Tropaeolum majus

An old recipe for pickled nasturtium seeds

Gather your little knobs quickly after your blossoms are off; put them in cold water and salt for three days, shifting them once a day; then make a pickle (but do not boil it at all) of some white wine, shallot, horse-radish, pepper, salt, cloves, and mace whole and nutmeg quartered; then put in your seeds and stop them close; they are to be eaten as capers. *The Complete Housewife*, 1736.

A simple modern version of pickled nasturtium seeds

Collect the nasturtium seeds while they are still green, until you have about 50 g/2 oz. Stir 25 g (1 oz) salt into 300 ml /1/2 pint/1 1/4 cup water, add the nasturtium seeds and leave for 24 hours. Then strain them and rinse well in fresh water. Put the seeds into a jar with a muslin bag filled with mixed pickling spice, top up with malt vinegar and seal with an airtight lid. Leave for 3–4 weeks before eating.

Growth It is an invasive plant that needs no cultivation. Propagated from seed or by division.
Parts used Leaves, flowers – fresh or dried.

USES Medicinal Coltsfoot is said to have tonic effects and contain mucilage, which is soothing to the mucous membranes. It is still recommended by herbalists to be taken in infusions for coughs and applied externally as a wash or compress, or as fresh leaves mixed in a paste of honey, for sores, ulcers, skin inflammation and insect bites.
Culinary Traditionally, leaves were added to springtime salads and soups.

Above *The leaves of* Tussilago farfara *appear after the flowers have faded.*

COMPOSITAE/ASTERACEAE
Tussilago farfara
Coltsfoot

History and traditions Known since the days of Dioscorides and Pliny as a herb to relieve coughs, often taken in the form of a smoking mixture, it is still a basic ingredient of herbal tobaccos. The generic name comes from *tussis*, a cough (from which we get the word tussive), and *agere*, to take away. In the Middle Ages it was sometimes known as *Filius ante patrem* (son before father), because the flowers appear before the leaves. Although still used in herbal medicine for cough remedies, recent tests have revealed that it contains low quantities of pyrrolizidine alkaloids, which are carcinogenic in high doses. (Also found in *Symphytum officinale* – comfrey).

Description A small perennial, on a creeping rhizome, 15–20 cm (6–8 in) in height. The bright-yellow, dandelion-like flowers, borne singly, appear before the rosette of toothed heart-shaped leaves.

Habitat/distribution Native to Europe, western Asia and northern Africa, introduced elsewhere including North America. Found on roadsides, wastelands, fields and hedgerows, in moist, loamy soil.

Tussilago farfara

ULMACEAE
Ulmus rubra
Slippery elm

History and traditions The common name is taken from the slippery texture of the inner bark when moistened. It was a traditional medicine of Native Americans, used mainly for gastric problems and healing wounds, and was taken up by early settlers, who made the powdered bark into a nutritious gruel for invalids with weak digestions.

Description A deciduous tree 15–20 m (50–65 ft) in height, it has dark-brown, rough bark and obovate, toothed, deeply-veined leaves. Inconspicuous clusters of red-stamened flowers are followed by reddish-brown, winged fruits.

Habitat/distribution Native to eastern and central North America and eastern Canada. It is found in moist woodlands.

Growth This tree grows well in poorish soil and is propagated by seed or cuttings. It is liable to Dutch elm disease.

Parts used Inner bark – dried and ground into powder. (Bark should not be stripped from wild trees, which are becoming rare, only from those cultivated for the purpose.)

USES Medicinal Rich in mucilage, slippery elm powder is taken for stomach and bowel disorders, gastric ulcers, cystitis and urinary complaints. It is soothing to sore throats and applied in poultices for skin inflammations, boils, abscesses and ulcers and to encourage the healing of wounds.

Other name Red elm.

CAUTION Subject to legal restrictions in some countries, especially as whole bark.

Urtica dioica

URTICACEAE

Urtica dioica
Stinging nettle

History and traditions The common stinging nettle may be an unpopular weed, but over the centuries it has been put to many practical uses, remaining an important nutritious and medicinal herb. It was named *Urtica* by Pliny, from *urere*, to burn. Roman legionaries are said to have flailed themselves with nettles against the bone-chilling cold of a northern British winter. They even brought their own seeds, in case no plants grew locally. Whipping with nettles later became an established cure for rheumatism. The nettle was a common source of fibre (similar to that of flax and hemp) in many northern European nations. One of Hans Andersen's fairy-tales tells of the Princess who wove nettle coats for swans. Above all, in former times, it made a valuable springtime pot-herb, tonic and anti-scorbutic after the deprivations of winter and was made into all manner of soups, puddings and porridges, as well as nettle beer.

Description A tough, spreading perennial, the erect stems grow to 1.5 m (5 ft) tall, on creeping roots. The stems and ovate, toothed, dull-green leaves are covered in stinging hairs. Inconspicuous greenish-yellow flowers (male and female on separate plants) appear in mid to late summer.

Related species *U. urens* is a small, annual nettle, found in cool, northern temperate regions. *U. pilulifera* (Roman nettle) originates in southern Europe.

Habitat/distribution Found in waste ground, grassland, field edges, gardens, near human habitation or ruins, in nitrogen-rich soil.

Growth Cultivation is usually unnecessary for domestic use as nettles are plentiful in wild and semi-wild areas and can be invasive in the garden. Grown as a crop they require moist, nitrogen-rich soil. Cut back before flowering to ensure a second crop of young leaves.

Parts used Leafy stems – cut in spring, before flowering, fresh for cookery, fresh or dried for infusions, extracts, lotions and ointments. Roots – fresh or dried for decoctions for hair use.

USES Medicinal Constituents include histamine and formic acid, which causes the sting, vitamins A, B, C, iron and other minerals. The high vitamin C content ensures proper absorption of iron and the juice is taken for anaemia. Its diuretic properties help rid the body of uric acid and it is taken as an infusion for rheumatism, arthritis and gout, or applied as a compress to ease pain. It also stimulates the circulation and is said to lower blood pressure. Decoctions of the root and leaves are applied for dry scalp, dandruff and are said to help prevent baldness.

Culinary Only fresh young leaves should be used, cooked as a spinach-like vegetable or made into soup. Leaves should not be eaten raw as they are highly irritant in this state.

VALERIANACEAE

Valeriana officinalis
Valerian

History and traditions This is thought to be the same plant known to the medical authorities of ancient Greece, Dioscorides and Galen, as *phu*, for the offensive odour of its roots, and recommended by them for its diuretic properties. The name *Valeriana* dates from about the 10th century and is said to be from the Latin *valere*, to be in good health. It was promoted by the Arabian physicians of this era, appears in Anglo-Saxon leech-books of the 11th century and became known in medieval Europe as "All-Heal" for its supposed therapeutic powers. Despite the early Greek name, the smell of the root was not unpleasant to everybody: it was appreciated as a perfume in the 16th century and Turner's *Herbal*, 1568, describes laying the aromatic dried roots among linen. In fact it has a musky scent, similar to *Nardostachys*

Above *Flowers of* Centranthus ruber.

jatamansi (once classified as a valerian), and the essential oil is a perfumery ingredient to this day. It is also attractive to cats and rats.

Description A tall, hardy perennial, growing to 1.5 m (5 ft), it has grooved stems and pinnate leaves with lanceolate, toothed leaflets. The white, sometimes pinkish, flowers are borne in terminal clusters in summer. *V. officinalis* should not be confused with red valerian, *Centranthus ruber*, which has no medicinal value, but is grown as a herb garden ornamental.

Habitat/distribution Native to Europe and western Asia, introduced to many temperate regions and naturalized in North America. Found in damp meadows and ditches, often near streams.

Growth Grow in damp, fertile soil in a sunny position. Propagated by seed sown in spring, or by division in spring or autumn. It is inclined to be invasive.

Parts used Roots – dried for use in decoctions, medicinal preparations and extracts; essential oil – distilled from roots.

USES Medicinal It has sedative properties and is taken as a tea for insomnia, nervous tension, anxiety, headaches and indigestion. Also said to lower blood pressure.

Aromatic The essential oil is used in perfumery, and extracts as a flavouring in the food industry.

> CAUTION Excess doses are harmful and may cause headaches or a racing heart. It can be addictive and should not be taken for long periods. It should not be taken by anyone with liver disease.

SCROPHULARIACEAE
Verbascum thapsus
Mullein

History and traditions "Candlewick plant" and "hag's taper" are two of the many country names for this plant and refer to its former use, when dried, as a lamp wick or taper. The tall flower spires also look like giant candles, as described by Henry Lyte: "the whole toppe, with its pleasant yellow floures sheweth like to a wax candle or taper cunningly wrought" (*The Niewe Herball*, 1578). As a medicinal herb, it was taken for colds, in the form of "mullein tea", as indeed it still is, and was sometimes smoked as a tobacco for coughs and asthma (which must have made things worse). It also made a yellow hair dye. Throughout Europe and Asia mullein had an ancient reputation as a magic plant, capable of driving away evil spirits.

Description A tall, hardy biennial, growing to 2 m (6 ft), it has a basal rosette of soft, downy, blue-grey leaves, broadly ovate in shape, in the first year. Yellow flowers are borne on tall spikes in the second year.

Habitat/distribution Native to Europe, Asia and northern Africa, found on shallow, stony soils in grassland and wasteland.

Growth Thrives in dry, stony or gravelly soil and a sunny position. Propagated by seed sown in autumn. Often self-seeds.

Parts used Leaves – dried for use in infusions and liquid extracts; flowers – fresh or dried for infusions. Preparations must be carefully strained to eliminate irritating fine particles.

USES Medicinal It has antiseptic properties and is rich in soothing mucilage. Its main use is for coughs, colds, influenza and respiratory infections, when it is taken as an infusion. It is also sometimes recommended for colic, digestive upsets, nervous tension and insomnia. An infused oil, made of the flowers, has been applied to sores and chapped skin.

Other name Aaron's rod.

Above *The tall flower spikes of* Verbascum thapsus *appear in the second year.*

Verbena officinalis
Vervain

History and traditions This unspectacular plant has a long history as a magical herb of exceptional powers and features widely in the folklore of Celtic and northern European cultures. It was venerated by the Romans, who scattered it on their temple altars and whose soldiers carried sprigs to protect them. A story began that it grew at the site of Christ's crucifixion and was used to staunch his wounds on the cross. It was called *herba sacra*, a holy herb, when used in religious ceremonies, and *herba veneris* for its supposed aphrodisiac powers. In Anglo-Saxon and medieval times it was worn as an amulet to protect against plague, snakebites and evil in general. And, with so much going for it, by the 16th century it became an "official" herb of the apothecaries, used for at least 30 complaints. Although it had largely fallen from favour by the early 19th century, it does have a place in herbal medicine today and in traditional Chinese medicine.

Related species Many of the ornamental verbenas grown in gardens come from Brazil and South America. Others with medicinal properties include a West Indian species and *V. hastata*, with blue flowers, which is indigenous to eastern North America.

Description A hardy, rather straggly perennial, with an erect, branched stem, it has ovate, deeply lobed, sometimes pinnate, leaves, which are dull green and slightly hairy. Small, pale-lilac flowers are sparsely arranged in terminal spikes.

Habitat/distribution Native to Europe, western Asia and northern Africa, found in waste places and roadsides, usually in a sheltered, sunny position.

Growth Grow in well-drained but moist soil in full sun. Propagated by seed sown in spring.

Parts used Leaves, flowering stems – dried for use in infusions, ointments, liquid extracts and other medicinal preparations.

USES Medicinal Vervain has mildly sedative and hypnotic properties and is taken in infusions for nervous exhaustion, anxiety, insomnia, tension headaches and migraine. Also for disorders associated with the stomach, kidneys, liver and gall bladder. Externally it is used in compresses and lotions for skin complaints and as a gargle for sore gums and mouth ulcers.

Verbena officinalis

Vetiveria zizanioides
Vetiver

History and traditions A large coarse grass with many economic uses in the East, it was at one time planted on Sri Lankan tea estates to control erosion. An Indian name for it is *khus-khus*, and it has been used since the time of the Moghul Emperors to make scented screens, popularly known as "*khus-khus* tatties" which were sprinkled with water to keep buildings cool before the days of air conditioning, and which deterred insects as well. It is now widely cultivated for the volatile oil contained in its roots, especially in Réunion, which produces more than 35 tons annually.

Description A clump-forming grass, which grows to about 1.5 m (5 ft), with aromatic, rhizomatous roots, it has linear spears of leaves and brownish flowers produced on long stalks.

Habitat/distribution Grows wild in tropical Asia, eastern Africa and Central America and is widely cultivated there as well; also in Java, Réunion, the Seychelles, New Guinea and Brazil.

Growth A tender, tropical plant. Propagated by division or layering.

Parts used Roots – distilled for essential oil.

USES Aromatic The essential oil has a woody, musky odour, is strongly insect-repellent and antiseptic, and has sedative properties. It is used as a fixative for perfumes and as an ingredient of soaps and cosmetics.

APOCYNACEAE

Vinca major
Greater periwinkle

History and traditions The periwinkle is mentioned by Pliny and was woven into garlands in ancient Greece and Rome to decorate rooms, or to wear at celebratory banquets. An old name for it is "sorcerer's violet" and it has a long tradition in early herbal literature as an anti-witchcraft herb. *Macer's Herbal*, dating from the 11th century, writes of its power against "wykked spirits", and the *Herbal of Apuleius* (1481 – translated from a manuscript of c. AD 400) recommends it "against devil sickness and demoniacal possession". The always imaginative *Boke of Secrets of Albertus Magnus,* 14th century, tells of a recipe for wrapping it in earthworms, reducing it to a powder and mixing it with houseleek, to be eaten with a meal for inducing love between man and wife. In European cultures it has variously been seen as a flower of death, of immortality and of friendship. The generic term *Vinca* is from the Latin, *vincire*, to bind, a reference to the plant's twining stems. The name periwinkle is derived from the full Latin version of the name, *pervinca*.

Description A trailing evergreen perennial, to 45 cm (18 in), it has prostrate stems, which root at the nodes, and glossy, ovate, dark-green leaves. Five-petalled, violet-blue flowers appear in the axils of the upper leaves in summer.

Related species *V. minor* is quite similar in appearance, but lower-growing and with smaller flowers; it also has similar medicinal properties. The Madagascan periwinkle, *Catharanthus roseus*, formerly *Vinca rosea*, contains the toxic alkaloids vincristine and vinblastine. These are isolated to make drugs used in the treatment of certain cancers.

Habitat/distribution Periwinkle is native to Europe, found on loamy calcareous (alkaline) soils, often in woodland.

Growth Tolerates dry conditions, but prefers moist soil and shade or partial shade. It is

Above left Vinca major *is often used as a climber, scrambling through shrubs and hedges. It retains its glossy green leaves throughout the winter and produces bright blue flowers in early spring.*

Above Vinca major *'Variegata' looks good against dark hedges.*

propagated by division throughout the dormant period. Periwinkle makes useful ground cover, but can be invasive. Cut back hard in autumn to restrict its spread.

Parts used Leaves, flowering stems – processed for extraction of alkaloids.

USES Medicinal Both *V. major* and *V. minor* contain the alkaloid vincamine, which dilates blood vessels and reduces blood pressure, and is used in pharmaceutical preparations for cardiovascular disorders.

CAUTION All parts of the plant are poisonous if eaten. Self-treatment is not advised.

VIOLACEAE
Viola odorata
Sweet violet

History and traditions Violets were greatly esteemed in the classical world and are mentioned by Theophrastus (400 BC) as well as appearing in the works of Horace, Pliny and Juvenal. The Greek word for violet is *io* and in Greek mythology Io, daughter of the King of Argos, was ravished by Zeus and then turned into a heifer so that his wife Hera wouldn't find him out. But at least he had the decency to provide sweet-scented flowers (later named after her) for Io in heifer-form to eat. Violet was the favourite perfume of Josephine and the flowers became the emblem of the Bonapartes after Napoleon became sentimentally attached to them. Despite its elusive scent, the violet has long been an emblem of constancy. Many medicinal uses are listed in old herbals and syrup of violets was a gentle laxative, still in use at the beginning of the 20th century. Household recipe books from the 16th to the 19th centuries give many examples of violet flower syrups, honey, conserve, cakes and vinegar. John Evelyn suggests eating the leaves and this is his recipe: "Violet Leaves, at the entrance of spring fried brownish and eaten with Orange or Lemon Juice and Sugar is one of the most agreeable of all the herbaceous dishes" (*Acetaria*, 1719).

Description A low-growing, hardy perennial, 15 cm (6 in) tall, with a short rhizome and creeping stolons that root at the tips. The toothed, heart-shaped leaves form a basal rosette from which the solitary, drooping, purple or white flowers arise on long stalks, in spring.

Related species *V. tricolor*, heartsease, or wild pansy, is a hardy annual or perennial, which has branched stems and alternately arranged, lobed or toothed, ovate to lanceolate leaves. The flowers, like small pansies, are in combinations of yellow, white, purple or mauve borne on leafless stems sprouting from the leaf axils. Medicinal uses are similar to those of *V. odorata*. Strong doses may cause vomiting and allergic skin reactions. The common dog violet and wood violets are unscented and have no herbal value.

Habitat/distribution Native to Europe, Asia and northern Africa, introduced elsewhere. Found on damp soils in shady woodland.

Growth Grow in humus-rich, moist but well-drained soil, in sun or partial shade. The easiest method of propagation is by division in autumn. Also grown from seed sown in spring or autumn.

Parts used Flowers – fresh for culinary use; leaves, flowers, rhizomes – fresh or dried for use in infusions and medicinal preparations; essential oil – extracted from flowers.

USES Medicinal A healing, anti-inflammatory herb with expectorant, diuretic properties, it is taken internally as a tea for coughs, colds and rheumatism. Applied externally in compresses and lotions for skin complaints, swellings and ulcers and in gargles for mouth and throat infections. The essential oil is used in aromatherapy. *V. tricolor* is known to be a heart tonic, used to treat high blood pressure, colds and indigestion.

Culinary The flowers are candied, made into jellies, jams, conserves and vinegars, or added fresh to salads and desserts.

Aromatic The essential oil is used in perfumery.

Top Viola tricolor *(heartsease or wild pansy) has some medicinal value, but the flowers are not scented.*

Centre Viola tricolor *with golden feverfew leaves.*

Above Leaves of Viola cornuta, *the horned violet, which has lightly scented flowers.*

Fresh ginger root and crystallized ginger.

VERBENACEAE
Vitex agnus-castus
Chaste tree

History and traditions The association of this tree with chastity probably stems from its former use as a pepper substitute (made from the dried, powdered fruits) said to have been served in monasteries to suppress libido. The herb has, in fact, been established in recent times to have an effect on the hormonal balance of the body. It was also used in earlier times to relieve aches and pains, and other popular names for it are "Abraham's balm" and "hemp tree", because the leaves are similar in shape to those of *Cannabis sativa*.

Description A hardy deciduous shrub or small tree, up to 5 m (16 ft) tall, it has palmate leaves, dull-green on the upper surfaces, downy and greyish beneath, with long spikes of fragrant lilac flowers in summer, followed by small black fruits.

Habitat/distribution Originates in southern Europe and western Asia, also found in North and South America. Found on dry coastal sites.

Growth Grows in most soils and tolerates dry conditions well. Propagated by seed, sown in spring or autumn, or by semi-ripe cuttings taken in summer.

Parts used Fruits.

USES Medicinal A relaxant herb with pain-relieving properties, sometimes used by herbalists for hormonal complaints and imbalances.

ZINGIBERACEAE
Zingiber officinale
Ginger

History and traditions Ginger has been known in China and India since earliest times, valued for its medicinal properties and as a potent culinary flavouring. It was imported by the Greeks and Romans from the East, by way of the Red Sea, and its names in Greek, *zingiberis*, and Latin, *zingiber*, are derived from the Sanskrit, *singabera*. During the Middle Ages it was an important trading commodity, appearing on import-duty tariffs at European ports from 1170 onwards. It was known in Britain at this time and is frequently referred to in Anglo-Saxon leech-books, and in the 13th and 14th centuries it was second only to pepper as an imported spice. At the start of the 16th century, ginger was taken by the Spaniards from the East Indies to the Americas and West Indies, where it soon became established and was exported to Europe in large quantities as early as 1547. Ginger is one of the most popular culinary flavourings worldwide today. It is an important ingredient in both Chinese and Ayurvedic medicine, known in the latter as *maha-aushadi*, "the great medicine", and has an eastern tradition as an aphrodisiac, probably because it stimulates circulation and increases blood flow.

Description A perennial reed-like plant, it has thick, branching rhizomes and grows 1–1.2 m (3–4 ft) tall, with bright-green, lanceolate, alternately arranged leaves, on short, sheathed stems. The yellow-green flowers are borne in dense cones on separate stalks from the leaves.

Habitat/distribution Native to south-east Asia, introduced and widely grown in tropical zones.

Growth A tender, tropical plant, grown in fertile, humus-rich, well-drained soil with plenty of moisture and humidity. It is usually treated as an annual crop. Propagated by division.

Parts used Rhizomes – fresh, or dried, whole or ground.

USES Medicinal Ginger has antiseptic, expectorant properties, promotes sweating and is taken in decoctions for colds, chills and feverish infections. It is taken in tablet form or as a tincture for nausea, travel sickness, indigestion, stomach upsets and menstrual pain, and is said to be safe in small doses for morning sickness during pregnancy. The essential oil is taken in drops on sugar lumps for fevers, nausea and digestive upsets, and added to massage oil to ease rheumatic pain and aching joints.

Culinary Fresh ginger is grated and added to stir-fry dishes, and widely used, fresh or dried, in Chinese and Thai cuisines. Dried ground ginger is an ingredient of curry powder, pickles and chutneys and used in Western cookery in biscuits, cakes and desserts. Whole fresh ginger is crystallized in sugar syrup and made into chocolates and confectionery.

Aromatic The essential oil is used in perfumery and as a flavouring in the food industry.

Glossary

Salvia officinalis *'Icterina'*

ALKALOID – a nitrogen-based compound contained in a plant, usually capable of having a powerful effect on bodily systems, such as painkilling or poisoning.

ALLERGEN – a substance which causes an allergic reaction.

ALTERNATE – refers to leaves arranged successively on either side of a stem.

ANALGESIC – pain relieving.

ANTISCORBUTIC – counteracts scurvy, a disease caused by Vitamin C deficiency.

ARIL – seed-covering, often fleshy and brightly coloured, of certain plants, such as *Taxus baccata* (common yew).

ASTRINGENT – has a binding, contracting effect on bodily tissue and stops bleeding.

AXIL – the upper angle between a leaf or bract and the stem on which it grows.

AXILLARY – growing in the axil.

BASAL (of leaves) – growing or forming at the base of the stem.

BOLT – to run to seed prematurely.

BRACT – a small, modified leaf.

BULBIL – a small, bulb-like structure growing in a leaf axil or flower cluster.

CALCAREOUS – containing lime; chalky.

CALYX (pl. **CALYCES**) – the outer circle of sepals, joined or divided, which surround a flower head or bud.

CORYMB – a flat-topped or convex flower cluster having flower stalks arising from different points on the stem.

CULTIVAR – a plant produced or selected from a natural species, its distinctive characteristics maintained by cultivation.

DECIDUOUS – describes a tree or shrub that loses its leaves annually, regrowing them the following season.

DECOCTION – an extraction of the water-soluble constituents of a medicinal plant, made by boiling it in water.

DECUMBENT – growing along the ground, with a tendency to turn upwards at the tips.

DIOECIOUS – produces male and female flowers on different plants.

DISC-FLORET – small, often tubular floret, which, along with many, forms the centre of a compound flower head, such as a daisy.

DIURETIC – promotes the flow of urine.

DROPSY – (oedema) a disease characterized by excessive build-up of fluid in bodily tissues.

DRUPE – fleshy fruit with one or more seeds enclosed in a stony casing.

ELLIPTIC – oval-shaped, tapering to a point at each end.

EMETIC – causes vomiting.

EMOLLIENT – softens and smoothes the skin.

ENTIRE – refers to smooth, untoothed leaf margins.

EXPECTORANT – encourages the ejection of phlegm from the respiratory tract.

GLOBOSE – spherical.

HYBRID – a plant produced by cross-fertilization between two species.

INFUSION – an extraction of water-soluble constituents of a medicinal plant, made by steeping it in water that has been brought to boiling point.

LANCEOLATE – (of leaves) narrow and tapering to a point at the tip.

Below *A colourful border display.*

Below *An espaliered fruit tree.*

Below Calendula officinalis.

Monoecious – bears separate male and female flowers on the same plant.

Mucilage – a glutinous substance contained in a plant.

Obovate – an inverted egg-shape, narrow at the base and broader at the top.

Opposite – (of leaves) growing in pairs at the same level, on opposite sides of the stem.

Ovate – egg-shaped, with the broader part at the base, narrow at the top.

Ovoid – a solid egg-shape with the broader end at the base, usually applied to fruit.

Palmate – describes a compound leaf with several leaflets arising from a common point.

Panicle – branched, compound flower cluster.

Perfoliate – describes a stalkless leaf, or leaves, which encircle and enclose the stem.

Pinnate – describes a compound leaf, made up of two rows of leaflets on either side of the central stem.

Prophylactic – protects from disease.

Purgative – strongly laxative.

Raceme – an unbranched, often conical-shaped, flower cluster.

Ray-floret – the usually strap-shaped outer petal (floret) of a compound flower head such as a daisy.

Rhizome – an underground, often ground-level, branched, swollen root-like stem, that usually grows horizontally and bears leafy shoots.

Spadix – a flower spike with a thick, fleshy stem, usually encased in a spathe.

Spathe – a leaf or bract wrapped round a central spike of flowers.

Taproot – the main, downward-growing root of a plant, which is often cylindrical or a cone shape.

Tincture – a solution, usually in alcohol, of the active constituents of a medicinal plant.

Trifoliate – describes leaves with three lobes or leaflets.

Umbel – an umbrella-shaped flower cluster.

Vermifuge – expels or destroys intestinal worms.

Vulnerary – promotes the healing of wounds.

Whorl – leaves or flowers arising from the same point and encircling the stem.

Left *A border of purple and green sage.*

Above *A bed of mixed thymes.*

Below *Catmint and a yellow climbing rose.*

Bibliography

HISTORY AND TRADITIONS
Old Herbals – See pages 16–17.

Anderson, Frank J., *An Illustrated History of the Herbals* (Columbia University Press, New York, 1977)

Baker, Margaret, *Discovering the Folklore of Plants* (Shire Publications Ltd, Princes Risborough, 1969/1980)

Cockayne, Oswald, *Leechdoms, Wortcunning and Starcraft of Early England* (2 vols. London, 1864)

Encyclopaedia Britannica (New York, 1910)

Folkard, R., *Plant Lore, Legends and Lyric* (London, 1892)

Grieve, Maud, *A Modern Herbal* (Jonathan Cape, 1931, Penguin Books, London, 1980)

Griggs, Barbara, *Green Pharmacy* (Jill Norman & Hobhouse, London, 1981)

Hepper, F. N., *Bible Plants at Kew and Pharaoh's Flowers – the botanical treasures of Tutankhamun* (HMSO, London, 1981/1990)

Manniche, Lise, *An Ancient Egyptian Herbal* (British Museum Publications, London, 1989)

Rohde, Eleanour Sinclair, *The Old English Herbals* (Minerva Press, London, 1972)

A Garden of Herbs (P. Lee Warner & Medici Society)

Shakespeare's Wild Flowers, Fairy Lore, Gardens, Herbs, Gatherers of Simples and Bee Lore (The Medici Society, London, 1935)

MEDICINAL

Bakhru, H. K., *Herbs that Heal, and Foods that Heal* (Orient Paperbacks, Delhi, 1997)

Britt, Jennifer and Keen, Lesley, *Feverfew* (Century Hutchinson, London, 1987)

Buchman, Dian Dincin, *Herbal Medicine* (The Herb Society/Rider, London, 1983)

Frawley, David and Lad, Vasant, *The Yoga of Herbs: An Ayurvedic Guide to Herbal Medicine* (Lotus Press, Sante Fe, 1988)

Heyn, Birgit, *Ayurvedic Medicine* (Thorsons, London, 1987)

Kaptchuk, Ted, *Chinese Medicine -The Web that has no Weaver* (Rider, London, 1983)

Kreig, Margaret, *Green Medicine – the Search for Plants that Heal* (George Harrap, London, Toronto, Wellington, Sydney, 1965)

Leung, Albert, *Chinese Herbal Remedies* (Wildwood House, London, 1985)

Mills, Simon Y., *A Dictionary of Modern Herbalism* (Thorsons, Wellingborough, 1985)

Ody, Penelope, *The Herb Society's Complete Medicinal Herbal* (Dorling Kindersley, London 1993)

Saynor, Reg, *The Garlic Effect* (Hodder & Stoughton, London, 1995)

Squire, Peter Wyatt, *Squire's Companion to the British Pharmacopoeia* (J. & A. Churchill, London, 1908)

Stary, Frantisek, *The Natural Guide to Medicinal Herbs and Plants* (Tiger Books International, Twickenham, 1998)

Vogel, Virgil, *American Indian Medicine* (University of Oklahoma Press, US, 1970)

Weiss, R. F., *Herbal Medicine* (Beaconsfield Publishers, Beaconsfield, 1988)

Wren, R. C., *Potter's New Cyclopaedia of Botanical Drugs and Preparations* (C.W. Daniel, Saffron Walden, 1988)

CULINARY

Jaffrey, Madhur, *An Invitation to Indian Cooking* (Jonathon Cape, 1976)

McWhirter, Alasdair and Clasen, Liz (eds), *Foods that Harm, Foods that Heal* (The Reader's Digest Association Ltd, London, 1996)

Richardson, Rosamund, *Hedgerow Cookery* (Penguin Books, 1980)

Stobart, Tom, *Herbs, Spices and Flavourings* (Penguin Books, 1977)

AROMATIC AND ESSENTIAL OILS

Arctander, Steffan, *Perfume and Flavour Materials of Natural Origin* (Steffan Arctander, New York, 1960)

Day, Ivan, *Perfumery with Herbs* (Darton, Longman & Todd/The Herb Society, London, 1979)

Genders, Roy, *Scented Wild Flowers of Britain* (Collins, London, 1971)

A History of Scent (Hamish Hamilton, UK, 1972)

Poucher, William A., *Perfumes, Cosmetics and Soaps* (3 vols, Chapman and Hall, London, 1950)

Price, Shirley, *Practical Aromatherapy* (Thorsons, Wellingborough, 1983)

Rimmel, Eugene, *The Book of Perfumes* (Chapman and Hall, London, 1865)

Tisserand, Robert, *The Art of Aromatherapy* (C. W. Daniel, Saffron Walden, 1977)

PLANTS AND GARDENING

Achele, Dietmar, *A Field Guide in Colour to Wild Flowers* (Octopus Books, London, 1975)

Anthony, John, *The Renaissance Garden in Britain* (Shire Publications, Princes Risborough, 1991)

Davis, P.H., *Flora of Turkey and the East Aegean Islands* (Edinburgh University Press, 1965)

Bown, Deni, *The RHS Encyclopedia of Herbs* (Dorling Kindersley, London, 1995)

Below *A herb border flourishes in the shelter of a wall at Poyntzfield Nursery, Scotland.*

Brickell, Christopher (Ed-in-Chief), *The RHS A–Z Encyclopedia of Garden Plants* (Dorling Kindersley, London, 1992)

Britton, Nathaniel and Brown, Addison, *An Illustrated Flora of the Northern United States and Canada* (3 vols, Dover Publications Inc., New York, 1970)

Buczacki, Stefan, and Harris, Keith, *Pests, Diseases and Disorders of Garden Plants* (Harper Collins, London, 1981, 1988)

Harvey, John, *Restoring Period Gardens* (Shire, Princes Risborough, 1988)

Hills, Lawrence D., *Comfrey for Gardeners and Smallholders* (Henry Doubleday Research Association, Coventry, 1985)

Hooker, J.D., *The Flora of British India* (vols 1–7, Reeve & Co, London, 1872–1897)

Huxley, Anthony and Taylor, William, *Flowers of Greece and the Aegean* (Chatto and Windus, London, 1977)

Lancaster, Roy, *A Plantsman in Nepal* (Antique Collectors Club, Woodbridge, 1995)

Lord, Tony (Ed.) and Botanists of RHS Gardens, Wisley, *The Plant Finder 1998–99* (Dorling Kindersley, London, 1998)

Mabberley, D. J., *The Plant Book – A Portable Dictionary of the Vascular Plants* (Cambridge University Press, Cambridge, 1997)

McVicar, Jekka, *Jekka's Complete Herb Book* (Kyle Cathie Ltd, London, 1997)

Miller, A.G. and Morris, M, *Plants of Dhofar* (Office of the Advisor for Conservation of the Environment (Oman, 1988)

Phillips, Roger and Foy, Nicky, *Herbs* (Pan Books Ltd, London, 1990)

Polunin, Oleg, and Stainton, A., *Flowers of the Himalaya* (Oxford University Press, Delhi, 1985)

Rice, Elsie Garrett and Compton, Robert Harold, *Wild Flowers of the Cape of Good Hope* (Botanical Society of South Africa, Kirstenbosch, S.A., 1950)

Ridley, H.N., *The Flora of the Malay Peninsula* (L. Reeve & Co., London, 1922–25)

Sharma, B.D. et al (eds.) *Flora of India* (Botanical Survey of India, Calcutta, 1993)

Simonetti, Gualtiero, *The Macdonald Encyclopedia of Herbs and Spices* (Macdonald & Co (Publishers) Ltd., London 1991)

Stodola, Jiri and Volak, Jan, *The Illustrated Book of Herbs* (Octopus Books, London and Artia, Prague, 1984)

Stuart, Malcolm (ed.), *The Colour Dictionary of Herbs and Herbalism* (Orbis Publishing, London, 1979)

Watt, J.M. and Breyer-Brankdwijk, M.G.,*Medicinal and Poisonous Plants of Southern and Eastern Africa* (E. S. Livingstone, Edinburgh and London, 1962)

PERIODICALS AND PAPERS

Abstracts of papers on Neem, published by the Neem Foundation, India

The Herbal Review and *Herbs* (various volumes, The Herb Society, Warmington, Oxfordshire, 1977–97)

Balandrin et al, "Plant-Derived Natural Products in Drug Discovery and Development" (*American Chemical Society*, 1993)

Buchbauer, G. and Jirovetz, L., "Aromatherapy – Use of Fragrances and Essential Oils as Medicaments" (*Flavour and Fragrance Journal*, 1994)

Deans, S. G. and Ritchie, G., "Antibacterial Properties of Plant Essential Oils" (*International Journal of Food Microbiology*, 1987)

Fellows, Linda, "Botany Breaks into the Candy Store" (*New Scientist*, 1989)

O'Neill, M.J. and Lewis, J.A., "The Renaissance of Plant Research in the Pharmaceutical Industry" (*American Chemical Society*, 1993)

Above left *Fragrant herbs surround a bench.*

Above *Chives in a raised bed.*

Below *An arched walkway of herbs.*

Useful sources and suppliers

UNITED KINGDOM

SUPPLIERS OF ESSENTIAL OILS

Culpeper Ltd
Hadstock Road
Linton
Cambridge CB1 6NJ
Tel 01440 788196

The Fragrant Earth Co. Ltd
PO Box 182
Taunton
Somerset TA1 1YR
Tel 01823 335734 for mail order catalogue.

Neal's Yard Remedies
5 Golden Cross
Cornmarket Street
Oxford OX1 3EU
Tel 01865 245436 for mail order catalogue.

Shirley Price
Essentia House
Upper Bond Street
Hinckley
Leicestershire LE10 1RS
Tel 0455 615466 for mail order catalogue.

MEDICINAL AND CULINARY HERBS

G. Baldwin & Co.
171–173 Walworth Road
London SE17 1RN
Tel 0171 703 5550

Potters Herbal Supplies
Leyland Mill Lane
Lancashire WN1 2SB
Tel 01942 405100 for mail order cut herbs.

Poyntzfield Herb Nursery
Black Isle by Dingwall
Ross & Cromarty
IV7 8LX
Tel 01381 610352 for mail order plants.
Informative catalogue sent on receipt of four
first class stamps.

Rosemary Titterington
Iden Croft Herbs
Frittenden Road
Kent TN12 0DH
Tel 01580 891432 for mail order.

NORTH AMERICA

SUPPLIERS OF ESSENTIAL OILS

The Body Shop
2870 Janitell Road
Colorado Springs, CO 80906
Tel (800) 263 9746

Lorann Oils
PO Box 22009
Lansing, MI 48909–2009
Tel (800) 248 1302 for mail order.

Above left *Golden feverfew.*

Below *A deeply-coloured knot garden.*

MEDICINAL AND CULINARY HERBS

Caprilands Herb Farm
Silver Street
North Coventry, CT 06238

Richter's Herbs
Goodwood
Ontario
Canada LOC 1AO
Tel (905) 640 6677

Seeds Blum
HC 33 Box 2057
Boise, ID 83706
Tel (208) 342 0858
Order tel (800) 538 3658

AUSTRALIA

MEDICINAL AND CULINARY HERBS

Bundanoon Village Nursery
71 Penrose Road
Bundanoon 2578
NSW
Tel (02) 4883-6303
e-mail: cabbage@pbq.com.au. A nursery in a
garden. Classes on use of herbs, seeds and
some Chinese medicinal herb tubers available
by mail order.

Above Helianthus annuus.

Above Monarda didyma *'Cambridge Scarlet'.*

Above *Wild strawberry and marjoram pot.*

Chamomile Farm
79 Monbulk Road
Emerald 3782
Victoria
Tel (03) 5968-4807. No mail order.

Darling Mills Farm
62 Francis Street
Castle Hill 2154
NSW
Tel (02) 9634-2843
Fax (02) 9894-7439
Wide variety of salad leaves and the more
common herbs as well as some Asian herbs.

Herbie's Spices
745 Darling Street
Rozelle 2039
NSW
Tel (02) 9555-6035
Website:http://www.herbies.com.au
All culinary herbs and spices in one place.
Huge range. Mail order for dried herbs
nationally and throughout the Pacific.

House of Herbs
1 Digney Street
Sandy Bay
Tasmania 7005
Tel (03) 6224-3788. Wide range to show size
and shape under Tasmanian conditions.

Right Tanacetum cinerariifolium.

Lillydale Herb Farm
Mangans Road
Lilydale 3140
Victoria
Tel (03) 9735-0486
Display gardens with medicinal, culinary,
fragrant, companion and insect repellent
plants. Shop with range of herbal items and
books.

Renaissance Herbs
Lot 521
Hakone Road
Warnervale 2259
Tel (02) 4392-4600
Fax (02) 4393-1221
Largest range – supplies to nurseries
nationally through franchised growers
throughout Australia.

TLC Herbs
Lot 10
Old Coach Road
Aldinga 5173 SA
Tel (08) 8577-7161
Many varieties, including more unusual ones.
Mail order.

RESOURCE INFORMATION

For information on any aspect of the herb
industry in Australia, the Australian Herb
Industry Resource Guide by Kim Fletcher is
invaluable. Regularly updated. Available from:

Focus on Herbs
Consultancy & Information Service
PO Box 203, Launceston
Tasmania 7250

The publisher would like to thank the following people for assisting with the photography for this book:

Roger and Linda Bastin
Kruidenkwekerij Herb Nursery
Trichterweg 148a
6446 AT Brunssum
Holland

Christine and Peter Bench and Mrs
    Nancy Bench
The Herb Nursery
Thistleton
Oakham
Rutland LE15 7RE
Tel 01572 767658

Chris and Mandie Dennis
Proprietors
The Citrus Centre
Marehill Nursery
West Mare Lane
Marehill
Pulborough
Sussex RH20 2EA
Tel 01798 872786

Adam Gordon
Rochfords
Joseph Rochford Gardens Ltd
Pipers End
Letty Green
Hertford SG14 2PB
Tel 01707 261370

Henry Doubleday Research
Association
Ryton Organic Gardens
Coventry
CV8 3LG
Tel 01203 303517

Simon and Judith Hopkinson
(and Anne)
Hollington Nurseries
Woolton Hill
Newbury
Berkshire RG20 9XT
Tel 01653 253908

Victoria Ker
Bedwyn Common
Wiltshire

The Kew Gardener
4a Station Approach
Kew Gardens
Surrey TW9 3QB
Tel 0181 332 9630

Anne Marie Powell
Garden Designer
West London
Tel 0181 840 1230

Letta Proper Pranger
Castle Hex
Belgium

Sally Reed
Braxton Gardens
Braxton Courtyard
Lymore Lane
Melford-on-Sea
Hampshire SO41 0TX
Tel 01590 642008

Duncan and Susan Ross
Poyntzfield Herb Nursery
Black Isle by Dingwall
Ross & Cromarty
Scotland IV7 8LX
Tel 01381 610352

The Royal Botanic Gardens
Kew
Surrey TW9 3AB
Tel 0181 332 5000

Lord Salisbury/Michael Pickard
(Curator)
Hatfield House
Hatfield
Hertfordshire AL9 5NQ
Tel 01707 262823

Richard Scott
The Herb Farm
Peppard Road
Sonning Common
Reading
Berkshire RG4 9NJ

The Shakespeare Birthplace Trust
Shakespeare Centre
Henley Street
Stratford-upon-Avon CV37 6QW
Tel 01789 204016

The Shrewsbury Quest
Abbey Foregate
Shrewsbury
Shropshire SY2 6AH
Tel 01743 366355

Roger Souvereyns
Scholteshof Restaurant and Hotel
    with Gardens
Belgium

Phillip C Stallard
Site Facilities Officer
(Tretower Court)
CADW Welsh Historic Monuments

Peter Turner
The National Herb Centre
Banbury Road
Warmington
Near Banbury
Oxfordshire OX17 1DF
Tel 01295 690999

Stijn Vanormelingen
De Horne Restaurant and Gardens
Brugstraat 30a Vechmaal
Belgium

Susie & Kevin White
Hexham Herbs
Chesters Walled Garden
Chollerford
Hexham
Northumberland NE46 4BQ
Tel 01434 681483

AUTHOR'S ACKNOWLEDGMENTS

My thanks to the following people for specialist information: Alan Gear of the Henry Doubleday Research Association, on the use of comfrey in the garden; Dr. Stanley Deans on thyme oil; Duncan Ross of Poyntzfield Herb Nursery on ginseng; Dr. Rosita Arvigo and the Traditional Healers Foundation of Belize, on plants of Central America; and also to Dr. Katya Svoboda of the Scottish Agricultural College, Dr. Rosemary Cole of the National Herb Centre and Dr. Charles Hill.

PICTURE CREDITS

Pages 10 bl, 14 bl, 17 tl ET Archive; pages 14 tr, 15 bl Edimedia; pages 15 tr, 16 bl, 17br, 20 bl The Bridgeman Art Library; pages 11 tr & 123 Vaughn Fleming, 20 tr Clay Perry, 26 rc David Askham, 43 br Steven Wooster, 100 tl, 134 tr, 145 tr John Glover, 123 bc, 128 tr Brigitte Thomas, 135 tr Sunniva Harte, 136 tr Clive Boursnell, 144 tl Lamontagne, 144/5 tc Christopher Gallagher, 149 tr Ron Evans, 213 b Clive Nichols – The Garden Picture Library; pages 21t, 41 br, 53 cl, 78 tr & cr, 79, 97 bc, 98 tl, 100 br, 106 tl, 107 tl 108 tc, 113 bl, 118 tl, 119 tl, 121 tr, 122 tl, 125 tl, 129 tl, 132 tl, 143 tc, 147 bl, tr, 155 tc, 156, 157 tl, 159 bc, 164 tl, 165 tl, 171 bc, 181 tr, 197 tr, 204 tr, 208 tr, 209 tl, tr, 213 t, 214 br, 215 tr, 216 b, 218 tl, 222 tl Jessica Houdret; pages 21 bl, 40 bl, 41 bl, 102 tr Lucy Mason; pages 21 tr, 24 tr, 36 bl, 48 tr, 51 br, 59 tr Jacqui Hurst; pages 32 br, 226 tr Adrian Thomas, 44 bl Neil Joy, 57 Michael Jones, 60 tr Geoffrey S. Chapman, 124 tc K. Jayara, 127 bl Malcolm Richards, 138 tr Michael R. Chandler, 232 tl Anthony Cooper, 233 tr E. Mole, 235 tl Bjorn Svensson 235 tr – A–Z Botanical Collection Ltd; pages 34 bl, 41 tr & tl, 67, 68, 69 tl, tc, tr, 73 tr & bl, 80/81, 82 br, 85 tr, 86, 88 bc, 90 tr, 122 cr, br, 149 br, 153 br, 161 bl, 169 br, 171c, 218 tr Michelle Garrett; pages 82 bl, 83 br, 85 br & bl, 86 cl, 88 tl & tr, 89 bl, 91 cr Polly Wreford; pages 95 tr, 126 tl, 134 tc, 136 tl, 151 tr, 194 tl, 197 bl, 225 tl Harry Smith Collection; page 98 tr Brenda Szabo – Kirstenbosch Botanic Garden, South Africa; pages 99 tl, 204 tl Dr. Eckart Pott, 113 br Bob & Clara Calhoun, 185 tc, tr, 191 tl Staffen Widstrand, 191 cl N. Schwihtz, 206 tl Harald Lange, 206 cr Hans Reinhard – Bruce Coleman Ltd.; pages 116 tl, 185 tl, 192 tr Deni Bown; pages 140 tl, 142 tl, 156 br, 158 tl Dr. John Feltwell, Garden & Wildlife Matters; page 194 br Duncan Ross, Poyntzfield Nursery.
key t = top, b = bottom,
c = centre, l = left, r = right

Index

Note: *italics* refer to photographs and diagrams.

Above Borago officinalis.

Above Buxus sempervirens 'Elegantissima'.

Above Echinacea purpurea.

Above Helianthus annuus 'Velvet Queen'.

Above Watermint growing in a pond.

Above Myrtus communis *'Tarentina'*.

N

O

Above Polemonium caeruleum.

Above Primula veris.

Above *Purple sage.*

Above Thymus vulgaris *'Silver Posie'.*

Above Tropaeolum majus.

U

V

W

Y

Z

Below *Herb nurseries often have attractive display gardens where you can see how big the plants will grow before deciding what to buy.*